The Hellenistic Greeks

The Hellenistic Greeks

From Alexander to Cleopatra

MICHAEL GRANT

Weidenfeld & Nicolson
London

© by Michael Grant Publications Ltd, 1982
New Edition © 1990
The First Edition was published under the title
From Alexander to Cleopatra: The Hellenistic World

George Weidenfeld and Nicolson Ltd
91 Clapham High Street, London sw4

ISBN 0 297 82057 5

Printed in Great Britain by
Butler & Tanner Ltd
Frome and London

Contents

———— ▪ ————

Part II Reality and Withdrawal

Maps

————— ▪ —————

Preface

This book is about the brilliant, crowded, lively age of those Greeks who lived in the three centuries following what is generally described as the classical epoch.

The history of Greece is customarily presented before our eyes in an unbalanced manner. A great deal is said about 'classical' Greece, and very little about the long period that followed – and continued until the Greeks were engulfed by Rome. 'Classical Greece' culminated in the fifth century BC when, first, a large number of the city-states of which the country was composed joined together (as they never had before) in order to defeat the invading armies of the Persian empire (490, 480–479)*; and then the two leaders among those states, Athens and Sparta, fell out with each other, and fought the long and disastrous Peloponnesian War (431–404), finally won by the Spartans. The epoch also witnessed an unparalleled burst of literary and artistic brilliance, represented by the great names of tragic and comic poetry, history, architecture and sculpture, and accompanied by a mighty stirring up of people's minds: in which Athens played the predominant part, as the names of its leading citizen Pericles and inspiring thinker Socrates (d. 399) testify.

After the Peloponnesian War was over, the city-states continued their uneasy bickerings; and Plato wrote his dialogues. Thereafter, the situation was transformed, because King Philip II of Macedonia reduced the traditional city-states to powerlessness for evermore, at the battle of Chaeronea (338). Next, his son Alexander III the Great broke into Asia and overwhelmed and annexed the enormous Persian empire, pressing onwards as far as India. Something will be said in this book about what he did and planned, but it is with his early death (323) that the story truly begins. It deals with an age in which the Greek world, fantastically enlarged by the exploits of Alexander, split up into a number of kingdoms which, after a period of brilliant independence, fell in turn to the

* All dates in the text are BC unless otherwise indicated.

Romans, the last major state to succumb being the Egypt of Cleopatra (VII) in 30 BC: though the remote Hellenistic kingdom of the Indo-Greeks in Afghanistan and Pakistan still held out for another generation. It is the intervening period of approximately three hundred years preceding the disappearance of these states that I shall try to cover. They are years that were eventful in the highest degree; and what happened, and what was thought, is in many ways much closer to modern times, not merely in a chronological sense, than the developments of the foregoing classical age. Moreover, these three centuries contained even more remarkable personalities than the age that had gone before.

They were men and women who inherited the full continuity of the Greek past. But they also rapidly endowed their civilization with novel and original features. For one thing, the conquests of Alexander, while transforming the geographical dimensions of the Greek world, had brought it into connexion with quite other, foreign, ancient, ways of life. Yet despite all the migrations, settlements and annexations that made such contacts inevitable, these new Greeks, and the way of life that they continued to develop, still remained essentially Greek. Nevertheless, this was a Greekness which, for a variety of reasons, came to differ considerably from what had been seen hitherto. Indeed, so different was it that a new label is used for this Greek civilization that flourished after the time of Alexander. It is called the 'Hellenistic' age, in contrast to the 'Hellenic' world of the classical Greeks from which it had sprung. The term 'Hellenistic', which is not ancient – it was given its modern meaning in the early nineteenth century[1] – has never really been widely accepted or understood, outside scholarly circles. Yet it remains a convenient enough designation to distinguish the new epoch starting after Alexander the Great, which had evolved from the age of the classical Hellenes but formed novel characteristics of its own.

One of the most significant of these developments was the pre-eminence of large, monarchic states, the kingdoms deriving from Alexander's successors; and, in particular, the power of the great kingdoms that evolved not only under the Antigonids (Macedonia) – whose régime was an ancient one – but under the new dynasties of the Ptolemies (Egypt and its dependencies) and Seleucids (based on Syria and Babylonia and lands farther east). In addition to their own intrinsic peculiarities, these kingdoms were important because they moulded the future far ahead of their own times, since it was they, to a large extent, which supplied the models for the even more extensive Roman empire to come. In terms of military and political strength, the great Hellenistic monarchies cast the ancient, traditional Greek city-states into the shade. Yet these city-states continued to exist all the same, and even, in some cases, flourished, and originated interesting new features of their own. In particular, some of the cities (and older, tribal units too) learnt the knack of uniting into politically viable federations or leagues, a feat which had escaped the grasp of the self-contained city-states of earlier eras. Rome learnt something from these federations, as well as from the monarchies; and it improved upon the institutions of both types of unit alike – thereby becoming strong enough to defeat them.

Yet the Hellenistic age must emphatically not be seen as just the forerunner of the Roman epoch, any more than it must be seen as a sort of appendix of classical Greece. For the epoch was rich and fertile in versatile creations which, despite all debts to the past, were very much its own. It was with good reason, for example, that Hellenistic writers, when they drew up a list of Seven Wonders of the World for a new public that was interested in travelling, included in their final list no less than two marvels of their own epoch (the Pharos of Alexandria and the Colossus of Rhodes), as well as another dating from its very commencement (the Mausoleum at Halicarnassus).

The Colossus of Rhodes, had it survived, would have vividly illustrated a potent new realism which was in the air – and which made the drama and poetry of the age, in addition to its sculpture, curiously different from their classical forerunners and models. One of the most significant aspects of this realism was a greatly enhanced interest in the individual human being and his mind and emotions, an interest given vigorous expression by biographers and portrait artists. And this concern for the individual was extended not only to men but to women, whose position in society, literature and art underwent an unprecedented transformation that was one of the most remarkable evolutionary changes of the age.

All these developments owed something to the eclipse of the old, self-sufficient, city-state ideal, cut down to size (despite the survival of the city-states themselves) by the rise of the vast kingdoms. The individual person no longer had this cosy, local, civic and corporative institution to lean on – and to lean, instead, on the remote institutions of the great new states was of little use or comfort. So he and she were compelled to think again and devise new explanations and foundations for their lives, and new consolations to fill the place of those that had gone. How their minds worked as they tackled this challenging situation is one of the outstanding and fascinating aspects of the Hellenistic age.

The old idea that these people collectively suffered from a loss of nerve can no longer be maintained. True, a very large number of Greeks did succumb to profoundly depressing convictions that everything was immutably governed by blind chance (or fate) and the stars. More hopeful and more emotional men and women clung to new, ecstatic pagan Saviour (Mystery) Cults that increasingly, in people's hearts, replaced the worship of the old Olympian gods, who no longer seemed very efficacious. Yet many thoughtful persons remained unimpressed by this sort of exciting salvation, whether in the present world or the next, and instead decided that the purpose of their lives should be something quite different: the attainment of *ataraxia* – philosophical peace of mind, a condition of imperturbable, invulnerable, impregnable security and tranquillity against which the buffetings of fate or chance could do no harm. It may not be an ideal which fully satisfies the selfless demands of the Jewish or Christian ethic. Yet it has a grandeur of its own; and one of the most remarkable episodes in the intellectual history of the world is provided by the very diverse attempts of the Cynics, Stoics, Epicureans and Sceptics of Hellenistic times to achieve this single common aim.

Writers outside those schools, too, or influenced by them in a secondary fashion, devised means of their own for attaining the same *ataraxia*. For one thing, repeated literary endeavours were made to devise a Utopia, a cosmopolis freed from the trammels of the old, limited city or polis – a community in which everyone would be free to develop his or her existence in perfect conditions. As for the major writers of the age, many of them decided that the best solution was another sort of escapism that they could achieve in their own lives – subsidized by the Museum and Library at Alexandria, which gave them the opportunity to set themselves against the prevailing realism of the age and write, instead, for the fellow-members of their own small élite groups, exercising their finely tuned imaginations and inherited, modified linguistic skills to achieve new and rarefied insights. Yet one of these men, Theocritus, also did more: not only did he, almost alone, in his own person and imagination, bridge the gulf between realism and withdrawal, but his own private, peculiar recipe for peace of mind amounted to a flash of genius. It consisted of a haunting pastoral or bucolic type of poetry. A hundred times more stimulating than the Dresden-shepherdess affectations of his remote literary descendants, this was a form of art which, operating simultaneously at many levels of feeling and intelligence, could effectively lead those who had enough discernment to the *ataraxia* that was so widely longed for.

I am very grateful to Professor Marylin B. Arthur, Professor David M. Halperin and Professor Sara B. Pomeroy for sending me books and articles, to Dr William Brashear, Professor G. S. Kirk, Prof. Sir Hugh

Lloyd-Jones and Mrs Eva Neurath for other valuable assistance, to Mrs Flora Powell-Jones for bibliographical help, to Miss Linden Lawson and Miss Paula Iley of Messrs Weidenfeld & Nicolson for preparing the original edition (*From Alexander to Cleopatra*) for the press, to Mr Malcolm Gerratt and Mr Marcus Harpur for looking after this corrected edition (with revised bibliography), to Mr Charles Scribner Junior for constructive advice about what the book should contain, and to my wife for her partnership in the enterprise.

Michael Grant

1982, 1990

Introduction

The Greek World Transformed

I Alexander III the Great

Philip II of Macedonia (359–336), who made his country into a major power, virtually controlling the mainland Greek city-states, intended to lead his and their forces against the two-centuries-old Persian (Achaemenid) empire, which ruled over huge territories extending from the Aegean to Egypt and central Asia. Philip's motives were mixed: revenge for the Persian invasion of Macedonia and Greece in the previous century, annoyance because the contemporary Persians had at times aided the king's own Greek opponents, a desire to wipe out the only large-scale potential enemy to the Macedonians that was still in existence – and pure lust for expansion.

When Philip II was murdered at the age of forty-six, his nineteen-year-old son Alexander III (the Great) inherited the plan with enthusiasm. In 334 BC, at the head of 40,000 Macedonian and Greek troops, he crossed the Hellespont (Dardanelles) and confronted the Persian advance forces on the river Granicus (Çan Çayi), winning a victory which enabled him to conquer western and southern Asia Minor. In the following year, at Issus on the borders of Asia Minor and Syria, he defeated the Persian king Darius III Codomannus himself, whose mother, wife and children fell into his hands. Rejecting favourable offers of peace, Alexander next captured the great Phoenician city of Tyre after a long siege (332), and occupied Egypt (a Persian province since 525), where he founded Alexandria (331). Then, moving onwards into the heart of the Persian empire, Alexander overran Mesopotamia, crossed the Tigris, and outmanoeuvred and overwhelmed Darius at Gaugamela (Arbela). The victory enabled him to capture the Persian capital cities of Babylon, Susa and Persepolis (which went down in flames), and Darius fled to Media, south of the Caspian Sea, where he was murdered. Thereupon Alexander assumed the dead man's royal title.

During the next three years, he extended his frontiers extraordinarily far to the east. After marrying Roxane, the daughter of an eastern

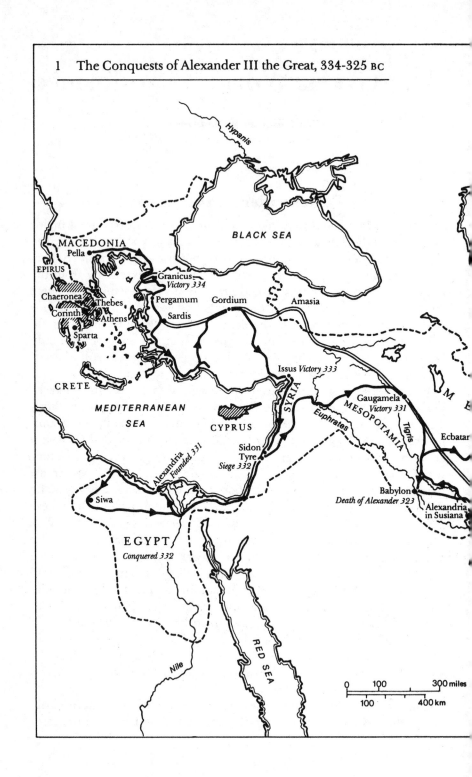

1   The Conquests of Alexander III the Great, 334-325 BC

Hypanis

BLACK SEA

MACEDONIA
Pella

EPIRUS

Granicus
Victory 334

Pergamum   Gordium   Amasia

Chaeronea
Thebes
Corinth   Athens   Sardis

Sparta

Issus *Victory 333*

CRETE

SYRIA

Gaugamela
Victory 331

MESOPOTAMIA

Euphrates

Tigris

MEDITERRANEAN
SEA

CYPRUS

Ecbatar

Sidon
Tyre
Siege 332

*Alexandria
Founded 331*

Babylon
Death of Alexander 323

Alexandria
in Susiana

Siwa

EGYPT
Conquered 332

RED SEA

Nile

0   100   300 miles

100   400 km

Empire of Alexander the Great

Dependent states

Routes of Alexander the Great

Persian Royal Road

Conquered 328

SOGDIANA

Alexandria Eschate (?) (Leninabad)

Aï Khanum

Alexandria Margiana (Merv)

Bactra-Zariaspa (Balkh)

Paropamisus (Hindu Kush) Mts.

BACTRIA

Conquered 328

Cabura (Kabul)

GANDHARA

Taxila

PARTHIA

PAROPAMISADAE

Alexandria in Aria (Herat)

Alexandria (Ghazni)

Victory over Indian king Porus 326

Hydaspes

PUNJAB

Kandahar

Hyphasis

ARACHOSIA

CASPIAN SEA

Persepolis
Occupied 331

Indus

GEDROSIA

PERSIAN GULF

Alexandria (Portus)

INDIAN OCEAN

Iranian chieftain, he pressed on beyond the Paropamisus (Hindu Kush) mountains, securing the submission of Omphis (Ambhi), whose capital at Taxila (Sirkap) controlled Gandhara, between the rivers Hydaspes (Jhelum) and Acesines (Chenab). But after invading the Punjab (326) Alexander finally turned back, because his army refused to go with him any further. Moving down the Indus as far as its delta he withdrew westwards by the terrible land route through the deserts of southern Gedrosia (the Makran, in Baluchistan and south-eastern Iran), while his fleet, under Nearchus, disappeared into the unknown sea route along the coasts of the Indian Ocean and Persian Gulf. For a long time there was no sign of the ships and he began to think that they had perished. Then one or two straggling sailors appeared, and finally Nearchus himself. It was a moment of extreme emotion for Alexander, who swore both by Zeus of the Greeks and Ammon of the Libyans that he was more pleased by this news than by the conquest of all Asia.

Arriving back in Susa, the king executed governors and officers accused of misconduct in his absence, and dealt savagely with alleged plots among his own intimate friends. A serious mutiny among his Macedonian soldiers was caused by his project for a mixed army – part of a spectacular new plan, announced at Opis on the Tigris in 324, to govern his empire in collaboration with the Iranians: a policy for which he himself set an example by marrying Barsine Statira, daughter of Darius III (without repudiating Roxane). However, in the summer of 323, Alexander died of fever – aggravated by an Indian wound, and perhaps by drink as well; but suspicions of poison were not conclusive.

He was only thirty-two when he died, but he left an empire stretching from the Adriatic and Cyrenaica to India and what is now Soviet central Asia. After such startling conquests, the world could never be anything like the same again. His motives for undertaking these vast enterprises seem to have been mixed. As a Macedonian, he wanted to show that he could do better than any of the Greeks, who considered his people barbarians. As a son, he wanted to show himself greater than his great father, and to carry out his father's proposed vengeance on the Persians – with all the more enthusiasm because his own personal hero was his mythical ancestor Achilles, conqueror of that earlier Asian power, Troy. And new motives crowded in: notably a growing desire to reach the uttermost confines of the world. That was part of what he described as his imperative yearning (*pothos*) to achieve each successive, distant, impossible target. This urge was a dominant feature of his tricky, adventurous, alluring, frightening character: a character which, like his dramatic appearance, gave a decisive impetus to the arts of biography and portraiture. Moreover, unlike almost everybody else in the world, Alexander possessed the ability and genius to put his yearnings into practice to an almost immeasurable extent.

He and his helpers explored many lands, he brought the title of king into the Greek world, he helped decisively to inspire a long-lived religious cult of rulers, he founded a number of Greek cities, he issued a fine, uniform, empire-wide currency. But the everlasting legend that sprang up around his life and personality – one of the most astonishing, prolonged imaginative phenomena in the history of the world – was far more enormous than anything he himself left behind: for the implementation of his marvellous plan of partnership with the Persians remained in the air – and almost everything else, too, still remained to be done.

If his beloved friend Hephaestion had lived – the man for whom he revived the Persian title of vizier – he might have become Alexander's successor. But Hephaestion had died in 324, and when the king was asked on his deathbed to whom he bequeathed his empire he could only reply (so it was said): 'to the strongest'. There is thus a bitter irony in the story that when a storm rages in the Aegean the mermaids emerge and cry out to passing ships, 'Where is Alexander the Great?'; and the captain cries back along the wind, 'Alexander the Great lives and rules, and keeps the world at peace.' To keep the world at peace was exactly what Alexander failed to do. On the contrary, his early death was followed by four decades of warfare between his generals.

2 The Successors

Most of the competitors had played important parts in his army. The monarchy was at first officially represented by two kings appointed in his place, Philip III Arrhidaeus (his mentally retarded half-brother) and Alexander IV (his posthumous son by Roxane). A few of the commanders still wanted to preserve the unity of the empire that this kingship purported to represent. Most of their colleagues, however, were intent on breaking up these dominions, so as to carve out kingdoms for themselves. From a military and political viewpoint, therefore, the period of forty-two years in which the Successors fought against one another is highly confused. Moreover, although the aims of the participants were simple enough – the seizure of territory and assertion of personal status – the detailed events seem chaotic and purposeless. Nevertheless, the appearances and disappearances of the leading notable figures, and the kaleidoscopic readjustments of the relations between them, make it possible to divide the period up into a few successive, distinguishable stages.

To begin with, after Alexander was dead, the central government was partially and imperfectly represented, not by the kings who were powerless, but by three other principal Macedonian personages. Antipater, formerly one of Philip II's chief advisers, had been left in Europe by Alexander as his viceroy. Perdiccas had become Alexander's second-in-command, and after the king's death was virtually regent of the empire; it was his intention to come to some arrangement which would look legitimate, while concentrating the real power in his own hands. The third of these figures was Craterus, who had been transferred back home by Alexander with discharged Macedonian soldiers, and now became the guardian of King Philip III Arrhidaeus, perhaps under the supervision of Perdiccas.

Other officers quickly set themselves up as local rulers on their own account. Alexander's associate Ptolemy I - later known as Soter (Saviour) - arrived in Egypt as representative of Philip III Arrhidaeus, but quickly asserted his virtual independence, founding the Ptolemaic state in that country and adding Cyrenaica to its territory. Antigonus I Monophthalmos (One-Eyed) had served Alexander for ten years as governor of Phrygia (west-central Asia Minor), and now extended his control to the south coast of the peninsula. Alexander's former bodyguard and commander Lysimachus was given a principality consisting of Thrace and north-western Asia Minor. Eumenes - not a Macedonian like the others, but a Greek from Cardia in Thrace - had been secretary both to Philip II and to Alexander. After the latter's death, he was installed as governor of Cappadocia in east-central Asia Minor, though the territory still had to be conquered.

In the first phase of the struggle that followed, Antipater crushed a rebellion of the Greek city-states - led by Athens - known as the Lamian War, and a revolt of Alexander's mercenaries left behind in Bactria (Afghanistan) was likewise suppressed. Ptolemy's kidnapping of Alexander's corpse and its removal to Egypt led to a war in which Perdiccas and Craterus were killed, in a Macedonian mutiny and a battle against Eumenes respectively. At the conference of Triparadisus in northern Syria (321) Antipater was made sole guardian and viceroy of the two young kings, while Antigonus I Monophthalmos, who was his friend, gained the command of the royal army in Asia. Seleucus I, later known as Nicator (Conqueror) - who had been a friend of Alexander, but was not one of his prominent generals - became governor of Babylon.

The next five years witnessed a decisive weakening of the central government, especially after the death of Antipater (319). His successor

6

Polyperchon associated himself with Eumenes – ostensibly as champion of imperial unity – but was driven from Macedonia and most of Greece by Antipater's son Cassander; while Eumenes, expelled from Asia Minor by Antigonus I, found himself deserted by his own troops, and was put to death (316). In the previous year, Philip III Arrhidaeus had been captured and killed by Olympias, the mother of Alexander the Great, out of a desire to obtain the eventual sole rule for her infant grandchild Alexander IV.

The five years that followed saw powerful attempts by Antigonus I, supported by his son Demetrius I, to make himself sole ruler of the whole of Alexander's empire. These ambitions caused Cassander, Ptolemy I Soter and Lysimachus to unite against the pair. In 312 Demetrius I was defeated by Ptolemy I at Gaza, and Seleucus I, who had been ejected from Babylon by Antigonus four years earlier, regained the city and, with it, Alexander's eastern territories, thus laying the foundations of the Seleucid kingdom.

A truce was agreed upon in 311, but only lasted for a single year. King Alexander IV was soon put to death by Cassander, who also made strenuous and partially successful efforts to master Greece and Macedonia. Antigonus I found it impossible to suppress Seleucus I (310–309); and Antigonus' son Demetrius I (in spite of a naval victory over Ptolemy I off Cyprus) failed to take Rhodes by siege, unable to live up to his nickname Poliorcetes (the Besieger). In 306 Antigonus I assumed the title of king (without naming any particular territory), and Ptolemy I and Seleucus I did likewise in 305-304. By this time it had become increasingly clear that the principal danger to all the other leaders came from the imperial ambitions of Antigonus I: but finally Lysimachus and Seleucus I defeated and killed him at 'the battle of the kings', fought at Ipsus between 75,000 men on either side (301), and won by elephants which Seleucus had obtained from the Indian king Chandragupta Maurya in return for the cession of his eastern territories. This outcome of the battle, by eliminating the only potential reunifier, meant the irrevocable dismemberment of the empire of Alexander, which was now divided into four separate kingdoms: those of Seleucus I, Lysimachus, Ptolemy I and Cassander.

Yet another, and final, phase of the wars of the Successors was still to follow. Recovering from his father's disaster at Ipsus, Demetrius I reoccupied Greece and, after the death of Cassander (297), gained control of Macedonia as well. But in 288 his Macedonian territory was simultaneously invaded by Lysimachus and Pyrrhus I of Epirus – the western neighbour of the Macedonians – with such success that Demetrius I lost his entire territories and fled to Asia Minor, where, three years later, he

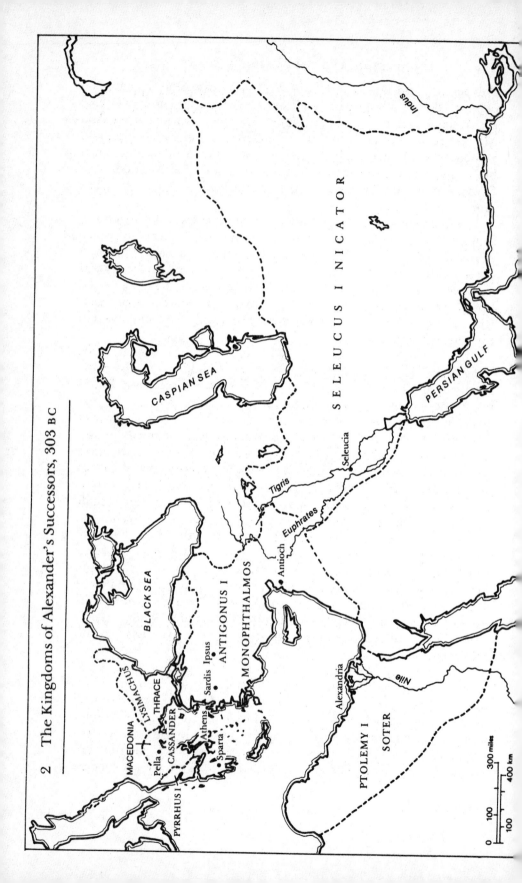

2   The Kingdoms of Alexander's Successors, 303 BC

SELEUCUS I NICATOR

CASPIAN SEA

PERSIAN GULF

Seleucia

BLACK SEA

Tigris

Euphrates

Antioch

ANTIGONUS I

Sardis   Ipsus

MONOPHTHALMOS

MACEDONIA

LYSIMACHUS

THRACE

Pella

CASSANDER

Athens

Sparta

Alexandria

Nile

PYRRHUS I

PTOLEMY I

SOTER

Indus

| 300 miles |
| 400 km |
0   100   100   300

0   100

died of drink, supplied freely by Seleucus I. Demetrius' son Antigonus II Gonatas maintained himself precariously in Greece, but meanwhile Lysimachus, by a series of lightning actions, was greatly extending his own territories, which now included not only Macedonia itself, but also Thrace, Thessaly and a large part of Asia Minor. In 281, however, he was attacked by his former ally Seleucus I, and at Corupedium in Lydia (western Asia Minor), these two last survivors of Alexander's generals, both over eighty years of age, fought a battle that confirmed Seleucid power, since Lysimachus lost and fell: but shortly afterwards Seleucus died too, at the hands of an assassin.

The scene was now transformed by the invasion of the Balkans by the warlike Celts (Gauls). Antigonus II Gonatas triumphantly repelled them near Lysimachia in Thrace (278/277), so that many of them moved across the straits (Hellespont) into Asia Minor, enabling their victor to establish control over Macedonia. The 'Age of the Successors' was now over, and the three great Hellenistic dynasties had fully established themselves: the Antigonids in Macedonia, the Seleucids in Syria and Babylonia and lands farther east, and the Ptolemies in their empire based on Egypt.

Meanwhile, beyond the fringes of this uneasy balance of power, other Greek or partially Hellenized kingdoms asserted or maintained their independence. On the northern shores of the Black Sea the state of the Spartocids on the Cimmerian (Crimean) Bosphorus (Straits of Kertch) attained considerable power and prosperity, and in the regions of Asia Minor that had remained more or less untouched by Alexander's conquests – Bithynia and Pontus in the north, and Cappadocia in the eastern central parts of the peninsula – effective dynasties held their own.

As for Greek lands in the west, a large part of Sicily was under the control of the dictatorial leader of Syracuse, Agathocles (317-289). The other city-states of the island appealed to the great Semitic power of Carthage in north Africa – originally a colony of Tyre in Phoenicia – which had established a naval and commercial hegemony over major areas of the western and central Mediterranean, including the western part of Sicily. When, in response to these appeals, the Carthaginians besieged Syracuse, Agathocles boldly crossed the sea and attacked Carthage itself; but in 306 peace was re-established on the basis of the *status quo*. Meanwhile, in Apulia – part of the large Hellenized region of southern Italy known as 'Magna Graecia' – the rulers of the ancient, wealthy agricultural city of Taras (Tarentum, now Taranto) dominated a league of neighbouring Greek cities and frequently invited commanders from Greece itself to help them repel their various Italian enemies.

9

3 The Balance of Power

The period that now followed was the great age of the Hellenistic world, though the relations between the various kingdoms were anything but harmonious.

Antigonus II Gonatas, for example, was severely threatened by his neighbour, Pyrrhus I of Epirus. For a time, Pyrrhus was tempted away to the west, where, at the request of Taras, he invaded south Italy and Sicily (280–275) – in order to help resist the encroachments of the rapidly rising Romans, who had formed the whole of central Italy, including civilized Etruria, into a single formidable confederation. But the king eventually left Taras at Rome's mercy and returned home, with a new and different intention, that of raising the Greek city-states against Antigonus II. However, in 272 Pyrrhus met his death at Argos.

Freed of this menace, Macedonia was virtually back in the strong position Philip II had won seventy years earlier. Yet there was one important difference. For Macedonia could no longer be seen as the only powerful Greek state in the eastern Mediterranean: the Seleucids and Ptolemies were there as well. Indeed, the Ptolemies possessed coastal territories in Asia Minor right up to the Aegean. The Seleucid monarchy, on the other hand, now under Antiochus I Soter (281–261), had to look in the opposite direction towards the south and east of its dominions, where a massive and historic colonization drive was under way. This drive also extended to the key central region of his empire, combining Syria and Lebanon. However, the Seleucid border with the Egyptians in those countries, though sometimes theoretically fixed on the river Eleutherus (Nahr el Kelb) dividing northern from southern Syria, was hotly disputed between the two great powers for decade after decade. The first of the many wars for the region broke out in 274, between Antiochus I and Ptolemy II Philadelphus (who had succeeded his father Ptolemy I Soter nine years earlier). But Antiochus I was in no position to contest the issue with any real determination, since he also needed to keep his gaze on Asia Minor. It is true that he had won a great victory in that country over the invading Gauls (275). Yet they remained a permanent menace, and he was obliged to accept their presence in the centre of the peninsula, in the land which was named Galatia after them.

In these circumstances Antiochus I agreed in 272 (with mental reservations) to recognize Egyptian suzerainty over southern Syria. This freed Ptolemy II Philadelphus to look further afield and intervene in Europe, adopting a policy of opposition to Macedonian control over Greek affairs. With this aim, he incited King Areus of Sparta (a city which still maintained its traditional authority in the Peloponnese) to attack Macedonia. Among the states which rallied to the same cause was Athens, which hoped to put the clock back to its prestigious past. But the war that followed (267–262) – known as the Chremonidean War, after its leading Athenian advocate – resulted in the utter collapse of this anti-Macedonian coalition formed at Egypt's prompting.

In Asia, on the other hand, Egyptian influence was strengthened by the secession of huge peripheral areas from the empire of its Seleucid rivals. First, at Pergamum, in western Asia Minor, Philetaerus (282–263), founder of the Attalid dynasty, became self-governing in fact though not yet in name. Next, after the accession of Antiochus II Theos (261–246) to the Seleucid throne, the huge eastern lands of Persia and Bactria broke away, under Iranian (Parthian) and Greek dynasties respectively. Meanwhile, however, Antiochus II had attempted to shore up his position by forming an alliance with Antigonus II Gonatas of Macedonia (259). In the following year, Antigonus defeated the Egyptian fleet off Cos, repeating the process in 245 when he beat Ptolemy III Euergetes (246–221) off another island, Andros.

These victories seemed to have elevated Antigonus to a dominant position in the Aegean. Somewhat unexpectedly, however, two groups of minor communities, which had merged with one another to form federations, now confronted him in continental Greece. One was the Aetolian League, a confederacy of obscure tribes in the centre of the country which had gained prestige by playing a leading part in pushing back the invasion of eastern Europe by the Celts (Gauls) (279). The second federation was the Achaean League, consisting of an amalgamation of little towns south of the Gulf of Corinth, to which the leader of the union, Aratus, was able to add his own native town of Sicyon in 251. Then in 243 Aratus, backed by Ptolemy III Euergetes behind the scenes, seized Corinth which was Macedonia's principal fortress in Greece. However, Aratus subsequently changed sides and joined Antigonus III Doson (229–221) against the Spartans, because their king Cleomenes III (following the example of Agis IV) had sought to introduce social reforms which seemed to Aratus, as to many others, to bear a perilously revolutionary aspect; and at Sellasia Cleomenes was decisively defeated (222).

The Seleucids had fared none too well under Seleucus II Callinicus Pogon (the Bearded) (246–226). A treaty of 241 had safeguarded his frontier against Ptolemy III, but at the cost of the sacrifice of the Syrian coastline, which passed into Egyptian hands. Then a quarrel which broke out between Seleucus II and his brother Antiochus Hierax (the Hawk) lasted for a whole decade, so that Seleucus' attempts to recapture the breakaway kingdoms of Pergamum, Parthia and Bactria failed.

After the murder of Seleucus II, a new period began in which all three states had youthful rulers. The Seleucid kingdom came into the hands of the dead man's eighteen-year-old brother Antiochus III the Great (223-187). Ptolemy III Euergetes was succeeded by his son Ptolemy IV Philopator (221-205), and the new Macedonian king was Antigonus III Doson's adopted son Philip V (221-179). Antiochus III and Ptolemy IV soon clashed, as the struggle for southern Syria was renewed. Mobilizing native Egyptians to supplement his Greek soldiery, Ptolemy IV repelled a Seleucid invasion at Raphia, south of Gaza (217), so that Antiochus III lost the greater part of his Syrian possessions. Nevertheless, he later embarked on one of the most remarkable enterprises of the age, an eastern expedition in imitation of Alexander the Great (212-206), culminating in his crossing of the Paropamisus (Hindu Kush). But the adventure had few permanent results, though Antiochus III did subsequently succeed in re-annexing southern Syria (together with Palestine) from Ptolemy V Epiphanes (205-180), as a result of the battle of Panion (200).

4 The Rise of Rome

Meanwhile the power of Rome was making itself ever increasingly felt. The Romans had first encountered Greek forces during Pyrrhus I's abortive invasion of southern Italy and Sicily (280-275). Subsequently, their victory over Carthage in the First Punic War (264-241) had gained them their first overseas province, the island of Sicily, which included many Greek city-states – though they left Hiero II of Syracuse (269-215) as an independent monarch, under their own ultimate control. Next, Roman fleets crossed the Adriatic Sea in order to suppress the hostile and piratical activities of the Illyrian queen Teuta (229) and their own former client Demetrius of Pharos (219). These expeditions were seen as an encroachment by the young King Philip V of Macedonia, who took advantage of Rome's immersion in the Second Punic War (218-201) to conclude an alliance with its Carthaginian arch-enemy Hannibal and invade the Peloponnesian regions of Greece. But the Romans' so-called First Macedonian War (215-205) was a minor and peripheral affair, in which they left their Greek allies (the Aetolians) in the lurch by concluding the Peace of Phoenice with Philip.

At this point, he saw an opportunity to turn against the outposts of the Egyptian empire along the coasts of Asia Minor. This, however, was interpreted as a threat to themselves both by Attalus I Soter of Pergamum (241-197) and by the leading maritime city-state of the Rhodians, who fought a damaging though indecisive sea-battle against the Macedonian fleet off Chios. Alarmed by the Macedonian menace, Pergamum, Rhodes and Egypt all appealed for help to the Romans, whose prestige was at its height following the victorious conclusion of the Second Punic War. Rome responded to their appeals, and the result was its Second Macedonian War. After several campaigns (200-197), the Roman general Flamininus was victorious at Cynoscephalae in Boeotia; his victory was only the first of many such successes against Greek states which sealed the ultimate downfall of the Hellenistic world. For the time being, Macedonia (and Philip) continued to exist. But Flamininus' declaration of the 'freedom' of Greece meant, in effect, that the city-states of the Greek mainland were destined henceforward to be Roman rather than Macedonian dependencies, though for the time being one of the major political units in the country, the Achaean League, was actually able to increase its power, under Philopoemen (d. 183).

Soon afterwards it was the turn of the Seleucids to feel Roman might. In 192, at the invitation of the Aetolian League, Antiochus III the Great invaded Greece, but he was driven out by the Romans after a battle at Thermopylae (191), defeated off Myonnesus (190), and then again at Magnesia by Sipylus in western Asia Minor. By the Treaty of Apamea that followed (188) Antiochus was forced to evacuate, permanently, the whole of Asia Minor west of the Taurus, ceding a large region to Eumenes II Soter of Pergamum (197-160/59) who had contributed to the Roman victory.

The next rulers of the major states were Seleucus IV Philopator (187-175) and Antiochus IV (Theos Epiphanes Nicephorus) (175-163) in the Seleucid kingdom, Ptolemy VI Philometor (180-145) in the dominions controlled by Egypt, and Philip V's son Perseus (179-168) in Macedonia. When Eumenes II Soter denounced Perseus to Rome for allegedly hostile intentions against Pergamum, the Romans embarked on their Third Macedonian War, and after operations lasting three years defeated Perseus' army at Pydna (168). Thereupon the king surrendered, and the Macedonian monarchy was suppressed in favour of four client 'republics', thus becoming the first of the great Hellenistic monarchies to succumb totally to Roman power.

Indeed, Pydna meant the end of any real independence throughout all parts of the Greek east, this side of Bactria and India, for Rome now felt free to attend to Antiochus IV Epiphanes. He, holding a pre-emptive

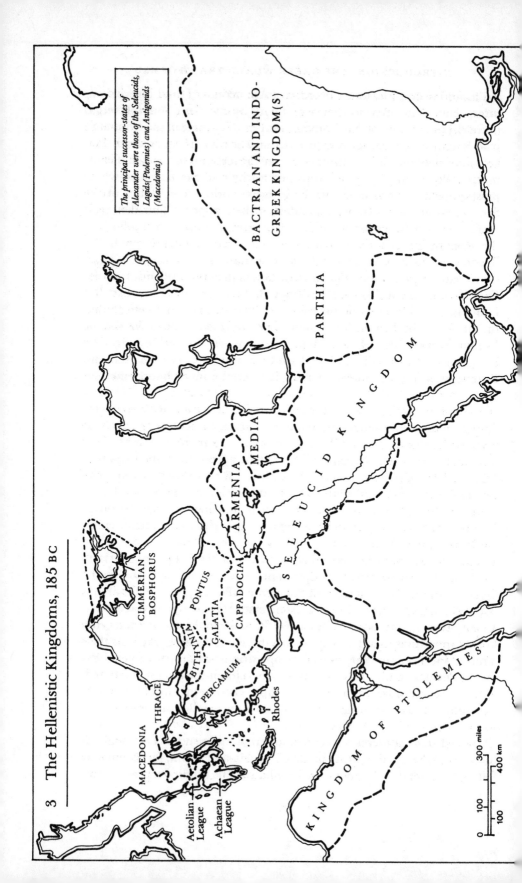

3 The Hellenistic Kingdoms, 185 BC

The principal successor-states of
Alexander were those of the Seleucids,
Lagids (Ptolemies) and Antigonids
(Macedonia)

BACTRIAN AND INDO-
GREEK KINGDOM(S)

PARTHIA

MEDIA

ARMENIA

S E L E U C I D   K I N G D O M

CIMMERIAN
BOSPHORUS

PONTUS

BITHYNIA

GALATIA

CAPPADOCIA

PERGAMUM

MACEDONIA

THRACE

Rhodes

Aetolian
League

Achaean
League

K I N G D O M   O F   P T O L E M I E S

300 miles

400 km

100

100

0

strike against the Ptolemaic kingdom to be necessary, had invaded the delta of the Nile. But control over Egypt would have made him too powerful in the eyes of the Romans, and at Pelusium on the border he submitted to their peremptory order to withdraw (168). Nevertheless, he still felt able to take repressive action against one of his own clients, the Jewish priestly state of Judaea, fearing pro-Ptolemaic subversion. But Antiochus IV's attempt, in the interests of universal Hellenism, to turn Jerusalem into a Greek community city ('Antiochia'), worshipping Zeus instead of the Hebrew God, precipitated a revolt among the Jews that eventually led to the proclamation of their independence, under the dynasty of the Hasmonaeans (Maccabeans).

An insurrection by Andriscus in Macedonia was put down by the Romans, who abolished the local republics and converted the country into a province (148); it included Greece as well, for when the leaders of the Achaean League remained obstinately determined to invade Sparta against Roman wishes, their army was defeated by Lucius Mummius, who sacked and destroyed their chief city, Corinth (146). In the same year the Third Punic War between the Romans and Carthaginians was concluded by the total destruction of Carthage, followed by the creation of the great Roman province of Africa, rich in grain. Twelve years later Attalus III Philometor Euergetes of Pergamum bequeathed his kingdom to Rome – probably in order to avoid social revolution; and the Romans converted its whole territory into their fabulously wealthy new province of Asia, putting down the rising of Aristonicus who sought to oppose the annexation.

During these years the historic Ptolemaic and Seleucid states, racked by internal disunities, were both in full decline, and came increasingly under the power of the Romans. On the other hand, the Greek kingdom of Bactria (northern Afghanistan), which even the long hand of Rome could not reach, was attaining extraordinary dimensions and power. Since its original secession from the Seleucids (c. 256–5), its dominions had been greatly expanded by the founder of a new dynasty, Euthydemus I Theos (c. 235–200). Early in the following century members of his house were established as far afield as Taxila beyond the Indus, and then a triumphant imperial drive into north-western India was conducted by Menander Soter Dikaios, who ruled from the second quarter of the second century until c. 140–130. He was the most powerful Greek monarch of his time in any land. His death, however, brought dynastic strife, amid which his empire split into a number of Bactrian and Indo-Greek kingdoms; and then these, one after another, succumbed to a variety of nomadic or formerly nomadic peoples of mixed Scythian, Parthian and Indian origins, who overran or sub-

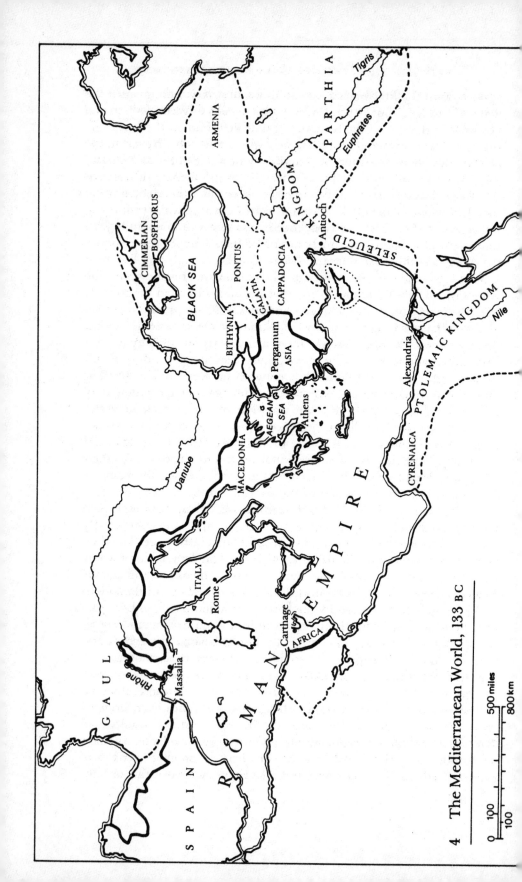

4 The Mediterranean World, 133 BC

ordinated all the Greek-ruled principalities, first in Bactria (*c.* 133–129) and next in the Indo-Greek states, which outlived it for more than a century.

At the other extremity of the Seleucid dominions, a major attempt to resist Rome had come from the partially Hellenized kingdom of Pontus in northern Asia Minor, where Mithridates VI Eupator, known also as Dionysus and the Great, ascended the throne in about 120 BC and conquered enormous extensions of territory. He temporarily suppressed the three-hundred-year-old kingdom of the Cimmerian Bosphorus (Crimea) across the Black Sea, and in Asia Minor itself seized control, for a period, of the hitherto independent states of Cappadocia and Bithynia. In 88 BC, when the Romans were preoccupied with an Italian rebellion (the Social War), Mithridates VI declared war against them – reportedly inciting the massacre of 80,000 Italians in Asia Minor – and proceeded to cross the Aegean and invade Macedonia and Greece, where Athens and other city-states supported his cause. Driven out of Europe by a Roman army led by Sulla, he renewed aggressive warfare in 74, and it was not until another eight years had passed that Rome finally defeated him. Pompey, the victorious general, combined the western part of Pontus with Bithynia to form a single Roman province, extending along the south coast of the Black Sea. Not long afterwards, the ancient, prosperous groups of Greek cities on the western shores of that sea (including Istrus in what is now Rumania, and Odessus and Mesambria, later Nessebur in Bulgaria) were plundered and subordinated by a native (Dacian) ruler from the interior, Burebistas, who established a powerful but short-lived kingdom uniting the tribes of the northern Balkans (*c.* 60–44 BC).

When Pompey had reorganized the affairs of the near east, he suppressed what little still remained of the Seleucid kingdom, and converted it into the Roman province of Syria. At this point, the only major Hellenistic state that still remained formally independent of Rome was Egypt, although it was coming more and more under the influence of Rome and Roman adventurers, tempted by its wealth. The last Egyptian monarch, Cleopatra (51–30 BC) – formally Cleopatra VII Philadelphus Philopator Philopatris – formed a mighty plan to revive the great Ptolemaic empire of the past by maintaining associations with two successive Roman leaders, Gaius Julius Caesar and Marcus Antonius (Antony), who both in turn became her lovers. But the dream collapsed in 31 when Antony's fleet, including a strong Egyptian flotilla, was defeated at Actium off north-western Greece by Caesar's great-nephew Octavian, soon to be known as Augustus. In the following year Egypt was annexed by Rome, and became its principal granary. Now, at last, the great Hellenistic kingdoms, which had arisen out of the heritage of Alexander's empire, were no more; though Hermaeus Soter continued to rule in Indo-Greek lands for another three decades before he fell to the Kushans.

Part I
The Hellenistic World

Chapter One

The Hellenistic Kingdoms

1 The Kingdoms of Europe

The ancient kingdom of Macedonia was centred upon the lower plain of the country, which is drained by the rivers Haliacmon and Axius and their tributaries and ringed around by mountains. The national rulers had from an early date regarded themselves as Hellenic, but their subjects, who were of very mixed race, tended to see the Greeks as foreigners, an attitude that was generally reciprocated. Nevertheless a form of the Greek language was spoken in Macedonia, and Hellenization began to make headway from the early fifth century onwards – when King Alexander I (*c.* 495–450) was recognized as a Greek by the presidents of the Olympic Games. Yet even in Hellenistic times the distinction between Greeks and Macedonians remained a feature of the political scene in Europe, though it tended to become partly effaced among settlers overseas.

The continued existence of kingship in Macedonia had in archaic (pre-classical) and classical times – that is to say, before the Hellenistic period – struck Greeks as foreign or anachronistic. And indeed the Macedonian monarchs retained some of the characteristics of a chieftain of the Heroic Age. They were on frank and familiar social terms with the nobles, who ranked as their kinsmen and provided their Companions. Yet the king continued to personify the state, and exercised supremacy in every aspect of public life. The army, it is true, retained certain traditional, limited powers, including the right to appoint the monarch by acclamation; but in the classical epoch it had already ceased, once the royal appointment had been made, to go on playing a leading part as an assembly of free men in arms, as has sometimes been supposed.

The country's greatest asset was its peasantry, which had to be tough because the Macedonians' tribal neighbours were warlike and threatening; it combined independent-mindedness with staunch reliability and loyalty. The country was also rich in timber, grain and wine. Its original royal residence at inland Aegae (now identified with Vergina, where

21

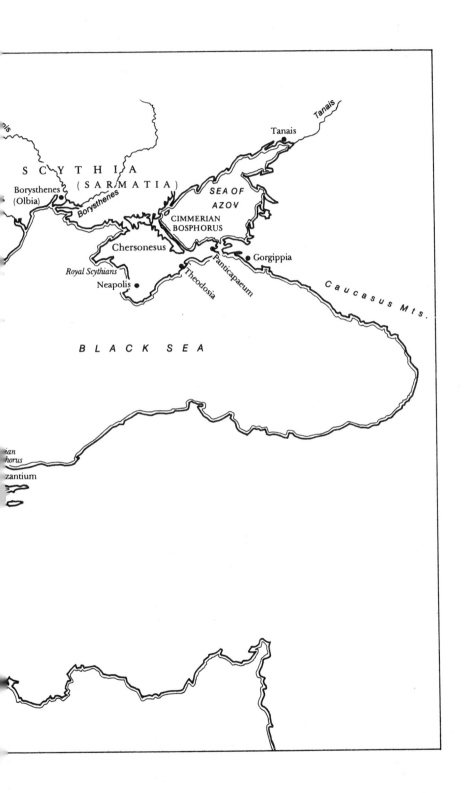

 nis

S C Y T H I A
(S A R M A T I A)

Borysthenes
(Olbia)

Borysthenes

Tanais

Tanais

SEA OF
AZOV

CIMMERIAN
BOSPHORUS

Chersonesus

Gorgippia

Royal Scythians

Panticapaeum

Neapolis

Theodosia

Caucasus Mts.

B L A C K   S E A

ian
horus

zantium

sensational archaeological discoveries dating from *c.* 340 have recently brought the number of tombs found there up to eight) was known as the Garden of Midas – proverbial for his wealth – because of its vines, orchards and roses. But when urbanization began to take place it was Pella, fifteen miles from the sea but linked to it by a river and lake (now silted up), which became the country's capital and largest city.

This perhaps occurred in the reign of Archelaus (413–399), who built straight roads and well-fortified strongholds and developed his heavy cavalry. But the decisive figure in the rise of the country was Philip II (359–336), who vastly increased its power and strength in every field. He seized and exploited the enormous riches of Mount Pangaeum's gold and silver mines – the major source of supply of these metals in Greek lands – using this wealth to create and pay for a first-class, up-to-date infantry army. He transformed the adjacent highlanders, it was said, from shepherds wearing skins into civilized citizens. And finally he crushed the Greek city-states at Chaeronea (338), compelling them to form the Federal League of Corinth under his own leadership.

Philip had set the stage for the conquering expedition of his son Alexander III the Great – an enterprise he would have conducted himself, had he not been murdered at the age of forty-six. To Demosthenes (d. 322), who had tried vainly to whip up the Greeks against him, he was a treacherous despot; but another influential Athenian orator, Isocrates (d. 338) saw him as precisely the man whom Greece needed. Their younger contemporary Theopompus of Chios paid the monarch the compliment of planning his history of the epoch, the *Philippica*, round his career, even though he was prepared to criticize his Companions as a bunch of debauchees from all over Greece. Philip's exploits continued to arouse violent controversy among the Greeks: yet all had to agree that it was he, quite as much as his son Alexander, who created the new epoch, the Hellenistic age, that was to follow.

Alexander worked to transform the army from a predominantly Macedonian institution into a cosmopolitan force owing loyalty only to himself. But the wars between his successors tossed the land of Macedonia, and its army, disastrously from hand to hand, and left the country ravaged, mutilated and partitioned. By unprecedentedly sweeping amalgamations of small communities, Cassander founded the new cities of Cassandrea (316, on the site of old Potidaea), and Thessalonica (the modern Salonica), which was made out of twenty-six former communities in 316/315 and replaced Pella as Macedonia's principal port; though Cassander rebuilt Pella as well. His brother Alexarchus created Uranopolis (City of Heaven) on the peninsula that separates Mount

Athos from the mainland. Then Demetrius I Poliorcetes (the Besieger) founded Demetrias on the Gulf of Pagasae in Thessaly (*c.* 293), once again by merging numerous small local towns. Demetrias was designed to assume a vital role as a garrison, one of the 'fetters' (along with Corinth on the isthmus and Chalcis in Euboea) by which the Macedonians controlled Greece, since they could not afford to see the country united or intriguing against them; yet none of these new foundations regarded themselves as integral parts of the Macedonian kingdom.

Indeed, the fortunes of the kingdom still remained highly uncertain, until Antigonus II Gonatas (284-239) revived them. In the earlier 280s, restricted and harassed by his neighbour Pyrrhus I of Epirus, he had just managed to hold on to the strategic 'fetters'. But then in 278/7, near Lysimachia in Thrace, he scored his resounding success against the invading Celts (Gauls), whose threat to Macedonia and Greece was thus averted, so that Antigonus II had played a major part in saving Hellenism from the barbarians.

Thus began a new and tenacious line of Macedonian kings, devoting close personal attention to government, and drawing the bulk of their revenue from their own personal estates, without the need to impose oppressive taxation. They were still the national rulers of a free Macedonian people. But the day of Philip II's professional long-term force was over: the Macedonian part of the army had once again become a levy of farmers, called up only when they were needed. By this time, however, these potential Macedonian warriors only numbered 30,000 at most, since wars and emigrations had eaten their numbers away. The bulk of the armed forces consisted, instead, of mercenary soldiers - Greeks and Illyrian and northern tribesmen, many of whom had been settled on Macedonian soil to replace gaps in the peasantry. These were the men the monarchs employed to garrison the strongpoints of Greece.

Meanwhile the Hellenization of Macedonia itself continued. In the third century the national dialect was largely replaced by the current, uniform Greek speech (*koine*), and the native pantheon gave way to the Olympian deities. Prosperity continued under Philip V (221-179) and Perseus (179-168), who developed Demetrias as a flourishing cosmopolitan port, now revealed by excavations. Grain was stored in Macedonian warehouses against the hour of need. And that hour was soon at hand, because both monarchs in turn overreached themselves and became disastrously embroiled with Rome, the latter with terminal results for his kingdom: after Perseus' defeat at Pydna in 168 it was converted into four weak republics, which were in their turn abolished to form a Roman province in 148.

The Macedonians had been defeated because Rome's armies and generals had achieved overall superiority: the Greek phalanx of the time was no match for the more flexible Roman legionary tactics. But Macedonia also succumbed to Rome because there were so few Macedonians. There had never been more than four million, and now there were less – too few to stand up successfully to the manpower of Italy.

One of the numerous conquests of Philip II around the borders of Macedonia had been its eastern neighbour, Thrace. The coast of the country had been colonized by Greeks from the eighth century BC onwards – their settlements included Byzantium (the future Constantinople) and Abdera (place of origin of leading intellectuals, Protagoras, Democritus and the historian Hecataeus) – but they had not Hellenized the interior. Its mountains and plains were inhabited by warlike tribes, speaking an Indo-European language that was not, however, closely connected with Greek. In the fifth century one of these tribes or tribal groups, the Odrysae, asserted their control over a large part of Thrace, extracting tribute from the Greek coastal cities. The subsequent fragmentation of this Odrysian empire gave Philip II the opportunity to invade the whole land and reduce its princes to tributary status; and in 342 he founded a military colony at Philippopolis (known informally as Poneropolis, 'Scoundrelton' – the modern Plovdiv), which commanded the route from Macedonia to the Greek settlements on the Black Sea.

After the death of Alexander the Great, Thrace was assigned, together with a portion of north-western Asia Minor, to Lysimachus, whose name was perpetuated at his new capital Lysimachia on the Thracian Chersonese, now the Gallipoli (Gelibolu) peninsula (309). However, at least two of the country's native principalities eluded his grasp. Yet they were open to Greek cultural influences. Thus Kazanlik, lying far into the interior of what is now Bulgaria, displays tombs (c. 300) containing paintings in emphatically Greek styles. Elsewhere, however, gold and silver drinking horns, although executed by Greek artists (notably the objects of the magnificent Lukovit and Panagyurishte treasures, probably the property of the native king Seuthes III), display compromises between Greek and Iranian tastes. At Strelca, nearby, the grave of one of the Thracian notables of the time has recently come to light.

The strife between Lysimachus and other Successors tempted the Celts (Gauls), when they were prevented from overrunning Macedonia, to invade Thrace instead, where those of them who did not move on to Asia Minor (Galatia) founded a kingdom of their own (279), forcing Byzantium to pay tribute. The Gaulish state was overthrown by a Thracian rebellion sponsored by Macedonia (216), but after that country succumbed to the Romans the Gaulish chieftains asserted control over the coastal Greek cities and gradually made the native Thracian tribes of the interior their vassals. Yet a high Thracian culture continued to exist – a superb ritual silver cauldron of the second or first century BC, found at Gundestrup in Denmark, seems to have been one of its products. During the latter part of this period, the rulers of Thrace played a considerable part in Roman politics; and the country, although thereafter it passed under Rome's indirect control in the form of client states, did not become a province of the empire until AD 46.

Princes who were Thracian in origin, more or less Hellenized, also played a large part in the histories of other countries in the Black Sea region. A Thracian dynasty established itself in Bithynia (north-west Asia Minor) in 298 BC (Chapter One, section 4). But long before that, other rulers of Thracian race, the Spartocids, had formed a powerful state on the Cimmerian (Crimean) Bosphorus, the strait which links the Black Sea with the Sea of Azov. The foundations of the principality had been laid in the 480s when the Archaeanactid ruling house of the old Greek colony of Panticapaeum ('Way of Fishes' in Iranian, now Kertch) unified the Greek cities on either bank of the narrows for better defence against Scythian, Sarmatian and other barbarian neighbours. Then in 438 Spartocus I, a Thracian mercenary commander, developed a régime displaying a highly centralized government, conducted by a Greek or Graecized minority dominating over local populations, which foreshadowed the Hellenistic kingdoms of the future. During the centuries that followed, this Spartocid state, together with its dependencies and neighbours in other parts of South Russia, formed a very extensive, prosperous and diversified complex of Hellenism which constituted a major autonomous factor in the history of the age.

Its rulers adopted thoroughly Greek ways. Leucon I (389/8–349/8) described himself as 'archon' (the title of city magistrates) of the Bosphorus and of Theodosia (a Greek harbour city in the south-east Crimea) and 'king' of various tribes. Paerisades I (349/8–311/10) fought off the Royal Scyths of the Crimean interior (a partially Hellenized military people whose capital was later at Neapolis, near the modern Simferopol) and exercised suzerainty as far as, or beyond, Gorgippia (Anapa) at the foot of the Caucasus, and up to Tanais at the mouth of the river of that name (the Don). Spartocus III (304/3–284/3) assumed the title of King of the Bosphorus, and in the course of the third century Eupatoria in the south-west Crimea (neighbour of independent Chersonesus) became part of the Spartocid territories.

A strong fishing industry was one of the national assets, but, above all, the country had invaluable access to the endless grain-lands of the Russian interior, exporting wheat extensively to other Hellenistic kingdoms and to the Aegean city-states, notably Athens (from which came oil, wine, luxury goods and plays of the New Comedy in exchange). These activities of the Bosphoran state, supported by local non-Greek serf labour, brought in great wealth, attested by a fine royal coinage and extensive municipal issues of Panticapaeum (including fourth-century gold pieces) executed in superior Greek styles. A series of splendidly equipped rock-tombs at the same city reflected Mesopotamian and Egyptian as well as Greek influences; and extremely sumptuous goldwork and jewellery, made by artists who may have been Graeco-Iranians from Parthia or Bactria, displayed novel Hellenized versions of the animal style favoured by the Scythian and Sarmatian tribes.

These tribes collaborated with the Greek and Hellenized coastal community in a highly profitable slave trade. Nevertheless, they also, from time to time, presented a grave threat to that community, so that the independent city-state of Borysthenes (Olbia), for example – near the mouth of the river Hypanis (Bug) – could only keep the native ruler Saitaphernes at bay by the subsidies paid him by an Olbian millionaire, Protogenes.

And the Scythians and Sarmatians terrorized and weakened the kings of the Bosphorus as well, from the time of Spartocus IV (245-215) onwards, until Paerisades V felt compelled to appeal to Rome's famous enemy Mithridates VI Eupator of Pontus, who responded with alacrity – being interested in forming a Black Sea empire – and annexed the entire Bosphoran kingdom, adding it to his own possessions (108/7). After Mithridates' death following eventual defeat by the Romans, the victors granted the Bosphorus to his son and betrayer Pharnaces II. Pharnaces also tried to establish himself in Pontus (Chapter One, section 4), but after his defeat by Julius Caesar at Zela fled back to the Bosphorus where he was killed by a rebel. The Bosphoran kingdom, however, continued its existence for another three hundred and fifty years, as a strategically and commercially important and privileged Roman client.

To the west of Macedonia lay Epirus, which for a brief moment at the beginning of the Hellenistic age played a leading part in Greek affairs. It was a rugged country bordering on small coastal plains beside the Ionian Sea; behind the plains were narrow, wooded, well-watered valleys and plateaus separated by three mountain ranges parallel to the shore. The rough tribesmen in the interior, who were partly non-Greek but spoke an Indo-European tongue (Illyrian) and claimed Homeric origins, gradually became subject to commercial and cultural influences from a few Greek maritime colonies (including Ambracia and the island cities of Leucas and Corcyra, the modern Corfu), and from the inland oracle of Dodona which drew pilgrims from all Greece.

It was the tribe holding the plain near Dodona, the Molossi, which first unified the greater part of Epirus, in a confederacy under its king Alexander I (342–330), brother-in-law of Philip II of Macedonia. In the spirit of a Heroic Age adventurer, Alexander I responded to a call by Taras and occupied most of southern Italy in alliance with Rome, but was subsequently defeated and killed. Then Pyrrhus I (297–272) extended the frontiers of his kingdom northwards to include parts of the Illyrian coastline (probably as far as Epidamnus, later known as Dyrrhachium). He also expanded to the east and south at the expense of the Macedonians and emancipated himself from their dominant influence, occupying Leucas, Corcyra and Ambracia which he embellished and enlarged and made into his capital. A war with Macedonia brought him further territorial gains. He proved unable to keep them; but he had forced his backward country into the contemporary Hellenistic world.

Next, like Alexander I before him, Pyrrhus I accepted an appeal by Taras to invade south Italy, this time to ward off Roman encroachments (280). He won important battles against the Romans –their first historic encounter with a Greek enemy – but decided to pass onwards to Sicily to confront the Carthaginians, who were at that time Rome's allies. Their expulsion from the island, where they had been established for centuries, seemed almost within reach, when Pyrrhus after all made up his mind to try his luck in Italy once again. There, however, a battle at Beneventum (275), though not unsuccessful, cost him more losses than he could afford (hence the phrase 'Pyrrhic victory'), and he returned to Epirus with only one-third of his force still surviving. He then decided to attack Antigonus II Gonatas, but, changing his plans again, moved off to the Peloponnese, where he died at Argos, stunned by a tile thrown from a roof by an old woman and then decapitated by a Macedonian soldier.

Despite his achievements at home, Pyrrhus I had failed to impose his influence over the rest of the Greek mainland, just as he had failed to impose it over the Greek west. Moreover, the history of Epirus as a notable power virtually began and ended with himself. His successors were involved in wars on all sides, and in about 232 the monarchy came to an end. The league that replaced it split up, and the Molossians, in opposition to neighbouring tribes, fatally chose to support the losing cause of Perseus of Macedonia against the Romans. In consequence, a Roman army devastated the country and deported 150,000 of its inhabitants (167), attaching those who were left to Rome's new Macedonian province in 146.

The Illyrian tribes on the Adriatic coast farther north spoke an Indo-European tongue like the Epirots, but were even slower to embark on material development. In the latter half of the second century BC, however, King Agron succeeded in controlling a state which extended from Dalmatia to the river Aous, though it stopped short of the Greek colonies on the Adriatic shore (notably Apollonia), which served as channels for its trade. After his death (231) his widow Teuta defied Rome openly, besieging the Greek port of Epidamnus (Dyrrhachium), but was obliged to submit to a Roman fleet (229) and withdraw from most of her coastland. In 219, however, she provoked the Romans into sending a second expedition against her, whereupon Philip v of Macedonia came to her help; this started the train of events which brought Rome fatefully into the Balkan peninsula. In continuation of this process, the Illyrian king Genthius, who issued portrait-coins with Greek inscriptions, was induced by Philip v's son Perseus to attack the Romans, but suffered immediate defeat (168) and was taken prisoner. At this juncture, Rome abolished the Illyrian kingdom and divided it into three autonomous but not truly independent regions. Subsequently, however, a number of punitive expeditions proved necessary before Roman governors were regularly sent to the country in the first century BC.

Two states that were small but owned valuable territory, Sparta in the Peloponnese and Syracuse in Sicily, possessed kingships of earlier origins which nevertheless, in the Hellenistic epoch, took on many of the essential characteristics of the monarchies of the time.

The constitution of Sparta was antique and exceptional. Two kings, belonging to the Agiad and Eurypontid families, traditionally held equal power. They were the military commanders, but, in the archaic (pre-classical) and classical periods, they resembled state functionaries rather than the Hellenistic monarchs of the future. Moreover, the executive, judicial and disciplinary powers of the state were not in their hands, but were exercised by the annually elected ephors, who, in the fifth century, were five in number. Sparta thus had a 'mixed' constitution, which was subsequently admired by the Hellenistic historian Polybius and greatly interested the founders of the United States of America.

Sparta, the most prominent of the states speaking the Doric dialect they had inherited from their remote immigrant forebears, the Dorian Greeks, had for centuries exercised domination over the inhabitants of Laconia and Messenia in the southern Peloponnese. These included peoples of mixed race, 'the dwellers round about' (*perioikoi*), who ranked as a kind of second-class Spartan citizen, possessing rights that did not extend beyond their own localities. The rest of the population were Helots, state slaves who worked on the land. The ownership of the soil, on the other hand, belonged to the true Spartan citizens (Spartiates), each of whom possessed an equal portion of soil. This relatively small élite, unceasingly and vigilantly aware that the *perioikoi* and Helots overwhelmingly outnumbered and menaced them, had their lives regulated to meet this perpetual threat. For they were placed under state control from birth, underwent a ruthlessly tough education and training, and thereafter continued to lead lives of the utmost austerity based on communal messes. This brutal but logical system, of which the origin was attributed to a semi-legendary personage, Lycurgus, continued to attract interested comment throughout the Greek world – and a good deal of admiration among people of the most diverse views, including militaristic conservatives and egalitarian theorists alike.

By 500 BC Sparta dominated a league extending over most of the Peloponnese, and exerting influence far beyond its borders. The Spartans shared with Athens the credit for winning the Persian Wars, and then, after the two cities had come to blows in the Peloponnesian War (431) it was Sparta that gained the final victory (404). But its disastrous defeat at Leuctra (371), at the hands of the briefly ascendant power of Thebes, was followed by the secession of Messenia and marked the end of Spartan hegemony. Thereafter, the Spartans did not join the Greek movement that tried to confront Philip II of Macedonia, and their subsequent belated resistance to the Macedonians, while Alexander was away in Persia, was crushed by his regent Antipater.

Subsequently, the Spartan king Areus (309/8–265) sought to create an anti-Macedonian coalition, but was killed when it was defeated in the Chremonidean War.

The currency of Sparta, uninterested in trade, had always been limited to iron bars; but Areus, eager to assert himself as a modern Hellenistic ruler, innovated by striking silver coins, on which he stamped his own head. This not only meant that the old ban on a money economy had been reversed, but provided a sign that the old Spartan austerity in general was being rapidly eroded. The ancient, rigorous training and communal eating of the Spartiate citizenry had been abandoned, just as its Doric dialect had been eroded by the common Greek speech (the *koine*). The traditional equality of their land-holdings, too, was a thing of the past; there were now about a hundred very rich men and women, whose wealth caused great ill-will. The other Spartiates had to have recourse to mortgages – and these had become oppressively heavy, so that many borrowers from their ranks became so impoverished that they no longer satisfied the property qualification which was a condition for the holding of citizen status. In consequence, the number of Spartiates diminished to such a catastrophic extent that no more than seven hundred of them remained, while another two thousand had been disfranchised recently enough to retain feelings of extreme bitterness and resentment. Sparta, in fact, was faced with a ruinous crisis – and had become the early forcing-ground of many of the troubles which were to appear in the rest of Greece in the years that lay ahead.

King Agis IV (244–241) felt that everything would be better if the old traditional training and common mess-life were revived – and with them the old equal allotments of land. He had been taught that in antique times Lycurgus had carried out a land distribution: and that is what he, too, intended to do, in order to create 4,500 equal lots. In addition, he proposed to increase the number of Spartiates by cancelling mortgage debts (which would allow many people to regain their lost citizen rights) and enfranchising some of the *perioikoi*. Opposition, however, was strong. The owners of the large properties, though glad enough to have their debts cancelled, were naturally hostile to the redistribution of their own land; and some of the ephors, horrified at what sounded like a recipe for revolution, supported these objections. Moreover, even those who had earlier lost their citizen status, while keen to regain it by having their debts cancelled, found it very distasteful to have *perioikoi* as fellow-citizens and sharers in their new prosperity. Agis did his best; he enlisted the help of his mother Agesistrata (who, together with his grandmother Archidamia, was the richest of the rich Spartan women), he deposed reactionary ephors, and he forced his equally hostile fellow monarch Leonidas II into exile. But when he burnt the mortgages, Leonidas returned, and Agis was killed by the ephors.

Cleomenes III (235–219), Leonidas' son, learnt about all Agis' convictions from his wife, who was the dead man's widow; and he became determined to put these ideas into practice. But although an admirer of the Stoic philosophy (Chapter Four, section 2) – and of his Stoic guest Sphaerus of Borysthenes (Olbia), a writer on the Spartan constitution, like other members of his school – Cleomenes came to the conclusion that forceful rather than persuasive methods would have to be used to introduce such changes. Reform inside his territory, and military victory outside it, should go together, he felt, each reinforcing the other. So he moved his troops north, and annexed Peloponnesian cities belonging to the Aetolian Confederacy (229). Next he confronted Aratus, the Achaean League's famous leader; it was a tragedy for the Greeks that their two most able men of the age, outside the great kingdoms, should have clashed in this way.

The poor in many other cities flocked to Cleomenes' side, hoping that his reforms would spread to their cities as well. But once he had won two victories against the Achaeans, he chose to return home, and concentrated on Spartan affairs instead. First he executed four of the ephors – and abolished their historic office altogether. Then he cancelled debts, enrolled *perioikoi* and mercenaries as citizens, redistributed the land into 4,000 equal holdings and sold some thousands of Helots their freedom – which was a step that Agis had never taken, and caused alarm in slave-owning circles throughout Greece. Cleomenes' action was an emergency measure intended to increase the size of his army. For it was now his intention to fight the Achaean League again, and with a more formidable force than before. To the Achaean leader Aratus the threat seemed so severe that he reversed the policy of a lifetime and turned to the Macedonian kingdom for help. Antigonus III Doson contributed the most substantial army he could muster, and he and the Achaeans defeated Cleomenes at Sellasia on the Laconian border (222). Almost the entire Spartan force was destroyed, and Sparta itself fell to the invaders. Thereupon Cleomenes fled to Egypt where (after an abortive revolt) he committed suicide.

Before long, another Spartan, Nabis (207–192), probably descended from an exiled branch of the Eurypontid royal family, became guardian of the youthful king Pelops, and after the young man's somewhat mysterious death seized the crown for himself, becoming not so much a traditional Spartan monarch as a typical autocrat of the Hellenistic type. Forming a bodyguard of mercenaries, enlisting Cretan pirates as allies, and 'freeing slaves'[1] (who were probably Helots), he revived the full reformist programme of Cleomenes, but with even more whole-hearted ruthlessness. This made him popular, especially among the poorer classes; and his popularity spread when, like Cleomenes, he exported his ideas to other cities. After a clash with the Achaean League under Philopoemen, Nabis changed sides in the second war between Macedonia and Rome (200–197), deserting Philip V in favour of the Romans. But it was not long before his relations with the Roman commander Flamininus, who distrusted his aggressive behaviour, gravely deteriorated, and in 192 an officer of the Aetolian League, which likewise found Nabis an unreliable ally, struck him down.

The Spartan 'revolutions' had failed, because they were backward-looking and made no attempt to create new wealth, of which there was not enough to go round. Nor were the three successive reformist leaders ever strong enough to win lasting dominance in the Peloponnese, despite all the attractions these programmes held out to its poorer inhabitants; the ruling classes in other states were frightened of these unusual Spartan kings – and Nabis, though at first maintaining his power adroitly, made a fatal mistake by alienating Rome.

After his death, Sparta passed into the hands of Philopoemen's Achaean League. When the Achaeans were destroyed by Rome, and Greece became part of a Roman province, the city remained technically a free city but had no real independence left, and lost its outlet to the sea; though at the end of the first century BC this was restored to its client-ruler Eurycles by Augustus.

The indigenous peoples of Sicily (Siceli, Sicani, Elymi) had been supplemented and partly overrun, ever since the eighth century BC, by two separate sets of immigrants. In the west of the island, there were Semitic-speaking people from the Syrian coastland of Phoenicia: originally settlers from the great maritime cities of Tyre and Sidon, whose descendants came under the control of their compatriots at Carthage in north Africa. The east of Sicily, on the other hand, was occupied by Greek colonies: the local historian Timaeus of Tauromenium (c. 356–260) was at pains to prove that the island had been Greek from very early times.

These numerous Greek settlements continued to exist as independent city-states. Outstanding among them was Syracuse, where Gelon I (c. 490–478), victor over the Carthaginians, sought to convert his 'tyranny' (the word the Greeks used for autocratic régimes when they possessed no dynastic basis) into a legitimate royal house. The dynasty was carried on by his son Hiero I (478–467/6). Subsequently, after the victorious repulse of an expedition sent by Athens during the Peloponnesian War (415–413), Dionysius I (406–367) established a new autocratic régime in the city. Continuing to keep the Carthaginians at bay, Syracuse achieved spectacular increases in wealth and population, becoming the most magnificent and best fortified of Greek townships anywhere in the world. It asserted control over the whole of the eastern half of the island, and possessed the most powerful of all Mediterranean fleets: so that it uniquely combined the features of a city-state and an imperial kingdom.

Dionysius' son Dionysius II (367–344) resisted attempts by Plato (friend of the young monarch's relative Dion) to turn him into a philosopher-king. Finally, however, blockaded by a fleet of Syracusan rebels and Carthaginians, Dionysius II was obliged to surrender to the newly arrived Timoleon, a Corinthian, who freed Syracuse and Greek Sicily from dictatorial rule and the Carthaginian threat alike. Although his praises by the patriotic Timaeus sound suspiciously fulsome, he must have been an inspiring and altruistic leader under whom, as the archaeological evidence shows, the island enjoyed a notable revival of urban growth and prosperity.

Timoleon retired from public life when his eyesight was failing (337). Twenty years later, however, the Republican government of Syracuse was overthrown by Agathocles of Thermae Himeraeae (317–289), with the help of a mixed force of Sicels and exiles from other Greek cities. Agathocles then proceeded to rule as dictator, mobilizing the lower classes as his supporters and subjecting the nobility to terrorist atrocities (possibly exaggerated by Timaeus, whom he banished). But the Carthaginians, who had supported his coup, soon turned against him; whereupon Agathocles took the unprecedentedly bold step of invading north Africa and attacking Carthage itself (310). Forced, after initial successes, to withdraw from African soil (307), he nevertheless imposed his rule over most of Sicily itself (placing its three-legged emblem, the *triskelis*, on his coins) and subsequently intervened in Italy and even captured Corcyra (*c.* 300). Four years earlier, he had declared himself king, and was unmistakably the outstanding figure of the western Mediterranean world. Thus, in his last years, he felt able to afford somewhat milder methods, and Syracuse and its dependencies enjoyed peace and prosperity.

Agathocles' death was followed by a period of chaos. A new autocrat, Hicetas (288–278), was defeated by the Carthaginians, who would probably have taken over the whole island had it not been for the arrival of King Pyrrhus I of Epirus (278–276). After his departure one of his Syracusan officers, Hiero II, seized power and ruled Syracuse for no less than fifty-four years (*c.* 269–215). He made a grave initial mistake by siding with Carthage against Rome at the beginning of the First Punic War, but changed sides rapidly enough to benefit from the final Roman victory in 241. For when, in the subsequent settlement, the rest of Sicily became Rome's first overseas province, Hiero II was allowed to retain control over most of the eastern part of the island.

His wife Philistis helped his claim to legitimacy by her descent from the family of Dionysius I, but Hiero also boasted of renewing the older glories of Gelon I and Hiero I. Protected by the Romans from his own potentially disaffected subjects, and prudently avoiding expansionist adventures of every kind, he was able to dispense with severe political or financial measures. His taxation system (the *Lex Hieronica*), partially modelled on the Revenue Laws of Ptolemy II Philadelphus of Egypt, impressed the Romans so much that they subsequently took it over for employment in their own province. In its original form (unlike its partial Egyptian prototype), it claimed for the monarch a tenth part (tithe) of all crops produced in his kingdom. Hiero was a technocrat who wrote a handbook on agronomy and used the exportation of the wheat piled up in his massive, fortified granary as a potent economic and political instrument. With an eye on the Egyptian and Rhodian trade, he also maintained an impressive fleet, including the unique 5,000 tonner *Alexandria*.

Although Sicily had produced the great fifth-century philosopher Empedocles of Acragas, Plato's idea of converting the Syracusan court to philosophical ways had proved a dismal failure; and thereafter, too, *nouveau riche* Hellenistic Sicily was by no means in the cultural forefront. It is true that Centuripe, north-west of Syracuse, produced some of the best vase-paintings of the time, and that Hiero erected grandiose buildings, including perhaps the largest altar in the world (650 × 74 feet). But local writers were relatively few, though in the field of history Timaeus found a single successor in Philinus of Acragas, who wrote an anti-Roman account of the First Punic War. However, Sicily did possess its own specific literary traditions: the origins of pastoral poetry were traditionally ascribed to the island, and Sophron, who in the fifth century created the literary mime, had been a Syracusan. So was Theocritus, who endowed both these genres with genius (Chapter Three, section 2; Chapter Four, section 3). But when Theocritus appealed to Hiero II (in the early days of both) for patronage, Hiero evidently failed to respond, or responded inadequately, for Theocritus went to live in Cos and Alexandria instead. However, his younger contemporary Archimedes, the greatest scientist of the age, was also a Syracusan, and Hiero became his intimate friend – finding his engineering inventions useful for military purposes.

Hiero II lived long enough to come to the Romans' help in the Second Punic War, thus creating a vital barrier between Hannibal's army in Italy and the home base in Africa on which he relied for reinforcements. But after Hiero's death, his grandson Hieronymus sided with Carthage, which he believed to be winning the war. He was overthrown by a plot, but Syracuse had to stand siege from the Romans (213–212) and eventually fell and was sacked, despite the defensive schemes of Archimedes – who was killed by a Roman soldier. The kingdom was abolished and assigned to the Roman province of Sicily.

The island was never again to play an independent part in ancient Mediterranean history. Henceforward, it was chiefly remarkable for the grain it supplied to Rome, and for its large landed estates, manned by gangs of maltreated slaves who broke out into the gravest slave-revolts that the Romans ever experienced (135–132, 104–100).

2 The Ptolemies

Uniquely shaped by the narrow but immensely fertile Nile valley, Egypt possessed formidable potential resources and strength: and Greeks had always been well aware of this. During the two centuries before Alexander, the country had been under the domination of the Achaemenid Persian empire, whose ruler Cambyses had invaded the country in 525 and dethroned the Egyptian Pharaoh. A native revolt in *c.* 410-404 was successful, but Artaxerxes III Ochus re-established Persian authority in 341. Nine years later, however, Alexander the Great occupied the whole of Egyptian territory without opposition, its population welcoming him as a liberator.

He left the ancient Egyptian city of Memphis as the capital of the country, but immediately set about the foundation of a new Greek colony at Alexandria. It was a mark of genius to see in the meagre fishing village of Rhacotis the immense and spectacular city of the future. Whereas most of Alexander's colonies were located and planned for a military purpose, it is probable that he founded Alexandria for commercial reasons, to take the place of Tyre in Phoenicia, which he had destroyed.

Alexandria faced both ways, and was defensible from either side: it was linked to the interior of the country by Nile canals debouching in Lake Mareotis, and to the north it had two fine harbours opening on to the Mediterranean. With the Pharos lighthouse planned by Sostratus of Cnidus under Ptolemy I Soter, and completed under his son Ptolemy II Philadelphus (*c.* 279), as their symbol and unfailing guide (it ranked as one of the Seven Wonders of the World), these harbours were fully able to accommodate the large ships of the epoch. Alexandria made one set of fortunes by exporting the surpluses of Egypt, and another by its maritime trading all over the near and middle east.

With dazzling speed it became the largest of all Greek cities. Dominated by a principal avenue of unprecedented width, it extended over a rectangular area measuring four miles by three-quarters of a mile, and contained, before the end of the third century, something like half a million inhabitants. These included the largest Greek (and partly Macedonian) population of any colonial foundation; the place persistently maintained its Greek customs – and for a long time preserved sentimental ties with the city-states of the homeland. The Greeks of Alexandria had their own exceptional privileges and organization (*politeuma*), but no assembly and probably no council (or had one at first, but soon lost it). The large Jewish community, too, possessed an autonomous *politeuma* of its own (Chapter One, section 4). But in addition, outside any

37

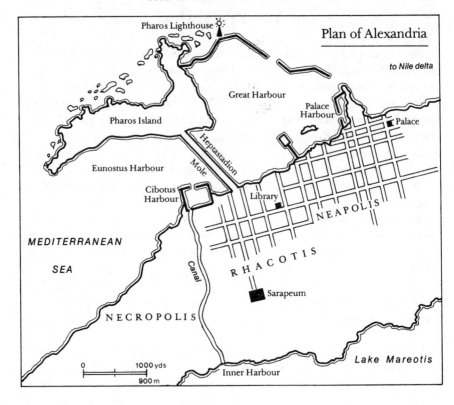

Plan of Alexandria

civic organization, Alexandria housed tens of thousands of Egyptians and people of innumerable other races. For it was an immensely cosmopolitan centre, the first and greatest universal city, the supreme Hellenistic melting-pot. Alexandria was a place that beckoned to young and lively people of all races and creeds to come and join in its seething and infinitely varied activities.

Much of the city was magnificently constructed of stone: a Roman general later remarked that it could never be burnt down, because there was no wood to burn. Many of its buildings were world-famous – not only the Pharos, but the Museum and Library, and the temple of Sarapis. And there were also the palaces of the Ptolemies, a cluster of Greek halls and living rooms arranged round elegant parks. Remains of these buildings have now been discovered in the eastern section of the harbour area. This was where the ruling house lived, because Ptolemy I Soter, son of a Macedonian named Lagus, moved the capital to Alexandria from Memphis. Alexander had sent Ptolemy I to Egypt as his governor, and after Alexander's death he asserted his control over the country (and Cyrenaica) as an independent ruler, taking the Greek title of king in 305-304. His Lagid dynasty outlasted those of the other two major successor kingdoms, continuing, despite many ups and downs, until the death of Cleopatra VII in 30 BC.

Ptolemy I's brilliant administrative powers rapidly brought the country, which had not been devastated in the recent wars, into fairly full working order. Theocritus, who hoped for Ptolemaic patronage, declared that 'Lagus' son boldly achieved such grand schemes as no man but he could ever have thought of.' And then Theocritus spoke up once again, to offer more detailed flattery of Ptolemy II Philadelphus (283-246) – who made Egypt even richer.[2]

In their dependencies in Syria and Asia Minor the Ptolemies founded colonies in the Greek style, but they decided not to do so in Egypt, where the population was already so dense (probably between six and seven millions), and thoroughly and intricately organized on traditional lines of its own.

The exceptions were Alexandria in the north and Ptolemais Hermiou in the south. Ptolemais Hermiou was intended as a centre of Hellenism in upper Egypt, as a rival to Egyptian Thebes. And on a far larger scale that was the role of Alexandria in the north, in competition with Memphis. The purpose of Alexandria was to provide the whole country with a Greek rallying point. Ptolemy I Soter himself set a seal on the city's new status by seizing the embalmed body of Alexander the Great, and, after a brief period of lodgement at Memphis, moving it to Alexandria and laying it there with great pomp. This had been the late king's foundation, and now it was to be his permanent resting-place: its presence supported Ptolemy's claim to be, in a very special sense, Alexander's successor.

Yet Alexandria was a curious capital, because, despite its links with the interior by way of the Nile, it never quite belonged to the country; the city was not so much its centre as its superstructure. People spoke of travelling from Alexandria 'to Egypt': after its role as a Greek headquarters, its other primary function was to be the chief port of the eastern Mediterranean, the capital of an empire.

For although a Ptolemy was 'king' in the eyes of the Greeks, he was not king 'of Egypt', but (like the other Successors) king in general and undefined terms – and this situation was reflected and demonstrated by his overseas dominions. They were intended to put Egypt right back into the centre of international affairs: and the monarchs made continual endeavours to keep and increase these territories. At their most, they included Cyrenaica (with the ancient city of Cyrene), Cyprus (where the old local kingships were replaced by city-states) and many other islands; and the empire extended all along the coast of Asia Minor. But the greatest efforts had to be expended on southern Syria and Lebanon. This territory (to which the name of 'Hollow Syria', Coelesyria – hitherto used more loosely – came to be applied) was fought over with the Seleucids in no less than five wars, won from them (together with the north Syrian coast) in 241, and finally lost to them definitively at the battle of Panion in 200.

The Ptolemaic empire served very important purposes. It was designed as an advanced screen to protect Egypt from its enemies. It was also intended to bring immense commercial profit. The Ptolemies needed a positive cash balance, based on economic self-sufficiency, in order to finance their military expenditure. And by means of their foreign dominions they were able to control a massive proportion of the Aegean market, which still played a pre-eminent part in Mediterranean and near-eastern trade. In particular, these Aegean dependencies provided pitch and metals and ships' timbers, which Egypt itself did not possess. In addition, the same lands supplied the Ptolemies with the shipwrights and navigators they so greatly needed.

But the monarchs simultaneously looked towards the south and east as well, abandoning none of the old trading routes and creating many new ones. The first four Ptolemies' seamen opened up the Red Sea and went much further afield as well, and later mariners continued to explore sea-routes of Africa and India, guarding the maritime terminals of the south Arabian caravans and suppressing the pirates who threatened the passage of their merchandise. Goods came into Egypt from the south and were re-exported into the Mediterranean area, including many materials which came in raw and unworked and left the country in manufactured form. Exports were the essence of Ptolemaic policy and profit.

In order to develop all such activities as efficiently as possible, it was necessary to raise internal organization to the highest pitch of vigorous productivity. Ptolemy I Soter began this task, but it was greatly developed and elaborated by his son Ptolemy II Philadelphus, who took excellent advantage of the country's temporary exemption from the blood-letting that was going on elsewhere. One of the remarkable features of his system was the creation of the most elaborate and far-reaching bureaucracy the world had ever known. And, at first, these Greek bureaucrats in Egypt served their state with efficient skill. A dominant figure in this process was the formidably active and versatile Apollonius, finance minister of the government from c. 268/7 for over twenty years, of whom we know a great deal from the archives of his trusted agent and estate administrator, Zeno of Caunus. This information comes to us from papyri; and indeed we owe most of our knowledge of what was happening in Egypt to such papyri, which its sands have so abundantly and uniquely preserved.

One of the most enlightening among these documents contains an official assertion that 'no one has the right to do what he wants to do, but everything is regulated for the best'![3] The governing idea was that the country belonged to the kings, who had the full right to use it for the general good. In pursuance of this doctrine, the Ptolemies tended to merge the civil and military power, so as to be able to organize the government and its pervasive police with ever greater thoroughness on the lines of military discipline.

Everything the monarchs did served the exploitation of all possible resources for their own advantage, subordinating the economy to state power; the whole structure was meant to buzz like a disciplined hive so that every conceivable form of enrichment could be extracted for the benefit of the king, at minimum expense. Efficiency was not, of course, complete; the Ptolemies often had to take over what they found, and compromises, laxities and incompetences were numerous. Nevertheless, the Ptolemies pursued their mercantilist programmes far more single-mindedly than any other Hellenistic monarchs (though the Attalids of Pergamum, and Hiero II of Syracuse, did their best to compete). In this task the kings were assisted by the obligatory, universal compilation of demographic and economic registers of startlingly detailed character. Through these, the government ought to have been in a position to know what most of their subjects were doing, and were worth, at any given time, although the functionaries later became swamped in their own statistics.

The system was to be seen in its most elaborate form in its application to agriculture. Spurred on by Egypt's fabulous natural resources, the first two Ptolemies were the most impressive land-improvers in Greek history. Ptolemy II Philadelphus reclaimed large tracts of desert in the Fayum, and Greek engineers introduced more scientific methods of irrigation (one of the few major technological advances of the period): so that the peasants, previously content with primitive ways of working their beneficently Nile-flooded soil, found themselves dragged sharply out of the Bronze Age into the present – that is to say, into the Iron Age, since iron tools had not been used in the country before.

A very considerable proportion of this soil was 'royal land', belonging to the kings themselves and operated by their representatives. Exactly how large this category of land may have been, we cannot say:

perhaps more, proportionately, than in any other Hellenistic monarchy, since the Ptolemies were said to be able to feed half a million people from their own estates. Theoretically the *whole* of Egypt (except for the Greek cities) was 'spear-won' territory, that is to say, it belonged to the king: but much of it was leased out by grants, tenable at his will. Choice pieces of real estate were assigned to Greeks and Macedonians under the name of 'cleruchies', of which the monarch himself still retained the ultimate ownership. And in particular allotments were rented out on favourable terms – indeed, often without the need for any payment at all – to senior officers and civil servants, as incentives to loyalty, for although it was the policy of the Ptolemies to take much and give little away, they showed calculated generosity in their distribution of favours to privileged persons. Thus the finance minister Apollonius was leased three square miles of reclaimed land at Philadelphia (a foundation of Ptolemy II in the Fayum), which he cultivated and developed by the most varied and advanced means. Moreover, royal lands were also let out (on terms varying between leniency and stiffness) to a wide range of less important individuals, often of Egyptian race, as well as to institutions, including temples, or occasionally whole urban communities.

The government also lent the lessees cattle, seed and tools. But in return they were expected to do just what they were told. For example, they had to plant whatever the official schedules (revised each year) instructed them to plant, and the seasons and dates at which each crop should be sown were meticulously stated and specified. Moreover, a very high proportion of what they grew had to be sold to the government, or handed over in lieu of rent and taxes. Especially careful supervision was exercised, not only at the moment of sowing but again at harvest time, when those parts of the crop designated as rent were separated out, collected together at district capitals, and shipped to the granaries at Alexandria.

The Ptolemaic system has been described as a system of monopolistic nationalization or state socialism, perhaps the most thoroughgoing until the present century. But this is not entirely accurate. For the men directly working for the kings on their royal land form only part of the picture. The numerous remaining farmers and peasants in the country were cultivating portions of land that they had leased from the monarchs, so that the latter, although they told them in such detail what to do, were not their direct employers. It was not, that is to say, so much a monopolistic state socialism as a command economy.

The results, for a century, were unprecedented and spectacular. Their most impressive manifestation was to be seen in the production of grain, especially wheat – which was Egypt's staple crop – but also barley. The grain, like other produce, had to be cultivated in every region according to an official timetable, annually adjusted to meet the king's requirements. This grain trade exceeded all others in importance, for it was Egypt's principal resource: in a society in which wheat and barley played a far larger part as foodstuffs than they do today, the Ptolemies were the greatest of all the grain merchants in the world, the greatest it had ever seen. Millions of bushels were exported by the kings' agents every year, using Rhodes and Delos as their international distribution centres. Rhodes was also the depot for the spices which formed the principal luxury commodity (if luxuries they could be called, when they were so necessary for the preservation of food). At home in Alexandria, this spice trade was so carefully controlled that workers going home at night were stripped and searched before they could leave the factories.

The same command economy methods were once again strictly applied to the production, sale and export of the highly serviceable papyrus, which grew in Egypt and nowhere else, and not only provided materials for writing – which was now far more widespread, ensuring a huge foreign demand – but could also be employed to make sails, mats, ropes, baskets and clothes. And there was equally tight control of a product which was intended for exclusively Egyptian consumption, namely oil: not, in general, olive oil – since olives were rare or non-existent in most parts of Egypt, and were only used as fruit – but the oil of sesame (the best), safflower (a thistle-like plant), colocynth (the gourd), linseed (flax, used in manufacturing) and croton (a laxative) – all of which grew widely in the valley and delta of the Nile. This industry, well-known from papyri, again had to conform to a fixed but constantly adjusted time-schedule: once more official control, whether exerted directly over royal employees or indirectly over lessees, was extraordinarily strict at every stage, regulating the extent of the oil-producing land, the timing of the production, and the sales-rights which were leased out at fixed prices subject to annual adjustment. Workmen were allowed a share of the profits: but they were watched over so closely that even to change their place of residence was forbidden.

Facilities were also made available to assist the cultivation of the vine (already not unknown earlier, though the Egyptians preferred barley beer); and new strains of food-plants, including fruits, were developed for marginal land. Moreover, the monarchs and their expert staffs showed equally bold initiatives in the breeding of cattle. Bulls, rams and boars of high quality were brought into the country, and pasturage was enormously extended and improved, in order to increase the wool-trade and provide fodder for the royal cavalry. Other activities in which the kings were equally interested included textiles, perfumes, the curing of fish, the management of baths, the brewing of beer, the making of bricks, the processes of glazing, the working of metals, and the manufacture of all manner of utility and luxury goods, for which highly trained Egyptian craftsmen were available in abundance. All these industries, in so far as they were not undertaken by the monarch's direct employees, were entrusted to his concessionaires, who, subject to the payment of a fee and the usual meticulous control (variously organized to suit the different needs of each industry), received a licence granting them the right to conduct their activities, to the exclusion of all unlicensed persons.

Ptolemaic taxation was equally far-reaching. A direct, uniform land tax, on the lines adopted by some other Hellenistic states, was not levied. However, the subjects of the Ptolemies paid taxes of a size and diversity that were unprecedented in the ancient world. Every detail of more than two hundred of these impositions is recorded, and Ptolemy II Philadelphus, in particular, extorted an abundance of taxation which could scarcely be equalled even today. Everyone, at every level, paid heavy taxes in order to buy from the producers, who suffered equally heavy burdens themselves. Furthermore, in order to prevent competition from other countries, not only did the Ptolemies maintain a separate coin standard all their own (the light 'Phoenician' standard), but another expedient was resorted to as well: an import tax of 50 per cent was applied to all imported oil (notably the olive-oil of Greece, superior to the local seed products). Moreover, if oil was imported all the same, it had to be sold to the king at a fixed price, cases of evasion being punished with confiscation and heavy fines. The collection of a great deal of this revenue was entrusted, for a price, to tax-farmers, middlemen between the taxpayers and the government. This, as the experience of the Roman empire later showed, was a system easily liable to abuse, but the Ptolemies – at least to begin with – controlled the tax-farmers with exemplary strictness.

Taxation was one of the facts of life that prompted the Ptolemies to encourage a massive development of banking. This was already an ancient institution in the Greek world: but amid the far-flung transactions and exchange requirements of the Ptolemaic kingdom, as elsewhere in the Hellenistic world (Chapter Two, section 2), a new and more professional kind of bank arose, replacing the old oral management of business by insistence upon written documents. Another novelty of the banking system was centralization, based on the establishment of a central state bank at Alexandria, with branches elsewhere. It was these royal institutions that guaranteed the contracts between the state and the tax-farmers; and the banks acted as receiving agents for taxes paid either in kind or in cash. They had many other functions as well. For example, it was their duty to effect payments that needed to be made from the king's treasury – and, conversely, to develop every means of bringing more wealth into its coffers. The banks also found time to look after private funds.

Banks were sometimes attached to the temples, which had been, for millennia, the basic stable institutions of Egyptian society, and still remained powerful economic, intellectual and artistic units. It was only in these temple societies that the indigenous Egyptian upper class still survived; they remained the principal centres of the national civilization and script and craftsmanship, enabling the literary, epigraphic, architectural and sculptural traditions of Egypt to resist obliteration, and remain largely independent of the imported Greek culture. These survivals were encouraged by the Ptolemies, who reduced the temples to indirect dependence upon themselves by granting them privileges and allocating them funds. In response, Manetho, the Egyptian high-priest at Heliopolis (On), wrote a history of Egypt in Greek (later added to and amended by anonymous hands) and dedicated it to Ptolemy II Philadelphus. The latter's son Ptolemy III Euergetes (246–221) made particularly strong attempts to gain favour with the native priesthood. The cults of Isis and Sarapis, which the Ptolemies indefatigably stimulated, were Hellenized versions of Egyptian traditions (Chapter Four, section 1). In other respects, however, the monarchs accepted the separate existence of Egypt's religion just as it was, without attempting to convert or modify its ancient, native characteristics. The new rulers also wanted themselves to be seen not only as Greek kings but as Pharaohs of Egypt, and Ptolemy V Epiphanes (205–180) was crowned at Memphis according to Egyptian rites.

And yet, despite all these moves, Egyptian culture tended to wilt. For the relationship between Greeks (and Macedonians) on the one hand, and Egyptians on the other, remained fundamentally unsatisfactory. The trouble was that the Greeks enjoyed a markedly superior status. True, some of the ordinary Egyptians under the early Ptolemies were better off than they had been for a good many centuries past, since the monarchs felt it necessary to protect them from the worst oppressions – if only out of self-interest. Nor could it be said that these rulers consciously or deliberately followed racialistic principles: their policy was not racial but royal – the pursuit of their own advantage. Nevertheless, it was the Greeks who were, to an overwhelming extent, the principal agents and supports of their régime, and this situation inevitably made itself felt and caused friction.

The Greeks, it is true, were impressed by the antiquity of Egypt. Their authors had long been writing with strong, if inaccurate, admiration about its local institutions; their doctors were prepared to learn from Egyptian medicine, and their novelists borrowed Egyptian themes (for example in the *Dream of Nectanebus*). Moreover, the poorer members of their community sometimes intermarried with Egyptians, at least from the time of Ptolemy II Philadelphus onwards. Yet the Greeks had brought with them into the country the conviction that every individual Egyptian was violent and dishonest, and it was a conviction that most of them persistently retained. Greek judges were grossly biased against Egyptians. Native peasants – who cheaply performed the lowest kinds of manual labour, reserved for slaves in other countries – paid much heavier taxes than Greek residents, and lived virtually in a state of profitless bondage, which, at its worst, could degenerate into horrifying cruelty: for example, in the convict labour of the Nubian gold mines, described in the second century by Agatharchides of Cnidus.[4] In the old Greek cities elsewhere in the Mediterranean world, state prisons had always been rudimentary (such as the Athenian lock-up in which Socrates spent his last days), and still were more or less unchanged. Those on the great slave plantations (*ergasteria*) in the new Hellenistic world were much nastier; but nothing could compare for horror with the gold mines of the Ptolemies. Most Egyptians, of course, did not suffer these extremities of misery. But they, too, saw their properties and whole lives placed at the disposal of interests that were entirely alien from their own.

Besides, the successes of the Ptolemaic economy did not last. For the centralized, bureaucratic system could only work adequately under men who possessed exceptional drive – and were immune from ordinary human failings. For a time the former requirement was met. But in the nature of things this could not go on for ever, and the Egyptians, under the impact of increasing ill-treatment, inevitably became dangerously embittered, and finally desperate. The deterioration was gradual, and uneven. But already in the reign of Ptolemy II Philadelphus, the correspondence of Apollonius' agent Zeno of Caunus shows that discrimination could be found, and was resented. 'I do not know how to behave like a Greek (*hellenizein*)' mourns a camel-driver (perhaps an Arab). And under Ptolemy III Euergetes, a priest complains that the Greek billeted in his home looks down on him 'because he is an Egyptian'.[5]

But then, by way of contrast, Ptolemy IV Philopator (221–205) felt himself forced to the conclusion that association with the natives might, gradually and partially, replace Greek domination as his guiding principle. For he was under the pressure of growing political isolation, including the suspension of the country's western trade, which helped to create a ruinous inflation of the currency. To meet this crisis, he made up his mind to shore up his power at home by calling upon the Egyptians to cooperate: and his decisive military victory over the Seleucid monarch Antiochus III the Great at Raphia (217) was only gained by extensive mobilization of native-born soldiers.

Yet opening the door ajar, as so often, only precipitated further trouble. From now onwards, a new class of Egyptian was to be seen, with novel, aggressive pretensions. Moreover, at the same time, native revolts broke out, and then proved impossible to stop. For two decades (208/7–187/6), almost the whole of the Thebaid in Upper Egypt, always the breeding-ground for Pharaonic nationalism, fell under the independent rule of secessionist Nubian kings, and the breakaway was only terminated by Ptolemy V Epiphanes (205–180) amid savage repression.

This was an epoch of chaotic local uprisings, sieges and robberies; and Nile transport became perilously insecure. In these years, moreover, it was not only the Egyptians but the ruling race who felt unsafe; for example, a recluse (named Ptolemy) is found complaining that he has been assaulted because he is a Macedonian. Furthermore, Ptolemy V's loss of most of his imperial possessions to the Seleucid Antiochus IV Epiphanes at the battle of Panion (200) isolated Egypt from its eastern commerce, and thus caused even worse impoverishment. Besides, the dynastic quarrels and court scandals that characterized the next reigns – in addition to new bouts of currency inflation (174–3) – meant that the welfare of the Egyptian populace declined still further.

The workers on the land had already formed the habit of registering their protests by the withdrawal of their labour – not for better wages or conditions, because clearly these were not to be had, but merely out of total despair: which was converted into this sort of protest action, from time to time, by some fortuitous irritation or hold-up. But as the second century BC continued on its way, something much more serious began to happen as well. For the peasants (and even tax-farmers unable to meet their obligations) increasingly went on strike by fleeing from their jobs and homes, usually in groups, and taking refuge in sanctuaries or going underground. 'We are worn out,' declares a papyrus letter, 'we will run away.'[6] And so the economic recession got worse still, because now there were not enough people left to cultivate the soil. Ptolemy VIII Euergetes II, who had the reputation of favouring the native population, produced a remarkable decree (not the first of its kind) ordering alleviations (118):[7] amnesties, the lightening of burdens, tax exemptions, counsels of moderation to officials. But it was too late. Egypt continued to lurch towards collapse and dependence on unscrupulous Romans –

and on Rome itself, to which more than one later Ptolemy contemplated leaving his kingdom, as Attalus III Philometor had made a bequest of the Pergamene state.

One of the worst problems that confronted the authorities – and these profit-seeking Roman adventurers as well – was the condition of the vast city of Alexandria. Its Graeco-Macedonian population had by now become a mixed race of exceptional liveliness, addicted to over-excitement and rioting. The palace, too, was sometimes in the hands of shady personages, notably the cunning and murderous Sosibius and his friends, who directed the régime of Ptolemy IV Philopator; and subsequently the court, although it remained Greek in culture, was dominated – like the courts of eastern states – by eunuchs, who were sometimes of sinister character. This volatile Alexandria was the power-base of Cleopatra VII Philadelphus Philopator Philopatris, who came to the throne in 51 BC and made a last determined attempt to revive the kingdom and empire by means of her successive associations with Julius Caesar (allegedly the father of her son, Ptolemy XV Caesar or Caesarion) and then Marcus Antonius (Antony) (by whom she had additional children). But the attempt failed – shortly before the last Indo-Greek kingdom, too, had collapsed – and after nearly three hundred years of Ptolemaic kingship the country became a Roman province in 30 BC. In spite of all the disasters it had suffered, it was still rich enough, especially in grain, to revolutionize the Roman economy. During the rule of the Romans, however, the Egyptian people did not fare even as well as they had under the Ptolemaic house – or at least under its earlier monarchs.

3 The Seleucids

The Seleucids in their great early days – even after Seleucus I Nicator had ceded his easternmost territories to the Indian emperor Chandragupta Maurya in exchange for war elephants (c. 303) – ruled over an empire of a million and a half square miles, extending from the Aegean Sea as far as Afghanistan and Turkestan, and containing perhaps thirty million people (compared with less than seven million in Egypt, and four million in Macedonia). The unique size of these enormous dominions enabled the Seleucids to claim that they themselves, rather than the Ptolemies or Antigonids, were in a very special sense the heirs of Alexander the Great, who had ruled the world. The overworked Seleucid monarchs, able to appeal to no unifying principle except their own persons and troops – a standing army of not more than 70,000, supplemented by mercenaries – had to devote their major energies just to holding on to this cumbersome realm.

And indeed it displayed numerous factors positively encouraging disunity. This was evident from the co-existence of two capitals, two new cities in different countries: Antioch in Syria, and Seleucia on the Tigris in Babylonia. There was also, inside each separate territory of the empire, a sharp distinction between the central, directly controlled region or regions and the less accessible outlying districts. Moreover, in the latter, as in lands under even looser, indirect control outside the royal frontiers, the local rulers were often not Seleucid governors (though even they were relatively autonomous) but partially independent kings or dynasts or tribal chiefs, or the priestly rulers of ancient temple states. The dynasts of these temple states, great and small – especially in Asia Minor and Syria – operated antique feudal systems that the monarchs habitually tried to restrict, annexing and secularizing as much of their land as they could, but never terminating their existence altogether.

This was a situation with which the now vanished Achaemenid Persian rulers had been familiar. But unlike the Persian empire, the Seleucid dominions also contained very numerous self-administering settlements or colonies containing Greek or Hellenized populations. Greek colonization had been in abeyance for two or three centuries until Philip ii, in Thrace, and his son Alexander iii the Great, much more comprehensively, revived the programme, seeing it as a fundamental feature of the new historical epoch that they were bringing into existence. Twenty such cities founded by Alexander (not the unlikely seventy recorded in the second century AD by Plutarch[8]) have been located with some probability: thirteen are certainly identified, extending east of the Euphrates and onwards, by way of 'Alexandria in Caucasus' in the Paropamisus (Hindu Kush), as far as the remote Punjab.

Alexander does not seem to have been deliberately acting as an apostle of Hellenism, for the purpose of his settlements (other than Alexandria in Egypt) was primarily military. Their sites were chosen – often in places where towns existed already – with a view to guarding strategic points, such as passes or fords, or supervising tracts of the surrounding recently conquered territories (with an eye on trade). The new communities were equipped with the fortifications needed to ensure their defence. The new settlers at these various Alexandrias were mostly conscripted ex-mercenaries capable of fighting again if they had to – men performing the function of a trained reserve to be called up in emergencies. About the constitutional status of the new settlements we

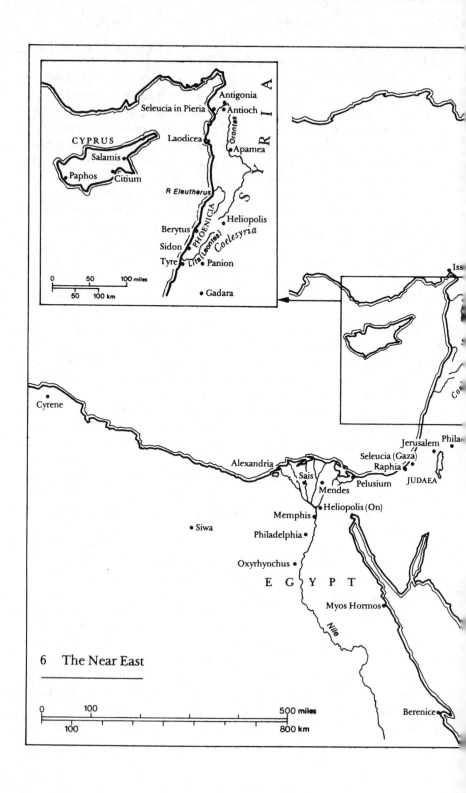

Antigonia
Seleucia in Pieria
Antioch
CYPRUS
Laodicea
Orontes
Apamea
Salamis
Paphos
Citium
R Eleutherus
SYRIA
Heliopolis
Berytus
PHOENICIA
Coelesyria
Sidon
Lita(Leontes)
Tyre
Panion
Gadara

0   50   100 miles
0 50 100 km

Iss

Co

Cyrene

Jerusalem
Phila
Seleucia (Gaza)
Raphia
Alexandria
Sais
Pelusium
JUDAEA
Mendes
Heliopolis (On)
Memphis
Siwa
Philadelphia
Oxyrhynchus

E G Y P T

Myos Hormos

Nile

Berenice

6   The Near East

0   100   500 miles
0   100   800 km

mosata

iochia (Edessa-
Orrhoe)   • Antiochia
                   (Nisibis)
• Carrhae   Gaugamela

apolis
Bambyce)

A S S Y R I A

M E S O P O T A M I A

Euphrates

Tigris

Dura-Europus•

Ctesiphon
Seleucia (Opis)

Babylon•
Borsippa•   B A B Y L O N I A

• Orchoi

R A B I A

C H A L D A E A

P E R S I A N   G U L F

:uce Come

Gerrha•

know little. Most of them probably lacked the formal organization of a city (*polis*) and remained under the authority of the royal governors; though promotion to city status, it was envisaged, could come later, if the foundations proved successful. For a colony to have a fairly advanced urban organization from the beginning, like Alexandria in Egypt, was probably exceptional.

Things did not go altogether well, since both before and after Alexander's death there were serious revolts among his settlers in Bactria, and in the event many of these people, and others elsewhere, packed up and returned to their homeland. Some settlements, too, were suppressed by Chandragupta Maurya when Seleucus I Nicator ceded him the eastern lands, and others again in the course of a great invasion of Iran by nomad Sacae (Scythians) in 293. Apart from the famous Egyptian foundation, most of Alexander's colonies failed to take root.

Yet his pioneer example had fired his successors, and especially the Seleucids, to make further attempts to people the enormous spaces they controlled, either by resuscitating Alexander's vanished settlements or by creating new ones on their own account. Like Alexander's colonies, most of the Seleucid foundations started as military settlements initially lacking full urban organization. Whether veterans or still, in a sense, active soldiers, the first settlers of these Seleucid foundations once again performed the duties of a trained reserve, ready to defend their fortified posts at any time.

The most remarkable work in this field was done by the first two Seleucid monarchs, Seleucus I Nicator (312–281) and Antiochus I Soter (281–261). Not every city that bears a Seleucid name was a Seleucid colony, since some ancient urban foundations merely took on Seleucid names without any influx of new settlers. Thus Appian's attribution of fifty colonies to Seleucus I Nicator is probably an exaggeration. Yet the king's achievement is remarkable enough if, as seems likely, he founded more than half of that number: namely, sixteen colonies named Antiochia (after his father, a Macedonian called Antiochus), five Laodiceas (after his mother Laodice), four Apameas (after his Iranian wife Apama), one Stratonicea (after his Macedonian wife Stratonice, whom he married after Apama's death), and nine settlements named Seleucia after himself. His son Antiochus I Soter, too, although otherwise a shadowy figure, somehow made the time – amid the unending troubles of his unwieldy empire – to establish something like twenty more foundations, though some of these may have been the work of Antiochus II Theos (261–246). Later, Antiochus IV Epiphanes (Theos Epiphanes Nicephorus, 175–163) renewed the process, as well as transforming many oriental towns into cities of the Greek type by the donation of new civic charters.

The seventy-odd colonies were spread throughout the Seleucid empire. Many of them were in Syria-Cilicia, Asia Minor and Mesopotamia, countries in which the Greek city-organization thus established was to continue onwards into Roman and Byzantine times. But there was also a far-reaching, if less long-lived, horseshoe of foundations around the fertile fringes of the Iranian plateau – and in lands even farther east as well. Two settlements in this distant region that could belong to early Seleucid times have now been unearthed. One is at Aï Khanum, on the bank of the river Oxus in Bactria (Afghanistan), beyond the Paropamisus (Hindu Kush) range. It is a purely Greek city, with a gymnasium, a walled sanctuary, a peristyle courtyard, statues by Greek sculptors, and an inscription telling how a certain Clearchus went to Delphi to copy out the moral maxims of the oracular shrine. The existing remains date from about 300 BC, and the colony may well have been a foundation of Seleucus I Nicator (though it has alternatively been identified with Alexander's Alexandria Eschate, 'the furthest', more generally supposed to be Leninabad, formerly Khodjend). A second colony of comparable date and Greek character, again with a walled sanctuary, has come to light at Kandahar in a more southerly region of Afghanistan (the ancient Arachosia). This, too, is likely to be a very early Seleucid colony, though, once again, Alexander could have been the original founder. A statue-base of about 275, dedicated to the son of a certain Aristonax, indicates that when part of Afghanistan was ceded to Chandragupta Maurya in about 303 the new frontier was drawn east of Kandahar, which evidently remained, for the time being, under Seleucid control. In about 260, however, the city passed into the hands of Chandragupta Maurya's grandson Asoka (c. 274-232).

These Seleucid attempts to colonize vast tracts of the continent of Asia were planned with systematic determination, and carried out with speed, energy and skill. It was one of the most remarkable enterprises of ancient times, exceeding even the great archaic age of Greek colonization in the size of the territory it covered. Indeed, only the Spaniards, in Mexico and Peru, have equalled it: like Spanish America, the Seleucid east was open to all who were adventurous enough to take their chance.

The new colonies brought in relatively few Macedonian settlers, but attracted many Greeks, mainly from the poorer regions of the homeland, who wanted to escape poverty and unemployment at home. Like Alexander, as we have seen, the first intention of the Seleucids was that their colonies should serve a military purpose. But traces have also been found of certain settlements that seem to have possessed a civilian character from the outset. This was a sign that various non-military aims quite soon supplemented the original military purpose. Above all, the Seleucids were clearly interested in the unification of their heterogeneous territories. These lands were to be, as far as possible, a union of cities. As in Alexander's day, the settlements were intended, at a later stage, to develop into fully-fledged cities of the usual Greek pattern: and in fact many Seleucid colonies (unlike Alexander's) were allowed the necessary time to reach the second phase, and duly did so. That is to say, they became equipped with the normal institutions of Greek cities – a code of law of their own, the traditional civic governing bodies and magistrates (state officials), a council, usually an assembly, and temples and gymnasia.

All this meant that the Seleucid empire – to a far greater extent than rival monarchies – became an aggregate of Greek cities, linked one with the other. And it also meant something else. For the founders of new cities were traditionally accorded divine honours, and so the Seleucid colonies established cults of their monarchs: this was a potent bond, especially as no formal constitutional link between kings and cities had been devised. The only link that existed, other than these royal cults, consisted of such individual privileges as the rulers may have conferred and felt obliged to respect. These privileges were substantial, including liberal grants of municipal autonomy – often a virtue of necessity on the part of the monarchs in times of stress when the collaboration of the local communities was urgently needed. The Seleucids were strongly on the side of the cities against the native feudal landowners, whom (like the temple states) they tried to cut down to size. In consequence, the cities were loyal, like Rome's later colonies in Italy.

Economic and agricultural considerations were not usually paramount in Seleucid plans, but some of the colonies, notably Seleucia on the Tigris, became large-scale trading centres. Moreover, the strips of cultivable territory granted to the new foundations were sometimes of remarkably large dimensions, comparable only to those of Athens and Sparta in the homeland. These pieces of land allotted to the new settlements had formerly belonged to the monarchy. Their cession to the cities meant gain as well as loss for the royal exchequer, since the recipients had to pay taxes on the land that they thus acquired. The existence of the cities was a financial help to the central authority in another way as well, since their ability to govern themselves made it possible for the rulers to cut down their own administrative staffs.

The new colonial enterprises also brought the local native populations into the picture. In the first place, a number of Asians (notably Persians) were included among the colonists – and indeed at the civilian colonies natives often constituted the bulk of the settlers. Furthermore, it was the people of local origin who provided the labour force working the land for the Greek and Macedonian colonists (supplemented by nomads of the region, imported and settled for the purpose). Conversely, too, Greeks were sometimes introduced into pre-existing native villages or cities; or when amalgamations (synoecisms) of two, or several, such communities took place, a further Greek ingredient was added. Besides, settlers, being short of women of their own race, often took local women as their wives.

These developments meant that a considerable number of local inhabitants were included within the orbit of the new foundations, so that some formula of racial co-existence, however empirical, had to be worked out. Now, cooperation with these foreigners on liberal terms does not seem to have figured explicitly among Seleucid aims: the Athenian orator Isocrates' insistence that Greekness depended less on blood than on common education, Alexander's enlightened attitude towards the Persians, contemporary Greek studies of foreign customs, a new interest in ethnic types among artists – these were all phenomena of the time, yet they barely dented the classical prejudice against barbarians.

Nevertheless, the more thoughtful of the Seleucid rulers and administrators must have hoped that the natives involved with the new cities would at least become sufficiently assimilated to ensure effective collaboration – and to increase the empire's reservoir of utilizable manpower. The earlier Seleucid colonies, therefore, although they did not usually confer citizenship upon Asians, were at least prepared to concede them certain lesser rights; and it was with the same intention of gaining their cooperative services that Antiochus IV Epiphanes was so ready to grant Greek civic charters to whole native communities.

In some countries such policies enjoyed a measure of success; for example, the more cultured classes in Syria and certain regions of Asia Minor were happy enough to become partially Hellenized. Elsewhere, however, further east, this scarcely happened. True, the Asians in those lands sometimes accepted the Greek forms, or even became wholly or partly 'culture-Greeks', speaking the universal Greek dialect, the *koine*. But they rarely took on the Greek spirit. And so they outstayed their visitors – and the success of the Seleucid colonizing effort had, after all, only been limited.

The fault also lay to a large extent with the Greek (and Macedonian) settlers, who, despite the inevitable links that have been mentioned, for the most part still passionately practised linguistic and cultural *apartheid*.

Moreover, since they let the natives till the land, that meant they did not go on it themselves; thus the ancient antagonism between town-dwellers and peasants remained undiminished, and became an antagonism between Greeks and natives. Besides, the settlers were not numerous enough: the immigration of useful elements into Asia gradually waned and ceased in the second century BC, when Greece no longer had a surplus population (of any value) to send. Besides, by that time, after a last brave effort by Antiochus IV Epiphanes, the Seleucid rulers were too critically beset by their enemies to have funds or time for major colonial programmes. Their most dangerous threat came from the Romans, who, indeed, finally suppressed their kingdom. And yet, by a curious paradox, it was also the Romans who saved and perpetuated the Seleucid colonies in Asia Minor and Syria.

The Seleucids had taken what measures they could to whip up the resources needed for the prosecution of these extremely costly colonizing efforts. Seleucid taxation was organized on a highly systematic basis, from which no section of the community escaped. It included a uniform land tax, which became fixed at the high rate of one third of every crop. Much of the empire's cultivable soil, however, remained directly under the kings themselves, whose henchmen organized its cultivation on old-fashioned lines, employing peasants on a hereditary basis.

But although agriculture was important to the Seleucids, it was not as important as international trade, which they elevated to unprecedented dimensions. Every Seleucid king was a tycoon on an enormous scale, making millions from the great trade routes from the Mediterranean to central Asia, India and Arabia: routes which passed through their empire and were served by a network of good roads. Trading was also facilitated by the creation of an impressive unified coinage, which the rulers issued themselves and made the basic currency of the whole of their huge territories, speeding up the process, begun by the Persians, of transforming an economy of kind on to a monetary basis. Even if, therefore, they were occasionally hard pressed by the ambitious dimensions of their policies, the Seleucid kings remained immensely rich; and they were surrounded by an increasingly elaborate hierarchy of court officials, including for example Hermias – minister of Antiochus III the Great – who could pay an army out of his own personal resources.

A word will now be said about the different regions of the empire in turn.

In Syria the first Seleucid rulers, by organizing foundations and encouraging settlers to immigrate and man them, tried to convert the northern part of the country into nothing less than a replica of the

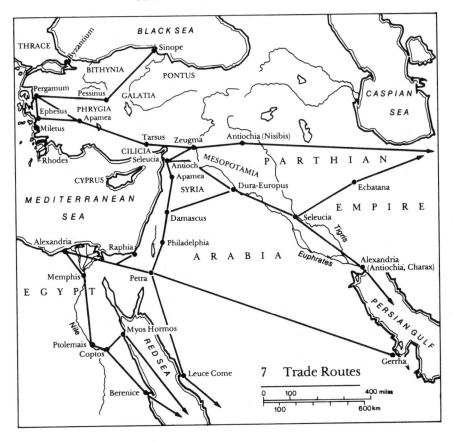

7 Trade Routes

homeland itself: the echoes of the old country provided by an abundance
of Macedonian place-names were intended to create a sense of continuity and make the newcomers feel at home.

It was the overall purpose of Seleucid policy to protect this Syrian
territory from all quarters and particularly from the south, where the
menace of Ptolemaic Egypt was unceasing. For this was a very rich
land. Agriculture (including cultivation of the vine) was profitably
intensified, and cities and ports provided the western terminals for two
of the major caravan routes to the east, one passing through Petra and
Palmyra, the other leading along the Euphrates valley.

The new foundation of Seleucus I Nicator at Antioch on the Orontes
(c. 300), receiving 5,300 Athenian and Macedonian ex-soldier settlers
(transferred from Antigonus I Monophthalmos' short-lived foundation
of Antigonia), became the capital of his western dominions, supplanting
Seleucia in Pieria which became its harbour. Antioch grew to be one

of the greatest cities in the world, and a model of rich urban sophistication. Its massive trade as terminus for the eastern traffic, temporarily diverted by the loss of Seleucia in Pieria to Egypt (241), revived after the recapture of the port in 219.

Despite the many wars fought with the Ptolemies over the possession of Syria, the Hellenistic age was one of the most brilliant epochs in the whole history of the country. Syria's record of comparatively successful Hellenization is illustrated by a remarkable series of Greek philosophers it produced, especially Stoics. Yet the land remained essentially bi-cultural; thus the huge, autonomous shrines of Syrian deities survived and prospered, disguised under Greek names (Baalbek as Heliopolis, Bambyce as Hieropolis; while in Cilicia (south-east Asia Minor), usually an adjunct of Seleucid Syria, Castabala became Hieropolis – though the Cilician temple-state of Olba retained its own name and dynasty). The leading Syrian (and Phoenician) cities had an ever stronger Greek veneer; for example, a certain Diotimus of Sidon, in the third century BC, was even able to satisfy the Olympic judges about the authenticity of his Greek race (regarded as an essential qualification) by urging a mythical link between his city and Thebes in Boeotia. And indeed, one of the Sidonian kings (c. 325–300) had been buried in the 'Alexander Sarcophagus' (now at Istanbul) which was decorated with reliefs by the most eminent Greek sculptors of the day. Sidon subsequently became a republic, which formed part of the territory (also including Tyre, recovered from its destruction by Alexander) which passed under the control of Antiochus III the Great after his victory at Panion (200).

This success partly compensated the Seleucids for grave losses of territory in other parts of Asia. In Asia Minor, where their governor-general resided at Sardis, they had initially controlled the western and southern parts of the country, except for coastal areas which belonged to the Ptolemies or Rhodes. But the presence of warlike Galatian immigrants in the hinterland weakened the hold of the Seleucids over the peninsula – especially when they themselves short-sightedly mobilized the Galatians to help them in civil wars. In 263, Eumenes I of Pergamum, in the west, threw off the suzerainty of the Seleucids with Egyptian assistance, and henceforward his territory remained independent (Chapter One, section 4). After the defeat of Antiochus III the Great by the Romans at Thermopylae (191), and then again off Myonnesus and at Magnesia by Sipylus (190), followed by the Treaty of Apamea two years later, the Seleucid frontiers were thrown back to the Taurus mountains on the borders of Cilicia, not far from the confines of Syria itself.

While Syria was one of the principal Seleucid strongholds, a second was another Semitic-speaking country, Babylonia, further to the east. On conquering this part of Mesopotamia from the Achaemenid Persians (against whom its people had repeatedly revolted), Alexander the Great had retained the former governor, Mazaeus, without change: and he had deliberately represented himself as the legitimate successor of the ancient rulers of the land. Subsequently Seleucus I Nicator, after victoriously asserting his claim to Babylonia against the other Successors, made a similar claim, respecting the country as the original nucleus of his rise to special power, and granting it protection and privilege. Babylonia had preserved, and was still allowed to retain, large parts of its own native, traditional, centralized governmental and social system. In particular, its ancient law – the most sophisticated legal system in the world outside Greece, Rome and China – was still very much alive, and represented a potent unifying factor. Moreover, the Seleucid monarchs took over the antique Babylonian theocracy. Like Alexander before him (who had rebuilt the temple of the god Bel), Seleucus I Nicator publicly ascribed his rule to Bel and Marduk, and he and his dynasty carefully maintained good relations with the local priesthood of the Magi. Lavishly reconstructed under the sponsorship of the Seleucids (once again taking their cue from Alexander), the temples of Marduk (at Babylon), Anu (at Orchoi or Uruk) and Nabu (at Borsippa) regained their prosperity and transacted their own business in their own language and according to their own code. After the loss of the Seleucids' western territories, the retention of the Babylonians' goodwill became even more essential as a counterweight, and they were able to infiltrate senior posts in the royal bureaucracy and army.

However, the Seleucid monarchs also created a remarkable cluster of Graeco-Macedonian colonies on the middle Tigris and Euphrates. Outstanding among them was Seleucia on the Tigris. Founded by Seleucus I Nicator in *c.* 312 – shortly after his conquest of the country – upon the site of the ancient town of Opis, beside the canal which linked the two great rivers, it rapidly became the second capital of the empire, in which the heir to the throne resided. It served as a Greek counterpoise to the power of the Magi, whom the Seleucids, however outwardly deferential, were not sorry to subject to competition.

The new foundation, so conveniently located, contributed enormously to Seleucid trade. The role of Mesopotamia as a source of commercial revenue for the kings was specially important. In the bloody rivalries between the successors of Alexander, the country had been fiercely fought over, and suffered ruinous losses. But under the Seleucids it became extremely productive once again. Its great potential fertility was exploited by efficient irrigation, its millennial textile industry flourished, and trading and banking reached a high degree of development, discreetly supervised, but without too great interference. Much of this prosperity was due to Seleucia on the Tigris, the supplanter of Babylon (which stood on a less satisfactory swampy site) as the principal commercial centre of the country. Seleucia was a river port for maritime shipping, linked with settlements on the Persian Gulf (notably Alexandria in Susiana) where vessels from southern Arabia and India called on their way up the Tigris. But Seleucia was also the centre upon which all the main land-routes converged. One of them led, safely, to Antioch on the Orontes, the other capital of the empire. And a further great caravan road ran in the opposite direction, by way of Ecbatana (Epiphania) in Media (Hamadan, northern Iran) and across the remote Seleucid frontier towards the far east. Few places have ever so effectively dominated the business affairs of half a continent as Seleucia on the Tigris. It became one of the greatest cities in the world.

The place also witnessed a memorable ethnic experiment, on a scale not far short of Alexandria in the rival Ptolemaic kingdom. By the first century AD, according to Pliny the elder, the population of Seleucia on the Tigris was said to have reached a figure of six hundred thousand.[9] Many of these people were of Greek or Macedonian descent, and Seleucia always maintained its predominantly Greek character right on into Roman times. However, as was seen earlier, collaboration between Greeks and natives inevitably occurred in Seleucid colonies; and this phenomenon was most notable of all at Seleucia, which possessed not only substantial numbers of Syrian and Jewish inhabitants, but also a large Babylonian element. Moreover, these Babylonians may have received some exceptional recognition in the community, since local coins display a pair of city personifications (Fortunes, Tychai) joining hands, instead of the single Fortune who usually appears elsewhere. For the same reason, another of Seleucus I's Mesopotamian colonies, Antiochia-by-Callirhoe (Edessa Orrhoe, now Urfa), was described as a semi-barbarian city.[10] A further colony of Seleucus I was Dura Europus on the Euphrates, which stood on the road from Seleucia on the Tigris to Antioch and was destined to have an equally long and remarkable future: its first Graeco-Macedonian settlers married natives, but their descendants considered themselves Greeks.

Babylonian customs and institutions were not unknown in the Greek world. That they should become more familiar was the intention of Berossus, a priest of Bel at Babylon, who compiled a three-book history of his native land, the *Babyloniaca* (or *Chaldaica*, from Chaldaea which lay between Babylon and the Persian Gulf), dedicating the work to

Antiochus I Soter. Like Manetho in Egypt, and other such writers in a variety of fringe lands, he wrote about his people in Greek, with the aim of making their achievements better appreciated among their Greek masters and settlers and visitors.

In fact, however, the Babylonian influence on the Greeks can only be detected in a number of specific, specialized fields. First of all, there was a notable, if rather vague, Greek interest in Babylonian religion and its priests, loosely known as 'Chaldaeans'. Alexander and the Seleucids were attentive to Bel, and Alexander consulted the clergy about the ways in which the god should be worshipped. Plato had allegedly admitted a Chaldaean to his Academy, and the worship of heavenly bodies described in his *Laws* – and in the *Epinomis* of uncertain authorship which seems to reflect his beliefs – bears a Semitic, Chaldaean air, which again becomes apparent in the ordered Stoic cosmos of Zeno (who came from Citium in Semitic-speaking Cyprus).

Indeed, it was in relation to the heavenly bodies that Mesopotamian influence on Greek culture is most clearly detectable. Contact between 'Chaldaean' astrologers and the Greeks had been established as early as the fifth century BC. But it was in the more truly scientific field of astronomy that the contact was particularly fruitful. Profiting by the clear air and long seasons without rain, Babylonian astronomers had recorded extensive observations from very early times; and the remarkable Greek astronomical advances from the third century onwards (Chapter Three, section 1) were manifestly stimulated by Babylonian studies, despite different methods of calculation. Indeed, the astronomer Seleucus, who probably worked in about 150 and stood alone as an all-out supporter of Aristarchus' hypothesis that the earth revolved round the sun, originated from Seleucia on the Tigris, and was described as a 'Chaldaean'. His great contemporary Hipparchus of Nicaea, too, had access to Babylonian eclipse records and used them extensively. Furthermore, one of the outstanding achievements of the Seleucids was the creation of a notable and widely employed calendar, which included Babylonian (as well as Persian) months. The Babylonians also possessed a very sophisticated algebra, and its techniques reappear in later Greek mathematics. In the literary field, too, the Hellenistic Greek novel revealed strong influences from this region; indeed, the theme of what may well be its earliest known example, the *Ninus Romance*, is Assyrian.

However, these instances of cultural movement between the Greeks and the land of the Tigris and Euphrates are not only somewhat specialized but form an almost wholly one-way traffic. Despite all the impetus towards collaboration exerted by Seleucia on the Tigris and other colonies, the peoples of Mesopotamia and the territories around it remained very little affected by Hellenization, because the roots of their own civilization were so deep and irremovable: and there were too few Greeks in the country to make a serious impact.

The Seleucid rule also extended over what had once been the empire of the Achaemenid Persians. That was the greatest state ever established, to date, this side of China: a huge, heterogeneous, self-sufficient fabric that held together for two whole centuries (549–330) because of a sensible, flexible policy of decentralization.

Because Achaemenid Persia ruled over so many Greeks, and was so often involved in wars with their city-states, it was the only foreign nation that they had thought about at all carefully. It is possible that certain of the pre-Socratic philosophers borrowed some of its ideas; this was said, for example, of Democritus of Abdera. Then, in the 360s, the Achaemenid founder Cyrus I the Great (549–529) was treated in the *Cyropaedia* of the Athenian writer Xenophon as a model hero. Next, Philip II of Macedonia deliberately copied many aspects of the Persian military and administrative machines, and leading Persians were living in exile at his court when Alexander the Great was a boy. After Alexander, by superior generalship, had defeated the armies of the Persians and annexed their entire empire from Asia Minor to India – thus transforming the face of the world (334–327) – by far the most imaginative act of his life was his prayer at Opis (the later Seleucia on the Tigris) that Macedonians and Persians might live in harmony, and jointly rule this enormous commonwealth.[11] It was a firm rejection of the narrowly Panhellenic, anti-Persian views of the Athenian orator Isocrates (436–338) and Alexander's own teacher Aristotle, and a vast step forward towards the cosmopolis which was beginning to take shape in people's minds (Chapter Four, section 3). Moreover, Alexander arguably began to put this plan into action by inducing eighty of his officers and some ten thousand of his soldiers to marry Persian girls, and by retaining and appointing Persian governors of his provinces.

Yet out of eighteen of these original appointees only three were still in office by the time of his death, and thereafter the policy was virtually dropped. Many Macedonians and Greeks, true to their traditions, had found the whole idea thoroughly shocking. Nor did they like Alexander's adoption, while in Persian territory, of Iranian costume and court etiquette, including the obeisance (although their belief that this practice involved a claim to divinity was mistaken, since the Persian monarchs had been 'rulers by the grace of God' and not god-kings).

When, therefore, Seleucus I Nicator gained possession of Iran he struck a new balance. Unlike almost all the other officers who had married Persian women, he did not put away his wife, Apama, an Iranian who came from remote Sogdiana (Afghanistan). But he abandoned Alexander's Iranian costume and obeisance, and, while retaining the Persian administrative framework, built it into a system in which the Greek element was entirely predominant: for the first two generations there seem to have been no foreigners in the Seleucid ruling class, and even afterwards they never constituted more than two or three per cent of its numbers.

While the Syrian and Mesopotamian regions of the Seleucid empire were inhabited by peoples of Semitic language and culture, the populations of its eastern, Persian, regions spoke Iranian (Indo-European) tongues and dialects. Now the Seleucids regarded their hold over the Iranian plateau as essential for the protection of their central, Mesopotamian territories – and thus for competition with their Egyptian and Macedonian rivals on equal terms. Once again, as in Semitic Mesopotamia, a primary method of asserting this control was by the establishment of colonies: and once again the cultural interchange between the Greek settlers and the natives is not very easy to assess. By this time, in Greek literary circles, the figure of Zoroaster, the legendary founder of Persia's sun-worship, had replaced Cyrus I – with the assistance of fictitious and forged accounts – as the most typical Iranian personage. This was a characteristic development in an age when the Greeks were looking more carefully at foreign worships (Chapter Four, section I). However, the syncretism – identification between Greek and foreign deities – which elsewhere sometimes arose from this process did not occur very much in Seleucid Iran. Instead, the Greek and oriental forms of worship lived separately side by side. And so did their cultures, each too strong – despite whatever contacts there had been in the past – to encroach seriously on the other. Apart from a certain amount of writing on Iranian history and geography by Greeks living in Iran and by Hellenized Iranians, the influence of Persian ideas on the Greeks remained fragmentary and inaccurate; and the Iranian tongues were still unknown to them. As for the Persians, even if a noble might occasionally leave his fortified country mansion and muster up a superficial Greek social habit or two, they were, taken all in all, not Hellenized in the slightest degree. Hellenization failed to compete in Iran. Generations of peace and stability might conceivably have made the story different. But these peaceful epochs never materialized.

Instead, in the disturbed conditions of the time, religious, political and cultural resistance to Hellenism stiffened. The result was the total breakaway of the various Iranian countries of the empire, one after another. These secessions were encouraged by repeated conflicts within the Seleucid royal house, and by continual nomad threats from central Asia, which the regional governors could not effectively confront owing to their masters' insistence that they should fight the Ptolemies, or internal usurpers, instead. The best of the Seleucid kings tried to stem the tide by timely concessions of local autonomy, in exchange for military assistance and occasional tribute. But no such solutions proved able to stem the continuing fragmentation of the empire.

Thus the revolt of Diodotus I Soter against Antiochus II Theos (*c.* 256-255) meant that the entire, huge eastern lands of Bactria and the Indian border, containing massive Iranian and Indian populations, were lost to the Seleucid empire for ever. At least, however, Diodotus' dynasty was still Greek – and more adroit than the Seleucids at reconciling the various races of their country (Chapter One, section 4). In the central Persian area, on the other hand, it was a native Iranian dynasty that seized power from the Seleucids. The coup was the work of the Parthian Arsaces I, whose dynasty dated its era from 247 and before long ruled over the whole of Iran.

After Antiochus III the Great's wars of reconquest (212-206) had failed to achieve any lasting effect, the Parthians moved on to annex most of Mesopotamia as well (141), where the leading classes had become increasingly self-assertive against the weakened Seleucid régime. Antiochus VII Euergetes Sidetes' bold recapture of Babylonia and Media (130) came to nothing with his death the following year; and after that the Seleucid state dragged on a limited existence extending to Syria and very little else, by sufferance of the Romans, who finally extinguished its existence altogether in 63 BC. This they did by driving out Tigranes I the Great, 'King of Kings' (originally the ruler of Armenia), who had supplanted the last warring rivals of Seleucid blood twenty-one years earlier.

It was a melancholy ending to two and a half centuries of endeavours to realize Alexander's unformed plans for a multi-racial state. Despite exciting successes, these Seleucid attempts eventually failed, because the interchange between the Greek ruling class and the peoples among whom they had come to live never proved quite substantial or fruitful enough to turn the scale.

4 The Near-Eastern Border States

Because of its complex, difficult terrain, Asia Minor never came entirely under the rule either of Alexander the Great, who treated it as a land of passage, or of the Seleucids, who saw it as the theatre of their duel with the Ptolemies. Thus the northern and central regions of the peninsula remained divided into independent states. Deep inland was Galatia, consisting of Celtic (Gaulish) invaders – who crossed the Hellespont in 278 – and their descendants. These Galatians were organized in three associated tribal units which possessed a military strength that had to be reckoned with, but remained right outside Hellenism (their first coinages – inscribed in Greek – only appeared after 64, under Roman suzerainty). Three other states of Asia Minor, however – Bithynia, Pontus and Cappadocia – achieved vigorous new life under rulers who devoted much of their energy to warding off Seleucid encroachment. These princes were not Greek by origin but adopted Greek ways of life and Hellenistic institutions.

Bithynia, in the north-west of the peninsula, possessed a variety of agricultural crops, extensive pasturage and timber and fine marble, and was able to rely on useful harbours and land communications. The Bithynian leader Zipoetes I (328–280), who like many of his people was partly of Thracian ancestry, avoided submission to Alexander the Great, successfully resisted Lysimachus, assumed the title of king (297), and repelled the Seleucid Antiochus I Soter. In order to gain help in an internal dynastic quarrel, his son Nicomedes I (280–255) took the ominous step of inviting the Gauls (Galatians) into the peninsula. But he also started a tradition of showing an interest in Hellenistic culture, to which his kingdom's geographical position gave it ready access. Indeed, before long, Bithynia virtually became a Greek state, ruled from the port of Nicomedia (Izmit), which was founded by Nicomedes I (through a merger of two earlier Greek cities) in about 265.

By war and active diplomacy – financed by the labours of the native serf population – Bithynia achieved considerable dimensions, political power, and commercial strength. These efforts culminated under Prusias I Cholus (the Lame) (c. 230–182). In spite of various difficulties (including the embarrassing presence of the Carthaginian Hannibal (d. 183/2) as a refugee at his court), he avoided a breach with the Romans. The monarchs who came after him increasingly fell under their influence – most notably Prusias II Cynegus (the Huntsman) (c. 182–149), who grovelled humiliatingly before the senate – until, finally, Nicomedes IV Philopator (c. 94–74) bequeathed his kingdom to the Romans.

The neighbouring state of Pontus extended along the well-watered, fertile, wooded northern coastal territory of Asia Minor and into the

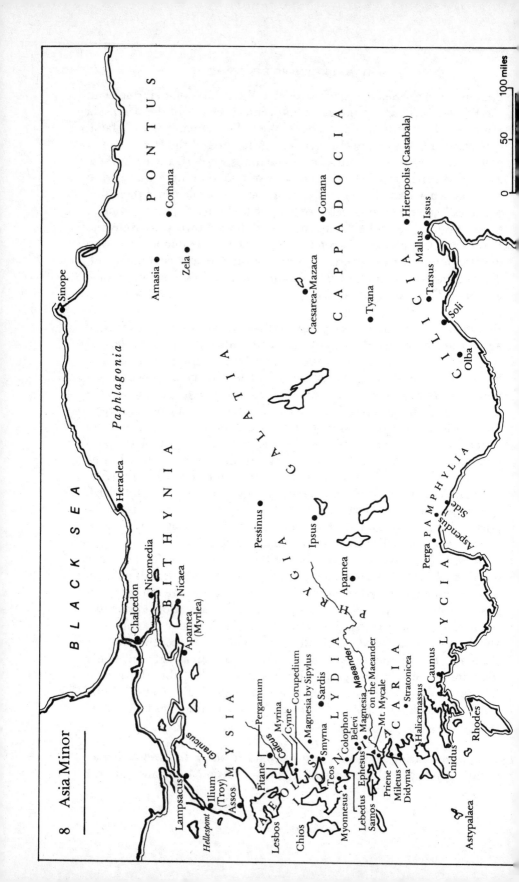

8   Asia Minor

metal-rich mountains of the hinterland. The country also possessed abundant salt. It was dominated by a feudal Iranian nobility, but the people who lived in the Pontic villages spoke no less than twenty-two different languages. Pontus also contained powerful, autonomous temple states, notably Comana ('the place of hymns') with its ancient cult of the nature-goddess and earth-mother Ma or Enyo (identified with the Greek Cybele), insisting upon a taboo on pigs and pork, and possessing extensive lands ruled over in patriarchal fashion by high priests who exercised absolute authority over a population of 6,000 male and female temple slaves.

King Mithridates I Ktistes, 'the Founder' (301-266), a partially Hellenized Persian who claimed descent from the Achaemenid monarchs, gained control over Pontus and asserted himself first against Antigonus I Monophthalmos and then against the Seleucids, collaborating with Bithynia in enticing the Gauls (Galatians) into Asia Minor. He established his capital at the city of Amasia (replaced in the early second century by Sinope).

The successors of Mithridates I continued to build up the strength of the country, employing many Greeks and obtaining recognition as a Hellenistic power. Some of the most remarkable and realistic coin-portraits in the entire Greek series are those of Mithridates III (c. 220-185) and Pharnaces I (185-169), this latter being a highly successful philhellenic ruler who formed the ambitious concept of a huge Pontic state extending all round the Black Sea. Profiting from his expansion, Mithridates V Euergetes (c. 150-120) became the most powerful king in Asia Minor.

Then his courageous and cunning son Mithridates VI Eupator Dionysus the Great (c. 120-63), a brilliant organizer and selector of subordinates, revived and put into practice Pharnaces' idea of a Black Sea empire by increasing his dominions to a breath-taking extent. The territories he thus overran far and wide around his kingdom included the Asian province of the Romans, to whom he offered, in a remarkably prolonged series of wars, the most dangerous challenge they had ever received from any Hellenistic ruler.

When Mithridates VI was finally defeated by Pompey (66), the core of his kingdom became part of the Roman province of Bithynia and Pontus, though large territories were also handed out to various client princes. At the same time Tigranes I, 'King of Kings', who during the past thirty years had used his position as Mithridates' ally to build up a large empire of his own round the Iranian, slightly Hellenized land of Armenia, was shorn of the territories he had conquered, but permitted to retain Armenia itself until his death in c. 56. Thereafter the Armenian highlands became a bone of contention between the Romans and Parthians for centuries.

Cappadocia, in the deep eastern central regions of Asia Minor, was a massive, rugged, isolated tract of tableland with extreme temperatures and poor crops, but huge numbers of horses, sheep and mules. The former Persian satrap Ariarathes I, who asserted that the Achaemenid Cyrus I the Great was his ancestor, evaded Alexander the Great's efforts to replace him, but was killed in 322 by Perdiccas who installed one of his fellow Successors, Eumenes of Cardia, on the Cappadocian throne. However, in 301 Ariarathes II recovered the country – nominally as a vassal of the Seleucids, though before 250 his son Ariaramnes secured their recognition of his independence; and then Ariaramnes' son Ariarathes III(c. 250–220) declared himself king, and placed the title on his coins. He and his son remained allies of the Seleucids until the defeat of Antiochus III the Great by the Romans (189/8), whom henceforward the Cappadocian monarchs were obliged to support. However, the country was not formally annexed by Rome until AD 17.

Under the Ariarathid monarchs, as in the earlier times of the Persian empire, the Iranian noblemen acted as local dynasts, using their strongholds to dominate the local peasantry, who were a byword for ignorance and boorishness. Thus the social structure resembled that of Pontus, and Cappadocia, like Pontus, had its temple states, once again including a Comana dedicated to the mother-goddess Ma. Cities were very few, and Hellenization slow, but the court of Mazaca (later Caesarea, now Kayseri) kept up a superficial Hellenistic appearance, which is also displayed by the royal coinage. Ariarathes V Eusebes Philopator (163–130), in particular, promoted Greek culture as far as he could, becoming an honorary citizen of Athens.

Bithynia, Pontus and Cappadocia were units that had at all times escaped incorporation into the Seleucid dominions. But there was another state of Asia Minor that only achieved independence by breaking away from that empire. This was Pergamum, a city in the territory of a non-Greek people, the Mysians, situated fifteen miles from the sea at a strategic point commanding the rich agricultural land of the Caicus (Bakir Çay) valley. The place began to become important under Philetaerus, a eunuch of mixed Macedonian (?) and non-Greek (Paphlagonian) parentage. Philetaerus was first an officer of Antigonus I Monophthalmos and then military governor of Pergamum under Lysimachus, whom he subsequently deserted for Seleucus I Nicator (282), taking with him an enormous treasure to facilitate his passage.

Thereafter, until his death nineteen years later, he ruled Pergamum under Seleucid overlordship, gaining distinction from his successful resistance to the Gaulish invaders who were consequently obliged to move further east to their eventual home in Galatia. Philetaerus' successors dutifully retained his portrait on their coins.

His nephew and adopted son Eumenes I (263-241), aided by Ptolemy III Euergetes, threw off the suzerainty of the Seleucids and made territorial acquisitions at their expense; and although the Seleucid régime regained them after a time it could not shake his independence. The annexations of Attalus I Soter (241-197) from the Seleucids once again were not lasting; but he won a spectacular victory over the Galatians, which caused him to assume the royal title and reassert his dynasty's claims to be the protector of Hellenism. Moreover, by his 'western' policy involving intervention across the Aegean, he gave a new turn to Pergamene history. In particular, Attalus I sought to block the alleged ambitions of Philip V of Macedonia by helping his successive enemies, the Aetolian League and the Romans; and he cooperated with Rome in its second war against Philip (200-197).

His son Eumenes II Soter (197-160/159) continued this policy of collaboration with the Romans, thus securing important gains from the defeated Seleucid Antiochus III the Great in 189-188. This meant that his territories, although still conveniently compact, now included five or six million inhabitants and occupied no less than half the total surface of Asia Minor, and far the most advanced half at that, including areas of ancient civilization such as Lydia and Phrygia. Subsequently, however, Eumenes II forfeited the confidence and goodwill of Rome, allegedly conducting secret negotiations with its Macedonian enemy Perseus. But his brother Attalus II Philadelphus (160/159-138) managed to regain the favour of the Romans, who helped him in local wars.

These Attalid kings lived more modestly than their Seleucid and Ptolemaic counterparts, but were equally absolute rulers. They kept and increased their power by maintaining an unusual internal freedom from disputed successions, usurpations and family feuds. Keenly devoted to cultural activities, these monarchs – and particularly Eumenes II Soter – made their capital Pergamum into one of the most magnificent architectural and artistic centres of the world. And perhaps the city of Pergamum spread rather more Hellenization round its fringes than Alexandria ever succeeded in doing. Yet in the last resort, like Alexandria, it was merely the Greek façade of a state consisting of non-Greek natives, who practised their own religious cults in villages that were still the principal economic and social units of the kingdom.

It was from the labours of these natives that the Attalids derived the wealth that caused them to be regarded as the richest rulers in Asia. Their prosperity, symbolized by a widely circulating coinage, was owed to a strict and skilful control (on somewhat Ptolemaic lines) of the country's resources. These included silver mines, an abundance of wheat, and active stock-breeding. Guided by technical handbooks, the cattle breeders produced important subsidiary industries of woollen textiles and parchment – employed to make the books in Pergamum's library, which deliberately rivalled Alexandria's.

The Attalids controlled the native population directly, establishing Greek military settlements in their midst, like those of the Seleucids. Pergamum and adjacent Greek towns were conceded the usual city-state institutions, although the monarchs exercised a good deal of inter-ference – which they justified by philhellenic claims that they were providing a defence from Galatian incursions. When, however, after 189-188, the Attalid house acquired numerous ancient Aegean city-states from Antiochus III the Great as tributary dependencies, it treated them with greater tact and restraint, imposing considerable taxes, it is true, but also granting subsidies with calculated generosity. The kings also allowed autonomous vassal rank to ancient, commercially flourish-ing religious states such as the shrine of the deities Agdistis (Cybele) and Attis at Pessinus, during the years (183-166) when this sanctuary was under their control; Eumenes II gave its community a new temple and porticoes, writing to its priest-king as one monarch to another.

The Attalids, for the most part, were efficient, single-minded and self-sacrificing. They showed a considerable flair for government, and created an impressive army and navy: their troops were good enough to have achieved the success of which they continually bragged, their defeat of the Galatians. Expert diplomats, they bought up allies, bought off enemies and played on rivalries, with equal dexterity. But the essential element in the Attalids' foreign policy – only briefly endan-gered – was their friendly relationship with Rome and dependence on Roman support. This produced spectacular short-term results, but in the long term, by strengthening Rome's position against other Greek states, it contributed to the downfall of the Hellenistic world, deserving the accusations of betrayal that the Pergamene rulers incurred on all sides, in contrast to their own patriotic Greek boasts.

The last, eccentric monarch of Pergamum, Attalus III Philometor Euergetes (138-133), surprised many people by leaving his royal estates and personal treasures – in fact, so it was interpreted, his whole kingdom – to Rome, perhaps in order to protect the Greek upper class against threatened social disturbances. Thereupon the Romans, after putting down a formidable revolt by Aristonicus (133–130), an illegitimate son of Eumenes II Soter, converted the whole territory into the province of Asia, which wholly transformed their imperial economy by its great wealth.

At just about the time when the kingdom of Pergamum was coming to an end, another Seleucid offshoot in the eastern Mediterranean was just embarking on independence. This was the religious state of the Jews.

Politically, as in so many other respects, Judaea (Palestine) presented an exceptional picture during the Hellenistic period, because it went through three different political phases. For after Alexander the Great's conquest of the country from the Achaemenid Persian empire, it came under the Ptolemies and Seleucids in turn – and then achieved national independence.

Syria's Hellenization inevitably spilt over into its neighbour and adjunct Judaea. Yet there the process was bound to encounter greater resistance, since the Hebrew population maintained its wholeheartedly monotheistic beliefs and forms of worship, based on the Bible, which the Christians were later to call the Old Testament. There had already been Greek influences in Judaea as early as the seventh century BC (if not earlier), and a quarter of a millennium later this influence was becoming quite extensive; fourth-century silver coins from the Persian province of 'Yehud' imitate Greek issues for trading with Greeks. But it was thereafter, when Alexander the Great occupied the country in 332, that the Jews for the first time felt the direct, large-scale impact of the Greek world and way of life, and the subsequent clash and interrelation between the Hellenic and Hebrew (Syriac) cultures had notable effects on their country.

After Alexander's death, Judaea was one of the numerous territories outside Egypt that were annexed by the Ptolemies. Many Jews from their homeland (as well as from Alexandria) served like other foreigners in the Ptolemaic forces. There were also Greek government officials and merchants in every Judaean village. And, above all, there were cities of Greek type round the fringes of the central Jewish territory. Before the Hellenistic period was over, the number of such cities on the Judaean periphery, including towns which had exchanged oriental for Hellenistic structures, came to as many as thirty. Perhaps Gaza, partly destroyed and then repeopled by Alexander, was one of the first of such foundations (later it was given the name of Seleucia); and either Alexander or Perdiccas sent Macedonian settlers into the town of Samaria. Among the other Greek foundations in the region, Gadara became especially significant because, remote from Greece and multilingual though it was, it produced very distinguished Greek literary figures, including Philodemus the Epicurean, Menippus the satirist, and the poet Meleager. The foundation of this screen of fortified Greek-style communities round the edges of the central Jewish plateau had a military purpose; for it was intended by the Hellenistic monarchs to help them keep the frequently recalcitrant Jews in order – a task which the cities enthusiastically undertook.

The Ptolemies saw Judaea as another of the temple states so well known in the near east, of which there were such famous examples in Asia Minor and Syria. In consequence, subject to their own ultimate control, they readily recognized the hereditary High Priests as the rulers of the country, and mediators between the Jewish community and themselves. When, however, the High Priest Onias II, probably inspired by pro-Seleucid sentiments, withheld Judaean taxes from Ptolemy III Euergetes (242–240), the king transferred the lay branches of the High Priest's authority, and other powers as well, to a Jewish sheikh, soldier and businessman from across the Jordan named Tobias. He, in turn, was succeeded by his financially gifted son Joseph, who although not a deliberate or cultivated Hellenizer was sufficiently Greek in his behaviour to be welcome at the court of Alexandria – and even to refer in a letter to Apollonius, the Ptolemaic minister of finance, to 'the gods'.[12] And many other Jews also – perhaps extending beyond the wealthy priestly families to an actual majority of the entire educated class – were likewise prepared to accept a measure of Hellenism. 'Let us make a covenant with the Gentiles [Goyim] about us', the Jewish *First Book of Maccabees* reports them as saying, 'for since we have been different from them, we have found many evils.'[13] Even, therefore, in a country so culturally remote as Judaea, Greek was rapidly becoming the language of government and big business – and the language of educated conversation, too, in place of Hebrew, which was largely literary, legal and liturgical (while the population as a whole continued to speak Aramaic).

In 200, the Seleucid monarch Antiochus III the Great, by his victory at Panion, annexed Judaea from the Ptolemies. It was he and his successors, henceforward, to whom the taxes must be paid, and it was they who appointed the High Priests, and, through them, enforced the sovereignty of the Seleucid state. But these procedures were conducted, at first, with some measure of tact, since Antiochus III issued an edict upholding the customs of the Jews, and confirming that the Temple at Jerusalem, the centre of their religion, was (like the shrines of temple states elsewhere) exempt from tax and entitled to a subsidy. However, the Tobiad family, while maintaining its local pre-eminence, soon showed that its allegiance was divided. In about 180 the High Priest

Onias III, of this Tobiad house, adopted what was regarded as a subversive pro-Ptolemaic stance – in contrast to his brother Jason (Joshua) who supported the newly installed Seleucid régime. Jason also offered Antiochus IV Epiphanes a larger tribute than hitherto, in order to secure promotion to the High Priesthood (175-172) – an appointment which contravened the traditional hereditary character of the office. What is more, Jason also bought from the monarch the 'privilege' of converting Jerusalem into a Greek-style city (*polis*) – or, possibly, establishing a Greek communal organization (*politeuma*) alongside the temple authority,[14] under the new name of Antiochia in Judaea, complete with gymnasium and naked uncircumcised young athletes. This not only shocked Jason's orthodox co-religionists but made an already deep gulf between the social and economic classes deeper still, because the poorer people did not obtain citizenship of the new Greek community – and no doubt many of them did not want to either.

Jason was in due course unseated and driven into exile (to Sparta, with which the Jews claimed a fictitious kinship, since both had strong traditional disciplines). His overthrower and successor, however, a certain Menelaus, was not an orthodox personage at all, but an even more lax Jew, who promised the king still larger sums of money (laying his hands on Temple plate for the purpose) and proclaimed such unrestrictedly Hellenizing views that he was actually prepared to admit a Greek garrison into the citadel at Jerusalem. In 168 Jason returned, imprisoned Menelaus, and overturned the Greek-style administration.

Unfortunately for him, however, he was believed by Antiochus IV Epiphanes – heavily engaged in warfare with Egypt – to be planning a pro-Ptolemaic coup, though whether the charge was justified or not we cannot tell. In the previous year, Antiochus had himself despoiled the Temple treasury, and now he entered Jerusalem again, massacred his opponents, reintroduced the Syrian garrison, and, with its approval, dedicated the Temple of the Hebrew God to Olympian Zeus. His reason was that he had found the Jews troublesome, and felt it best to merge the local religion into the main current of paganism, in keeping with his general empire-wide policy of Hellenizing the constitutions of local communities: although even he, while a keen plunderer of sacred funds, had never actually tried to extirpate the cults of the other temple states in his dominions.

No doubt, since the blending (syncretism) of deities was so much in the air, it was suggested that Zeus and the local Jewish God were much the same, and could easily be merged and assimilated. But the assessment of Antiochus, or his advisers, that the Jews would take this action lying down showed very faulty intelligence. On the contrary, his action united the entire population – except Hellenizing extremists – in opposition to his plans: and a popular revolt broke out. It was led by Judas Maccabaeus, a priest of the house of Hasmon, and was supported by the fanatical movement of the Hasidim, who popularized the idea of martyrdom and enjoyed great support in the towns and villages. The Maccabean movement proved so successful that the Temple was reconsecrated to the God of the Jews in 164. The new holder of the High Priesthood, Alcimus, a moderate Hellenizer, retained that office (with difficulty) until his death in 159. In the previous year Judas had died and was succeeded by his brother Jonathan (Yehonatan), who gave the Seleucids military assistance and thus secured their recognition, not only as High Priest (152), but as 'governor of Judaea' (150). Then in 142 Simon, brother of Judas and Jonathan, expelled the Seleucid garrison and was confirmed as High Priest by a national Jewish assembly, subsequently receiving coronation in the manner of a Hellenistic king – though he did not assume the title.

For the next eighty years, apart from a short interlude of subjection to Antiochus VII Euergetes Sidetes the Great (139–129), the Jews were independent, under the rule of the Hasmonaean (Maccabean) High Priests, who claimed the post as a hereditary right. Supported, in general, by the Romans, who valued them as a counterweight against the convulsed Seleucid state, the Hasmonaean dynasty relied on the aristocratic Sadducee party – based on the Temple, but superficially Hellenized – and gradually lost popular support. However, from the time of John Hyrcanus (Yehohanan) I (134–104) – who may have issued his dynasty's first coins, though a later date for these is also possible – the régime greatly increased its military strength, expanding in all directions at the expense of the Greek cities on its periphery, and transformed itself from a religious community into a secular state on Greek lines. Thus the pro-Hasmonaean books *I* and *II Maccabees*, though totally pro-Jewish, are both written in Greek (the former from a Hebrew original). Aristobulus (Yehudah) I (104–103) even adopted the title 'Philhellene',[15] while Alexander I Jannaeus (Yehonatan, 103–76) assumed the title of king,[16] and displayed luxurious Hellenistic trappings at his court – though as far as aggression against his hostile Greek neighbours was concerned, and their forcible conversion to Judaism, both Aristobulus I and Alexander Jannaeus were as patriotic as can be. Judaea again reached a peak of material power under Herod I the Great (37–4), founder of a new (Idumaean) dynasty under Roman protection.

Yet the people whom these men ruled were mostly Jewish in a more emphatic and doctrinal fashion than their monarchs. For the Maccabean revolt, and then the nationalistic but enlightened movement of the Pharisees – based on the local meeting-places (synagogues) instead of the Temple, and opposed to the Hasmonaean plan that the kings should occupy the High Priesthood – ultimately meant the defeat of Hellenism at the hands of the Jewish faith and way of life. Other oriental cultures, too, such as those of Babylonia and Persia, were managing to avoid becoming Hellenized to any considerable extent. But Judaea went further than any of them in violently rejecting all that the Hellenistic world had to offer. The Jews proved not only unassimilated, but unassimilable, and in spite of the smallness of their numbers the demonstration that this was so proved one of the most significant turning-points in Greek history, owing to the gigantic influence exerted throughout subsequent ages by their religion, which not only survived intact, but subsequently gave birth to Christianity as well.

Another essential and unique feature of Jewish life was the Dispersion (Diaspora). When Sargon II of Assyria had annexed Israel (the more northerly of the two Jewish Palestinian kingdoms) in 722–721 BC, he had removed more than twenty-seven thousand of its most prosperous inhabitants into areas within his own empire, where these 'Lost Ten Tribes' disappeared without a trace. Then in 597–586 the southern kingdom, Judah, including its capital Jerusalem, succumbed to the Babylonian King Nebuchadrezzar II, who deported many thousands of its people to his own Mesopotamian homeland. Although their families were permitted by the Persian king Cyrus I to return to Judaea in the sixth century, many preferred to remain in Mesopotamia, though they kept up contacts with Jerusalem and its reconstructed Temple from afar. Later, another Persian monarch, Artaxerxes III Ochus (358–338), settled a considerable number of Jews in his northern territory of Hyrcania, beside the Caspian Sea.

Next, after his successor Darius III Codomannus had been overthrown by Alexander, the conqueror's new foundation of Alexandria in Egypt rapidly became one of the most important centres of Jewish settlement in the world: more Jews lived in Alexandria than at Jerusalem itself. There had been Jews in Egypt before, probably from at least the sixth century onwards. But now Ptolemy I Soter introduced a lot more of them, mainly prisoners of war or ex-mercenaries, and Ptolemy VI Philometor (180–145) welcomed many others, appointing some to high offices of state. These Jews in Alexandria probably lived scattered among the city's Greek population until the middle of the second century BC, when many or most of them decided, no doubt with official encouragement, to occupy their own separate area instead, in the palace (Delta) quarter of the city. There they were permitted a largely autonomous organization – lacking the Alexandrian citizenship enjoyed by the Greeks but enjoying equality of rights with them by custom if not by law, and ranking above the native Egyptian population. The Jews were ruled by their own Council of Elders, and possessed synagogues (the earliest known anywhere). Their services were often conducted in Greek, which soon replaced Aramaic as the spoken language of the Jewish communities in Egypt.

Meanwhile the Greek historian Hecataeus of Abdera had written a historical study of the Jews (now lost), perhaps as part of a history of Egypt (*c.* 315). Although, apparently, treating their record with respect, he seems to have indicated that they liked to keep themselves apart because, encouraged by Moses, they hated foreigners and Gentiles. And this was precisely the tone of the large and much more anti-Semitic literature that was soon to arise (long before the existence of the Christians, who in due course took up the same theme). Manetho, an Egyptian chief priest, dedicated to Ptolemy II Philadelphus (283–246) a history of Egypt into which some Greek inserted a declaration that the legendary Exodus from that country had taken place in circumstances entirely discreditable to the Jews. Then Mnaseas of Lycia, in the later second century, told stories of how the deity worshipped by the Jews in the Temple (mysterious because inaccessible to visitors) was merely the head of a donkey – so that its worshippers, therefore, were no better than atheists. It was the unfamiliarity of their practices, not to speak of resentment because of the privileges they were allowed to enjoy, that told against them: and the persecutions of Antiochus IV Epiphanes, of course, encouraged the surrounding Greek cities to act against them in every way they could. In all the known world, it was only between Greeks and Jews that racial prejudice, in these Hellenistic times, was really strong.

Meanwhile, however, the Jews of Alexandria themselves had begun to produce their own Greek writings. Most important of all was their Greek translation of the Bible. This version was known as the Septuagint after its supposed seventy (or seventy-two) translators. However, the work was not undertaken at the request of Ptolemy II Philadelphus – as a legendary tale intended to give the work authority suggested – but came to be composed at various times from about his time onwards. The creation of the Septuagint contradicted the old belief that to translate the sacred text meant handing over part of its efficacy to the enemy; and it weakened the Jewish insistence on total separateness. Yet, at the same time, it successfully brought the Bible within reach of very many Jews who could no longer read the original with any ease.

The Septuagint also provided a massive stimulus to other Jewish writers in Greek. None of their endeavours, it is true – including the Septuagint itself – made much missionary impression on the Greeks, who found any approach based on the Bible too incomprehensible to possess any relevance to their own lives. But Jewish authors in Alexandria continued to write in Greek, not so much in order to gain new converts as for the benefit of their own community, because what they were interested in was, first, comforting their fellow-Jews and bolstering up their self-confidence, and, secondly, attempting to achieve effective equality or assimilation with the Alexandrian Greeks. The outcome was a Jewish literature – in the Greek language – that was unique among non-Greek peoples this side of the far east in quantity and quality alike.

Above all, in order to rebut writers like Hecataeus of Abdera, one Jewish apologist after another proceeded to claim that Judaism, not Hellenism, was the source of all human knowledge – adding, however, that the two could be reconciled. Thus one such Alexandrian Jew, a certain Demetrius living in the third century BC, composed a work, *On the Kings of Judaea*, which inaugurated a considerable series of similar Jewish histories in Greek. Eupolemus, who although a diplomat wrote execrable Greek, argued that it was only by the instruction of Moses that the Greeks had ever learnt to write at all (*c.* 150). Another Jew, Aristobulus (not one of the Hasmonaean rulers of that name), gave currency to many other comparable Mosaic legends as well, in order to show that Hebrew wisdom was much more antique and venerable than Greek philosophy (*c.* 100). He also quoted Greek writings (real or invented) to support his case; and indeed all the Jewish works of this kind inevitably showed considerable Greek influence. So did works in Hebrew such as *Ecclesiastes* (the Preacher, *c.* 250(?)) – stressing the vanity of all human effort at a time when Judaism was challenged by Greek ideas – against which *Ecclesiasticus* (written by Ben Sira (Sirach) *c.* 190, and translated into Greek in 116) represents an orthodox Jewish reaction. Meanwhile, at about the end of the same century, the *Letter of Aristeas* reassured the Jews that they were not 'barbarians' and could share Greek ways without compromising the essentials of their religion. The author of *Joseph and Aseneth* illustrates the same point by writing a romance of the Greek type about a Jewish theme from the Book of Genesis, the marriage of Joseph, son of Jacob, to the daughter of the priest of Heliopolis (On) – probably the oldest novel in Greek to have come down to us. All this Jewish literature in Greek culminated in the magisterial philosophical works of Philo Judaeus (*c.* 30 BC–AD 45), which, in common with so many other Jewish phenomena at Alexandria, owed far more to the traditions of the Greeks than to those of the

Hebrews (whose language possessed a structure ill-adapted to philosophy), although he tried conscientiously to reconcile the two schools of
thought.

The Dispersion extended to many other countries besides Egypt. The
Jewish element in the population of Syria seems to have been the largest
of all. Seleucus I Nicator incorporated Jews in his foundation at Antioch;
then immigration continued under Antiochus III the Great, and reached
its peak in the time of Antiochus IV Epiphanes, when numerous Jewish
emigrants moved out of crisis-ridden Judaea into Syrian territory. There
were likewise many of their co-religionists in Mesopotamia, notably at
Seleucia on the Tigris. However, Antiochus III the Great moved two
hundred of these Jewish Mesopotamian families into Asia Minor to help
guard the interior – and this was not the first, or by any means the last,
transfer of Jews into that country. *I Maccabees* also mentions Jewish
groups upon the Aegean islands, and in Greece and Cyrene. Rome, too,
after Pompey's enslavements in the east (63 BC), possessed an important
community of Jews – which has existed without a break ever since. Well
might one of those popular anonymous prophecies, the 'Sibylline Oracles', declare that 'every land and every sea is filled with Jews'.[17]

In the alien cities to which these migrants came, whether under
Seleucid or Ptolemaic or Attalid control or still maintaining independent governments of their own, the Jewish settlers became inclined to
request separate residential quarters of their own, although these were
by no means ghetto societies, since a Jew was prepared to belong to all
the usual professions of the cities where he resided, and took part in the
farming of its hinterland. The close contact that these Jewish people in
foreign lands always maintained with Judaea was to the advantage of
the priestly class at Jerusalem, where contributions began to flow into
the Temple on a substantial scale from about the first century BC.

On the whole, these Jews of the Dispersion kept right apart from alien
faiths; and they were assisted to do so by official concessions granting
them the right to use their own laws. Nevertheless, not only at Alexandria but elsewhere as well, their religion and culture inevitably became
somewhat Hellenized. One result of this process was the emergence of
a large category of what may be called 'Judaizers', pagans who admired
and sympathized with the Jewish faith and accepted its monotheism,
Sabbath-observance, dietary laws, and most of the Hebrew moral code,
but shrank from such total commitments as circumcision for men, or
ritual baths for women, since they lived among populations that were
predominantly Greek and found these customs distasteful.

In the later Hellenistic period, the approximately eight million Jews
in the world (as against fourteen million today) included perhaps seven

million who, affected in various degrees by Hellenism or not at all, lived in one part or another of the lands that had earlier belonged to the Greek states and now formed part of the Roman empire.

The most important product of the Jewish Dispersion was Saint Paul (d. AD 64 or later) from the Hellenized city of Tarsus in Cilicia (southeast Asia Minor), who spoke and wrote in Greek and thus personified this classic interrelation between Hebraism and Hellenism. But only up to a point: for the local Jewish community at Tarsus to which he himself belonged was Pharisaical, and therefore remained untouched by the temptation to water down Judaism by infiltrating Hellenistic ways. Yet the Jews of Asia Minor mostly rejected Paul, because they regarded his doctrine of the divinity of Jesus Christ as a blasphemous betrayal of their tradition of monotheism. So he turned to the Gentiles instead, infusing his reinterpretation of Jesus' message, at times, with some degree of Hellenism in order to make it more palatable. But this, too, was unavailing, at least in the short run, since the Gentiles also refused to give him the absolute faith and submission he demanded of them. So for the time being his Gentile mission failed to take root, and such Christians as continued to exist scarcely extended beyond a small band of Jews who were the heirs of Jesus' original Jewish following. It was only after Paul's death, when the first Jewish Revolt (AD 66) discredited Jewish Christians as well as Jews in the eyes of the ruling Roman power, that Christianity took shape among the Gentiles instead. And it was in their hands that the future of the faith in later centuries was to remain, not in the hands of the Jews, since the original Jewish nucleus of Christianity died out before the ancient world had come to an end.

5 The East

Judaea and Pergamum were states that broke away from the western extremities of the Seleucid empire. But there were also vast lands at its eastern fringes which had likewise seceded from its rule.

Among these territories were the complex, far-reaching tracts containing the various Iranian and Mesopotamian peoples, speaking Indo-European and Semitic languages respectively.

Before and after 300 BC the Parni or Aparni, members of a confederacy of three semi-nomad Scythian (Indo-European) tribes, moved from central Asia into Parthia – which, in this original and limited sense, corresponded roughly to modern Iran's province of Khurasan, southeast of the Caspian Sea. There, in c. 247, their chieftain Arsaces I rebelled against the Seleucid governor Andragoras (himself in revolt from Antiochus II Theos), and asserted the independence of his people,

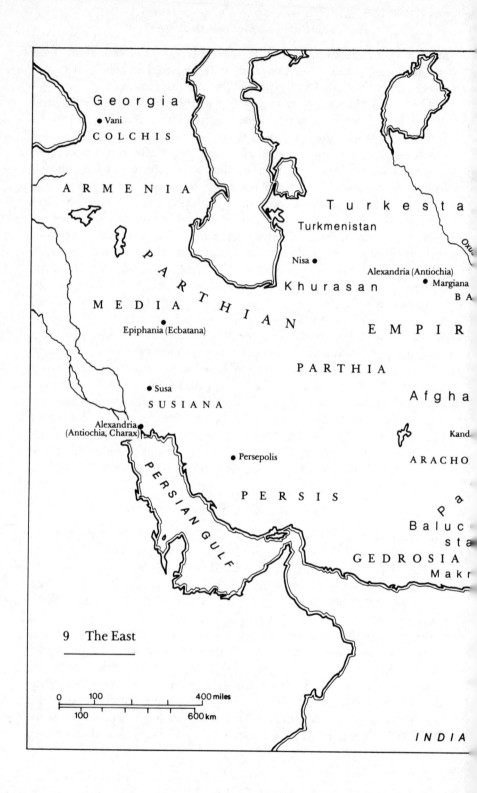

Georgia
● Vani
C O L C H I S

A R M E N I A

T u r k e s t a

Turkmenistan

Oxu

Nisa ●

Alexandria (Antiochia)
● Margiana
B A

Khurasan

M E D I A

P A R T H I A N

E M P I R

● Epiphania (Ecbatana)

P A R T H I A

● Susa

A f g h a

S U S I A N A

Alexandria ●
(Antiochia, Charax)

Kand

A R A C H O

● Persepolis

P E R S I S

P a

P E R S I A N   G U L F

P
B a l u c
s t a

G E D R O S I A
M a k r

9   The East

0   100   400 miles
    100   600 km

I N D I A

Sinkiang

• Alexandria Eschate (?)

DIANA Tadjikistan

• Aï Khanum

ctra-Zariaspa   Chitral   • Hunza
pamisus   • Gilgit
u Kush)   Alexandria by   Swat
ts.   • Caucasus   Gandhara
ura (Kabul)   • Pushkalavati
•   • Peshawar
PAMISADAE   • Gardez
n
• Demetrias   • Sacala

                    Jhelum
                    (Hydaspes)   Chenab
                                 (Acesines)
            a n   P u n j a b
                         Beas
                         (Hyphasis)
                                                    Ganges
         Indus
                                            Jumna
      R a j a s t h a n
   Sind   • Pataliputra

      Gujarat

E A N

whose dominions soon became considerably larger. The Parthians spoke the Pahlavi dialect of middle Persian, and adopted the Iranian religion of Mazdaism. The Seleucid Antiochus III the Great fought successfully against them, and for a time reasserted his suzerainty over large areas; yet he finally felt obliged to recognize their régime, concluding that he could not reoccupy such remote territory permanently.

Subsequently the Parthian monarch Mithridates I (c. 171–138) achieved an enormous geographical expansion, including the conquest of Media (northern Iran) and Babylonia (Mesopotamia), in the course of which he captured the Seleucid King Demetrius II Nicator Theos Philadelphus (140). Thus Mithridates I became the true founder of the huge Irano-Semitic Parthian empire, extending over half a million square miles. When an invasion by Antiochus VII Euergetes Sidetes 'the Great', which temporarily recovered Media and Babylon, ended in his failure and death (129), the Parthian acquisition of all territories east of Syria became definitive and permanent, despite temporary setbacks (including the loss of two monarchs' lives) at the hands of nomad tribesmen and Tigranes I the Great of Armenia (c. 87). By this time, the Parthian empire had shifted its gravity to Mesopotamia, where its rulers, encouraged by a resounding victory over the Roman triumvir Crassus at Carrhae (53), continued to hold sway for another three hundred years.

Instead of aiming at direct, centralized government of their varied territories, the Parthian monarchs favoured (or were obliged to accept) a much looser type of organization; so that their dominions not only consisted of provinces administered by their own nobility – mostly easy-going men, fond of hunting – but also included numerous vassal principalities governed by hereditary local dynasties. These also contributed their quotas to the royal army, which was based on heavy cavalry (*cataphracts*), armed with lances and bows.

Industry only played a minor role in the economy of the Parthians, which was founded on agriculture and commerce. Their principal customers were China and then Rome; and the Parthians took good care to keep the two of them apart. Their trading was based on towns, which they built on a considerable scale. The court tended to move from place to place. A favoured winter residence, after their capture of Babylonia, was Ctesiphon, founded as a Parthian military camp opposite Seleucia on the Tigris. Seleucia, however, was still by far the largest city of their empire, and despite its cosmopolitan population retained its predominantly Greek character: it even continued to date its coins by the Seleucid era.

The Parthian régime conceded the Greek cities the same measure of autonomy as they had received from the Seleucids, and tolerantly allowed them to worship as they pleased. Moreover, the official language of the royal administration was Greek, which it had inherited from the Seleucid bureaucracy. The Parthian kings also took over Greek administrative methods, legal practices, and titles; they employed Greeks as secretaries and members of their Council, and encouraged them to trade, explore, and write the history of the country. The Parthians made use, that is to say, of whatever Greek ideas or institutions they found useful. Indeed, Mithridates I, after his conquest of Babylonia, chose to adopt the designation of 'Philhellene', like monarchs in other lands. Moreover, Parthian artists were among the first easterners who made an attempt to absorb and adapt Greek art. At Mithradatkirt (Nisa), a Parthian foundation and royal residence at what is now Ashkhabad in Turkmenistan (USSR), excavations have revealed a Greek theatre and fine drinking cups blending Achaemenid, Parthian and Greek styles. The Parthian coinage, however, which under Mithridates I had included some pieces with a very Greek appearance, started to look much less Greek soon after his death. By the same token, more specifically Parthian styles of sculpture and architecture also began to emerge and develop, especially on the western fringes of the empire – for example at Dura Europus, an earlier Seleucid military colony which prospered under Parthian rule but became gradually and partially orientalized.

Parthia continued to survive as the only major power on Rome's frontiers until it succumbed to the Sassanian Persians in *c.* AD 224.

When it had become clear, in the third century BC, that Iran, under the Parthians, was preparing to become totally independent, the Seleucids no longer retained any possibility of holding on to Alexander's conquests still farther east – from Samarkand down to the Indus and beyond. From north to south, these lands at the farther extremity of Iranian territory included Sogdiana, roughly corresponding with what is now Soviet Tadjikistan; Bactria (Afghanistan), south of the river Oxus and north of the Paropamisus (Hindu Kush) mountains; Arachosia, south of that range and of the Cabura (Kabul) valley (which was the land of the Paropamisadae), in the southern part of Afghanistan; and finally the deserts of Gedrosia (Baluchistan and south-eastern Iran), the scene of Alexander's return from his Indian expedition. The Indian people he had encountered were, first, those of Gandhara in and around the vale of Peshawar, in northern Pakistan, east of the Khyber pass but on this side of the Indus; secondly, beyond its banks the kingdom of Taxila, whose ruler Omphis (Ambhi) had submitted to him in 327; and, thirdly, further south, another kingdom – between the rivers Jhelum and Chenab – where Alexander had defeated and reinstated a further Indian monarch, Porus (Parvataka or Parvatesha).

These huge territories had not been unknown to the Greeks even before the time of Alexander. The Achaemenid Persian king Darius I (521–486) had commissioned a Greek, Scylax of Caryanda, to sail down the Indus to its mouth, and a fifth-century Sanskrit grammarian from near Taxila, Panini by name, was acquainted with the Greeks and their script. The Achaemenids had also employed many Greek mercenaries whom they subsequently settled in eastern Iran, Afghanistan and the Indus valley, where their descendants lived on. Alexander, whose naval commander Nearchus of Crete wrote a valuable account of his Indian explorations, planted Greek colonial settlements at selected locations right up to the furthest extremities of his conquests, where he founded Alexandria 'by the Caucasus' (for which the Hindu Kush range was mistaken).

Across those mountains to the north lay the most prosperous of these eastern countries, Bactria, at the commercial cross-roads of Asia: rich in agricultural and pastural lands, 'country of a thousand cities', or at least of several hundred walled and fortified towns. But it had taken Alexander two seasons to pacify Bactria (and fertile Sogdiana) even superficially, and a grave rebellion of 13,000 Greek mercenary settlers that began in 325 and revived after his death – when it had to be put down by Perdiccas – showed that secessionist tendencies were already at work. To arrest the process, Seleucus I Nicator (if not Alexander before him) planted a new colony at the Bactrian centre of Aï Khanum, and another at Kandahar in Arachosia – part of a pattern of about a dozen colonies in these distant eastern regions. On Seleucus I's coins, his helmet is covered with a panther skin, alluding to the god Dionysus, the mythical conqueror of India. However, a native ruler Chandragupta Maurya (Sandracottus) – who had conquered the whole of north India – marched into his eastern lands, and in c. 303 Seleucus, proving unable to dislodge his forces, ceded to him the whole huge territory on the far side of Kandahar: eastern Arachosia, the land of the Paropamisadae, Gandhara, and the regions beyond the Indus. In exchange he obtained a number of elephants (stated to be 500, but probably less than half that figure) which he needed, and employed, to defeat his Greek enemies elsewhere.

In 256–255 Diodotus I Soter, the Seleucid governor of Bactria (and probably Sogdiana as well), declared himself virtually independent of his master Antiochus II Theos, while the latter was fighting a rival in the west. The Parthians, whose territory divided Bactria from the rest of the Seleucid dominions, were preparing their own total secession from Seleucid rule, and Diodotus I believed that Greek resistance to this and other non-Greek threats could be better organized from his own head-quarters Bactra-Zariaspa (Balkh) than from the distant Seleucid capitals.

But the coinage of this emergent Greek state in Bactria shows that full independence was only asserted gradually. Thus it seems to have been Diodotus I's son Diodotus II (c. 248–235) who, after first dutifully placing the head of Antiochus II Theos on his coins, subsequently assumed the title of king on his own account, after the Parthian rebellion had taken place and cut him off completely from the Seleucid empire. Diodotus II also appears, unlike his father, to have sought some kind of accommodation with the Parthian power.

Almost all we know about the subsequent rulers of this remarkable Hellenistic state, and its Indo-Pakistani offshoots, comes from their coins, which name – and strikingly portray – no less than forty monarchs, of whom scarcely more than half a dozen are recorded by extant ancient historians; and the circulation of their coinages gives us an idea of the dimensions of their power. The second and greatest founder of the Bactrian state, and creator of a new dynasty, was evidently Euthydemus I Theos (c. 235–200), who came from Magnesia by Sipylus (or Magnesia on the Meander) in western Asia Minor. After apparently killing and supplanting Diodotus II, Euthydemus I Theos greatly extended his frontiers. He strengthened his position against the Parthians in the west by the capture of Alexandria in Aria (Herat) on his south-western frontier. Moreover, to keep the barbarian Scythians on his northern borders at bay, he probed deeper into central Asia than any other Greek monarch ever had or ever would again, through Sogdiana as far as Sinkiang on the periphery of the Chinese empire, though he proved unable to maintain control of these territories. And then finally, with the help of his 10,000 cavalry, he resisted the invading armies of the Seleucid Antiochus III the Great, with whom he then concluded a treaty for the joint defence of Hellenism. Euthydemus' son Demetrius I (c. 200–185) seems to have retaken part of Arachosia from the Mauryan empire (which was failing) and to have founded a Greek colony in the territory he had captured – Demetrias, between two other settlements at Kandahar and Alexandria (Ghazni), and apparently the first such settlement founded by a Bactrian monarch (another was called Euthydemia). His coins show him wearing the elephant's scalp head-dress of Alexander the Great, but it has now been suggested that the Indian conquests thus implied were still only initiated or hoped for (at this stage) rather than effectively carried out.

The next kings, however, were able to profit from the impending collapse of the Mauryan state so as to extend their rule east of the Khyber pass into Gandhara. The heritage of Demetrius I was divided among three legitimate successors. One was Antimachus I Theos (an Antimachus Nicephorus also named on the coinage seems to have been the same man), who is known to us from exceptionally fine coin-portraits. At one time he controlled the whole of northern Pakistan, but for a time Demetrius' other two successors – who were probably his sons – Pantaleon and Agathocles Dikaios were able to issue coins at the Gandharan metropolis of Taxila. Another of their mints was Pushkalavati (Charsadda, on the approaches to the same territory), where their coinages show bilingual inscriptions in Greek and Brahmi. The parent of all modern Indian alphabets, Brahmi was the script of the Ganges and Jumna valleys, and its use suggests that by now the Indo-Greek kingdom had expanded its territories at least as far as the eastern Punjab. Another apparently powerful Indo-Greek monarch, Demetrius III Aniketos (Unconquered), who may have been connected with Pantaleon and Agathocles Dikaios, was perhaps the first to issue a further set of bilingual coins in Greek and Prakrit, written in the Kharosthi script – an adaptation of the Aramaic alphabet to Indian languages, employed in the Paropamisadae and Gandhara.

Eucratides I (c. 170/65–155), who described himself as 'the Great' (Maharajasa), was apparently the enemy and supplanter of Demetrius I's successors. He gained control, eventually, of a united Indo-Greek kingdom extending from Merv to Taxila. One of his generals was Menander Soter Dikaios, born (not of royal blood) near Sacala (east of Taxila), who coined early enough for Demetrius III Aniketos to imitate his issues, and then succeeded to Eucratides' dominions (c. 155–140/30). The Milinda of Buddhist tradition, Menander passed into history as the most memorable of the Indo-Greek kings. His coinage, and that of his sub-kings, is found over a wider area than the issues of any other Indo-Greek ruler. It seems that he not only consolidated Greek rule throughout the Punjab, establishing his capital at Sacala (Sialkot), but also launched an expedition down the Ganges valley as far as Pataliputra (Patna). To the north-west, his coins are found in parts of Bactria, which likewise evidently formed part of his dominions. Similar finds have also come to light in territories far to the south, including Sind, Gujarat and Rajasthan, though it is disputed whether their presence signifies his political control or merely commercial penetration.

Menander produced gold and extensive silver coinage at Pushkalavati, and further issues were made there by one of his successors, Strato I Epiphanes Soter Dikaios, with whom, in the course of a long reign (c. 130–75), his consort Agathocleia Theotropos ('godlike in character') was prominently associated as a monarch in her own right. The beginning of his reign witnessed the permanent detachment of Bactria and adjacent territories from the Hellenistic world, succumbing, province by province, to nomad or quasi-nomad tribesmen from central Asia. Thus the Yüeh-Chih (Tochari) occupied Sogdiana, dividing it into five principalities, while their enemies the Sacae (Scythians) overran and settled most of northern and western Afghanistan, creating a group of city-states, one of which was centred upon Bactria. Nevertheless, Strato I, like other Indo-Greek kings, maintained mints at Taxila, Alexandria by the Caucasus, and Gardez (south of Kabul). Under his rule, the old rival families of Euthydemus I and Eucratides I found unity. But the respite was brief, for the extraordinary variety of royal names on the Indo-Greek coinages of this time vividly testifies to a welter of dynastic feuds; they resulted in successive kaleidoscopic fragmentations of the kingdom into four or five small warring states, generally divided into a western and an eastern group, based on the Kabul valley and Gandhara respectively. However, some of their princes still boasted their moments of glory. Thus Amyntas (c. 100–75) – apparently a descendant of Eucratides I – reconquered Demetrias, Alexandria (Ghazni) and other areas from the Scythians; and at Kapisa in the Paropamisadae he issued the largest silver piece ever to be seen in the ancient world, on which, depicted in a particularly individual portrait, he describes himself as Nicator (Conqueror), like Seleucus I before him.[18]

At about the time of Amyntas' death, however, the Scythian Sacae advanced from the Kandahar valley to capture Gardez, while other invaders known as Indo-Scythians moved up the Indus to capture Taxila, where their leader Azes I (c. 57–35) – successor to Maues (Moga), 'Great King of Kings' – overthrew the last local Greek ruler. Nevertheless, there was still one remarkable Hellenistic monarch to come in these distant lands. He was Hermaeus Soter. The son or kinsman of Amyntas Nicator, he succeeded to the western Indo-Greek kingdom in c. 40 and, ruling with his wife Calliope, he reconquered for a time the eastern half of the region as well, as far as the Indus. In c. 30, however, the Yüeh Chih crossed the Oxus and occupied his western territories; and at about the beginning of the Christian era one of their tribal chiefs, Kudjula Kadphises I, obliterated his Indo-Greek kingdom altogether, incorporating it into the huge Kushan empire that he was bringing into being.

And so came the end of the last Hellenistic rulers in the world to have survived beyond the reach of Rome. It was remarkable that these states, so far from the Mediterranean zone, had lasted as long as they did. In the end, they proved too remote to strike permanent political roots. Yet they had carried out a most notable series of inter-racial experiments. True, the extent to which, during the three centuries that now came to an end, Iranian Bactria (Afghanistan) had become Hellenized remains unknown; but the descendants of the Greek settlers planted by the Achaemenids were no doubt still there, and Alexander, the Seleucids and the Bactrian monarchs themselves had added colonies of their own. And there does appear to have been a better understanding between the Greek and Iranian communities than in any other Iranian country. The feudal native society benefited from the increased wealth and frontier security that the Greek régime was able to guarantee; while Bactria's inaccessible distance from Hellas compelled the Greeks to adopt a more friendly and equal attitude to the Iranians, especially as foreign menaces, threatening both parties alike, were apparent on all sides. Nevertheless, the Greeks and Iranians in Bactria, even if they enjoyed fairly amicable mutual relations, did not absorb each other's ways of life to any great extent.

In Pakistan and north-western India the situation was more positive. It is uncertain how many Greeks had penetrated to India before the time of Alexander. Subsequently, however, although the Indo-Greek dominions beyond the Indus were even farther away from Greece than Bactria was, a closer partnership and understanding seems to have developed between its two peoples: indeed, closer than between the Greeks and their subjects in any other land. This was all the easier to achieve because the rulers of the Indian, Mauryan empire that lay beyond showed markedly pro-Greek tendencies. Chandragupta Maurya, after his confrontation with Seleucus I, received at court his ambassador Megasthenes (writer of a history of India), and entered into a marriage alliance with the Seleucid family. Subsequently, Chandragupta's heir Amitraghata (Amitrochaites) maintained favourable relations with Antiochus I Soter, who was said to have sent him, in response to a request, figs and wine, but not the sophist (philosopher) he had also asked for, since these were in shorter supply.

This desire for a philosopher has a bearing on the alleged relationships between Hellenistic and Indian culture. In spite of reports that Greek philosophers, notably the Sceptic Pyrrho (Chapter Four, section 2), met Indian sages, the links between their philosophies may not have amounted to very much. The Greeks respected Indian wisdom in principle, yet knew nothing of its primary sources or current developments. But the Indians did borrow considerably from the sciences of the Hellenistic world. In the words of the *Gargi Samhita* (an astronomical work of c. AD 230, containing certain material dating from two centuries earlier) 'the Yavanas [Ionians, i.e. Greeks] are barbarians, yet the science of astronomy originated with them, and for this they must be reverenced like gods'.

Chandragupta Maurya's remarkable grandson Asoka (*c.* 274–232) may have been partly Greek by blood; in any case he was deeply affected by Greek culture. One of his edicts found near Kandahar (by now under his control) is bilingual, inscribed in Greek and Aramaic. Moreover, his monuments display Greek stone-carving techniques and were probably made by Greek immigrants or settlers, since in Asoka's reign a large Greek population of India is increasingly evident. He was eager to convert them to Buddhism, and one of his Buddhist Councils dispatched missionaries to leading Greek rulers (Antiochus I or II, Ptolemy II Philadelphus, Antigonus II Gonatas, Alexander II of Epirus, and Magas of Cyrene).

Subsequently, evidence indicating some kind of ethnic and cultural symbiosis is provided by the bilingual character of the coinages issued by the Greek kings; moreover, these pieces are often square in shape, to suit the taste of the Indian bazaars. Their designs also display a variety of Indian religious allusions. Pantaleon shows Lakshmi, goddess of Brahmin merchants, with tight trousers, long ear-rings and a flower in her hair, while Agathocles Dikaios, on the other hand, depicts the holiest symbols of Buddhism: the sacred tree in a railing, the pyramid stufa, the lotus plant. It was largely due to the influence of the Greek settlers and rulers – responsible for a general atmosphere of emancipation – that Buddhism, after the death of Asoka, had moved out of its monastic seclusion; and it was asserted that the great Menander (Milinda) himself – who enrolled Indian princes on his Council – embraced the Buddhist faith after a discussion with its scholar-priest Nagasena recorded in the *Milindapanha* (*Questions of Milinda*), a quasi-Platonic Prakrit dialogue. Indeed, the wheel that appears on Menander's coins may be the Wheel of the Law (Dharma Chakra) connected with Buddhism. It seems probable, in fact, that he did not actually become one of its adherents, but he does seem to have transformed it into a kind of state church.

The Greeks came and saw (it has been claimed – modifying a famous statement of Julius Caesar), but India conquered. However, Greek cultural influence still remained strong in the area even after the Indo-Greek régimes had disappeared. The Pahlava (Indo-Parthian) Gondophares (?AD 19–45) – who was said to have received St Thomas at his court – placed not only Shiva but Zeus, Athena and Nike on his coins; and the issues of Kushan rulers likewise honoured Greek as well as Zoroastrian and Brahmanic gods and Buddha, in addition to imitating the coins of the Indo-Greek ruler Hermaeus Soter. Moreover, the flourishing school of sculpture and architecture that developed in Gandhara from the first century AD onwards contained strong Greek as well as Indian ingredients – styles and motifs presumably derived from the Indo-Greeks, or perhaps in some cases from Syrian Hellenism. For a thousand years, until the fifth century AD, there were still Greeks in India, and there are people there even today who believe they are descended from Alexander's settlers. They are to be found in Chitral, Gilgit and Hunza, on the northern fringes of the peninsula, where it borders upon the Chinese empire.

China, which has been compared to ancient Egypt because of its conservative, hierarchic social system, rivalled the Hellenistic world in the brilliance of its contemporary civilization. At the time of Alexander – in the last century of the Chou period – the country was politically fragmented. But then, after a struggle to the death that is comparable with the almost contemporary events of the Second Punic War, Shih Huang Ti reunited the vast Chinese dominions; his burial site at Ch'ang An (Sian) is one of the most remarkable discoveries of modern times. The Ch'in dynasty which he established was short-lived (221–207): but the Han dynasty that followed (202 BC–AD 221) outdid all the Hellenistic kingdoms put together, and even rivalled Rome, in size, wealth, prestige and power.

Alexander knew nothing about China; and for a time its contacts with the Hellenistic world, too, remained slight, for the great transcontinental routes had not been systematically opened. Greek influences on Chinese manufactures and arts become apparent from the time of Euthydemus I Theos of Bactria, a country which had begun to import goods from China by way of Antiochia (formerly Alexandria) Margiana (Merv in Soviet Turkmenistan), including the gold and nickel the Bactrian and Indo-Greek rulers used for their coinage. Then a new epoch of more intensive contacts between east and west was launched by the remarkable central Asian travels of the Chinese explorer Chang Ch'ien (138–125). The Han emperor Wu-Ti (141–87) pushed forward the Chinese frontiers to include huge areas in the interior of the continent. Soon afterwards, China established much stronger commercial links with Parthia, and thus, indirectly at first, with the Seleucid and Ptolemaic kingdoms.

In particular, Chinese silk garments began to be exported to the west, in exchange for glass and metal-work. They were made from the cocoons of the mulberry silk-worm (*Bombyx mori*), unwound by methods which China long kept a secret. The sea-routes were used for these exports, and also a famous land-route, the Silk Road, passing by way of Antiochia

Margiana, Seleucia on the Tigris, and Antioch on the Orontes. Robes of this materal became very fashionable among rich Parthians and Greeks and Romans; the silks that were worn, the Roman poet Lucan tells us, by Cleopatra VII of Egypt[19] were surely the expensive genuine article rather than one of the substitutes which were provided from various inferior silk-worms and made into clothing at the Aegean island of Cos and elsewhere.

6 Monarchies and Monarchs

The states that have been discussed in the foregoing sections were all ruled by monarchs. The Greeks, before Hellenistic times, had experienced kings of a kind, at Syracuse where the leaders were often a cross between 'kings' (who were hereditary) and 'tyrants' (who were not); at Sparta where they were hereditary but not much more than army commanders; in the Cimmerian (Crimean) Bosphorus where they controlled a highly organized administration; in Cyprus and Caria where they presided over outposts of Persian rule; and in Macedonia where they represented a survival from the hereditary tribal chieftainship of heroic times. Alexander's career started as that of a Macedonian king, but the national character of this kingship became obscure when he subsequently conquered many other lands as well, and ruled them according to their own various traditions. Thus it was he who perpetuated the institution of monarchy and invested it with a new character – not bound up with any single country or race – as a widespread political necessity for the Hellenistic future.

After the deaths of the powerless 'kings' who came after him – his feeble-minded half-brother Philip III Arrhidaeus (d. 317) and his infant son by Roxane, Alexander IV (d. 311) – the surviving rulers took the title of king in this new style: Antigonus I Monophthalmos in 306 and Ptolemy I Soter and Seleucus I Nicator in 305/4. That meant that the fiction of a unified empire had finally been abandoned, and the time was ripe for the Successor states – if, indeed, the term 'state' is appropriate, since with the exception of ancient Macedonia, their kingly titles bore no territorial definition or limitation. Each king was himself the state and the law incarnate, irresponsible and absolute, and owner of all his subjects' land. Such, then, was the world of kingdoms that came into existence until the Romans were able to show that a big state could also be a Republic – and that only for a time, since they, too, eventually found that their large possessions needed an autocrat to govern them.

It was extremely hard work being an effective Hellenistic monarch. As

Seleucus I Nicator remarked, nobody who realized the quantity of his correspondence would want to pick up his crown if it was dropped at his feet.[20] The kings' 'Friends' were of some assistance. The Macedonian kings of old had appointed 'Companions', more or less hereditary chieftains themselves, but their Hellenistic successors maintained a constant, informal council of Friends, chosen with little regard for class or wealth, who could be given some of the more responsible jobs. However, the rulers also developed substantial bureaucracies. Indeed, one of their most notable achievements was the rapid absorption of whatever systems they inherited, and their development into unprecedentedly complex administrative machines.

However, the most important royal task of all was to be a victorious military leader. In the words of the pseudo-Platonic treatise *the First Alcibiades*, the main thing that the statesman has to know is 'when to go to war and how long and with whom'.[21] The decades of Alexander's successors were a period of almost ridiculously incessant wars, and even when the great monarchies took durable shape, frontier conflicts remained frequent. The kings needed this external warfare not only for the propaganda value of military glory (for example, when barbarian Gaulish invaders were repulsed) but also because war could be such a lucrative business concern, bringing territory and riches.

Alexander the Great had inherited both the Macedonian and the Greek traditions of warfare, and combined and improved upon them to become one of the most rapid and versatile and formidable and breathtakingly successful military commanders of all time: subsequent Hellenistic rulers could only admire his brilliance, and imitate it as far as they might. Each battle Alexander had directed was different from the last, each was fought as he wanted it to be fought, and each was crushingly conclusive. In the course of these engagements, Alexander met unprecedented hazards, on land and water alike, with unerring improvisation. His personal courage was unequalled: time after time he barely got away with his life. His men followed him for countless miles, through extremes of heat and cold – until finally, on the edge of the Indian sub-continent, they felt they could go on no longer to the uncertain lands that lay beyond.

His attacks, on the battlefield, combined infantry and cavalry with immense skill, transferring the decisive role to the latter. Alexander had also learnt the military value of elephants at his battle with the Indian King Porus, and subsequently Seleucus I Nicator won the battle of Ipsus against Antigonus I Monophthalmos because of the elephants he had obtained from Chandragupta in *c.* 303 in exchange for territory. At Raphia in 217, although Ptolemy IV Philopator finally proved victorious over Antiochus III the Great, his left wings had crumbled at the outset because its small African forest elephants – they were not the larger bush variety – could not stand the smell or trumpeting of the elephants on the other side. From about the same period the infantry phalanx, originally developed by Epaminondas of Thebes (d. 362) and Philip II of Macedonia, came back into prominence, dominating the military scene with its bristling, jabbing array of heavy lengthened spears, until the increasing rigidity of its tactical operations succumbed to the more flexible Roman legionary manoeuvring.

Even though no Hellenistic state was able to muster more than 100,000 soldiers for a decisive battle, their armies were far more varied, rapid and purposeful than anything that had ever been seen before in Greek lands. Above all, they were much more efficient, since they largely depended (like the Achaemenid Persian armies before them) on a strong class of professional mercenaries. Crete and Galatia were favourite sources of supply, but origin or nationality did not matter; men wanting this sort of occupation, wherever they came from, flocked for recruitment to international centres such as Taenarum (Laconia) and Aspendus (Pamphylia), near the southern coasts of the Peloponnese and Asia Minor respectively. We hear a great deal about the mercenaries from the playwright Menander and from the historians. They were a rough and uncultivated lot, but in great demand. By the second century, however, the high cost of obtaining them was increasingly painful for potential employers, and the men themselves were becoming harder and harder to find.

It was another sign of this military professionalism that war was one of the few fields in which Hellenistic technology made progress. Philip II and Alexander the Great had introduced marked improvements in siege technique, and these were elaborated upon still further by those who came after them, notably Demetrius I 'the Besieger' (Poliorcetes). Besiegers, that is to say, gained an increasing superiority over besieged: but this trend was countered, already before the fourth century was ended, by new developments in fortification design. Well-fortified harbours, too, made their appearance, because the royal and Rhodian fleets played an extremely prominent part in the continual contestation and commercial exploitation of the Aegean basin. The Ptolemies, for example, possessed ships of new and enormous dimensions, designed for shock and ram tactics; though Hiero II's *Alexandria* was larger still.

So above all the Hellenistic kings had to be the commanders of forces fighting wars: or at least that is how many of them interpreted their job. But they had many other tasks as well; Seleucus I Nicator, as we have seen, complained of their multiplicity. And so many intellectuals of the time, bearing in mind the weight of this burden, sought to build up a philosophical picture of Hellenistic monarchy as a whole.

Thinkers of the earlier and middle fourth century had already busied themselves with the characteristics and qualities of an ideal king. Plato, who was all in favour of a monarchical system – provided that it was designed on the right lines – presented a picture of the 'kingly man' of genius, placed above all positive law, and himself its source.[22] Isocrates (436–338), the orator who hailed the role of Philip II of Macedonia, had a follower who wrote that 'the will of the king is law';[23] and Philip II's historian Theopompus gradually modified his initial aristocratic ideals in favour of paternalistic monarchy. Aristotle saw kingship as a valid constitutional form, in which one man aimed at the common good – in contrast to its degenerate offshoot, despotic sole rule for the benefit of the sole ruler.

Then came treatises on kingship by all the Hellenistic philosophical schools, declaring it the best form of government and confirming that the kings were identical with the state and became its all-powerful incarnations – though not just arbitrary in their behaviour, because they must be fair and, being embodiments of the law, must behave in accordance with it. In particular the Stoics, with their belief that the world was governed by providence (*pronoia*), seemed to offer the perfect philosophy of monarchy, as providence's mirror. They attended the courts of rulers, including Antigonus II Gonatas, who used his knowledge of their doctrines to formulate a momentous definition of monarchy as a form of service, a 'noble servitude'.[24] In general, however, Stoic support of kingship tended to bolster up existing tendencies towards authoritarianism. For, the king being the state, the king's will is always right. That is what Demetrius I Poliorcetes and Seleucus I Nicator pronounced, and their declarations must have earned heartfelt approval from monarchs in Ptolemaic Egypt – and elsewhere, too, so that the Seleucid pretender Tryphon (Diodotus, 142–138) felt impelled to describe himself on his coins as *autokrator*, absolute ruler.

In keeping with such convictions, most Hellenistic kings were eager to present a grandiose impression. The ships they built were unnecessarily huge, and the festivals they staged seem remarkably extravagant. The palace or group of palaces of the Ptolemies, upon which archaeologists are now at work, was surely by no means a model of austerity: the tradition that they lived sumptuously is not to be disregarded. Even in relatively unpretentious Macedonia, the royal residence at Aegae (Palatitsa, Vergina) was imposing. And the provision for dead royalties in Aegae's tombs (*c.* 340) (for it would seem that the people buried there were royal, although the attribution of a tomb to Philip II is not confirmed) was equally sumptuous. For among these grave goods was a crown of gold leaves described as the finest piece of ancient jewellery ever seen, opulent gold- and silver-sheathed caskets, and a ceremonial parade shield ornamented with ivory of which the restoration is now under way.

This was all part of a general royal taste for large dimensions and monumental overstatement. A number of kings liked to be described as 'Great' (*megas*) – and Aristotle had argued that greater size meant greater excellence. He had also indicated that great-heartedness (*megalopsychia*) was a major virtue; and the monarchs took this sort of injunction very seriously, presenting the city-states, for example, with countless temples and porticoes and theatres, and lavishing substantial gifts and loans of money upon their administrations, in the hope of earning loyalty and gratitude.

All this made the kings seem to others, as well as themselves, a good deal larger than life. In consequence, the Hellenistic age witnessed the full development of ruler-worship. Though somewhat puzzling to ourselves, this came naturally enough to the Greeks. In spite of the recognized gulf between gods and human beings, it had been understood for a considerable time, first, that heroes – such as Heracles or Achilles – were halfway to gods, and secondly that they and other great figures, including the founders of cities, could receive reverential cults (though not quite the worship due to gods) after their deaths. Then in the fifth century a number of poets, including Pindar, began to stress that 'in greatness of mind or body we can be like the immortals'.[25] Before long, cults, including altars and games, were allocated to living men – famous athletes, frightening lunatics, the Spartan Lysander (d. 395) who won the Peloponnesian War, and Plato's friend Dion (d. 354) who competed with Dionysius II for the mastery of Syracuse. Indeed, philosophers such as Protagoras, Plato and Aristotle were all of the opinion that human beings in some way partook of divinity.

Alexander the Great was familiar enough with such ideas, since his family claimed descent from Zeus, through Heracles – and his father Philip II had already received various godlike honours in his lifetime. When Alexander paid a pilgrimage to the shrine of Amon-Ra (Ammon) at the Siwa oasis in Egypt (331), its priests addressed him as the god's son, which was the traditional salutation due to any Pharaoh of Egypt (such as Alexander had now become by conquest) but was also comprehensible to the Greeks, who were beginning to identify Ammon with Zeus. Nor is there any reason to doubt the report that in 324 Alexander ordered the Greek city-states 'to vote that he was a god'[26] – which means that he ordered them to institute a cult in his honour. In Greek lands, such honours to leading men were by now familiar enough, and Alexander saw his command as a convenient extra-constitutional formula for obtaining recognition of his universal status – a political device for unifying his empire. No doubt flatterers constantly offered him hints about his own divinity; and he himself was said to have echoed the current view that 'while God is the father of all mankind, it is the noblest and best whom he makes especially his own'.[27] In particular, he openly proclaimed his desire to emulate the arch-hero Achilles, who was supposedly the ancestor of his mother Olympias. Such ideas made it all the easier for him to demand devotion from the Greek city-states – a devotion which, not being strangers to adulation, they may even have exaggerated beyond his own requests. And it was these actions of theirs, not any oriental traditions, that directed the future course of Hellenistic thinking about the worship of kings.

In the years following Alexander the Great's death, Demetrius I Poliorcetes allowed his name to be associated with the most widely favoured of current divinities, Dionysus (whose eastern adventures were identified with Alexander's – Chapter Four, section I). His coins also displayed him wearing a bull's horn, which symbolized Poseidon, god of the sea. Moreover, an Athenian poet, celebrating the rescue of his city from the authoritarian local leader Demetrius of Phaleron, wrote a *Processional Song* in honour of Demetrius I Poliorcetes which summed up this whole institution of ruler-worship and its causes: 'For other gods are either far away or have not ears, or do not exist, or pay no heed to us at all: but you we can see in very presence, not in wood and not in stone, but in truth. And so we pray to you.'[28]

It was in Ptolemaic Egypt, however, that ruler-worship attained its greatest emphasis and complexity. Ptolemy I Soter, in order to stress his legitimacy, endowed his new capital Alexandria with the official state worship of its founder Alexander (dubiously alleged to have been a distant relation of Ptolemy's mother Arsinoe), who appears displaying various divine attributes on coins of the time – notably the ram's horns of Zeus Ammon, his reputed ancestor, and the elephant scalp of Dionysus. Then the authorities of the city-state of Rhodes, after Ptolemy I had helped them to repel Demetrius I Poliorcetes, were prompted by an oracle to hail the Egyptian monarch as Saviour and greet him as a god (304). Ptolemy's coins show him wearing the goatskin-cloak (*aegis*) of Zeus over his shoulders, with Zeus' eagle and thunderbolt on the reverse: and a small bronze bust at Baltimore may identify him with Dionysus. Next, when Ptolemy I died in 283 and his wife Berenice I four years later, they were in turn proclaimed Saviour Gods by their son

Ptolemy II Philadelphus. Subsequently, Ptolemy II created a cult for his own magnificent sister-wife Arsinoe II Philadelphus and sponsored their joint cult as Brother and Sister Gods – already, apparently, before her death in 270.

The evolution of Ptolemaic ruler-worship was now complete, and by the end of the century there were priests not only of Alexander the Great, but also of each pair of deceased Ptolemies since his time, in addition to the reigning king and queen themselves. The process may perhaps have been accelerated, or facilitated, by local precedent – and the desire to gain favour with the indigenous clergy – since Arsinoe II Philadelphus shared a temple with Egyptian gods and was worshipped as Isis, like many Ptolemaic queens after her. The male rulers, too, were equated with Egyptian deities. But they were identified with Greek gods as well, and Ptolemy IV Philopator (221–205) in particular (like other monarchs elsewhere) demonstrated a thoroughgoing desire to see himself as the popular Dionysus, from whom his house claimed descent through Arsinoe, the mother of Ptolemy I.

As for the Seleucids, they regarded Alexander as their forerunner, but did not claim any special connexion with him or include him in an official ruler cult. Moreover, drawing on the precedent of the Achaemenid Persians, they desired not so much to appear as incarnations of the gods like the Ptolemies, but rather to stand above all human standards by the gods' special grace. Nevertheless, there were lapses from this Seleucid purism. Thus a decree of the city-state of Ilium (Troy) in honour of Seleucus I, though it does not actually call him god, invests him with the attributes of a divinity.[29] Indeed, he himself was not averse to tracing his lineage back to Apollo; and a coin found at Pasargadae, and apparently issued at Persepolis – still the capital of its realm, Persis, though it had been burnt down by Alexander – equips Seleucus' portrait both with the bull's horn of Poseidon and with Dionysus' skin. It remained for his son Antiochus I Soter formally to deify his father as Nicator (Conqueror) (280). Not long afterwards a royal Seleucid ruler-cult was duly established, with high priests of the living king and his divine ancestors. Antiochus II (261–246), like the rulers of various states after him, bore the title 'God' (Theos), which seems not only to equate him with the traditional deities but also, in a sense, to differentiate him from them (one would not, for example, add 'Theos' to the name of Zeus). In an empire, however, in which ruler-worship was generally divided up in countless separate manifestations, in contrast to the centralized Ptolemaic arrangements, Antiochus III the Great was the first of his line to institute a state cult of himself and all his ancestors. The Seleucid, however, who made the greatest political capital out of his divinity – seeing it as a bond between the different peoples of his empire – was Antiochus IV, known as the victory-bringer (Nicephorus), who issued a gold coin showing Victory, held by Zeus, placing a crown upon the king's title (Theos) Epiphanes (God Manifest).

In the third great kingdom, Macedonia, official attitudes were, at times at least, very different. Antigonus II Gonatas, when a certain Hermodotus proclaimed him 'offspring of the sun, and a god', replied: 'the man who empties my chamber-pot has not noticed it.'[30] For Antigonus II belonged to the heroic tradition of Macedonian monarchy according to which the king was only the first man among equals: in consequence, like his grandfather Antipater – who had refused to worship Alexander himself – he saw ruler-cult as a sham, and refused to do anything to encourage it. However, the god Pan on his coins – the god who had spread panic among his enemies, the Gauls, at the battle of Lysimachia (277) – seems to possess the king's features and diadem. Antigonus II's grandson Philip V liked to trace the origin of his Argive wife back to the legendary slayer of the Gorgon, Perseus – and he gave the hero's name to his son and successor, who allowed himself to be depicted in this guise on his coinage. Another compromise was effected in the Pergamene kingdom, where the king and queen were honoured by special priesthoods in their lifetimes, but were only 'translated to the gods' after their deaths; while the Indo-Greek queen Agathocleia preferred to call herself Theotropos, '*godlike* in character'.

The key to the meaning of Hellenistic ruler-worship is provided by titles such as Soter, Euergetes, and Epiphanes – Saviour, Benefactor, and God Manifest. As the hymn to Demetrius I Poliorcetes pointed out, the ruler is present here and now: he is able to provide assistance in time of trouble, to fulfil hopes and repel dangers and allay anxieties, with an efficiency that the traditional Olympian deities, 'protectors of cities' though they were, seemed unable to equal. No veneration of a specifically religious character was involved; there is no record of any actual prayer addressed to a Hellenistic king. There were, however, pleas and poetic invocations, often spontaneously offered by helplessly dependent subjects who hoped for political and economic advantage, and addressed their appeals to all-powerful rulers who were often vain and amenable to flattery.

The cities, once again, led the way. What they particularly admired and looked for in a king was *philanthropia*, the generous quality of a benefactor (Euergetes), a term originally applied to the care of human beings by the gods, and extended in the fourth century to the monarchs. A monarch, for his part, took pains to deserve this reputation, because he found that this ruler-worship from cities gave him convenient honorific access to these communities – with which his purely constitutional links were ill-defined – and ensured the continued validity of his official acts and decrees relating to their affairs even after his death.

The treatises on monarchy, which were being published in such large numbers, sought ingenious means to explain and illuminate this divine character of their rulers. Thus at the very outset of the Hellenistic age, Euhemerus of Messene, in the service of Cassander – and perhaps also Hecataeus of Abdera, working for Ptolemy I Soter – developed the argument that the traditional gods themselves had once been kings on earth, who earned worship for their benefactions (an interpretation that was facilitated by the mortal motherhood ascribed to some of the gods). According to this theory, seeing that even Uranus, Cronus and Zeus themselves had formerly been living human kings, who had earned worship from their grateful subjects, there was every reason for contemporary royal benefactors to receive similar honours.

Particular play, in this respect, was made with the name of Heracles, the immensely revered hero who had laboured and suffered incessantly for the good of human kind: the Cynics idealized him as a man who had won moral kingship by his achievements and endurance, and it was generally believed that after his death he rose to become a demi-god. Alexander the Great, who hailed Heracles as his ancestor, was constantly compared with him because of their exploits. Enormous numbers of Alexander's coins show Heracles, wearing his characteristic lion's scalp, not only as the forebear of the monarch but with a considerable hint of his actual features. The Ptolemies, too, claimed descent not only from Dionysus but from Heracles as well.

All these and other aspects of Hellenistic kingship and its aims are illustrated by the wide range of honorific titles which are displayed by the monarchs – and sometimes their queens – on their coins (and which help, like their sometimes derogatory nicknames, to distinguish them from the confusingly numerous rulers who bore the same names). The following titles are found: Aniketos, unconquered; Callinicus, gloriously victorious; Dikaios, just; Dionysus, the god (sometimes Neos, 'young'); Epiphanes, (god) made manifest; Euergetes, benefactor; Eukairos, opportune, well-timed; Eupator, son of a noble father; Eusebes, pious; Ktistes, founder; Megas, great; Nicator, conqueror; Nicephorus, victory-bringing; Philadelphus, brother- (or sister-) loving; Philhellen, lover of the Greeks; Philometor, mother-loving; Philopator, father-loving; Philopatris, lover of his or her country; Philoromaios, lover of the Romans; Soter, saviour; Theopator, son of a divine father; Theophilos, loved by the gods; Theos, god (the female form, Thea, is found qualified by Eueteria, fertility, and Neotera, younger); Theotropos, godlike in character.

These titles made their various contributions to a flourishing, unceasing personality cult devoted to the admiration of the rulers. Nor did it limit itself to the generalities represented by these titles, but, in addition, focused sharply on the distinctive characteristics displayed by each one of them separately. A monarchy was what each of its monarchs made it, and in an age of individualism it was inevitable that their qualities and idiosyncrasies should be attentively studied, with emphasis on picturesque, dramatic qualities which set every one of them apart from the rest, and from other men.

The personality of Alexander the Great provided the most satisfying of all possible models for such speculations, which have continued to gather round his character and career ever since, and have filled thousands of books in all epochs. Within the past century alone he has been presented as a Nietzschean superman, as a missionary of Greek culture, and as a moderate, scholarly philosopher-king combining the virtues of an English public-schoolboy and a Scottish laird. More recently, he has been revealed, with equal diversity, as a reasonable, hard-drinking idealist and a ruthless scheming megalomaniac; emphasis has been laid upon his clement magnanimity and tolerant intellectual curiosity, or, alternatively, upon the appalling genocidal atrocities committed on his orders. His fabulous onward drive towards the east, as we saw, he himself attributed to an intense, uncontrollable yearning (*pothos*) – his use of the term seems to have been recorded by his contemporaries Ptolemy I Soter and Nearchus – which drove him to do and see things that nobody had ever done or seen before. This was the driving force within his glamorous, bisexual, perilous, obsessively daring personality, and it was a force set in motion not only by the desire to emulate his Homeric ancestor Achilles and surpass his father Philip II but also by two manifestations of genius peculiar to himself. In the first place, as we have seen, he was one of the greatest military commanders the world has ever known, in every sense of the word: and secondly, he conceived the soaringly enlightened idea that the Persian empire he had conquered should be ruled by a partnership between Macedonians (or Greeks) and Persians.

His officers, the warring Successors, were mostly Alexander written small – military commanders who were not in his own superlative class, but still very good: and indeed, those who managed to survive to found kingdoms showed truly formidable staying power.

Among those who did *not* survive, Antipater (d. 319) was unattractive (not that this was exceptional), yet, despite a certain parochiality, he was solid and unusually wise: although he alone refused to worship Alexander, he was one of the few who kept faith with the puppet kings who were his master's joint heirs. The loyalest of all the Successors was Eumenes of Cardia, not a Macedonian but a Greek, which meant that even his first-rate generalship could not gain him the continued support of Macedonian soldiery. Loyal, too, to the royal house was Perdiccas (d. 321), Alexander's second-in-command, a handsome and experienced man, not unreasonable and very popular with the army, yet compared with his rivals a light-weight. Antipater's son Cassander, who died in 297, perhaps of tuberculosis, had been disliked by Alexander, and intensely reciprocated the feeling; far from cherishing Alexander's family, he later wiped it out. He was a hard, unpleasant personage, guided by ruthless determination and logic.

Antigonus I Monophthalmos (d. 301) was the only Successor who for a time seemed within striking distance of seizing Alexander's united inheritance: a man of commanding presence and military gifts, who seesawed strangely between mild and overbearing behaviour but was notable for his honesty, munificence and courage. His son Demetrius I Poliorcetes (d. 283) – who enjoyed a touchingly good relationship with his father – was a feverishly energetic, spectacular, good-looking womanizer, whose career was a continuous series of impetuous enterprises,- glorious successes and crushing catastrophes, until finally, in exile, he drank himself to death. He regarded another of the great leaders, Lysimachus (d. 281), as hateful, vulgar and stingy (and was much disliked by him in return). But Lysimachus was an excellent general and financier, and was capable of taking a patient, long-term view. Not so his contemporary Pyrrhus I of Epirus (d. 272). This huge, red-haired monster, handicapped by a deformed mouth, was more chivalrous and generous than most, and an expert student of war; but he lacked staying power, failed to exploit his opportunities, and overstrained his resources. Neither he nor Lysimachus left anything behind them; and the ruthless adventurer Agathocles at Syracuse did not leave much.

Those who bequeathed more durable heritages included the successive rulers of the Cimmerian (Crimean) Bosphorus – notably the mild but highly efficient Paerisades I (349/8–311/10) – but above all the founders of the three great Hellenistic kingdoms, those of the Ptolemies, Seleucids and Antigonids. For in all three of these states (as does not always happen) it was the men with the greatest qualities who won through to perform their great tasks.

In Egypt, Ptolemy I Soter (d. 283) was not only a distinguished historian but showed prudent shrewdness of an advanced order in immediately staking out a claim for a specific, defensible, rich portion of

Alexander's empire; and he concentrated all his efforts on the successful management of this large but limited sphere. His son Ptolemy II Philadelphus (d. 246), though a judicious annexer of territory, was a civilian and an intellectual by temperament, with an eye for sophisticated administration and big business; but he was a cautious man, who needed his wife Arsinoe II to spur him on. Ptolemy VI Philometor (d. 145), though only a powerless boy when he came to the throne, showed himself capable of unusual diplomacy in dealing with Rome. Ptolemy VIII Euergetes II (d. 116), known as Physcon (Fat-paunch) because of his huge bulk – which he clothed in some sort of transparent gauzy garment –received portrayal as an appalling tyrant, but this was mainly a picture created by the Greeks, since he favoured the native population to their cost. Another highly complicated and probably neurotic character was Cleopatra VII's father Ptolemy XII Theos Philopator Philadelphus 'Auletes' (Oboe-Player), 'the new Dionysus' (d. 51), who spent his long reign coping with internal strife and Roman encroachment.

The founder of the Seleucid kingdom, Seleucus I Nicator (d. 281) – the youngest of the Successors – though an able commander, had not been among Alexander's most prominent generals, but excelled rather in political acumen and statesmanship; he was also humane, an unusual quality among contemporary leaders. The characters of the Seleucids who followed him are often unknown. Antiochus III the Great (d. 187), however, was seen in his youth to display extensive activity and efficient good sense, combined with a certain lordly generosity. His enormous eastern expedition earned him Alexander's title of 'Great', but any success the enterprise might have yielded failed to materialize because later he fatally miscalculated by deliberately confronting Rome, which crushingly defeated him. On the other hand, his energetic, combative, whimsical, impulsive showman son, Antiochus IV Epiphanes (Theos Epiphanes Nicephorus) (d. 163), was an admirer of Rome, where he had lived for fourteen years – though he suffered a severe Roman snub (169). But above all he was a keen devotee of Hellenism, which led him to underestimate the resistance of the Jews to its imposition on their way of life. Alexander I Theopator Euergetes Epiphanes Nicephorus (Balas) (d. 145) – whose claim to royal blood was fictitious – has been described as the one altogether contemptible monarch on the Seleucid throne, and Antiochus VII Euergetes 'Sidetes' (brought up at Side) was its last strong and effective occupant (as his title 'the Great' showed) though he suffered from a drink problem.

The shattered pieces of Macedonia, after the Successors' wars, were put together by the straightforward and doggedly persevering Antigonus II (d. 239) – snub-nosed, and 'with knotted knees' (Gonatas), like a soldier – so very different from his flashy father Demetrius I Poliorcetes and different again because he was keenly interested in philosophy, poetry and history. Antigonus III (d. 221), known as Doson, 'he who will give', because he saw himself modestly as guardian of Philip V, displayed a generous approach to the Greeks that proved him a statesman of vision. Philip V (d. 179) was a person of regal presence, excellent memory, and febrile dynamism, a daring, skilful general whose popularity as a defender of city-state freedoms was squandered by his increasingly savage temperament and disregard of scandal. Like others, he made the mistake (whichever side was ultimately more at fault) of coming into conflict with the Romans. His son Perseus' relief measures, and general relaxation of his father's severity, attracted goodwill among the people of Greece, but when the nerve-racking clash with Rome became inevitable (171–168), his very real gifts for tactical generalship were invalidated by meanness in buying support, and a hesitant lack of initiative.

The three kings who tried to introduce sensational reforms at Sparta all possessed remarkable characters. Agis IV (244–241) was a high-minded, nostalgic traditionalist, seeking to restore his state by the revival of austerity – which neither the poor nor the rich wanted. Cleomenes III (235–219), full of dynamic charm and affability and hospitality to philosophical guests, was nevertheless much tougher and less afraid to resort to force, which, however, proved his downfall because his seemingly revolutionary designs stirred up too many fears. Nabis (207–192) seems to have been even more ruthlessly set on change, so that he gained widespread popularity among the poor; but he proved himself shifty and aggressive in his dealings with outside leaders, who inevitably and fatally retaliated.

The Attalid line at Pergamum likewise produced a series of rulers whose characters had to be reckoned with. Philetaerus (d. 263), though a eunuch, was a forceful figure whose timely desertions from one allegiance to another brought the new state within the bounds of possibility. His adoptive son and nephew Eumenes I (d. 241), another adroit changer of sides, was a quiet, able man, unhampered by the conceited ambitions that spoilt so many Hellenistic monarchs. Attalus I Soter (d. 197), who gained the maximum propaganda value out of his victory over the Galatians, was another cunning statesman (and excellent general) who took the immediately successful but ultimately disastrous risk of aligning himself with Rome. Eumenes II Soter (d. 160/159), hard-working and likeable, adorned his city nobly, but also became Rome's sycophant-in-chief until his over-cleverness forfeited the senate's confidence. His brother Attalus II Philadelphus (d. 138) loyally resisted the temptation to undermine him. The personality of Attalus III Philometor Euergetes, son of Eumenes II, is hidden from us by the shocked feelings engendered by his bequest of his kingdom to Rome; his enemies represented him as a neurotic, mistrustful, stage tyrant, with a mania for pharmacology, but a terror of social change was what probably motivated his famous action.

About the rulers of the other kingdoms we do not usually know very much; but some sort of picture is available, for example, of Prusias I Cholus (the Lame) of Bithynia (c. 230–182), whose astute diplomacy played with fire in its near-provocation of Rome. Later, a monarch of neighbouring Pontus becomes much more clearly visible. He is Mithridates VI Eupator Dionysus the Great (d. 63 BC), who enlarged his dominions on an enormous scale and defied the Romans for almost half a century. He was brave and cunning, and capable of delegating authority to one of the best generals of the day, a certain Archelaus. Mithridates possessed keen philhellenic tastes: but at the same time he was a descendant of Persian kings and saw himself as the natural leader of all his non-Greek subjects, although neither they nor the Greeks could wholly identify with him. To resist the Romans for ever, he would have needed to be a supreme strategist, which he was not. Yet he stands out as a brilliant, belated figure in the series of remarkable leaders that the Hellenistic world produced.

However, he was not quite the last of them: Cleopatra VII was still to reign in Egypt (Chapter Three, section 4), and on the far eastern borders of Hellenism the Indo-Greek rulers still held out for a time. Our ignorance of their personalities is particularly tantalizing because of the extraordinary vivid portraits on their coins. But the greatest of them all, Menander Soter Dikaios in the mid-second century, has at least survived in an ample, if partly legendary, tradition preserved by the Buddhists, who claimed him, probably with exaggeration, as a convert to their faith.

Chapter Two

City-States and Leagues

1 The Principal Cities and Leagues

The kingdoms that have now been described by no means form the whole of the Hellenistic picture. There were also hundreds of city-states both within the kingdoms and outside them, extending over the entire Mediterranean and Black Sea areas, and as far afield as India and central Asia. Some old, some new, they still constituted the normal, basic form of Greek existence throughout the entire epoch. A certain number of them even remained wholly independent of any external power, for a duration of many centuries. This was easiest to achieve when they were geographically remote, like the commercially powerful, traditionally pro-Roman Massalia (Marseilles) on the south coast of France – with its own western Mediterranean colonies such as Emporion (Ampurias) in Spain – or like Illyrian Apollonia on the Adriatic, or Borysthenes (Olbia) at the mouth of the Russian river Bug.

Even if independent, however, the city-states, for the most part, did not fulfil the role of important powers any longer: their prestige as the pre-eminent Greek political norm and force was gone for ever. Philip II of Macedonia, an expert exploiter of disunion among the city-states, had put an end to this role at the battle of Chaeronea, although afterwards he was careful to treat them as 'free' allies and members of the League of Corinth over which he presided. And then the conquering career of Alexander the Great had – in the words of Polybius – 'relieved active men from the ambitions of a military or political career'.[1]

Alexander's various Successors, to whom Greece was still the most coveted prize, held two conflicting opinions of the city-states (with many nuances in between): that they were still free allies (a view upheld ostensibly, and perhaps genuinely, by the philhellenic Antigonus I Monophthalmos), and, conversely, that they were little better than subjects (the attitude of Antipater and Cassander). As for the cities, they too held two contradictory attitudes towards these relationships, and both attitudes often appeared simultaneously within a single community: they wanted protection, but they also wanted liberty – and so regarded protection, after all, with suspicion. Indeed, neither kingdom nor city wanted the constitutional relationship to be too abundantly clear. The Hellenistic kings talked a lot about 'liberating' cities, which (as the realistic Polybius remarked) generally meant seizing them from their rivals[2] – and only rarely signified their exemption from tax. However, the monarchs, for the most part, soon stopped proclaiming that all Greeks must be free, and instead offered 'freedom' as a reward or prize for loyalty to themselves, though this was often a matter of prestige rather than substance, since such freedom, in effect, did not make much difference to the cities one way or the other.

The kings made very little use of the city governments as administrative agents, since they preferred to keep taxation in the hands of their own functionaries and concessionaires. Thus whatever human ability existed in cities within the monarchical orbits found itself deprived of any significant outlet. Yet, by a paradox, the city-state organization survived intact under the Hellenistic kingdoms, and was even deliberately expanded by them on a very substantial scale – and continued to exist long after they themselves had disappeared.

The Antigonids of Macedonia felt it necessary to dominate the city-states of Greece by the fortress-towns they garrisoned, the 'fetters' of the land, Corinth, Chalcis and Demetrias (Chapter One, section 1). Yet Antigonus II Gonatas settled the Chremonidean War against Athens and its allies (267–262) with statesmanlike moderation. It was his policy and that of his successors to support the ruling classes in the Greek cities. However, the Macedonian monarchy eventually proved too weak to hold these cities against the Romans, whose proclamation of their 'liberty' by Flamininus (196) was a publicity move that enjoyed great success.

The Ptolemies supported the Greek cities against Macedonia by providing, not troops, but money and grain. They themselves interfered with the Greek cities of Asia Minor, though they left those on the islands more to themselves. The Attalids behaved in a rather similar way. Under the Seleucids, themselves city-founders and refounders on a particularly massive scale, city-states played an incomparably larger role than in any other kingdom. They remained fairly free (except in regard to taxes), and the monarchs were often elaborately polite and tactful in writing to their governments. The Seleucid régime also renewed the cities' privileges again and again, since it saw them – rather than the feudal proprietors in the hinterland – as its strongest supports and cohesive elements. Thus Ephesus, for example, enlarged by Lysimachus in about 294, and passing into Seleucid hands until 188, prospered enormously as the terminal of the eastern commercial route, and

Miletus, enriched by a wool trade run on socially advanced lines, still possessed a large, fertile and well-fortified territory.

But the first and foremost of all Greek city-states, in the eyes of nearly everyone, was still Athens.

After the glories of the Persian Wars (490-479) and the democratic régime guided by Pericles (d. 429), the Peloponnesian War against Sparta (431-404) had brought the empire of the Athenians down in ruins. However, as the fourth century proceeded, they regained some of their former possessions. As Philip II of Macedonia proceeded to inaugurate his policy of aggressive expansion (359), the orator Demosthenes tried to impel Athens to resist him in the cause of freedom, but when the Athenians and others finally moved into joint military action against him, they were decisively defeated at Chaeronea (338). Although the peace terms were mild, this was a conclusive set-back to the Athenian imperial dream.

After Alexander's death, they attempted to revolt, but defeat by Antipater in the Lamian War forced them to accept a Macedonian garrison. Cassander made the philosophical, authoritarian, luxury-loving Demetrius of Phaleron his agent in charge of Athens (317-307), where Demetrius maintained peace but believed that power should be in the hands of a few trained experts, who issued a mass of regulations on his behalf. After he had been driven out by his namesake Demetrius I Poliorcetes, the Athenians returned to their ostensibly democratic constitution (though the Assembly was no longer an effective decision-maker). Then, taking advantage of Macedonia's weakness at a time of Celtic (Gaulish) invasion, the Athenians briefly regained their independence of action; but their forces were defeated once again in the Chremonidean War (267-262) by Antigonus II Gonatas.

Though reinstating a Macedonian garrison, he remained respectful of Athens, treating it as his cultural capital. Moreover, the Athenians soon managed to recover economic strength (with the help of deeper and richer veins of their Laurion silver mines, of which the installations have been recently investigated), and recovered their position, for a time, as the wealthiest commercial state of the Aegean. In 229 they were even able to buy the Macedonian garrison out. At this juncture they also entered into friendly relations with Rome, enduring attacks on this account from Philip V of Macedonia (200-199) and his son Perseus; after the latter's defeat, the victorious Romans gratefully presented Delos, centre of the grain market, to Athens as a free port (166), and the Athenians retained it for three or four decades.

When Rome converted Macedonia and Greece (146), into a province, the Athenians remained technically free under Roman protection, and a considerable number of them continued to enjoy an Indian summer of material prosperity. But growing discontent among the lower classes was fanned by Mithridates VI Eupator of Pontus; and then even the city government itself decided to support him against Rome. After succumbing to a siege by Sulla (87–86), Athens appealed to the glories of its past. But Sulla replied that he was there to punish rebels and not to listen to ancient history lessons. The war left the city impoverished and deprived of its trade.

Yet the Athenians still remained in the forefront of Greek cultural life – as they had been throughout the entire Hellenistic period. In the years around 300, their city was the home of the New Comedy of Menander and of all the great philosophical movements: their founders had been born elsewhere, but chose Athens as the place where they must teach and found their schools. Even after the last of so many political débacles when it fell to Sulla, Athens remained a revered university town, frequented by people from all over the Mediterranean world – including numerous young Romans who later became leading figures, such as Cicero, Atticus, Brutus and Horace.

Rhodes, off the south-west coast of Asia Minor, has a good claim to be regarded as even more important, in this period, than Athens – indeed, as the outstanding city-state of the Hellenistic epoch.

Until the later fifth century BC, the island had contained no less than three separate political units. When, however, these towns changed sides from Athens to Sparta in the later stages of the Peloponnesian War, they united to form a single state, with a new federal capital, Rhodes, at the north-eastern extremity of the island. In the fourth century the new government at first found itself forced into subjection to one major power after another, falling eventually into the hands of Alexander. But after his death it expelled the Macedonian garrison and was henceforward independent and increasingly influential. In 305–304 the Rhodians successfully repelled a siege by Demetrius I, whose skills to which he owed his nickname Poliorcetes ('the Besieger') failed him here. They shared with Pergamum the fateful (and ultimately fatal) responsibility of soliciting the first major interventions in Hellenistic affairs by Rome, whose allies they became in its wars against Philip V of Macedonia and the Seleucid Antiochus III the Great, gaining coastal territories of Asia Minor as a reward.

Rhodes was ruled by a limited democracy – with an aristocratic tinge – which earned it the reputation of the best regulated city in the whole Greek world. Its government dealt with the acute economic and social problems of the time by measures of a remarkably judicious character. In particular, it introduced a system of compulsory food contributions framed so that, in addition to the admitted responsibility of the administration itself, all rich citizens accepted an undertaking to look after a certain number of the poor; Rhodes was one of the very first places to feed the proletariat systematically at the expense of the community and its wealthiest members (Chapter Two, section 2). But this was only part of a general policy of encouraging corporate spirit and enterprise. For example, public education was highly developed: and all citizens alike served for a time in the fleet, built for the most part by rich citizens who also, in wartime, provided the sailors' pay (later reimbursed to them by the state). When the seamen and officers had retired from the service, they continued to cherish their comradely relationship in ex-service associations. In consequence of these carefully devised social measures, mutual trust between the different income-groups in the community was exceptionally high.

Aided by this healthy situation at home, Rhodes rivalled or even replaced Athens as the principal commercial city-state of the Aegean in the later third and early second century BC, maintaining strong and lucrative links with the cities of the eastern Mediterranean and the Black Sea and Sicily. Its prosperity came mainly from its key position in the carrying trade, especially of grain, for which it charged other states a two per cent tax. This activity made it exceptionally rich.

In consequence, the city also became the centre of international finance and banking and exchange. Not unnaturally, therefore, it did everything possible to safeguard the economic and commercial unity of the Greek world. This was the purpose, for example, of the promulgation of a mercantile code, which was widely accepted. And the Rhodians, in the years following 200, made the first resolute attempt since the heyday of classical Athens to clear the eastern Mediterranean of pirates, a task which they carried out almost single-handed. Their efficient and highly trained fleet, designed to carry out this brave endeavour, was lodged in five harbours, furnished with first-class docks and arsenals, protected by a strict security system, and presided over by the bronze Colossus of Rhodes, a statue of the Sun-god standing a hundred and ten feet high – the emblem of the city, and one of the Seven Wonders of the World (Chapter Three, section 1).

The Rhodians' intense interest in trade prompted them to form a highly lucrative business partnership with the essentially commercial state of Ptolemaic Egypt. However, until they became linked with Rome, it was also their policy to aim at neutrality between the major

kingdoms, so as not to miss commercial opportunities. Their friendship was coveted by all the powers; after a severe earthquake in 227-226
(in which the Colossus crashed to the ground) all Greek states contributed to the restoration of the city, since they could not afford to see it
ruined.

However, the success of Rhodes did not last. Its government earned
the disapproval of the Romans by adopting an equivocal position in
their war against King Perseus of Macedonia (171-168); and it was as
a punishment for this offence that Rome declared Delos (hitherto the
distribution point and branch banking centre of Rhodes) a free port
under Athenian control, thus diverting a large proportion of the Rhodians' trade and depriving them of the funds needed to suppress piracy
(a step which Roman shipping had reason to regret later on). Despite
this setback they strenuously resisted Rome's enemy Mithridates VI
Eupator Dionysus the Great of Pontus, who failed in his attempt to take
their city by siege. In 43, however, Rhodes was captured by Caesar's
murderer Cassius, and suffered severe devastation. Its great days were
now over, though it remained technically free under the emperors.

Throughout the Hellenistic period Rhodes had been one of the
leading cultural centres of the Greek world. The Colossus had been a
symbol not only of the city's commerce but of its remarkable artistic
production as well – to which the sculptural group of Laocoön and his
sons later bore equally eloquent witness (Chapter Three, section 2).
The city had given a home to the third-century poet Apollonius
Rhodius, who found it more congenial than his native Egypt; and the
Stoic philosopher Panaetius (c. 185-109) famous at Athens and Rome,
was a Rhodian by origin. The polymath Posidonius (c. 135-50), after
studying with Panaetius at Athens, came to take up his residence at
Rhodes. So did Apollonius Molon, head of a local rhetorical school
which gained a widespread reputation; when Apollonius Molon visited
Rome in 87 and 81, Cicero became his pupil.

Not only Sicily – where Syracuse was dominant (Chapter One, section 1)
– but south Italy, too, was thickly planted with Greek-city-states,
some of which had been in existence for centuries; a substantial region
was so intensely Hellenized that it became known as Magna Graecia.

Outstanding among these south Italian cities, standing upon a deep
gulf of the Ionian Sea, was Taras (the Roman Tarentum, now Taranto),
which traditionally went back to a date before 700. By the fifth century,
this city, despite harassment by the surrounding Lucanians and other
native peoples, had become a leading power in the region. But it reached
the height of its power in the years before 350, when its democratic and

relatively stable (if somewhat excitable) government, protected by an almost impregnable citadel, came under the guidance of Plato's Pythagorean friend Archytas, who was not only a famous philosopher and scientist but had the reputation of never losing a battle.

Taras bestrode an isthmus between a tidal lagoon and a shallow protected bay, which formed the safest and most spacious harbour on any Italian coast. The bay also contained huge clusters of *murex* mussels, from which purple was extracted to dye the wool from flocks owned by Taras in the interior. This was the chief industry of the city, and brought it great prosperity. But the lands where the cattle lived and grazed were highly vulnerable to the adjacent Italian tribes: and for mutual protection against them a league of coastal Greek cities was formed, of which Taras became the leading member.

The Tarantines possessed the largest fleet in Italy, and an army of 15,000 men; but after the death of Archytas, they felt that this force was not sufficient, and in consequence invited a succession of Greek commanders from overseas to bring in mercenary reinforcements – two kings of Sparta (338, 303) and Alexander I of Epirus (c. 333). However, they soon found – like other Greeks after them – that the most serious problems of all came from Rome, which created a dramatic link with the south of Italy by building a new road, the Via Appia (312). Moreover, in 291 the Romans proceeded to found a large colony at Venusia (Venosa): it was primarily intended to dominate the tribal peoples of the interior, but lay only ninety miles from Taras which saw its establishment as a menacing provocation.

Then, in 282, the Greek city of Thurii (formerly Sybaris), across the Tarantine gulf, was attacked by Lucanian raiders and appealed to the Romans: and they responded by sending ships – thus breaking earlier agreements with Taras not to send ships into the gulf. The Tarantines sank the squadron, killing its admiral, and drove out a garrison the Romans had installed at Thurii – jeering at the bad Greek spoken by envoys sent from Rome. The city also invited Pyrrhus I of Epirus to come to its help (281), but despite victories he evacuated Italy in 275, leaving the country partly ruined and depopulated, and his garrison abandoned Taras three years later. In 272, therefore, the Tarantines felt obliged to accept the alliance the Romans proposed to them – thus gaining peace at the price of independence. During the Second Punic War their city fell to Hannibal by treachery (213), and was recaptured and devastated by the Romans four years later. Thereafter the place went into decline.

Taras was a considerable artistic centre. Already in the archaic and classical periods the number of its outstanding works of art had been enormous. Then, after Alexander's death, the sculptor Lysippus arrived there and made huge statues of Zeus and Heracles, symbolizing the city's leadership of the local federation. Subsequently, artists used the soft local stone to make hundreds of reliefs – which served as models for Etruscan sarcophagi. The jewellery and gold work of Taras, and its terracotta figurines, displayed great charm, and the city's craftsmen introduced a new style of moulded and ribbed pottery. There are also interesting vases of Hellenistic date showing designs relating to the popular theatre – which was a speciality of the place – and illustrating, in particular, the so-called *phlyax* farces to which the local dramatist Rhinthon gave a novel and more sophisticated form in the early third century BC (Chapter Three, section 2).

Through the Hellenistic period every one of the almost numberless city-states jealously continued to try to safeguard its independence from the rest, and, above all, from the kingdoms. But the process became increasingly difficult, so that attempts at collaboration between one city and another, however initially unwelcome, became inevitable. And perhaps the most significant feature of their story during this period was the resulting movement to break down the barriers which had always separated them from their neighbours.

One sign of this trend was a new and more civilized attitude to warfare. This emerged in the face of great difficulties, since the cities by no means stopped fighting each other. Massacres sometimes occurred, and there is no more depressing document than an inscription of *c.* 220 recording an oath by the people of the little Cretan city-state of Drerus that 'they would do all manner of harm to the people of Lyttus', their neighbour.[3] Nevertheless, this was a period when efforts were made on many sides to eliminate or restrict the worst excesses of warfare. Plato, while regarding it as normal enough for cities to be continually at war with one another, had nevertheless recognized, already, that such hostilities must be mitigated by civilized rules.[4] And now, in Hellenistic times, the more scientific nature of fighting – and the prominence of mercenaries, who were emotionally uninvolved in the rival causes – meant that quarter was more readily given. The release and ransom of captives (by states and pirates alike) also became much more frequent; indeed, some cities bound themselves not to enslave each other's citizens at all. Moreover, many communities sought to obtain recognition as holy (*hiera*, immune from war) and inviolable (*asylos*, immune from 'reprisals', or from acts of brigandage). These had been privileges traditionally granted to temples, and now the major powers sponsored their extension to cities, and particularly to those on the sea which had suffered from pirates – beginning, it appears, with Smyrna (Izmir), which received *asylia* from the Delphic priesthood in 245 on the recommendation of Seleucus II Callinicus Pogon.

These were signs that a new idea was beginning to take root, despite all the wars of the epoch: the idea that peace, not war, was the natural state of humankind. The dramatist Menander even went so far as to declare that a spirit of conciliation was a mark of the Greek character. Perhaps this seems too sanguine. Yet it was true that much of the warfare in which the cities were so often involved was forced on them by the kings, and that their hearts were not in the fighting as earlier. Some of the weaker communities even welcomed amalgamation in order to protect them better from its ravages. Besides, ideals such as the 'union of hearts' (*homonoia*) and humanity and cosmopolitanism were all under keen discussion at this time. Under the influence of such concepts, and under the pressure of the practical needs that prompted their formulation, the primitive view that the member of another city (unless you have to extend him hospitable guest-friendship) is automatically an enemy began to undergo modification.

And so the city-states of the Hellenistic age devised all sorts of new contacts with each other. The process was encouraged by the unification of such vast tracts of territory under Alexander's rule – and by some of its results, such as the uniformity and universality of his abundant silver coinage, all issued on the same standard. One notable example of the collaboration of city-states in this new atmosphere was the growth of *isopoliteia*, the granting of mutual citizenship between all the citizens of one state and another. In the legal field, too, there was progress in the same direction. Since each city-state had its own laws, there was, strictly speaking, no such thing as Greek Law, but only hundreds of sets of piecemeal local legislation. We obtain astonishing insight into the law-courts of Athens from the speeches of its principal orators, culminating in Demosthenes (384–322). The picture that emerges shows large boards of citizen judges or juries, manifesting a remarkable expression of democracy, it is true, but remaining amateurish, liable to fall behind schedule, and open to political influence.

In the Hellenistic epoch, however, there were certain notable improvements. It had long been customary, in some cities, for public or private arbitrators to be invited to rule on the settlement of claims (usually upon an equitable rather than a strictly legal basis), and it now became more and more frequent for cities to call in an arbitration judge – or a commission of two or more judges – from friendly neighbouring states to deal with civil, and also sometimes criminal, cases of which arrears had piled up under the old, ineffective, jury system. By the same token, the appointment of arbitrators from a third community to settle disputes between city-states, a custom attested since the mid-fifth century, also increased appreciably: some states bound themselves by treaty to refer all such questions to arbitrators. This practice encouraged the standardization, at long last, of some of the innumerable local codes or assemblages of past legislation, so that a tolerably functioning system of international law came to be applied to relations between the Greek states. This process received great encouragement from Rhodes, which was keen, for its own practical reasons, on facilitating economic and commercial transactions, and became famous, together with Priene in Ionia, for the excellent quality of its itinerant judges.

Furthermore, when the citizens of one city-state visited or resided in another, their hosts often honoured them with *proxenia*, an extension of the old guest-friendship tradition to include various practical immunities, and the right to hold land – with the underlying purpose that its beneficiaries should be available to act as ambassadors, advocates and go-betweens whenever required. Many city decrees honoured temporary residents in this way: lawyers, doctors, teachers, technicians, and athletes taking part in contests, especially the great quadriennial athletic Games – Olympic, Pythian (Delphi), Nemean, Isthmian (Corinth). Such functions, attended even by poorer people, offered notable opportunities of mobility; and so did the musical and dramatic festivals, attended by itinerant performers organized as members of the guild of the Artists (*technitai*) of Dionysus, centred on Athens, the Corinthian isthmus, and Teos in Ionia. In these times, men were coming to be classified according to their profession quite as much as by the city of their origin. This was an age of guide-books and sightseers – not to speak of mercenary soldiers, who travelled as widely as anybody. 'No country is far away', declared Apollonius Rhodius.[5]

Above all, the general erasure of barriers expressed itself in a growing tendency for whole groups of cities to join together as such, not only into military alliances (*symmachiai*) which were a familiar enough feature, but into leagues (*sympoliteiai*) in which the participants voluntarily limited their own independence by the creation of federal institutions to deal, for example, with foreign affairs or war. These leagues fell roughly into two categories, those dominated by a single powerful member-state, and those in which the members were more or less on a par with one another and collaborated equally to exercise joint control.

Within the former category, in which the league was the instrument of a single state, the earliest known and longest-lived example had been Sparta's Peloponnesian League, which lasted from the mid-sixth century until 336. The city of Thebes, which broke its power, had likewise formed an early Boeotian Confederacy; and after the Persian Wars Athens directed its own Delian League, which it subsequently converted into an empire. Then Philip II of Macedonia, following upon his victory at Chaeronea (338), united the defeated or over-awed Greek city-states into the League of Corinth under his own presidency – the first monarch to exercise this degree of control.

His move corresponded with the views of the Athenian orator Isocrates (436–338), who combined belief in Philip's leadership of Greece with an eloquently expressed conviction that the city-states – in order to unite with him against Persia – must break down their ancient, damaging attempts each to act on its own, and must act on a Pan-Hellenic basis instead. The 'Universal' History of Ephorus of Cyme (c. 405–330) was likewise Pan-Hellenic in character and aim. And even Aristotle (384–322), though still unquestioningly accepting the city-state as the basic political unit, threw off a casual suggestion of a possible unification of Greece – as a world-ruling power.[6] After this idea had seemed to receive confirmation from the conquests of Alexander, Aristotle's pupil Dicaearchus of Messana in Sicily (300) gave it shape in his *Life of Greece* (*Bios Hellados*), a universal history of the culture of the Greeks in which they were treated as a single unit like the life of a person.

So Pan-Hellenism was very much in the air, although it never escaped from the domination of one monarch after another; for the League of Corinth presided over by Philip II was successively renewed or adapted by Antigonus I Monophthalmos and Demetrius I Poliorcetes (against Cassander), and then by their Macedonian successors Antigonus III Doson and Philip V.

Meanwhile the other kind of Greek league, in which the members were more or less equal, never achieved anything like the Pan-Hellenic dimensions hankered after by philosophers and orators. All the same, the concept was given significant practical expression at a regional level. Leagues of this limited scope and range had existed, right back in archaic times, for religious purposes – the members meeting annually at a famous shrine; for example, the Amphictionic tribes who convened at Delphi, the Ionian cities across the Aegean sending delegates to the Panionion (Sanctuary of Poseidon) on Mount Mycale, and on the periphery of the Greek world the Etruscan cities attending annual rites at Volsinii. In due course, these religious associations amassed some political significance and ambitions, but the Delphic confederacy, apart from its religious prestige, remained weak, the Ionians' federal activity was only a flash in the pan, and the Etruscan League (which owed something to their example) turned out to be wholly disunited and

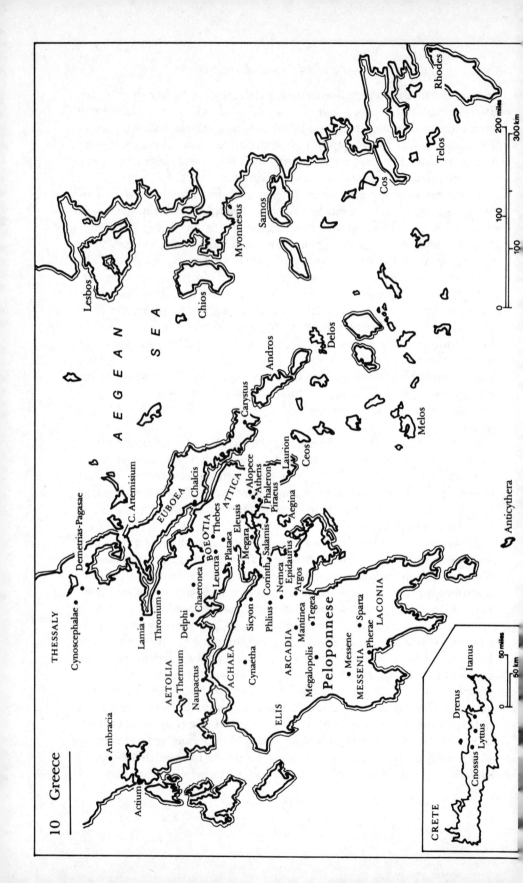

10 Greece

inadequate when faced with the Roman threat from the later fifth century onwards.

It remained for other groups to agree to sink parts of their political individualities and become federated equals in a more lasting and effective fashion, so that they showed the capacity to offer a really useful resistance to external threats. This was achieved, above all, in two regions of continental Greece that had never come into prominence before: Aetolia and Achaea, on the north and south sides of the Gulf of Corinth respectively. It proved practicable to form leagues in these areas because the local communities were weak and backward, and, in isolation, easily overrun.

The units in rugged Aetolia were not even cities (*poleis*) at all but merely tribes, living in half-savage little towns or mountain villages. In the later fifth century BC they had established some loose central organization, and by 367 at latest, for self-protection, they formed themselves into a federal league, which evolved an ingenious and flexible constitution. At its head was an annually elected General or President. There was also a primary Assembly which had two regular meetings a year (at the religious centre and hill-top of Thermum) and could be convened for special sessions as well. Apparently all adult males had votes, although those of the richer elements were dominant. Another feature was a federal Council consisting of a thousand delegates. Cities were represented upon the Council in proportion to their population; much of its business, however, was delegated to a committee of between thirty and forty persons (*apokletoi*). Although membership of the League extended outside Aetolia, its direction was always in Aetolian hands, because the more distant member communities only possessed a second-class form of the federal citizenship, conferring civil but not political rights. However, the League was not unwilling to enlarge its citizen body when territorial expansion made this desirable.

After capturing Naupactus on the Corinthian Gulf, and repelling attacks by Alexander's Successors, the Aetolians won possession of Delphi (*c.* 300), and a controlling interest in the sanctuary's Amphictionic organization. Their great triumph, however, was to resist the Gauls and protect Delphi against their invasion single-handed (279); to celebrate this occasion, they established a Delphic festival, the Soteria, three years later. In 245 the Aetolians subdued the Boeotians and thus gained control of all central Greece, following up this achievement by successful intervention in the Peloponnese. They were now second only, in eastern Europe, to Macedonia, against which they fought, alongside the Romans, in the Second Macedonian War (200–197). The hostilities culminated in the battle of Cynoscephalae (197) in which the Aetolians' cavalry greatly contributed to the Roman victory. When, however, Rome seemed insufficiently grateful, they earned its extreme disapproval by inviting the Seleucid Antiochus III the Great into Greece (192). Having defeated him, the Romans punished the Aetolians by restricting their territory to Aetolia itself and forcing them to accept a treaty as allies, which brought their independence to an end.

Their short career as a league had enjoyed mixed distinction. Their field force, though only twelve thousand strong, was among the best in the country. Their repulse of the Gauls earned them the name of defenders of Greece against barbarian encroachment; and their Macedonian wars caused them to claim a similar title of protectors of republicanism against monarchy. On the other hand, they acquired a deplorable reputation as encouragers of pirates. And, indeed, they themselves became active practitioners of piracy: which meant that if they bestowed a grant of *asylia* (inviolability), it was highly prized, as a guarantee against robberies by themselves.

Across the Gulf of Corinth the hitherto insignificant pastoral land of the Arcadians, in the centre of the Peloponnese, had set a local precedent for federalism in 370-362 by establishing a short-lived league based on the new city of Megalopolis, which they created out of the amalgamation of more than forty previously separate villages.

But the league which had a far greater future was that of their northern neighbours, the Achaeans, bordering on the Gulf. Their 'cities' – some of them scarcely more than fishing hamlets – had been formed in quite early times into an insignificant association, chiefly noteworthy (by the fourth century at least) because it was not averse to including non-Achaean members. In 280 this league was re-formed on a more impressive scale, at first with four and then with more numerous adherents, extending over 8,000 square miles – once again including non-Achaeans, among which was Sicyon, the western neighbour of Corinth (251). Thenceforward, under the direction of a Sicyonian, Aratus, the league became an important political force.

Its constitution was deliberately modelled on that of the Aetolians; but the Achaean League's President was also automatically its commander-in-chief. He could not be re-elected immediately after his term of office, which meant that Aratus (from 245 onwards) held the Presidency or generalship in alternate years. The President was assisted in the administration not only by a Council – limited to men over thirty years of age – but also by ten deputies (*demiourgoi*), who presided over the League's Assembly. This was open to all male citizens of the member states. So as to prevent the local population of the place in which the Assembly happened to be meeting at any one time from swamping the votes, these seem to have been taken not by heads (as in Aetolia), but by cities, a procedure which showed progress in the direction of representational government as we have it today. Nevertheless, as in Aetolia, the upper-class vote was decisive, since poorer people found it impossible to attend the meetings.

At first the Achaean Council and Assembly alike were both convened for four regular meetings a year. However, from the later third century onwards the Assembly may only have met on particular occasions, to deal with matters of exceptional significance. Thereafter, it would appear, the League was controlled by a new body, a Council of Representatives – who were perhaps elected by the member city-states on a proportional system, and thus displayed another interesting constitutional development. But the independence of the individual cities, in regard to such matters as foreign politics and war, was rather more heavily restricted than that of the Aetolian League members, at least after about 190 when the Achaean cities gave up their separate laws and local coinages.

Under Aratus, who organized or reorganized these constitutional arrangements, the Achaean League moved beyond its purely regional dimensions by seizing the ancient isthmus city and two-way-facing port of Corinth from the Macedonians (243). Next, in 235, they incorporated Megalopolis (in Arcadia), later the birthplace of the historian Polybius (who was to hold high office in the League, and, like the first American constitutionalists, greatly admired its mixed constitution). Thus enlarged, the League became famous as the leader of resistance to Macedonian encroachments. But in the end Aratus decided, fatefully, that the military and social threat from the Spartan king Cleomenes III was greater and more immediate than the menace of Macedonia: and, in consequence, he opened negotiations with King Antigonus III Doson, and helped him to destroy Cleomenes' army at Sellasia (222).

Aratus (d. 213) was one of the few Greek leaders of the time, outside the monarchies, to make a real mark on his age. No radical and no revolutionary, and not much of a military commander either, he was nevertheless an enterprising, incorruptible, ambitious guerrilla leader, a contradictory hero who often felt frightened, an idealist by no means incapable of rancour and not afraid to use despicable means to secure his purposes: a man who could sway any massed audience to his will, and who devoted his entire career to freeing the Peloponnese from autocrats – though finally he had to decide between two of them, and chose to help his lifelong Macedonian enemies against Sparta, which was so much nearer at hand.

Under Aratus' leadership, the star of the Achaean League had risen at the expense of the Aetolians. However, the Achaeans' relationship with Antigonus III Doson's adoptive son and successor Philip v deteriorated, and in 198 the League went over to Rome. This, however, was not in accordance with the wishes of the next great Achaean leader, Philopoemen of Megalopolis, who had first become general in 208–207: strongly distrusting the Romans' alleged desire to liberate Greece, he favoured neutrality in their war with Philip v of Macedonia. Philopoemen aroused vigorous military enthusiasm among the members of his confederation, and raised his army to a strength of fifteen to twenty thousand. In 192, after the assassination of King Nabis of Sparta, he was able to incorporate that city in the League, followed soon afterwards by Elis and Messenia. This meant that almost the whole of the peninsula was united as it had never been before, and the newly cohesive federation could almost rival the power of the kings. But in the course of a revolt in Messenia Philopoemen was captured and poisoned (182).

He had shown himself as curious a mixture as Aratus: once again a fine, independently and realistically minded patriot, austerely dedicating his burning energy to freedom – and, unlike Aratus, an able general as well. Yet – for all his engaging manners – he was harsh, quarrelsome and sometimes brutal: and inclined to press the Romans hard.

Once Philopoemen was gone, the Achaean League went further still in this same direction, allowing itself to engage in frequent clashes with Rome. These culminated in an attack on Sparta, in defiance of the senate's wishes (150). Four years later, the federal army was routed by Lucius Mummius, and the Romans dissolved the confederacy altogether (deporting 1,000 eminent Achaeans to Rome, including Polybius), though it was revived in a purely dependent capacity as an appendage to the new Roman province of Macedonia.

Meanwhile the Romans themselves, on the fringes of the Hellenistic world, had already made a durable success of another kind of federal formula, on Italian territory. They were aware of the partial Greek patterns, including those of the Aetolian and Achaean Leagues, and deliberately modified them to suit their own needs. After they had gradually worn the Etruscans down and broken up other recalcitrants as well, they found themselves in control (in the early third century) of a substantial Italian confederacy. They did not endow it with any central institutions, other than their own, and controlled it not by offering any overall, bureaucratic solutions, but by concluding painstaking piecemeal arrangements with each individual 'allied' city, as the facts of each separate case seemed to require.

Following this hard-headed, commonsense approach of 'divide and rule', and considering each case unvindictively and on its own merits, Rome developed a system which proved successful for generation after generation. As a result, when the first two Punic Wars broke out (264–241, 218–201), they were able to muster many thousands of allied Italian troops against Carthage: and even under supreme pressure most of these still remained conspicuously loyal. Then, in the second century, when the clash came with the Hellenistic kingdoms, they were too divided one from another to have any real chance against such a powerful and efficient organization.

Yet Rome too, as its consciousness of the Greek federal models made clear, was itself a strongly Hellenized community, despite all its native Roman and Italian characteristics. Heraclides Ponticus of Heraclea Pontica (c. 388–315) actually called it a 'Greek city',[7] and there were numberless legends ascribing to the Romans (like many other foreign or half-foreign cities) Greek origins. Timaeus of Tauromenium (c. 356–260), historian of Sicily, became the first Greek to collect extensive information about them and attempt to integrate their past systematically into Greek history. And indeed, it was true that, from very early times, Greek influence had infiltrated into Rome both directly (for example, from Cumae near Neapolis (Naples) and Sicily) and indirectly, through the Etruscans. The city-state concept on which Rome was based came from Greece, whether through Etruscan intermediaries or at first hand; and the Twelve Tables of the law (c. 450), to whatever extent they may or may not have been specifically modelled on Greek legislation, provided Rome with a legal system of Greek type.

Then, in the later fourth and early third centuries, when direct contact with the Greeks became so much more extensive, Rome experienced its full and permanent effects right across the board. Paintings of Greek style were to be seen in the city, similar to those in the city-states of Etruria, themselves long since partially Hellenized in their own peculiar fashion, and now under Roman domination. Subsequently, the Second Punic War brought the Romans into even closer direct touch with Greek communities and arts, especially after their plundering of Syracuse (211) and Taras (209). Incidentally, their enemy in the war, Carthage, was itself partially Hellenized – despite its endemic bad relations with the Greek cities of Sicily – and its great leader, Hannibal, in many ways resembled a Hellenistic prince, so that it was natural for him to employ a Greek teacher, Sosylus of Sparta, whom he prompted to become the historian of his own career.

The adoption of Greek models by the first Roman writers, who managed at the same time to preserve a sturdy independence, was one of the most famous balancing tricks between originality and indebtedness in all literary history. Another remarkable situation arose owing to the violent distaste for this Hellenizing process which was triggered off by its constant increase at Rome. In educated Roman circles (other than those of an ultra-conservative nature) admiration for the Greek cultural tradition was widespread and frequently awe-struck. But it was paradoxically accompanied, very often, by a considerable dislike of contemporary Hellenistic Greeks who were known to be hostile to uncultured Roman imperialism, and censured as cunning, untrustworthy, unscrupulous, quarrelsome, sex-mad, frivolous, inefficient, and readier with boastful words than with actions: sentiments of which pro-Roman Greeks such as Polybius were all too painfully conscious. The ambivalence is admirably summed up by a great many observations offered on both sides of the subject by Cicero.

In practical terms, this attitude among the Romans meant that after they had converted the Hellenistic states into provinces of their empire – of which, together with Africa, they were by far the richest and most populous portions – they put Romans in charge of them and not Greeks; although the Greek city-states still maintained their own self-government (subject to conformity in foreign affairs and payment of taxes), and a chain of 'client' states round the eastern fringes of the empire was left in the hands of Greek or Hellenized monarchs. When Antony ruled the east after Julius Caesar's death, this area of client states was increased (even to the extent of ceding Roman provincial land) in favour of Cleopatra VII; and it is possible that if the battle of Actium (31 BC) had gone in their favour, the future might have seen a more equal partnership between Romans and Greeks. But the victory of Octavian (Augustus) sealed the Roman hegemony, although the Greek city-state system still went on its way – unimpaired and even augmented, from time to time, by new foundations.

2 The Hellenistic Community

In the classical Greek city-states there had been great and violent disputes whether oligarchic or democratic systems should prevail. In Hellenistic times, the question had become largely meaningless, since what mattered now was whether you supported this or that monarchy. Formally speaking, it was democracy which for the most part prevailed in the cities, but this was heavily watered down for several reasons: because kings interfered, because only the more powerful local citizens played a prominent part, and because in any case the local citizen body was very often small. It was surrounded, in the population of each city, by a penumbra of non-citizens – resident aliens who were 'free' and shared in the social, cultural and economic life of the place but not in its government; and below that was a substratum of slaves, usually of considerable numbers. The social hierarchies of the kingdoms differed mainly because these large states possessed more rich people at the top.

Their wealth was stimulated by the production of a great mass of coinage, by the cities but above all by the kingdoms, following the example of Alexander. All this abundance of money in many parts of the Hellenistic world (despite the hardships it sometimes caused, in the form of increase of prices) brought about a large and positive development – the massive supersession of barter in kind by transactions in cash. Banking developed: bankers' orders were used for the payment of debts and letters of credit were known, though not apparently bills of exchange. Little use, however, could be made of capital – except to provide loans, and they were expensive. During the third century BC, the rate of legal interest (even when a loan was regarded as safe) became as high as 24 per cent per annum in the Hellenistic east, though the figure in Greece and Egypt was between a third and two-thirds lower.

Nevertheless, money-making engaged people's attention to an unprecedented degree. 'I've got an idea', says a character in one of Menander's plays, 'that the useful gods for you and me are silver and gold. Put up a shrine at home for those two; pray for them.'[8] The Greeks had expanded over a huge geographical space, and their total assets, too, though unevenly distributed, were correspondingly greater. In particular, maritime trade was on an unprecedented scale. Tin was imported from Britain, amber from the Baltic, spices from India and southern Arabia. These activities stimulated ambitious exploration. The Seleucids and Ptolemies sponsored remarkable eastern expeditions, and towards the end of the fourth century Pytheas of Massalia (Marseilles) set out from Gades (Cadiz) to Ushant and Cornwall, circumnavigated Britain, and continued his voyage up the coast of Europe, perhaps as far as Jutland, taking bearings throughout his journey. Such advances in scientific geography meant improved charts, and up-to-date coastal guides. Ships were often bigger – sometimes enormous, in comparison with the past – and there were superb new harbours designed on regular, improved plans, and providing impressive artificial protection. The great bronze statue, the Colossus, presiding over the port of Rhodes became known as one of the Seven Wonders of the World, and another was the lighthouse that stood on a peninsula beside the more important of Alexandria's two harbours, the Pharos designed by Sostratus of Cnidus for Ptolemy I Soter, and finished under his son Ptolemy II

Philadelphus in *c.* 279. Ascending in three storeys, of which the lowest (which contained three hundred rooms) was square, the next octagonal and the uppermost round, the Pharos (no longer to be seen today) was surmounted by eight columns supporting a huge statue; a furnace of resinous wood created a flame which was reflected by a great bronze mirror and could be seen over a distance of thirty-five miles. Yet, despite these sophisticated methods, the rudders of ships retained their old inefficient shape, and sailing into the wind, though bolder than before, was still avoided whenever possible. Piracy, too, made almost all major sea journeys additionally perilous.

The staple activity of the Greeks, as of all ancient societies, was still agriculture. The transportation of grain (by sea and land alike) was of overriding importance, and basic to the Hellenistic economy. Wheat entered the Aegean markets more plentifully, as Asia Minor, Syria and Egypt stepped up their supplies. But in spite of improvements here and there – for example, under the sponsorship of the Ptolemies and other monarchs, including Hiero II of Syracuse – there was no fundamental change for the better in the efficiency of agricultural production. In consequence, grievous shortages of grain often occurred, especially in the all too frequent times of political disturbance, and these shortages caused famines which produced grievous social distress.

Manufacturing industries were innumerable and varied, but mostly small: there was little or no progress towards large-scale industrialization, and little appreciable advance in technological methods, because there were few incentives – material or psychological – towards improving them. That is to say, technology was not generally seen as either practicable or desirable. Some engineers and architects, it is true, managed to earn a private income; but the concerted organizational drive that would have been needed to develop technical methods just was not there. The men of science, who registered important advances (Chapter Three, section 1), failed to make their knowledge a common possession, because the rest of the population, despite its improved education, showed no real capacity to advance abreast of them; the idea that science might hold the key to desirable material progress never made its appearance. Besides, labour, slave and free alike, was so cheap that research into sophisticated techniques seemed unnecessary, and rich men – aware that the buying power of the public was too low to create a market for mass consumption – had no desire to invest in new discoveries. This failure to develop technology was the principal reason why the gracious living of the few had inevitably to be supplied and counterbalanced by the labour of the many.

Economic imbalances and hardships were especially oppressive in continental Greece, with the partial exception of a few richer centres such as Athens and Corinth. The buffets inflicted by wars, political bullying and economic crises hit these mainland cities particularly hard, because they were far from self-sufficient – and increased birth-rates in the course of the fourth century had meant they had too many mouths to feed. For a short time, at least, fortunately for them, the expansion of the Greek world under Alexander and his Successors drew off much of this surplus population as mercenaries and settlers in Asia. Nevertheless, the years immediately preceding 300 already witnessed a steep rise in the prices of many foodstuffs, including wheat, wine and oil: and the cost of manufactured goods rose as well. This was due not so much to overall shortages as to an inadequate export market, an equally inadequate capacity to meet demands when they arose, the absence of any central body to regularize supplies and stabilize prices, and the overabundance of Alexander's fine silver coinage made from the huge treasure he had captured from the Persians – an event which sent down the value of gold and silver, and contributed further to the inflation of prices.

Thus wages of workers, in real terms, soon fell considerably below what they had been before the time of Alexander. It was not that any steady downgrading of living standards could be detected, as part of a uniform pattern. But alarming, uncontrollable fluctuations occurred, not only from place to place, but from one generation to another: thus the second quarter of the third century was a period, by and large, of prosperity, the third quarter was characterized by recession, and the fourth witnessed a certain recovery, bringing prices back, at last, to something like the pre-Hellenistic figure.

Nevertheless, many of the city-states, especially on the mainland, still experienced a deep and ever-deepening recession, accompanied by paralysing poverty. Poverty, of course, was nothing new. But now this endemic blight was greatly worsened by special factors. For as the monarchies became increasingly self-sufficient, the centre of the western world's commerce moved to Egypt and the coast of Asia. That is to say, it moved away from Greece. Many, now, were the factors which crowded in to reduce that country's labourers to a hopeless condition: not only the new loss of trade but persisting fluctuations of prices, a chronic series of bad harvests with no storage margin to offset them, inefficient or non-existent distribution arrangements, transport made more precarious than ever by recurrent disorders and wars, and a host of speculators ready to extract an unscrupulous profit from all these disasters.

There were poor in the kingdoms, too, and their grievances sometimes obtruded. But the monarchs' large resources – and watchful security services – usually prevented these discontents from getting out of control, though the later Ptolemies suffered, and it was probably because of his fears over this problem that Attalus III Philometor Euergetes left the Pergamene kingdom to Rome (133). But it was far more often the city-states who were confronted by mass starvation among their urban and rural proletariats. Indeed, scarcely any city was strong or efficient enough to stem the rapid deterioration and secure itself a steady income. Following upon the economic and social convulsions of the kingdom of Sparta (Chapter One, section 1), the republican city-states, too – except for a few of their fortunate or enterprising citizens – ran into grave difficulties. Since there were no longer massive civil and military emigrations to draw away surplus mouths, a floating, disaffected population of landless and workless appeared on the scene. Yet in spite of their uncomfortable presence, or because of it, the total number of inhabitants of continental Greece began to diminish. Polybius vividly notes how the earlier overpopulation came sharply to an end.[9] It was common, at this time, for a family to have only one child (or none at all), and to revert to the ancient custom of exposing infant daughters to die. Small-holdings diminished and vanished (in favour of huge estates manned by disaffected labour), and some smaller towns and rural areas became totally depopulated and deserted. Within the course of the second century alone, the number of people who lived in the city-state territories of continental Greece seems to have diminished by as much as a quarter.

Faced with such terrible threats to their welfare and security, the cities were mostly timid and ineffective – able to think of nothing better than to ask for contributions from the rich (who, however, thought it more glamorous to spend money on buildings and festivals). Only a few communities, mostly on and off the Asia Minor coast, created public funds (backed by staff) for the purchase of grain, so as not to rely on private generosity. In 303 Antigonus I Monophthalmos, while regulating the amalgamation of two cities in Ionia (Lebedos and Teos), agreed to the establishment of such a fund by the new joint community – but with reluctance, owing to the expense. In 246 Samos, alarmed by a series of famines, set up a permanent fund (reorganized in 200) of which the capital was to be loaned out, and the interest devoted to the annual purchase of grain, which was then distributed free to the poor. Rhodes, Ephesus and Delos had somewhat similar schemes, and Rhodes (like Cnidus) also tried to protect itself and its poor against emergencies by socialist projects, notably the state production of jars for the export of its merchants' wine. Miletus, too, maintained state ownership of the textile factories in the city, including the slave-weavers who conducted their operations.

However, such arrangements were few and sporadic, and they do not seem to have occurred on the Greek mainland. There, organized aid for the poor was scarcely to be seen. Indeed, pity for the poor had never had much place in the Greek character. The doctrine of the equality of all human beings, propounded by the fifth-century Athenian sophist Antiphon, had remained very theoretical; the generations that followed never faced the effort of questioning or mitigating poverty. Even Plato and Aristotle, who in many ways anticipated modern sociological ideas, offered few contributions to this problem; Aristotle contented himself with extolling kindness and generosity as the appropriate qualities of the Superior or Great-Souled Man.

In the Hellenistic age, the attitude of the Stoic school was scarcely less equivocal. While fatalistically describing the poor as 'hirelings for life', and commenting that some seats in the theatre must inevitably be better than others, they nevertheless showed themselves aware of the need to abolish class strife; Zeno was prepared to accept destitute and dirty followers, and his successor Chrysippus of Soli (d. 207) spoke warmly in favour of competitive generosity by the rich. Yet he attributed this, when it occurred, not to humane emotions but to the desire for personal praise and recognition (Anaximenes of Lampsacus, *c.* 380–320, attributed it to fear).[10] Nor, for that matter, were the Stoics in favour of feelings of pity, which they regarded as a weakness in the armour of self-sufficiency.

However, less forbidding attitudes began to emerge elsewhere. The playwright Menander, deploring the sharp division between rich and poor, admired any initiatives that cut through the barrier between them. The Cynics, too, deplored poverty in strong terms – though they were short of positive suggestions for getting rid of it. Crates of Thebes (*c.* 365–285), for example, consoled men and women in distress – but could only preach a gospel of voluntary austerity. Then, in the early part of the third century BC, several writers made it their particular business to show up the miseries of poor people. Thus Herodas paints an astonishingly acute picture of the depressed, truculent, lower-class world. Yet he treats his scabrous subjects satirically, clinically, as themes for picturesque treatment rather than sympathy – somewhat in the same spirit as the fashionable 'miserabilist' sculptors of the day who observed aged fishermen and drunken hags with the same close and rather cold exactitude (Chapter Three, section 2).

More deeply committed was another iambic poet, the Cynic philosopher Cercidas. Apparently he is to be identified with a statesman and general from Megalopolis, who helped to defeat the radical Spartan king Cleomenes III at Sellasia in 222. Nevertheless, he was also the most incisive social critic of the age. Cercidas eloquently laments the sufferings of the poor, scolds the gods for their unjust distribution of earthly goods, and warns the unrepentant rich to put an end to their spendthrift or miserly ways and give to those in need – otherwise, he says, trouble is in store for them. Iambulus' Utopian island envisaged the abolition of class distinction altogether (Chapter Four, sections 2 and 3).

The successful epigrammatists of the day also produced touching epitaphs of the destitute. Particularly vivid were the brief verses of the 'tramp-poet' Leonidas of Taras, in the first half of the third century, whose baroque artificial language contrasts startlingly with a tragic pessimistic sympathy for the poor, among whom he passionately counts himself. His humble fishermen, their hard daily tasks starkly elevated to poetry, are treated with far deeper feeling than the same themes handled by the sculptors.

Nevertheless, on a more practical plane, the widespread poverty continued to create a highly inflammable situation – and was recognized as such. Isocrates in his *Archidamus* (366) remarked that the poor wanted to revolt – hoping that wars would bring about drastic changes.[11] What less poor people feared about the three sensationally reformist Spartan monarchs Agis IV, Cleomenes III and Nabis (244-192) was the prospect that they would divide up land, cancel debts, and free slaves – and that the infection would spread elsewhere. These fears were not altogether unfamiliar. The military author Aeneas Tacticus, writing in the 350s, had already made the alarming admission that, in order to avoid local risings, the poor, who are 'numerous, on the watch for an opportunity, and exceedingly dangerous' – always ready to desert to the enemy – might have to be relieved of part or even all of their debts.[12] A treaty outlined in a speech attributed (wrongly) to Demosthenes (d. 322) in his last years stipulated that there should be 'no division of land nor cancellation of debts nor liberation of slaves with a view to revolution'.[13] The league of city-states sponsored by Antigonus I Monophthalmos and Demetrius I Poliorcetes (302) contained a similar provision, and the oath of loyalty sworn by new citizens of the Cretan town of Itanus likewise included the promise: 'I will not bring about any division of land ... or cancellation of debts.'[14]

These fears of revolution were by no means unjustified. Whereas we can only locate half-a-dozen cases of unrest, social strife and rebellion in the century before Alexander (and they are mostly among the Sicilian and south Italian Greeks), it is possible to identify no less than sixty instances of the same phenomena in the Hellenistic period. In the Peloponnese alone there were dozens of such outbreaks. Many of them were fomented by outside intervention. For instance, at Cynaetha in

Arcadia, where factions influenced by the Spartan upheavals fought bitterly for years about redistributing land, the Achaean and Aetolian Leagues competed to encourage violence among the local contestants. And Philip v of Macedonia (221–179), who came to the throne while this was happening, showed sympathy for the oppressed classes in the city-states – which caused some of their richer citizens to turn in a panic to Rome. Meanwhile, Polybius painted a bleak picture of the class-antagonism and demoralization in Boeotia in central Greece (192).[15] Similar distresses in Aetolia and Thessaly in the 170s, involving serious debt crises, gave the Romans a good opportunity to intervene and restore social order; and when in the 140s they set out to destroy the Achaean League, a mass of thoroughly discontented Achaeans, and other Greeks, were ready enough to join them, in the belief that any change would be for the better.

Once Greece had been annexed by the Romans, however, they supported the propertied classes in the now considerably diminished city-states and kept them in power as their clients, to reduce the risk of revolutionary movements. And yet, even before that time, revolutions, however alluringly or terrifyingly near they seemed to be, were never really likely to materialize or, if they did, to succeed. For one thing, the reformists or revolutionaries had no positive programme: at most, all that they envisaged was a simple reversal of roles between rich and poor, and indeed nothing more would have been possible without an increase in the level of production, which was not to be had. Further-more, the reformist leaders were scarcely ever members of the oppressed groups themselves; they nearly all belonged to the upper class. And in the third place – partly because of these social origins – their plans for revolution tended to shy away from the liberation of slaves – a step which would have formidably swollen the numbers at their disposal, but alienated and terrified almost everybody else. True, it was not unknown for reformers (for instance, at Sparta) to give or sell slaves their freedom. But this was only done in occasional emergencies, and never as part of a stated or systematic programme.

Until quite late in the Hellenistic period slaves did not become a major factor in the political scene, yet they existed in very large numbers. At Athens, for example, in 313 BC, there were 84,000 citizens, 35,000 resident aliens, and 400,000 slaves – a rise of 33 per cent since 338. And ever increasing quantities of slaves continued to come on the market as prisoners of war. Many were foreigners from Syria and Asia Minor; but many others were Greeks. Large numbers of men and women, too, were enslaved by pirates. These pirates – ex-mercenaries and men who had lost their citizenship or livelihood – were based on various centres, including particularly the island of Crete, which was racked by recurring social crises that its loose union of cities was powerless to control. Pirates raged and marauded throughout the Aegean in the third century BC, and in the second they developed the slave-trade to large dimensions. Side in Pamphylia (southern Asia Minor) became its principal centre, and Delos its main transshipment depot. This trade in human beings also became very active in south Italy and Sicily, to serve the great plantations that had grown up in these countries.

Just as a conqueror exercised absolute power over his defeated enemy, so too, according to the Greeks of the classical age, a master had absolute power over his slave. Yet already in the fifth century the questioning sophists, or popular philosophers, had begun to maintain that the distinction between free men and slaves is not a natural phenomenon at all, but purely artificial. The tragic poet Euripides, well aware of such doctrines, became the first writer to offer extensive discussions of the position of slaves and slavery. Or rather, his characters offer varied opinions on the subject; though he himself, as far as we can tell, concluded that slaves, even if they are noble according to their limited possibilities, cannot ever attain the complete stature of individual human beings.

Plato and Aristotle still accepted and justified the necessity of slavery. The author of a work known as *Estate Management (Oeconomica)*, wrongly included among Aristotle's works but possibly a work of his leading pupil, Theophrastus, once again defended the institution, and saw the slave as useful to the extent that he was cooperative: his life, maintained the writer, was one of work, punishment and food – plus the more enlightened incentive of future liberation at a predetermined date.[16] The Epicurean community, on the other hand, was prepared to admit a slave, named Mys ('Mouse'), as one of its members; and Zeno, founder of the Stoic philosophy, revived the sophists' opinion that there was no such thing as a *natural* slave. But the Stoics failed to draw the further conclusion that, since this was so, slavery ought to be abolished. Instead they concluded that the whole question was purely external and indifferent and irrelevant, because it did not affect the real self, which was the soul.

In New Comedy, domestic slaves played an enormous part. The view that no one was a slave by nature was echoed by one of these dramatists, Philemon of Soli (368/60–267/3), who added: 'even a slave is made of flesh and blood ... slavery's of the body and comes by chance'.[17] Menander (c.342–392) declared a well-disposed slave a unique asset[18] – his plays are full of resourceful, amusing, domestic slaves, portrayed very much as human beings and with a good deal of sympathy and variety: these characterizations are developed from the simpler lines of the faithful and thieving slave in Aristophanes' *Plutus* (408, 388) – and from the sketches of *paidagogoi*, the slaves who looked after children, in fifth-century tragedy. The frequency with which slaves continue to appear on terracotta statuettes from Myrina, representing stage figures of the years around 200, suggest that slave parts had by this time become even more prominent in the comedies and farces, now lost, that were popular on the stage at that time.

These privileged, quite cosily treated slaves, *paidagogoi* and nurses for babies and the sick, and so on, were well known not only in literature but in real life. And there were signs of improvement in both private and official attitudes to their status. Athens had already in the past set a limit to the penalties that could be inflicted on its urban slaves, and the third century witnessed a tendency for the rich to set some of them up in remunerative businesses, from which they were allowed to take their cut. Moreover, throughout the Hellenistic world, the emancipation of slaves (suggested in the *Oeconomica*) became more frequent; the practice which allowed them to purchase their freedom by fictitious sale to a god was encouraged by Delphi in *c.* 200. Opportunities for their education, too, showed signs of increasing, and certain cities granted them legal holidays. Moreover, as a work known as the *Epidemics* (written by a member of the school of Hippocrates, probably in the fourth century) indicates, their medical treatment had become a fairly regular occurrence. Religious worships, too, found room for slaves. The shrine of Demeter at Eleusis had traditionally admitted them to its rites, and now certain cult associations, especially those of eastern gods, accepted them as members. Slaves could sometimes become members of religious and social clubs (like women), and could place themselves under the protection of certain temples, where they could not be arrested.

But this only happened at a few places and in the event of extreme oppression. Indeed, this whole list of occasional official concessions to slaves, or acts of kindness by masters, must be seen in the context of a situation in which they still virtually lacked human rights altogether. A municipal or domestic slave might be treated solicitously, just as a washing-up machine receives careful treatment today, and for the same reasons. Furthermore, no such favourable treatment was to be seen in the great labour camps (*ergasteria*) which now reached formidable new dimensions. Some were on extensive agricultural estates, but Athens' silver mines at Laurion, too, employed 30,000 slave workers in the later fourth century, and were active again two hundred years later. These slaves worked in appalling conditions. And Agatharchides of Cnidus has left us a horrific account of the ruthless, murderous treatment of convict labourers in the gold mines of the Ptolemies.

It had long been realized that slaves represented a terrible potential threat to their masters, and in the fourth century this belief was vigorously expressed by Xenophon and Plato. Moreover, in due course, such revolts did break out. In the late fourth and early third centuries there were frightening slave-revolts in some of the semi-Hellenized city-states of Etruria. In Greek lands, the first of such recorded revolts occurred in c. 276, on the mercantile island of Chios, where the slave population was numerous.

Once started, the process had come to stay. But it was not until the latter half of the second century that the era of major slave-rebellions began. They first broke out in the western Greek lands, by this time under Roman rule, where agricultural plantations of unprecedented dimensions, growing olive and vine crops instead of cereals, were worked by slaves. In this respect they resembled the slaves on estates elsewhere in Italy, about whose treatment the Roman writer Cato the elder (*On Farming*) offered advice. Though entirely callous, he thought it counter-productive to work slaves to death. Other masters, however, did just that: and the result was that a great many desperate slaves deserted and went underground, massing together in armies which, in the end, openly confronted the Roman legions.

The first of these large-scale risings broke out in 135 on the large Sicilian properties, where ill-treatment had reached exceptional dimensions. The leader of the revolt, Eunus, issued coins on which he called himself King Antiochus, in memory of his Syrian homeland. Before the rebellion was put down in 131 – after immense loss of life – the slave army had swollen to 70,000 men, and its victories had stimulated outbreaks in other Mediterranean regions. And then, less than three decades later, at a time when Italy was threatened by a German invasion, the Sicilian slaves rose again (104–100), and 17,000 Roman soldiers were needed to put them down; their rising also sparked off an outbreak in Athens' silver mines at Laurion.

The last great insurrection was in southern Italy, where a 90,000-strong slave army mobilized by the Thracian gladiator Spartacus terrorized the entire Italian peninsula (73–71). The Roman general Crassus crucified 6,000 of them along the Via Appia, and the age of the great revolts had ended. But they had torn open a perilous gap in the precarious structure of Hellenistic and Roman society. Well might the Stoic Posidonius of Apamea (c. 135–50) observe that the ill-treatment of slaves by individual masters was a danger to the whole community.[19]

Between the slaves and 'free' poor on the one hand, and the rich on the other, lived those huge central sections of the population, which were far more numerous than ever before. They included the proprietors of industrial workshops, the owners or tenants of shops and warehouses and ships, money lenders, slave dealers, professional people of various kinds, tenant farmers and lesser landowners. That is to say, they were far from forming a homogeneous category of 'bourgeois' or 'middle-class'. For example, those near the top of this scale would have despised the men who did a job of work, especially if the latter were *technitai*, who laboured with their hands. What can be said, however, is that most of these varied groups of persons belonged to the non-political class: they had little interest in the communal activities that had occupied citizens in the classical age.

Such intermediate, non-political people are thoroughly well known to us from the plays of Menander, the *Characters* of Theophrastus, and the mimes of Theocritus and Herodas. They did not always prosper (notably in parts of the Greek homeland), since there was a tendency for the rich to become richer and the poor poorer. Yet they remained the core and nucleus of Hellenistic life.

They were bolstered up and justified, and given the cohesion which the variety of their occupations and statuses could not provide, by a common form of education, which is one of the most important phenomena of the Hellenistic age. This education is hard to grasp today, because it was so very predominantly rhetorical – based on the use of words. Indeed, that had been the main theme of Greek education since the distant past. Already in the *Iliad*, the ability to be a speaker of words was the second of the arts (next to being a man of action) taught to Achilles by Phoenix.[20] Then, in the fifth century, the sophists or popular philosophers, notably Gorgias of Leontini (*c.* 483–376), became the first teachers of the art of persuasive prose. Plato (d. 347) realized that general education had to go much deeper, and wanted to endow it with a basically philosophical character; but this proposal was not generally accepted.

What prevailed instead was the rhetorical type of education advocated by Isocrates (d. 338), who became the chief creator of rhetoric as a distinct science. For him, education above all meant developing the ability *to speak*, which distinguishes human beings from animals. Yet he, too, was at pains to advocate a broader and more liberal programme than the mere rules and techniques of the professional rhetoricians, which seemed to him to lack educational content and value. He would therefore have liked to reduce theory to a minimum, whereas Aristotle's *Rhetoric*, on the other hand, introduced a host of new definitions. However, Aristotle remained judiciously cautious about the quality of the rhetorical art, which he saw as useful yet dangerous – since we must not persuade what is wrong. Under the influence of his textbook, Greek education assumed its definitive form, which was fundamental to the whole picture of the Hellenistic world that lay ahead.

Further handbooks on rhetoric, of varying quality, continued to appear. They did good by teaching people to arrange their thoughts more clearly. Yet amid a proliferating mass of rules the basic idea that good speaking could only be derived from good thinking often tended to be lost sight of. Particularly famous, in the third century, was Hegesias of Magnesia by Sipylus, who displayed carefully thought-out principles of rhythm in his own flamboyant ('Asianic') speeches. Next, Hermagoras of Temnos produced the most elaborate system of rhetoric that had so far appeared, not only embodying general themes but discussing particular situations as well; and his views remained influential for many years to come.

In its most developed shape, the education of young Hellenistic males – of girls something will be said later (Chapter Three, section 4) – extended between the ages of seven and twenty, comprising three grades, each with its corresponding type of teacher: children (*paides*) of from seven to fourteen, pupils of secondary age (*epheboi*) from fifteen to seventeen, and youths at the tertiary stage (*neoi*) from eighteen to twenty.

In most Greek cities the primary, elementary stage of education was left to private enterprise, and paid for by parents' fees, without being in any way subject to public control, though in some places a civic post of controller, *paidonomos*, was brought into existence. Children were usually taught reading, writing, gymnastics and music, and sometimes painting as well. In secondary schools physical and musical training continued, and some mathematics and science were taught. But literary education played an exceedingly prominent part, and indeed constantly tended to push other studies out altogether: Homer, Euripides and other classical authors were studied in minute detail according to a meticulous plan.

Athens became a model for the ephebe (secondary) system of the Hellenistic world. Introduced in about 370 and remodelled in about 335 and 322, the Athenian ephebate was at first compulsory for citizen families; later, however, in the third century, it was placed on a voluntary basis. The institution had started as a sort of gentleman's militia, but, as the need for soldiers diminished, its military aspects gradually declined. Instead, the programmes increasingly concentrated not only on teaching but on training of character and instruction in social behaviour: that is to say, they became a sort of moral preparation for citizenship. In the late fourth century, when all these developments were occurring, there were probably between five and six hundred Attic ephebes at a time. It was somewhat ironical that this institution reached its height in the epoch of Athens' political eclipse. Once membership became voluntary, the ephebes, with their characteristic wide hats (*petasoi*) and black cloaks and short hair, tended to be a somewhat select and snobbish group, though it may be that a certain number of poorer applicants secured admission.

The ephebes congregated, in each city, at the gymnasium – usually comprising colonnaded porticoes and rooms round a rectangular open space – which was the centre and essential hall-mark of Hellenism. The gymnasia had been the foundation and support of Greek life and mentality since ancient times, and now their importance was even greater. For it was in these buildings that the boys did their physical training, were taught, and attended lectures by distinguished visitors. Fostering companionship, common ideas and esprit de corps, the gymnasia had increasingly replaced the old family life as the principal training ground of the young, and became the rallying points of all who possessed, or hoped to possess, Greek culture and education.

The cities appointed directors (*gymnasiarchs*) for public and private institutions alike. But the extent of civic responsibility varied widely. Miletus and Rhodes were among cities which recognized that education should be the business of the state. But private benefactions were also demanded and contributed on a massive scale, for example towards the cash prizes needed for the numerous public competitions between pupils. The kings saw the advantages of the system as clearly as the cities. Thus royal Pergamum had no less than five gymnasia of its own, including the largest surviving example, measuring 655 by 490 feet, and extending down the hillside on three levels, each reserved for one of the three educational grades. In Egypt, the state does not seem to have needed to subsidize the gymnasia, which were maintained by associations, perhaps consisting of old boys. Teachers (like athletic trainers and public doctors) received salaries. Some communities defrayed them from public funds, and exempted their recipients from taxes. But unless these men possessed exceptionally good qualifications, they were poorly paid, though their epitaphs are framed in respectful terms; and no doubt they received presents – including a share of the prizes their pupils won in competitions.

From the end of the fourth century onwards the institution of the gymnasium, together with the ephebate it served, spread rapidly to all Hellenistic cities, where it was seen as one of the indispensable bases of the Greek way of life. Established in new cities as well as old, in distant territories of the kingdoms as well as 'barbarian' lands beyond, it became the most important single denominator of Hellenization and unity, the factory stimulating the production of Greek-minded citizens, speaking the *koine*, the common dialect that every Greek and culture-Greek now spoke. One can only glimpse the difficulties the more remote cities experienced in getting teachers for their schools. According to Plutarch, for example, the Athenian rhetorician Amphicrates agreed to go to Seleucia on the Tigris as a visiting teacher, but when offered a permanent post there replied that a dolphin would not fit into a stew-pan.[21]

Amphicrates may have been asked to lecture to students of the tertiary grade, the *neoi* aged between eighteen and twenty. Students of this age-group are frequently found in the cities of Asia Minor. Like the younger pupils, they attended gymnasia, either sharing the premises with their juniors or possessing special buildings of their own. They usually came from the richest and most elegant families in their communities, and spent their time at the gymnasia acquiring an introduction to the adult life of civic affairs, high society and sport. In addition to athletics and music, they were expected to pursue literary and philosophical studies. But standards in these subjects were not high. For serious study one had to go to one of the great university towns – Athens or Pergamum or Rhodes for philosophy and rhetoric, Cos or Pergamum or Ephesus for medicine, Alexandria for a comprehensive range of subjects.

The Hellenistic educational system taught useful and stylish things, but tended to be superficial, élitist and nostalgic, and showed little or no concern for science and technology. Contemporary philosophers were well aware of some of its faults. Zeno, the founder of Stoicism (in his early *Republic*), had unkind words for the curriculum – and so had the Sceptics. Epicurus pronounced it an irrelevant waste of time, and the Cynics deplored the stress on athleticism – which was certainly in greater danger of running riot even than in earlier times when it had already been very prominent.

But public opinion was against such critics. To most Greeks the system seemed wonderful. Innumerable epitaphs tell us so – and promise that the chief delights of the Elysian fields will be cultural, a sort of continuation of one's schooldays. Cicero translated the Greek programme into his famous *humanitas*, which later became the basis of Renaissance education. But in its Greek form, too, Plutarch still admired the system immeasurably in the second century AD: 'of all our qualities, learning alone is immortal and divine'.[22] And even two hundred years later, the Roman emperor Julian the Apostate summed up what Greeks, and philhellenes like himself, so strongly felt: that this education developed boys as individuals, and not as cogs in a machine or bees in a hive. Any gifted person with a classical education, Julian declared, is capable of great things in any direction. He can take the lead in learning or politics, or war, or exploration, or heroism: 'he comes down among men like a gift from the gods'.[23]

However this may be, the result was an enormous quantitative diffusion and extension of Hellenistic education. It was an extension that created, as a significant by-product, a far wider public who wanted something to read. Aristotle recognized the existence of authors whose works were intended to be read instead of listened to,[24] and by his time the habit of reading was rapidly gaining ground: public and private libraries were being created everywhere to meet the demand, and copies of books (and commentaries on their contents) were reduplicated and multiplied to fill the library shelves.

Yet here something of a paradox must be noted. In one sense the new reading public – like its education – was remarkably uniform, part of a huge, widespread uniformity in daily habits and outward surroundings that characterized the epoch. And yet this very uniformity, often on a not very ambitious plane, had created an unfamiliar cultural split, because it did not satisfy the highbrows. This meant that the old homogeneous audiences – who had quailed and exulted together watching the great Athenian tragedies – had become sharply divided into two sections, one small and fastidious and intellectual and the other very large and middle brow.

The writers, therefore, were similarly divided. The cleverest and most refined of them wrote for the few people with tastes like their own, with some extraordinary results (Chapter Four, section 3). But it is clear that many others – whose works have scarcely survived – wrote for the vast new reading public, insatiable for popularization of every kind. Only at the beginning of the period was a real attempt made to bridge the widening gulf. Heraclides Ponticus of Heraclea, for example, who was still active in 322, made himself a very attractive popularizer of the best thought of his day, and then the *Characters* of Theophrastus and the New Comedy presented cleverly devised types and personages (and happy endings) that the ordinary person could recognize and understand. But then, very soon, things became different. Theocritus portrayed unintellectual women, and Herodas low life, but they did so in highly refined Greek and with patronizing sophistication, for the amusement of intellectuals like themselves (Chapter Three, section 2).

The historians of the time mirrored the new cultural gap with great accuracy, since they are sharply divided between highly responsible and accurate practitioners on the one hand (Ptolemy I Soter, Hieronymus, Polybius) – pursuing the truth with the same determination as contemporary scientists and realistic sculptors – and on the other hand a whole host of far less serious figures: quasi-fictitious historians of Alexander the Great (Callisthenes, Clitarchus and the writers of fabulous 'Alexander Romances'), fraudulent tale-spinners such as Antiphanes of Berge (fourth century), sensationalists like Duris of Samos (died *c.* 260), and scandalmongers of the calibre of Hermippus of Smyrna (third century). In the first century BC, Asclepiades of Myrlea remarked that narrative prose could be (1) true, (2) as it may probably have happened, (3) false.[25] And it was the last category that proliferated: the lack of interest in intellectual truth among the new semi-educated public produced not only this rash of collections of 'marvellous' happenings but deliberate pseudonymous writings, or, to put it less politely, deliberate fakes, for example, forgeries of famous people's letters.

A more durable product, however, of the new middle-brow diffusion of education was the Greek novel. Its development owed a good deal to romantic, semi-fictional 'histories', since the earliest extant novels still preserve a pseudo-historical shape and framework. But their plots are also similar to those of the New Comedy, and many other forms of literature and popular story-telling were mobilized to add their contributions – history, myth, science and religion, all are invoked: but the basic theme is sentimental love, the separation of virtuous lovers by cruel circumstances, and their triumphant reunion for a comfortable happy ending. The first novelists concealed their own names, probably to avoid the scorn of learned academics: but they could console themselves by the possession of an imposingly large public, which loved their works and could not cope with anything more intellectual.

Assyrian, Syrian, Judaean, Egyptian sources were ransacked for themes. Fragments of an early example of this type of writing, the *Ninus Romance,* have survived on papyri of the first century AD, but language and substance alike suggest that the work was written three hundred years earlier. The Romance tells of the chequered fortunes and eventual marriage of Ninus, traditionally the first Assyrian king, to Semiramis – chaste hero and bashful heroine. But it is possible that there is an older, or equally old, extant Greek novel, written by a Jew. This is the very popular *Joseph and Aseneth,* telling the story of the conversion of Joseph's Egyptian bride to Judaism, presented as a mystery religion. The *Dream of Nectanebus,* of the second or first century BC, is translated from the work of an unidentified Egyptian.

The huge diffusion of only moderately high educational standards, which created such novels and novelettes, also encouraged the bulk production of some not very elevated visual art; for a vastly expanded clientele demanded the creation of a great number of minor, trivial decorative objects. The graceful 'Tanagra' statuettes produced at various centres (Chapter Three, section 2) do not deserve relegation to this category. But larger Hellenistic figures sometimes display a remarkable degree of vulgarity. One enormously admired statue was of Aphrodite gazing backwards to admire her own bottom. And Delos possessed a statuary group showing the same goddess whimsically threatening to use her slipper on dirty-minded old Pan, while a flying Eros joins coyly in the fun.

This group was at the local club of the merchants from Phoenician Berytus (Beirut) on the island. Clubs and societies formed one of the principal phenomena of the age. Previously, the cities themselves, and their institutions, had provided most of the organized social life that people needed. But now that the city-states had lost much of their appeal, people resorted to club life instead to fill the vacuum. Clubs, mostly religious, had existed at least as far back as the sixth century, but in the Hellenistic age they became much more numerous and varied. Many of these institutions were still concerned with the maintenance of religious cults. Others, like the club for the Berytan merchants at Delos, were associations of merchants, and there existed many such guilds composed of fellow-workers in the same craft, industry or trade. It was not their purpose to act as trade unions, or to protest about working conditions. But general meetings are recorded,[26] and vigorous social activities. In the multi-national trade centres these clubs brought mixed populations together. And above all they kept people happy; even the watchful Ptolemies had no objection to their existence, provided their members made no political trouble.

Another way in which the régimes of the time tried to increase contentment was by adding greatly to the number of festivals which their citizenry, rich and poor alike, could enjoy. These celebrations, generally occurring at four-year intervals, sometimes included epic and dramatic contests. But the activities were mainly athletic and musical. They brought two typical movements of the time into play. First, they attracted important benefactions, which provided the prizes. And secondly, like so many other contemporary institutions, they overstepped the bounds of any single state. For Greek athletes flocked to the Olympic and other Games from far and wide. And the musical and dramatic performances were habitually undertaken by specialist guilds, officially of a religious character, known as the Dionysiac artists or craftsmen (*technitai*). One of the centres from which they moved on circuit was Teos, which belonged, for a time, to the kingdom of Pergamum. Moreover, the monarchs of the various kingdoms spent a lot of money on developing festivals of their own, to keep their volatile urban populations out of mischief. At Alexandria, in particular, we hear a lot about grandiose festivals. Theocritus was among those who dutifully praised their splendour, but Arsinoe III Philopator, wife of Ptolemy IV Philopator, described the Festival of Flagons as 'a dirty kind of party – a mixed crowd gorging up stale food'.[27]

The cities in which this Hellenistic life was lived underwent a profound architectural transformation during the Hellenistic age – in marked contrast to the miseries of the poor, who in many cases formed a large proportion of their inhabitants. Indeed, this epoch witnessed the climax of urbanization, directed, very often, by full-time public architects. These developments occurred not only at great centres like Alexandria or Pergamum, but at many or most of the other Greek cities as well, however insignificant.

The old Greek cities had grown up haphazardly, with narrow, winding streets. But in the period preceding the Hellenistic epoch there had already been increasingly widespread and systematic use of the axial, symmetrical 'gridiron' planning that is associated with the name of the fifth-century architect Hippodamus of Miletus, though it had been known for two or three hundred years before him. The town plan of Rhodes, commonly regarded as the most beautiful city of the Greek world, was sometimes attributed to Hippodamus, though probably wrongly. Alexandria was designed round an unprecedented main avenue, a hundred feet wide. But the most notable example of town planning extant today is Priene in Ionia, which was rebuilt in c. 350 as a compact, carefully laid out small city of about 4,000 inhabitants on a superb, steeply sloping, location.

Much more was to follow, for the Hellenistic age saw a growing interest in the plastic, pictorial grouping and integration of architectural blocks and masses, and an awareness of their rhythmical relationship to intangible space, with novel attention to light and shade. The builders of Priene imposed their will on the landscape, but the designers of royal Pergamum instead accommodated themselves to its contours, fanning out their buildings harmoniously up and down a crescent-shaped ridge, and employing ingenious asymmetries in order to establish an intimate relationship and unity with this challenging terrain: a lesson the Romans learnt from such models.

The most characteristic feature of Hellenistic town-planning is the *Stoa* (portico), a rectangular hall in which one of the long sides is formed not by a wall but by a colonnade. Such Stoas were often constructed along one or more of the sides of a city's Agora (market-place) – the traditional open space for meetings and commercial transactions, round which the civic offices were also grouped. The Stoa was not a new Hellenistic conception: the remains of the ninety-foot-long tile-roofed Stoa Poikile ('many-coloured') at Athens (460), decorated with paintings by Polygnotus and other famous artists, were discovered in 1981. But the formula underwent major developments – especially in the display of increasing sensitiveness to the environmental ensemble – during the later fourth century, when the South Stoa at Corinth attained a length of five hundred feet, extending almost from one end of the Agora to the other. Then at Morgantina in Sicily (c. 300), probably with the help of that city's ally Agathocles of Syracuse, a remarkable Agora was built on a slope – with flights of steps forming sides of a polygon, and serving also as seats for public meetings. This Agora at Morgantina was intended to have two-storeyed Stoas on three of its sides, though the plan was never completed.

Subsequently Stoas proliferated throughout the Hellenistic cities, providing shelter from sun, wind and rain for all who came to the Agora for meetings and talks. Architects liked the Stoa, because it increased available room, linked and integrated isolated buildings, and gave shape to spatial environment and landscape, in addition to the opportunities that it offered for artistic decoration. After 200, the rebuilding of cities increasingly centred upon these colonnaded structures. At the expense of Attalus II Philadelphus of Pergamum, the Agora at Athens was transformed so as to comprise two clearly defined spaces, unified by a single continuous two-tiered Stoa, with a row of shops at the back, and store-rooms underneath. At Pergamum the terraces on which the hill-side monuments rise one above the other were structured and defined by a series of Stoas. And most impressive of all, perhaps, is the large portico along the east side of the South Agora at Miletus, with its double colonnade and triple row of shops.

The fourth century and Hellenistic age also specialized in closed halls, and here once again Miletus possessed one of the most striking examples, presented by the Seleucid Antiochus IV Epiphanes. This hall was the externally two-storeyed Bouleuterion or Council House, containing seats in concentric semi-circles, like those in a theatre, and forming the dominant feature of an elaborate architectural complex. Two other such buildings, the Ecclesiasterion at Priene, with its seats arranged parallel to three walls and the speaker's platform on the fourth, and then the Hypostyle Hall at Delos (c. 210), look forward to the long series of Roman basilicas which were shortly to make their appearance. The

Romans notably improved on the formula, because the discovery and exploitation of concrete made it possible for them, first, to dispense with the forest of columns that had filled the Hellenistic edifices, and secondly, to erect round arches – which in the Greek buildings had mainly existed as secondary and invisible aids to construction, for example in drains and plain barrel-vaulted corridors (though arched gates were already to be found, especially in Etruria).

Greek theatres made of stone and marble began to be built in about the middle of the fourth century, and their possibilities as features of the urban landscape came to be more and more appreciated by architects. An early stage in this process was the introduction of the *proskenion*, a row of columns supporting a high platform which, in New Comedy, served as an elevated stage. (Old Comedy, like the classical tragic drama, had been acted in the flat *orchestra* in front.) The theatre at Miletus, dating from the third century, is the most spectacular of all its monuments; and the new high stage can be seen at the theatre at Epidaurus, of the same period. *Proskenia*, like other decorative monumental façades, gave opportunities for broken pediments, recessed entablatures, and orders on different scales combined in a single frontage – features reflecting much the same baroque desire to get away from pure classical simplicity which Bernini and his contemporaries were to display two thousand years later.

The temple had always been the model building of Greek architecture, and set the stylistic standards for the traditional orders which were exploited with a new flexibility in the Hellenistic age: the solid Doric order, with its capital consisting of a simple , convex, cushion moulding (*echinus*), whereas the more elegant Ionic capital was flanked by a pair of spiral scrolls (volutes); and now the ornate, acanthus-leaved Corinthian capital had come strongly into fashion. The temple was not, by tradition, a place of worship since the altar, at which both public and private sacrifices were made, normally stood outside the shrine itself – which served primarily as a place to house the sacred image (if there was one), and to offer room for ritual equipment and valuable offerings.

Hellenistic temples displayed vast dimensions, and various technical and aesthetic innovations, and new calculations of proportions. These developments were especially noteworthy in Ionia, where the Seleucids rebuilt the temple of Apollo at Didyma on a vast scale (*c.* 300); and subsequently the greatest temple architect of Hellenistic times, Hermogenes, built a famous shrine of Artemis Leucophryene at Magnesia on the Maeander (*c.* 130). The last big Greek temple to be erected in Asia Minor, it was a building that showed a masterly understanding of the correlation between solid masses and open space. In Etruria, too, there had been rebuildings and redecorations of major temples from the end of the fourth century onwards – constructed of wood, according to the native tradition, but adorned with terracotta ornaments in Hellenistic styles, learnt from Taras and elsewhere. And then, after 200, a further wave of activity was stimulated in Etruria by Greek artists whom the Romans brought back from their conquests.

Hellenistic shrines were increasingly envisaged as the central features of huge architectural precincts devoted to all manner of religious, social, oracular and curative purposes. Thus the modest temple of Asclepius, the increasingly popular god of healing, on the island of Cos – situated beside a gushing spring of medicinal water – was greatly expanded (with Attalid aid) to include an open reception court laid out below the original terrace; and a new group of imposing structures was added on a further terrace above, to become the crowning-piece of the whole massive group.

The Asclepieion illustrates an ambitious new plastic, pictorial, axial aesthetic. Another such elaborate complex was the Temple of Fortuna Primigenia (the equivalent of Tyche) at Praeneste (Palestrina) in Latium – an ancient, partly Hellenized, partly Etruscanized, partly Romanized city. The temple was already famous in 156-155 (when the philosopher Carneades commented on its widespread reputation).[28] But then in c. 80, on the initiative of Sulla, the whole slope on which part of the earlier town had been built was carved into tier upon tier of parallel, concrete-based, colonnaded terraces, Roman in detail but Hellenistic in grandiose overall conception.

There were also other extraordinary religious buildings, in addition to temples. Before his death in 353, Mausolus of Caria in south-western Asia Minor, a client prince of the Achaemenid Persians, had started work on his own Mausoleum at his new capital Halicarnassus (Bodrum). The building was continued by his widow Artemisia and then his sister Ada (deposed in 340 but reinstated by Alexander the Great), but still remained unfinished. Consisting of a twenty-four-step pyramid within a massive colonnade, and adorned by the leading sculptors of the epoch, the grandiose Mausoleum ranked as one of the Seven Wonders of the World, and inspired subsequent monumental funerary buildings, notably an exuberantly ornate rock-tomb façade at Belevi near Ephesus. The rectangular and barrel-vaulted graves of c. 340-320 at Aegae (Vergina), built to house the ashes of eminent Macedonians, provided no such architectural opportunity, because they were underground. But a slightly later grave at Lefkhadia Náousa in the same country is above ground level and displays a handsome two-storeyed façade.

As the Hellenistic age developed, religious structures of another sort came to be elaborated as well. These were altars of unprecedented size and monumental character. The Altar of King Hiero II at Syracuse, erected between 241 and 215 on a piece of land cut out of the living rock, was six hundred and fifty feet long: it had entrances at both ends, surmounted by statues, and its superstructure – which probably stood forty feet high – was crowned by a cornice with spouts in the form of lions' heads to carry rainwater from the roof. The resplendent Altar of Zeus and Athena at Pergamum, now reconstructed in East Berlin, was erected, it would appear, by King Eumenes II Soter and perhaps finished by Attalus II Philadelphus, to celebrate a victory, with Rome's help, over the Galatians (descendants of the Gaulish immigrants into central Asia Minor). Among the group of buildings arranged along the crescent-shaped Pergamene hill-side, the structure housing this altar formed the outstanding feature and focal point. It was made in the shape of a square colonnaded platform adorned with famous reliefs (Chapter Three, section 2) and flanked by two lateral, projecting bastions. The altar itself, which the framework enclosed, was approached up a flight of broad steps.

Another very notable feature of the age was the development of Greek private houses – the houses, that is to say, of the more prosperous citizens – into something far more commodious and artistic than had ever been seen before: a sign of the increasing individualism of an age when communal activities and values no longer seemed enough.

This process of evolution had started in the fifth and early fourth centuries, when Olynthus, capital of the Chalcidian League round the coast of Macedonia, showed houses of a hitherto unknown type. Decorated with graceful mosaics made of natural, unshaped pebbles, and displaying white on dark geometric and figured designs, these buildings consist of a long room (*pastas*) out of which a series of smaller rooms opened on one side, and a courtyard on the other. Dwellings of the same epoch at Athens look similar but plainer and less regular; but houses at Priene, after the mid-fourth century, are more attractive and comfortable.

In Macedonia, residences of a novel size and grandeur – built for royalties, and people who wanted to rival them – began to appear in the same period at Aegae (Palatitsia near Vergina), where large peristyle courts, double-storeyed colonnades and circular halls are to be seen, as well as at the national capital Pella, where more elaborately polychrome pebble pavements made a fine show. Improved by the replacement of pebbles by cubes in the period following Alexander's conquests, the mosaic technique spread far and wide, and in the mid-third century assumed a novel and sophisticated form at Morgantina in eastern Sicily, where carefully cut marble, stone and tile tesserae were composed into varied patterns. In the later third and second century this fully developed mosaic art spread to the houses of rich merchants at Delos.

In the tasteful houses of the same period, and later, at Pompeii and Herculaneum (formerly Heraclion) near Neapolis (now Naples) in Campania, the main feature is an unroofed or partially roofed courtyard (*atrium*) of Etruscan origin, but many luxurious features are Greek, including a superb and lavishly evolving series of mural paintings (sometimes developed from the styles of Delos) as well as stucco work and mosaics. But then the eruption of Vesuvius in AD 79 overwhelmed Pompeii and Herculaneum and the villas of the surrounding countryside – and preserved them for posterity. Campania, for all its sophistication, stood upon the utmost fringe of Hellenism. At the opposite, north-eastern extremity of the Greek world was Borysthenes (Olbia) at the mouth of the river Hypanis (Bug), where recent discoveries once again include Hellenistic dwellings – in this case notable for their well-built cellars.

The fine houses of the epoch belonged to a relatively small number of people who not only lived with considerable elegance but also had to play a very large part in keeping their city-states solvent. For the cities themselves, from their public corporate resources, were quite unable to afford their own upkeep. Indeed, they very rarely even drew up effective annual budgets, and facilities for floating city loans or running up public debts scarcely existed. On the frequent occasions, therefore, when a grave deficit occurred, a city had to call on its richest citizens to make it good. And they responded with remarkable generosity. It was they, too, who paid for most of the expensive communal buildings, and who financed other costly projects such as festivals and school prizes.

The men who footed these bills were, in consequence, annually elected to the top posts in the city governments; thus the principle that these were democratically elected was, in practice, modified by the custom that the rich should monopolize office, provided that they paid for it liberally. They had seized the various opportunities of the disturbed early Hellenistic age to invest in land, and it was from land, including rents, that they derived all their money. Yet what could they do with it? Investment possibilities were scarce; and large-scale capitalistic industry did not exist. So they had money to burn, and their highly developed love of distinction (*philotimia*) prompted them to spend it, not indeed on the welfare of the poor, but on more or less voluntary contributions towards the amenities and handsome appearance of their cities, including their own houses.

Part II
Reality and Withdrawal

Chapter Three

Reality and the Individual

1 Scientific Researches

Some men and women of the Hellenistic age wanted to get away, in mind at least, from the circumstances they found around them (Chapter Four). At the same time, many others became remarkably involved in a new, general, overall drive towards truly seeing things as they are – a drive towards greater reality and realism, and a conscious or unconscious jettisoning of some of the more idealistic, exalted conceptions of the classical Greek past. Writers and sculptors and painters showed a much stronger concern for realistic representations than had ever appeared in earlier times: but, above all, the scientific research of the epoch, building on past achievements, began to display – precariously but brilliantly – a new determination to discern the world as it really is.

The tendency had been launched by the development of mathematics. Well before the Hellenistic epoch started, the Greeks had discovered the use of mathematical calculation as a method of investigating natural phenomena. In particular, Pythagoras of Samos, who emigrated in about 531 to Croton in south Italy, became a legendary sage. Starting from the study of music, Pythagoras and his followers concluded that mathematical relations – number, geometrical pattern and the relation ('harmony') of numbers one to another – constitute the underlying, unifying essence of the apparent diversity of phenomena. In this conferment of a special and independent status upon Greek mathematics, another south Italian school, at Elea (Velia) in Lucania, also played a leading part. Next, these beginnings were built upon with great fervour by Plato, who made the Pythagorean doctrine one of the foundations of his whole philosophical system: so that mathematical universals (circle, line etc.) appear among the Forms which he saw as corresponding to every universal or general idea.

Although Aristotle did not share his master's view of the absolute pre-eminence of mathematics, it was the exercise in logic which the subject had imparted to the Greeks that led to his massive systematization of the laws of thought, accepted and applied by all subsequent thinkers.

But his unique contribution was to insist, at the same time, that enquiries into reality must start not with generalities – the discovery of principles by argument – but with particulars. For Aristotle, while believing that everything is placed where it is for a reason, capable of illustrating the purposefulness of the universe, nevertheless rejected Plato's view of the real world (his world of Forms) as something other than and outside the world of the senses. Quite on the contrary, Aristotle became increasingly convinced that empirical research, based on evidence and observation as well as reasoning, was needed to discover the truth. To this task he devoted not only an inspired commonsense but a passionate love of tidy orderliness which was not content until science became a separate set of disciplines from philosophy, organized into a coherent system marshalling the whole massive range of its subject matter under encyclopaedic classifications of genus and species. Above all, since individual human beings were the central features of his philosophy, he laid great stress on biology, in which the power and range of his observations and theoretical discussions alike were far ahead of his time. He was the true founder of the other natural and physical sciences as well: and it was with this whole vast corpus of scientific knowledge that he launched the Hellenistic age.

His successor Theophrastus of Eresus on the island of Lesbos (d. 288/5) established the Lyceum of the Aristotelians (or Peripatetics, walkers about while teaching and lecturing) as a school in its own right; and it became one of the leading research centres of the age. Theophrastus was said to have lectured to two thousand students. While dubious about the purposefulness of the universe envisaged by Aristotle – 'we must try to set a limit to the assignment of final causes'[1] – he was nevertheless a devoted disciple who inherited to the full his master's flair for classification: his surviving treatises are among the most complete and orderly of all extant Greek scientific writings, remarkable for the patient closeness with which their reasoning follows the observed facts. Employing these exacting methods, Theophrastus separated the animal from the vegetable kingdom, doing for botany what Aristotle had done for human beings and animals.

This efflorescence of biological science had been stimulated by Alexander's eastern campaigns, which brought in much new knowledge about peoples, animals and plants. But the burst of activity was short-lived, since Aristotle and Theophrastus proved impossible to equal or follow: and with their deaths pure research in these fields virtually came to an end until quite recent times.

Other scientific studies, however, showed greater progress during the first Hellenistic century and a half than in any other comparable period until the birth of modern science. Liberated at last from *a priori* speculations, scientists were able to come into their own. They were given very little help by the philosophers of the day, even when these claimed a materialistic basis for the universe, since the cast-iron, take-it-or-leave-it systems of the philosophical schools were quite unconcerned with empirical observation. Epicurus, for example, showed little respect for Plato, Aristotle or Theophrastus, since he deplored all research that did not fit in with his preconceived doctrines. The Sceptics, too, would obviously distrust scientific findings, and Diogenes the Cynic lumped science together with all the rest of learning as useless or worse (Chapter Four, section 2).

And yet, mathematics, astronomy, geography and medicine flourished in the Hellenistic age as never before. For one thing, while (as Plato complained[2]) the old city-state governments had never spent much money on research, the new monarchs felt differently. So the richer among these kings proceeded to establish more permanent foundations for learning, among which the Museum at Ptolemaic Alexandria, with its subsidized scholars, was outstanding. Admittedly, royal patronage was limited and unsystematic, and often had military purposes in mind – but not always, for mathematics and medicine were among its principal beneficiaries.

Indeed, the outstanding mathematician Euclid was one of the first men of learning to reside in Alexandria (*c.* 300). His great textbook, the *Elements*, contained thirteen books (1–6 on plane geometry, 7–9 on the theory of numbers, 10 on irrationals, 11–13 on solid geometry). By this choice of subject, Euclid was preserving the tradition of Plato, many of whose pupils had continued to stress mathematical learning. Mathematical *Elements* had also been compiled by earlier scholars: but Euclid superseded them all. He did so by incorporating everything of value that they had said, so that his own work was, in essence, the summing-up of all previous Greek mathematics: the culmination, closure and stocktaking of the classical epoch that had gone before, for the benefit of the new Hellenistic world of the present and future. Euclid's *Elements* are remarkable for the sagaciously chosen five hundred axioms or theorems from which he logically and systematically deduces the results of this past activity. His proofs are rigorous and compact, his presentations symmetrical, elegant and crystal clear. The western world learnt from the *Elements* how to reason at the highest point of exactitude. No other human creation has ever demonstrated so clearly how knowledge can be derived from rational methods alone, and no book except the Bible has enjoyed so long a reign.

Strato of Lampsacus (d. *c.* 269) confirmed the separation between philosophy and science, and converted the Lyceum – of which he succeeded Theophrastus as the head – from the former to the latter. He felt strongly that the processes of nature must be explained by natural causes, not by any god or providence; and he asserted the primacy of systematic experiment over logical proof. Ctesibius, who worked at Alexandria in the same period, gave these views a practical shape and twist. Not an outstanding theoretician himself, but a talented mechanic and inventor, he was the first to construct devices employing the action of air under pressure, and created a pump equipped with plunger and valve, a water-organ, and the first accurate water-clock, in addition to improvements in artillery. We know of Ctesibius' work from his third- or second-century follower Philo of Byzantium (writer of a compendium of technology, and *Seven Wonders of the World*), and from the mathematician and inventor Hero of Alexandria, who probably lived in the first century AD. Both were serious mechanical experts, though both, at the same time, shared a great love of gadgets and devices.

Archimedes of Syracuse (d. 212) was the most far-sighted Greek mathematician of all time, a wholly original genius who advanced far beyond the frontiers of knowledge into the unknown, and was declared by Voltaire to have an imagination finer than Homer's.

In solid geometry – fascinated by its logical consistency – he outstripped Euclid, and broke entirely new ground. He was consumed by a revolutionary determination to measure first, and only demonstrate afterwards. And what he measured, above all, was curvilinear area and volume: his work on the geometry of spheres and cylinders and on cones and conic sections was outstanding. Indeed, out of all Archimedes' multifarious activity, this remained the achievement of which he was evidently proudest. For he requested the sculptors of his tombstone to engrave on it a cylinder circumscribing a globe, with the ratio 2:3 written between them. This referred to his discovery that the ratio of the volume of a sphere inscribed in a cylinder to the volume of the cylinder, and the ratio of the surface of the sphere to the cylinder's surface, are as two is to three.

Archimedes' rigorous methods for determining areas and volumes led him close to the procedures of the first seventeenth-century practitioners of the integral calculus (the branch of mathematics that deals with variable quantities, and is based on the concept of the limit). He also devised a system for expressing large numbers, which no classical Greek had achieved: his *Sand-Reckoner* shows an understanding of the nature of a numerical system far in excess of the achievement of any other ancient mathematician.

His *Plane Equilibrium* can be regarded as the pioneer scientific treatise on the first principles of mechanics, which deals with the behaviour of matter under the action of force. His pioneer work in mechanics is illustrated by his alleged remark: 'give me a place to stand [i.e. with a long enough lever] and I will move the earth'.[3] He also built further on earlier researches to produce an epoch-making work on statics (the area of mechanics dealing with bodies at rest and forces in equilibrium) and hydrostatics (the study of the equilibrium of liquids and the pressures that they exert at rest). Indeed, he virtually invented the whole science of hydrostatics, and gave it a theoretical basis. One of his discoveries was that a body immersed in water is buoyed up by a force equal to the weight of the water displaced. According to one of the legends that proliferated round his career, this conclusion dawned upon him in his bath, whereupon he ran home without his clothes, crying *heureka, heureka* – 'I have found it'.[4]

Archimedes was also an outstanding engineer. By this time the lever, pulley, wedge and windlass were already known; but he himself was plausibly credited with the discovery of a screw (*cochlias*) for raising water, which is still used in many countries to irrigate land. Popular history also ascribed to him the invention of wonderful war-machines used against the Romans in their siege of Syracuse. It was during that siege that he lost his life, for while he was engaged in drawing a mathematical figure in the sand a Roman soldier ignored his request not to interrupt his process of thought and stabbed him to death.

About twelve years younger than Archimedes was Eratosthenes of Cyrene (*c.* 275–194), who worked at Athens and then became head of the Alexandrian Library. Part scientist, part humanist, he was a polymath who (despite the sneers that this versatility always evokes) rivalled Aristotle, or Leonardo da Vinci, in the breadth and range of his knowledge and work. But his particular achievement was in the field of geography, which had received such a mighty stimulus from the conquests of Alexander. Dicaearchus of Messana (*c.* 300), for his *Life of Greece*, had made a map of the world, and Eratosthenes revised it, using his mathematical knowledge (and observation that the sunlight strikes different parts of the earth at different angles) to determine the earth's circumference with a high degree of accuracy. He was the first systematic geographer, whose *Geographica* contributed more than any other single study by anyone else to an accurate delineation of the surface of the earth.

Greek mathematical geography was largely based on astronomy, and this was the branch of applied mathematics that especially fascinated the Hellenistic world. The first Greek constructor of a mathematical scheme to explain the apparent movement of the heavenly bodies had been Eudoxus of Cnidus (*c*. 390–340), an acquaintance of Plato, whose conclusions – which illustrate the strength of mathematics, and weakness of observation, at his time – were popularized in verse by the famous *Phaenomena* of Aratus of Soli (*c*. 315–240). Heraclides Ponticus of Heraclea on the Black Sea (*c*. 388–315) put forward a new planetary system, apparently suggesting that the earth (which was now recognized to be spherical) revolves on its axis.

It was Aristarchus of Samos, however, a pupil of Strato, who achieved far more enduring fame early in the third century BC by his discovery that the earth revolves round the sun. Seleucus of Seleucia on the Tigris (?*c*. 150) supported Aristarchus' heliocentric view, but Hipparchus of Nicaea (*c*. 190 – after 126), the greatest astronomer of antiquity, felt unable (like almost everyone else) to accept this conclusion because the known facts were insufficient to make any decision possible: we must abide, he felt, by the facts of observation – which could not confirm the immense distances required for Aristarchus' cosmos. Nevertheless, Hipparchus improved observational techniques out of all recognition, displaying a special talent for the selection of relevant data, which included Babylonian and Alexandrian records of eclipses, in addition to his own remarkably exact findings. He thus became the first to evolve a satisfactory theory for the motion of the sun and moon. Moreover, in the words of the Roman polymath Pliny the elder, Hipparchus 'did a bold thing, that would be reprehensible even for God – he dared to schedule the stars for posterity, and tick off the heavenly bodies by name on a list – thus bequeathing the heavens as a heritage to all humankind, supposing anyone could be found to claim the legacy!'[5]

Hellenistic astronomy lacked the close environmental control needed for the infinite repetitiveness of laboratory experiments, and the optical and other instruments at its disposal were limited. Yet its discoveries, and the developments of scientific method that accompanied them and made them possible, had been extraordinary. The sophistication of these techniques is illustrated by an astronomical clock, or calendrical computer, of *c*. 75–50 BC, found at the island of Aegilia or Ogylus, now Anticythera, between the Peloponnese and Crete. In this most complex of all the scientific objects that have come down to us from antiquity, an elaborate system of no less than thirty bronze dials and cog-wheels is applied to the plotting of the movements of sun, moon and stars.

Medicine, too, made notable advances during the Hellenistic age. The science was, of course, by no means new; for example, a vase-painting of 480–470 had displayed a whole series of medical procedures that were already in operation. Traditionally, the best-known medical centres of Greece were the shrines of Asclepius, hero and god of healing, especially at Epidaurus and Cos (founded *c.* 350). The sanctuaries included sanatoria, where healing took the form of incubation (sleeping in the temple and receiving guidance by dreams), described by the fifth-century poet of the Old Comedy, Aristophanes.[6] Many of the recorded cures display this element of miraculous intervention or auto-suggestion; but use was also made of dietetic régimes, baths and exercise.

How far the leading doctors of the day derived their science from the priests is hard to discover, but it seems likely that the foundation of the Cos temple was due to the disciples of Hippocrates, the greatest of all Greek physicians. Hippocrates, who was born on that island in the latter half of the fifth century, revolutionized medicine: researching, teaching and practising at many centres in the Greek world, he introduced reason into medical science at about the same time as Socrates was performing a similar function for philosophy. The Hippocratic Oath, however, prescribing the ethics of a doctor in memorable terms, seems, in its present form at least, to have been composed after 400; and the fifty-eight works in the Hippocratic Corpus likewise seem mostly to have been written at that time or, more usually, in the Hellenistic Age, of which they thus form one of the major achievements.

The various Hippocratic advances meant that the Greeks could now employ a system of medicine based not only on theoretical principles but on gradually accumulated observation. Moreover, Greek medicine managed to maintain itself as an autonomous subject, because of its obvious social relevance. Salaried public physicians had already been known earlier, but were now to be found much more widely. Medical writers were not slow to praise the profession, declaring it suitable for philosophers and demigods; though this insistence on assimilating their profession with philosophy – based on the traditional Greek preference for studies of an abstract nature – could be regarded as the sign of an inferiority complex that was never entirely overcome.

Nevertheless, the Hellenistic epoch witnessed practical developments in medicine fully worthy of the theoretical studies that were being undertaken during the period. Their most important centre was now the school founded at Alexandria, which, above all, developed the science of anatomy. The creation of this branch of medicine owed much to ancient Egyptian learning. It also owed a very great deal to its royal patrons, the Ptolemies, who in addition to paying the staff of the Alexandrian Faculty (linked in some way with the Museum), gave them opportunities, hitherto unavailable, for the dissection of human bodies by providing the corpses of criminals for the purpose. It was due to these facilities that anatomy, backed by much-improved surgical methods and instruments, led the way in Hellenistic medical research.

Thus Herophilus of Chalcedon, who had moved to Alexandria in the first half of the third century, employed dissection in order to transform knowledge of the brain, eye, duodenum, liver and reproductive organs. Though an eminent scholar, he was chiefly guided by the practical tasks and problems facing doctors, of whose obligations to the public he had a particularly high conception. Erasistratus, his younger colleague and perhaps pupil, made important discoveries in relation to digestion and the vascular (circulatory) system (though understanding of the circulation of the blood still lay in the future). If Herophilus is to be called the founder of anatomy, Erasistratus was the creator of physiology. Though a cautious clinical practitioner, he blended his careful, quantitative observation with flashes of bold, even rash, speculation. He was also the father of psychiatry: the first man to realize the existence of diseases of the nervous system and their possible causes.

Herophilus and Erasistratus represented the high-water mark of Hellenistic biology and medicine. After their deaths, dissection appears to have ceased. At this period, too, the profession became divided into warring sects, of which Dogmatists and Empiricists were among the best-known. The Dogmatists, followers of Herophilus, claimed to follow the classical Hippocratic methods of deduction, arguing that knowledge of the human condition and of what causes diseases is indispensable and can be obtained only by the employment of reasoning and conjecture to supplement experience. The Empirical school, on the other hand, were contemptuous of such abstract reasoning about what is invisible and preferred to base their conclusions on direct observation of patients' visible symptoms, rather in the spirit of contemporary philosophers who were concentrating on practical guidance of the individual. Thus Serapion of Alexandria (c. 200-150) – the school's founder (or second founder after Philinus of Cos, c. 250) – pronounced that it is not the cause but the cure of sickness which concerns the physician, not how we digest but what is digestible.

The scientific history of the Hellenistic age terminated with Posidonius of Syrian Apamea (c. 135-50). His works, like those of so many of his predecessors, are now lost: but he was evidently a polymath on a scale even more stupendous than Eratosthenes. Settling in Rhodes, and developing many contacts with Rome, he devoted himself not only to history but to every branch of science, not excluding ethnology. One of his motives was at long last to bring philosophical and scientific studies together again. Another was to illustrate his Stoic conviction that heaven and earth and all parts of the cosmos continually exchange influences with one another – and to suggest that this mutual 'sympathy' made the anti-scientific bias of most of his fellow-Stoics seem altogether misguided.

The observations Posidonius made and recorded on his widespread travels encouraged him to try to determine the distance and magnitude of the sun, to calculate the diameter of the earth, to draw a new map of the world, and to give an accurate description of the life and currents of the ocean, demonstrating the dependence of the tides upon the phases of the moon. When Aristotle had written of meteorology, he limited it to the study of the processes, conditions and phenomena of the atmosphere. But Posidonius, interpreting the same science much more widely, saw it as explaining the whole structure of the outer and upper world, within the context of a universal system which harmoniously blends matter, mind and spirit.

His almost unlimited range made him vulnerable to charges of superficiality. Yet he was the most learned man of his time; and people admiringly called him 'the athlete', with good reason. It was Posidonius' enormous achievement to collect and reshape a vast quantity of inherited Hellenic and Hellenistic erudition in a huge variety of fields, and to hand on the whole of this massive material to the Roman world and the Renaissance.

Two centuries earlier, as we saw, Hellenistic science had got off to a remarkable start. Aristotle and Theophrastus had laid the foundations for systematic research into imposingly numerous branches of learning. This inspired heady confidence. In the words of a poet of the Middle and New Comedy, Alexis of Thurii (c. 375-275), 'discovery attends on every quest, except for renegades who shirk the toil.... If men have probed worlds far remote, can problems of this earth, this common home to which we're born, defy them?'[7] The historian Polybius was later of the same opinion: 'all branches of science have made such progress among us that instruction in most of them has assumed the proportions of a system'.[8]

To us the story, for all its splendours, seems more patchy. Various lines of scientific thinking were carried so far, but then no further: continuous development, both in theory and practice, failed to materialize. The Hellenistic age knew nothing of chemistry, and little of physics or geology. For, in effect, the old classical aims had not been greatly changed or improved or expanded: aside from the unique genius of Archimedes, it was only that observations were better, and explanations more elaborate. There were various reasons why matters did not advance further. In the first place, although science had established its independence from philosophy, philosophy was still the goddess to be served – which must have been why mathematics, which was traditionally close to it, so far outstripped the other sciences. Besides, the dread of inconvenient research felt by the quasi-religious Stoic and Epicurean schools – and the general weakening of rationality which was the product of these fears – could not fail to exert a deadening influence.

Moreover, the time for advances in applied, experimental science had not yet come. For one thing, the basic laws of the universe, and the methods by which they operated, were even considerably less well known than they are today; and even when Hellenistic scientists propounded theories about such matters, they lacked the apparatus to subject their conjectures to experimental tests. But they also lacked the inclination to do so, and after breathtaking beginnings never consistently faced the unfettered application of the observational method to the problems of nature. Technology, as we saw in connexion with industry, was not thought of as worth trying to develop. Even the Ptolemies (for all their interest in bigger and better war machines) never thought of harnessing the inventiveness of a Ctesibius to practical application. Indeed – such was the continuing classical contempt for manual labour and the crafts – Ctesibius knew very well that as a theoretician he stood socially far higher than as an engineer or artisan (*technites*); and Archimedes was said by Plutarch to have 'looked down upon the work of an engineer and everything that ministers to the needs of life as ignoble and vulgar',[9] though whether this was really the view of the unique Archimedes, as it certainly was of Plutarch, we cannot say. At all events Hellenistic educationalists, whether aware of the possibility of technical development or not, were far too geared to the literary and rhetorical systems of the day to make the attempt, and simply refrained from doing so.

The Hellenistic age had begun with marvellous contributions to the quest for scientific truth. They formed part of a general urge to grasp reality; and an extremely notable part at that. Moreover, they continued with sporadic brilliance, though advances were all too often a matter of degree rather than of kind; and before long, as the drive towards realism was halted by a contrary wave of irrationality, even the talents of a polymath such as Posidonius did little to prevent them from petering out.

2 Literary and Artistic Realism

The drive towards finding out about reality which had set science, for a time, on such a prominent course, was paralleled in literature and art. It was a trend that had been given vivid expression in the harrowing character studies of Euripides. Aristotle too, showed in many passages of his *Ethics* how closely he kept a watch on social behaviour: while the *Metaphysics* reveal his realistic awareness that men and women can only live with pure reason for extremely short periods, and that in order to get an accurate view of their natures it is essential to study the irrational features in their behaviour. It was true that he and many of his followers generally believed that a person is born with his or her character ready-made. Yet this did not affect the keenness with which they noted and amassed evidence on differing patterns of human behaviour and on the relation they bore to free will.

One by-product of these diligent collections and classifications was the *Characters* of Aristotle's leading pupil Theophrastus. The title means 'features of character', for the work consists of thirty concentrated sketches of people who each possess an undesirable personal characteristic (there may have been a counterpart of more agreeable features, now lost). Dry and satirical and highly realistic, the author has no specific moral purpose in mind, but builds up a series of razor-sharp social observations, distinguishing the actions of each of his personages by some ridiculous failing or foible that they display – the lesser failures only, for the stronger vices are omitted. These are stock men and women who are neither very rich nor very poor, belonging to the huge and growing intermediate, non-political categories of the Greek population.

The literary antecedents of the *Characters*, if any, cannot be traced with any certainty. Probably the work is, to some extent, original, at least in regard to its amusing manner (Theophrastus is also said to have written a book on *The Absurd*). But it is possible that the *Characters* belong to a tradition of rhetorical handbooks or literary *Poetics* (no longer extant), after the fashion of Aristotle's work of that name, but relating especially to the characters of the comic stage. If Aristotle's work on *Comedy* had survived, a close connexion might well have been apparent.

It is no surprise, therefore, to learn that one of Theophrastus' pupils, for a time, was the outstanding practitioner of the New Comedy, Menander (*c.* 342–292). Menander wrote more than a hundred plays; following remarkable discoveries of papyri in recent years, substantial passages or fragments of ten of these are now available (the best of them is the *Epitrepontes* (Arbitrators), which is reasonably complete). The works of his seventy fellow playwrights of the New Comedy have not come down to us. Prominent among them was his older contemporary Philemon (probably a Syracusan), who wrote his first play in 326. In their own day Philemon was the more successful of the two; but Menander was notable enough for Ptolemy I Soter to invite him to Alexandria. Among posterity he gained extraordinary, dominant influence, extending from the Latin dramatists Plautus and Terence, in the third and second centuries BC, down to Molière and Richard Brinsley Sheridan. Menander has had the most abundant literary offspring of any Greek or Latin author.

He was keenly interested in human emotions – at a more practical, down-to-earth level than the tragic intensity of Euripides. This was part of his profound concern for realistic portrayal. The people Menander depicts, people like the subjects of Theophrastus' *Characters* and prostitutes (*hetairai*) and slaves, represent a big advance, in terms of realism, upon the stock figures of Aristophanes' fifth-century Athenian Old Comedy; or even, as far as we can tell, upon the more or less caricatured types of the heterogeneous, experimental Middle Comedy of Antiphanes and the long-lived Alexis, who won their first competitions in 385 and the 350s respectively. Menander's personages, instead, assume the three-dimensional shapes of individual human beings. This was why another Aristophanes, the scholar from Byzantium (*c.* 257–180), regarded him (somewhat exaggeratedly) as the second greatest of all Greek poets, because of his representation of life in such faithful terms: 'O Menander and Life,' he rhetorically asked, 'which of you imitated the other?'[10]

The 'life' which Menander reflected was, once again, not that of the Old Comedy of Aristophanes' Athenian synonym, for whereas the Old Comedy had been determinedly political, Menander's personages only show an occasional and indirect awareness of the outside world's excitements and convulsions. For in general, in pursuance of a trend already noted in Theophrastus, Menander preferred to detach the people he was portraying from important political activity – just as most men and women are removed from it in actual life. That is to say, like the Middle Comedy that had shortly preceded him he turned his attention instead to personal and domestic problems, which were gradually taking the place of civic affairs as people's principal interest and preoccupation.

At the same time he also deliberately imposed certain restrictions on his own realism – restrictions symbolized, one might say, by the fact that his actors, although clothed (unlike those of earlier comic drama) in ordinary everyday costume, nevertheless still wore masks. But there was more to it than that. For the problems Menander selected for dramatic treatment were not so much a typical selection from real life, or even from the particular section of it which he chose to portray, as the complaisantly accepted products of an established theatrical tradition: foundling children and their recognition tokens, kidnapped daughters, clever scheming slaves, extramarital pregnancies, costly entanglements with prostitutes, or the loss of merchant ships carrying family fortunes. No doubt all such things happened (and so, occasionally, did the improbable coincidences with which he laced his stories); but the concentration on these relatively few plots lent them a somewhat hackneyed and threadbare appearance, and imparted a rather lopsided, distorted view of life which owed scarcely less to mythology, it has been suggested, than to the realities of daily existence.

However, within a more or less unvarying structure of five acts (divided by choral interludes), these flaws were concealed or papered over by many ingenious constructional continuities, cunningly dovetailed interlockings of events, and rapidly flowing dialogues – all techniques with which Menander juggled like a master. By such means, although he does not delineate his personages in any psychological depth, his vivid, economical portrayal of detail skilfully coordinates their characterization with the development of his themes. Moreover, like Philemon, who had already specialized in such effects, he has some surprises in store for us; thus the characters, although standing for recognized contemporary stock types – the professional soldier, the professional cook, the *hetaira* – often stray with quite surprising nonconformity from the norms they might be expected to represent. For Menander, like many of his contemporaries, is deeply interested in human peculiarity.

Realism is also fostered by his handling of language. His metre, the iambic trimeter, though literary in origin, provides a kind of resemblance to the rhythms of contemporary spoken language. And while his personages, whatever their human qualities or social backgrounds, all normally speak the same dialect (approaching the dawning *koine* universal to the Hellenistic world), not only does it possess a markedly colloquial character, but the dramatist also allows a number of these men and women to exhibit distinctive tricks or habits of speech, subtly varied according to changes of situation and mood.

Menander is famous for the moralizing epigrams that crop up at appropriate intervals: 'whom the gods love die young' (asserted to annoy an old man) and probably 'I am a man; and think nothing that is human to be not mine' (spoken, as quoters fail to appreciate, by an unsympathetic character). But his special gifts lie rather in the nuances of social interaction, presented with inoffensive irony. He can rapidly delineate not only a person but a relationship: and he can make the situation it presents convincing, immediate, distinctive, a source of tears or laughter or both. His characters do not usually explain themselves explicitly, but one can detect their feelings and motives from what they say and do, which is, after all, how one perceives people in real life. There is controlled tension between what is familiar and what is exceptional: between convention and reality. That is to say, Menander's personages were as realistic as the conventions determining the drama of the day – or his chosen interpretation of them – permitted.

One of these conventions was the requirement of a happy ending. Despite all the conflicts and foolish, unnecessary sufferings – in the relations, for example, between parent and child, or between married couples and lovers – the good is sure to prevail, and crime, pomposity and villainy will be frustrated by kindness and friendship. Here, then, is realism modified by optimism (despite far from optimistic utterances as the plays have proceeded on their way). Not that human nature, however, even if it prevails over grim Chance and Misunderstanding (*Agnoia*), is always presented as reasonable: the pattern of qualities which Menander builds up into a character includes a fair measure of the irrationality noted by Aristotle and Theophrastus.

In the next generation, the remarkable literary mimes of Theocritus of Syracuse, and then those of Herodas, introduced a new sort of realism. The genre was not entirely new. In Greece, as elsewhere, mimetic dances had been popular from early times. They had first been presented, perhaps, by a soloist, and then by three or more performers together, who depicted short scenes from daily life or (heavily burlesqued) mythology, speaking or singing to the accompaniment of kettle-drums and cymbals, and making use of gestures and facial expressions, with emphasis rather upon character and situation than upon action. Such performances were closely associated with the name of the fifth-century Syracusan Sophron who gave literary form to these pieces, dividing his compositions into men's and women's mimes according to the sex of his characters (and, it was claimed, influencing the dialogue form of Plato).

In the centuries that followed, mime invaded the theatre in a variety of guises, and indeed replaced tragedy and, eventually, comedy too, as the only truly popular dramatic form. Closely linked with mime was the 'merry tragedy' or *phlyax* play (from *phluaros*, silly talk). This was particularly associated with the name of Rhinthon (*c.* 300), born at Taras and perhaps a resident of Syracuse, whose masked actors, wearing grotesquely padded costumes and enormous phalli, presented ludicrous versified scenes from daily life, and burlesque parodies of mythology.

The contemporary woman poet Nossis of Locri Epizephyrii praised Rhinthon for the invention of 'tragic' *phlyakes*, which seems to signify that he introduced a new literary and cultural note. In Alexandria, too, Sopater of Paphos introduced a mocking philosophical element into his mimes; for instance *The Gauls* – from which our longest surviving *phlyax* fragment comes – made fun of the Stoics.

Mimes of a much more realistic character soon became popular with people who wanted a more direct and unencumbered, though still humorous, view of the world. In particular, Theocritus (*c.* 300–260?), himself a product of Syracuse, gave an entirely new life to this kind of composition, including among his short poems a number which are unmistakably based on mimes by Sophron, adapted into his own sparkling form of hexameter verse. Several of Theocritus' poems (not his pastoral pieces – Chapter Four, section 3) resemble mimes, and may have been intended for semi-dramatic recitation. The second in his collection, *The Sorceress*, recalls that the largest surviving fragment of Sophron is also about popular magic. The colloquial ordinary speech of the fourteenth poem – a dialogue between Aeschinas and Thyonichus, full of clipped phrases, ellipses and proverbs – is also suggestive of mime. But it is above all the fifteenth poem, a presentation of two ladies of Syracusan origin attending the festival of Adonis at Alexandria in about 274 BC which, although containing echoes of the New Comedy (a witless slave), presents the most mime-like appearance of all his writings; Sophron, too, had composed a mime portraying women at Corinth's Isthmian festival.

Theocritus' women are quite well off, but trivial and low-brow, not to say vulgar. He is brilliantly deploying his powerful realistic gifts, laced with a strong sense of the ridiculous, to make fun of a vast section of contemporary urban life – just the people that the poet's refined circle despised. He brings to life their platitudinous thoughts and sentiments with unique felicity, and the joke is enhanced by the highly inappropriate literary diction that he puts into the mouths of these talkative females, adapting the originally popular mime-form to elegant, allusive verse.

It was probably in the next Egyptian reign, that of Ptolemy III Euergetes (246–221), that another type of literary mime came to the fore, developed by the talented 'Herodas (or Herondas), who may have come from Cos. Seven of his pieces, and fragments of others, have survived. These short, pithy, pungent sketches, sometimes adapted from Sophron and other writers of mimes, are composed in a mixed language of Herodas' own imagination and concoction; he employs an archaic variety of the iambic metre, the traditional metre of satire. In these *mimiambi*, as they were called, the characters include the ill-tempered

Cynno and naive Cocale, depositing their offerings at Asclepius' shrine at Cos; Bitinna, who is jealous because her lover has slept with a slave-girl; the oily and offensive shoemaker Cerdon, who offers a side-line in leather sex-substitutes for women; the crooked and unctuous brothel-keeper Battarus; and Metrotime, who urges a school-teacher to flog her drop-out son.

Herodas' *mimiambi* were probably recited by a speaker who personi-fied the different characters by variations of tone, style and gesture. As in the mimes of Theocritus, part of the joke is likely to escape us, because it derives from a highly naturalistic and realistic treatment paradoxi-cally presented in a thoroughly artificial dialect, replete with the erudite allusion of book poetry: popular content and literary speech are sur-prisingly and shockingly blended, for the entertainment of Herodas' sophisticated friends – so that Metrotime's illiterate boy, for example, employs entirely inappropriate poetic expressions. Nevertheless, despite this somewhat recondite form of humour, the sharp satire and acute reportage still strike home. With crisp finish and relentless precision, Herodas is unveiling part of the reality from which earlier literary society had traditionally averted its eyes. Later, the iambics of Cercidas, deploring the condition of the poor without any illusions, follow the same realistic tradition, abandoning humour in favour of a serious message.

Certain epigrammatists, too, had shown a similar trend at the outset of the Hellenistic age, notably Leonidas of Taras. Writing in language quite as artificial as that of Theocritus and Herodas, Leonidas gives a long, hard look, unhampered by misplaced optimism, at the lives of fishermen and peasants and other poor people, of whose miseries insuf-ficient account had been taken.

At the same period historians, too, were complaining of their fellow-writers' refusal to face facts. Thus Duris of Samos (*c.* 340–260) regarded *mimesis*, imitation, as an essential part of the historian's task, neglected in his view by his predecessors Theopompus of Chios (author of *Hellenica* and *Philippica*) and Ephorus of Cyme (*Universal History*).[11] Duris was using the term *mimesis* primarily to signify a vivid presentation of events in which emotion can be given free rein, but he also intended the term to stand for an ideal of 'reality' which he felt that historians ought to aim at. Yet he was too uncritical to achieve it himself, and it has been suggested that Hieronymus of Cardia (d. 250), a far more authentically realistic historian, wrote his authoritative *History of the Successors* in a deliberate attempt to offset Duris' exuberance and provide a more accurate and realistic 'imitation' of events.

Subsequently the conflict between the two sorts of historical 'realism' was renewed. Phylarchus, in the third century BC, wrote in Duris' colourful, melodramatic manner, for which he was sternly criticized by Polybius (c 200 – after 118). Polybius' own determination to achieve the highest historical standards, to see things and people clearly and steadily and whole, to detach himself from the past and discern it objectively as it was, represents the culmination of the urge towards realistic presentation that was one of the keynotes of Hellenistic literature. For Polybius observed and declared, first, that the whole Mediterranean world had been totally transformed since it first began to come under the control of Rome, and secondly, that Rome had gained this control because of its strength, and not just through the operation of the fashionable deity Chance.

These were tough conclusions but realistic ones, and their truth involved, and created, a revolution in the writing of history. As Polybius himself emphatically pointed out, once Rome's domination had stamped a unitary character on the course of events, universal history automatically became the only historical form adequate to deal truthfully with this phenomenon, since a plurality of separate or separable narratives could no longer rise to the occasion.[12] No wonder, then, that Polybius praised Ephorus of Cyme as the first historian ever to have attempted a universal history (even if, in practice, Ephorus had limited this endeavour to the Greek world). As for the fashionable sort of specialized monographs on limited themes, Polybius thought they were unrealistic and useless: in the new world conditions, he felt, only a vast, universal canvas could do justice to the novel necessities that were now imposing themselves.

That he has been denounced as all head and no heart is a tribute to the realistic interpretation which he aimed at and achieved. True, this achievement was not quite unbroken and invariable, for he could at times show bias and rancour, especially when he was writing of earlier historians. Another fault lies in his language, a literary version of the ordinary Greek of his time, the *koine*, but crabbed, verbose and sloppy. It is only because his style is so dreary that he falls a little short of the greatest historians of all time, not because of what he says or fails to say. For he understood the true nature of history better than anyone ever had before: better even than the great Athenian Thucydides, since Polybius' pragmatic approach showed keener realism than the patterns imposed on events by his predecessor's overpowering intellect could ever achieve. After Polybius, no one came anywhere near his objective standards for centuries.

The art of the Hellenistic period, while following on with direct continuity from the art of the previous age, at the same time rivalled contemporary literature in its novel, determined drive towards realism. The artists of archaic (pre-classical) and classical Greece, like their near-eastern forerunners for thousands of years past, had consciously adopted forms regarded as timeless and superior to the quirks of ordinary nature. Balanced symmetry, ideal serenity had been the keynotes. But already early in the fifth century frontal poses had begun to unstiffen and loosen up, and, by the middle of the fourth, statues were beginning to display softer modelling and more sensitive rhythms, and seemed at last as if they could move and breathe like real, spontaneously behaving human beings. The great sculptors of the age anticipated scientists such as Herophilus in their close acquaintance with anatomy (though they still employed their knowledge in the service of established canons), and were able to represent drapery exactly as well.

Scopas of Paros, working in this period, was a sculptor of drama and passion. The Athenian Praxiteles displayed the hinges of the human body, and examined its movements, employing eminent painters to add artful colouring. His Hermes at Olympia (*c.* 343) shows an accurately perceived displacement of weight, depicted by means of sinuous curves. Above all it was Praxiteles who devised nearly every formal idea for the female nude, in his efforts to portray the life-like essence of womanhood (Chapter Three, section 4). The same sculptor also extended his realism, we are told, to the depiction of children, old people, and exotic blacks – all of whom continued thereafter to be rendered by Hellenistic sculptors with keen and not unsympathetic observation. His son Cephisodotus developed a fashion for complex intertwined groups of multiple figures. Other Praxiteleans refined their modelling still further, in order to achieve sensuous or sentimental effects that had never been attempted before.

The Apoxyomenos (man scraping himself), created at a somewhat later date in the same century by Lysippus of Sicyon, shows a new set of physical proportions (smaller head, more slender body), a new degree of anatomical fidelity, a new sense of movement, and a new three-dimensional composition, so that those who wanted to see such figures properly must walk right round them. If we still had the bronze Helios or Sun-god (Colossus) of Rhodes, executed by Lysippus' pupil Chares of Lindos in 292–280, we should find – to judge from small-scale surviving adaptations – that the deity was standing in a pose and stance of equal liveliness, with his head and torso swivelling, and a hand shading his eyes. The figure was on a truly enormous scale: new skills in bronze-casting made it possible to create a free-standing figure more than a hundred feet high. This Wonder of the World stood beside the Rhodian harbour (not bestriding it, as Renaissance reconstructions preferred). But during an earthquake in 227/226 the statue collapsed at the knees, and despite all the relief contributions received by Rhodes from other cities it could not be restored. A millennium later nine hundred camels were needed to carry away the scrap metal.

Meanwhile another pupil of Lysippus created the most famous female statue of the age. This was Eutychides who, like his master, came from Sicyon, but worked away from the Greek mainland. Pre-eminent among his works was a gilded bronze statue of Tyche (Fortune) at Antioch in Syria. As marble copies and coins indicate, this fashionable goddess was shown seated, resting her foot on the figure of the river god Orontes; she held wheat ears in her hand, and the Seleucid monarchs Seleucus I Nicator and Antiochus I Soter were shown crowning her with a wreath, though their figures (which have not survived) may have been added by a later sculptor. The Tyche of Eutychides is virtually a programme piece for the new realistic ideas: her figure presents an extremely cunning three-dimensional structure of lines and folds set obliquely in different planes, so that our eyes cannot remain fixed on any single point.

The climax of these methods – and the proof once and for all, if further proof is needed, that Hellenistic art was not a decadent phenomenon – is to be seen in the Victory (Nike) of Samothrace, now in the Louvre. The masterpiece of an unknown sculptor, this statue of a goddess whose cult had received great stimulus from Alexander's victories and ministrations was created to celebrate a naval success by some later monarch or city – perhaps Rhodes, after it had helped the Romans to defeat Antiochus III the Great off Myonnesus in 190. Originally tinted, the figure alights exultantly upon a ship's prow, which in the location for which it was designed stood diagonally within a large two-level fountain filled with a mass of water cascading downwards between rocks and flowing past the monument on either side. As Victory leans forward to meet the rush of the wind, a calculated counter-twist or torsion of her swirling, wind-swept robes – a refinement of the simpler Lysippean spiral – conveys a breathtaking sense of movement on the wing.

At the very time when this new study of drapery as an object of independent interest was so dramatically developing, another opposite, yet cognate, aspect of realism had also begun to find vivid new forms of expression: the study of the naked or partly naked female form (Chapter Three, section 4). A superb marble Bathing Aphrodite, preserved in good copies, was possibly the work of a certain Daedalsas of Bithynia of the mid-third century BC. The sensuous crouching figure, her plump

stomach scored with horizontal rows of wrinkles, displays another pronounced twist, the body and legs facing in one direction, and the head
in the other.

Surviving copies of other Hellenistic Aphrodites are mostly chilly and
boring and the very opposite of sexually exciting. Yet a single extant
original of second-century date, the Venus of Milo (the island of Melos)
in the Louvre at Paris, is a superb evocation of womanhood. The planes
of the goddess' body are so ample and tranquil that their complexity at
first escapes notice: but they move and turn, on closer inspection, in
multiple, contrasting directions, and there are piquant contrasts, too,
between her smooth body and complicated drapery. Classical purity
and austerity have not been abandoned, but they are modified by all
the new ideas, utilized to exploit and elaborate the Hellenistic taste for
realistic interpretations.

While these various concepts of Aphrodite were being developed and
perfected, Hellenistic sculptural realism was moving to further triumphant achievements of quite another kind as well. These were the
bronze groups of statuary dedicated by King Attalus I of Pergamum
to the goddess Athena in his capital, perhaps c. 200 BC, to celebrate
the victories over the Galatians (Gauls) that gave him his title Soter
(Saviour). Owing to the mobility of Greek artists, Hellenistic 'schools' of
sculpture are hard to identify: but the group working at Pergamum
deserves such a title, since this was the only royal capital where sculptors
were engaged on extensive and important public works, with ample
official patronage behind them. One of the artists who created the
monument was a certain Antigonus (also a writer on art), who may
have been the biographer of that name from Carystus.

This was one of the most ambitious sculptural complexes ever attempted. The statue of the Dying Gaul (of which a fine copy can be
seen in the Capitoline Museum at Rome) was one of a circle of half-
recumbent figures whose slanting bodies converged to lead the eye
inwards and upwards to the contorted group in the middle. This centre-
piece, the 'Ludovisi Group' – designed, as can be seen from a copy in
the Roman National Museum, to be seen from every side – consisted of
a defeated, desperate Gaul and his dying wife, whose body he is holding
up with one arm as he plunges a dagger into his own neck with the
other. It is an extravagantly theatrical work, in which the wild tension
of the man's pose strikes a violent painful contrast with the limp,
inanimate form of the woman. To modern eyes, however, the Dying
Gaul among the circle of figures surrounding this central ensemble is
more poignant. His stricken figure combines the traditional simplifying

pattern of Greek classicism with the novel directness of observation from nature, and emotional impact, which were such features of the new age.

There is also a message, however. The Gaul is a foreigner, and the sculptor is conscious of this. But he does not see the man in a patronizing way. It is a strange thing that the conquerors have been omitted from the monument altogether. Only the vanquished are shown – not as embodiments of evil, but in all the defiant, savage grandeur and agony of their defeat. It is by this oblique, sophisticated means that the Pergamene victory is enhanced; while at the same time the tragedy and suffering of warfare, however heroic and necessary it may have been, are universalized, as they had been in the *Iliad* long ago and would again be in Virgil's *Aeneid*.

These statues are all more than life-size. But four groups of smaller figures made of bronze – a number of which survive in marble copies – were also erected by Attalus I Soter on the Acropolis of Athens, in honour of the same victory. The groups represented the battles of the gods against the giants, of the Athenians against the Amazons, of the Athenians once more against the Persians at the battle of Marathon (490), and (in the immediate past) of the Pergamenes against the Gauls. The deliberate juxtaposition of these themes claims for Pergamum's repulse of the barbarians a godlike glory equal to the renown that Athens had won in days gone by. And indeed Athena, to whom the monument was dedicated, was the patron deity not only of Athens but also of Pergamum, through the city's legendary founder Telephus, son of the priestess of the goddess. Building on this link, Eumenes I (d. 241) had brought Athenian artists into his new kingdom, and his successor Attalus I Soter (an early example of an art collector) imported Athenian works of art, including those of the fifth century: so that these new sculptures he commissioned combine the baroque realism of the latest Hellenistic style with deliberate echoes of the classical Parthenon.

This type of excitable, dynamic art reached its climax in a statuary group in the Vatican museum, which represents Laocoön and his two sons writhing in the grip of a monstrous serpent. The scene is from the Trojan cycle; Laocoön, the son of King Priam of Troy, and a priest of Apollo, had shown distrust of the wooden horse that the Greeks insinuated into the city, but Athena sent a huge snake which crushed him and his sons to death. This virtuoso structure of complex cross-rhythms is deliberately intended to shock by its fierce expression of physical tension and anguish; the artists are exploiting the clinical interest in the human physique that was aroused by the current anatomical researches of Hellenistic scientists such as Herophilus and Erasistratus. The work, as we have it, may be an original of the second century BC;

or it may be a copy made in the first century AD and taken from such an original (if that is the case, the original may have portrayed one of the two sons differently, or omitted him altogether). The sculptors, Hagesandrus, Polydorus and Athenodorus, came from Rhodes, which was still a leading centre of their art; but it is possible that the Laocoön was made for royal Pergamum.

Other sculptors of the time showed the human body in languid stillness instead. The massively muscular, sleeping Barberini Faun at Munich echoes the Dionysiac satyr theme that appealed to Hellenistic city-dwellers. An excellent copy of a Greek original of *c.* 200–150 BC (which stimulated sculptors of the Italian Renaissance), this study of satisfied physical exhaustion once again displays complete mastery of anatomical understanding. But this absorption in the complexities of the human frame could also lead to the depiction of brainless toughs, such as a Heracles (the 'Farnese Hercules') made by Glycon in the first century BC.

The same serious interest in bodily details and peculiarities – as well as in the social or pathetic or philosophical reflections that they evoked – prompted Greek sculptors not only to follow up Praxiteles' taste for the realistic depiction of children, old people and foreigners, but to express a taste, conveniently described as 'miserabilistic', for depicting hunchback dwarfs and old people of a particularly eccentric or forbidding appearance, such as craggy fishermen and maudlin female drunkards. Such themes were sometimes employed for large-scale statues, but generally seemed more suitable for small-scale figures which did not need to conform to traditional canons of subject-matter and manner. Alexandria, in particular, developed this picturesque, anecdotal style. An excellent example is a little bronze figure of a frantically straining boy-jockey (*c.* 150–100), found off Cape Artemision and now at the National Museum in Athens, where he is reunited with his mount. This is a closer and more detailed impression of life observed in action than can be provided by most larger works.

From the late fourth century onwards, there was a notable production of terracotta statuettes reflecting everyday life in this sort of way. They are known as 'Tanagra' figures, after the city in Boeotia where many were found, although their principal centre of production was probably Athens, anticipated, perhaps from *c.* 350, by Taras in south Italy. Subsequently, from the later third century, another major producer of these statuettes was Myrina, south of Pergamum, which first adopted the styles of the 'Tanagran' figurines and then struck out by the production of amusing and distinctive types of its own; while their colleagues at Alexandria, true to their custom, added a note of farcical caricature.

These were objects made from a mould, or from several moulds in combination – the creations of a relatively large-scale industry – and in consequence they have sometimes been dismissed as scarcely art at all. But such disparagements are often derived from the misleading classical idea that small objects must necessarily be less important than larger ones: whereas in fact at their best these little figures, while intentionally far removed from classical solemnity, display an inimitably graceful style and freedom of pose. Many of the figures represent the characters of everyday life, barbers, bakers and cooks; and they tell us what ordinary urban Greeks – the characters of Menander – thought about, liked and found amusing. A Myrina group of two women gossiping on a couch (perhaps a married lady advising a young bride) is typical for its slightly, but not excessively, sentimental charm, mildly satirical yet not without sympathy, but above all for the lively accuracy with which the momentary attitudes of the figures are captured.

Meanwhile, small-scale statuary in other media sometimes reached quite as impressive levels of quality as any larger work. One of the most talented productions of the age is a small bronze dancing girl in the Metropolitan Museum at New York, known as the Baker statuette and perhaps datable to about 230 BC. The figure displays a subtle treatment of drapery that could not have been bettered in any full-size statue. It is designed as a sharply ridged diagonal pattern of triangles set in different planes, a more developed version of the Fortune of Eutychides made two or three generations earlier.

The Roman historian, natural historian, and amateur art critic Pliny the elder, writing in the first century AD, declared that 'art' – he is referring to the art of statuary – ceased to exist from the 290s to the 150s BC.[13] This surprising assertion, comfortably reflecting an old-fashioned classical taste, was possibly encouraged by the drying-up of his literary sources for the period, so that he had no information to go on. But, whatever the cause, it was a strangely misguided artistic judgement of a period that witnessed remarkable achievements. For the best of the Hellenistic sculptors, while still respectful of the overpowering past, had thrown off many of its oppressive norms and limitations. They were deeply interested in exploring the mechanics of perception, and enthusiastically accepted the alluring opportunity to express the results in their art. Until the last century of the Hellenistic period introduced a boring taste for Neo-Attic nostalgia, it was always greater realism that beckoned, including the careful portrayal of emotion. And that is what the public wanted, too. The numerous ancient descriptions of these statues (ekphraseis, a recognized literary form) continually and emphatically praise and admire their faithfulness to nature, even to the extent of disregarding almost every other technical aspect of their sculptor's achievement.

The faithfulness was not, of course, complete (any more than it was in contemporary portraiture – Chapter Three, section 3): the idealistic tradition saw to that. Besides, what first-class artist does not impose his own pattern on what would otherwise be just the more unimaginative kind of photographic accuracy?

The tendency towards vigorous realism that is to be seen in the statues of the Hellenistic age reappears in its major reliefs, which are so important that they virtually form a separate art of their own.

The great tradition of the Parthenon reliefs found worthy continuation in the Tomb of Mausolus (d. 353), Persia's client prince in Caria. The sculptors of this monument, which is accounted one of the Seven Wonders of the World, included four famous figures, Scopas, Timotheus, Leochares and Bryaxis. Their work shows a fashionable concern for dramatic diagonals, twisted leanings, and cross-legged stances; and Mausolus himself is no less fashionably presented by his Greek sculptor as a foreigner whose distinctive foreignness is deliberately indicated. On a smaller scale, the vivid hunting scene on the Alexander Sarcophagus of c. 325–300 at Istanbul, found at Sidon, likewise renders contrasted national types of Greeks and Persians with care and sympathy.

But the climax of the entire contemporary drive towards realism – including a free play given to the emotions – was the stupendous frieze of the Gigantomachy, the battle of the Gods against the Giants, on the Altar of Zeus and Athena commissioned at Pergamum by Eumenes II Soter (197–160/59), a large part of which survives in East Berlin. The reliefs ran in a single continuous band, seven feet high and more than four hundred feet long, without any frame or moulding to separate it from the colonnade above. The artists of this frieze, the largest Greek sculptural work still in existence, inscribed it with their signatures, though only the name of a certain Orestes of Pergamum has survived.

More than twelve hundred divinities and part-human, part-animal giants were shown in this enormous series of reliefs; and each of them was originally identified by name. The extraordinary turmoil into which this mass of writhing figures is plunged has been intensified by every possible device of contorted limbs, wildly waving hair, contrasted textures, and facial expressions conveying every extremity of exultation, pain, anguish and terror. What is depicted is chaos: but it was out of this chaos that the gods asserted the triumph of civilization – like the triumph the Attalids themselves claimed to have won over contemporary Galatians (Gauls).

On the victorious side, the chief ally of Zeus is Athena. She was the patron goddess of Pergamum, as she was of Athens; and to preside over his library Eumenes II Soter set up a marble copy of the Athena of Phidias (438), the original of which was in the Athenian Parthenon. This Pergamene frieze of the Gods and Giants deliberately owes much to the depiction of the same subject on Parthenon reliefs. These have not come down to us, but it is clear that they, too, depicted violence, in contrast to the tranquil Parthenon sculptures that have survived. And yet a long artistic journey had been made since those days. For the Pergamene artists, while entirely content to employ the classical themes and styles, were willing to do so only in order to exploit and transform them. This they did by the injection of every sort of dramatic, baroque irregularity and tension, all dedicated to the expert presentation of illusionistic realism, emotion, and the conversion of the wildly flying moment into permanence.

Virtuosity of an entirely different kind is displayed by a smaller frieze carved round the interior wall of the Pergamum altar. This tells the story of Pergamum's legendary founder Telephus. In total contrast to the violent battle of gods and giants, the Telephus frieze is entirely quiet and inactive. This, too, is an epic tale of a king, but it is an epic which is romantic, picturesque and intimate. The frieze portrays a visual chronicle, divided into episodic scenes which unfold in what is intended to be a chronological succession – an experimental precursor of the great narrative reliefs of Roman imperial times, such as those spiralling upwards on the Column of Trajan (AD 98–117). The sculptors of the Telephus frieze have brought the current task for depicting drapery to a new zenith of cleverness. Even the inside and outside surfaces of a piece of cloth are distinguishable one from the other; outer robes, too, are now shown as completely transparent, with the folds of the inner garment visible underneath.

The early Hellenistic temples had their sculptural friezes, but these were, on the whole, not particularly imaginative, and did not take up very effectively the challenge of the Mausoleum at Halicarnassus. On other fringes of the Greek world, however – Etruria, and the adjoining regions of Italy – pedimental groups of impressively realistic Hellenistic technique were created in the local medium of terracotta.

One such group comes from Lo Scasato at Falerii Veteres (Città Castellana), chief city of the culturally advanced Faliscan territory which bordered Etruria across the Tiber. There a shrine of c. 300 BC was adorned by a series of terracotta figures in very high relief (so that they were virtually in the round), which were fitted together in jigsaw fashion upon plaques nailed to the wooden frames of the temple pediment. Male and female heads from these scenes reflect the styles of Scopas and Praxiteles respectively, while an especially fine torso of Apollo, with long curling hair and a pensive expression – perhaps the figure was seated in the chariot of the sun – is reminiscent of Lysippus' portraits of Alexander the Great, though superimposition of other styles as well suggests a date about 120 years after his death.

Another major extant group in the Hellenistic manner comes from a temple at Telamon (Talamone), on a hill above the Etruscan coast, erected to celebrate a Roman victory over the Gauls in 225 BC. The vigorous, dramatic reliefs on its pediment, of which numerous pieces (including some very recently discovered) have been fitted together in the National Archaeological Museum at Florence, show episodes from the attack of the Seven against Thebes, treated as a mythical prototype of the Gallic War. A further important set of temple reliefs, datable to the later second century, comes from Sentinum (Città Alba) in Umbria. They include scenes of the discovery of the sleeping Ariadne by Dionysus.

Whereas these compositions were influenced in their arrangement by local Etruscan tastes (which sometimes, deliberately or capriciously, deviated from Greek canons), their actual style and execution are purely Greek. While capable of displaying an impetuous freshness all their own, the artists were aware not only of the fourth-century Greek masters but of current Pergamene sculptural tendencies as well.

They were also deeply conscious of contemporary painted pictures; for the wall-painting of the Hellenistic world was advancing towards realism at the same time as its sculpture in relief and in the round. Surviving examples of the art, however, are very much fewer, though our knowledge can be eked out not only by the studies of surviving copies of its major wall-pictures, but also from the works of vase-painters, mosaicists and relief-sculptors, in addition to references in literary sources.

We are told that the murals of Polygnotus of Thasos, who worked in the 470s and subsequent decades, displayed more lifelike groupings, postures, features and drapery than had been seen before; though he himself significantly claimed, and warned, that his aim was not to achieve realism, but to show people as 'better than ourselves' – an assertion of the true classical spirit. Zeuxis of Heraclea in Lucania wanted to depict feeling rather than morality, and Parrhasius of Ephesus was said by Xenophon to have discussed with Socrates (d. 399) whether it was possible to reproduce psychological characteristics in a painting.[14] In the fourth century, shading and foreshortening (an advance towards perspective) were already fairly sophisticated. Some idea of the work of the time can be obtained from the bronze Ficoroni casket – the finest of a series of such objects from Praeneste in Latium – presenting an elaborate engraved group of the Argonauts. This composition is apparently a copy of a famous painting of *c*. 350 by Cydias from the island of Cythnos (?), which seems to have been on show at Rome.

Pamphilus of Sicyon, earlier in the century, had founded the leading painting school of the day. But by far the greatest influence on the Hellenistic art of the future came from his pupil Apelles of Colophon. Apelles, who enjoyed the patronage of Alexander, Ptolemy I Soter and Antigonus I Monophthalmos, innovated by using mixed instead of pure colours; his exploitation of illusionistic *trompe l'oeil* and foreshortening effects was particularly renowned, and he was careful to show men and women displaying a whole range of emotions, which he regarded, in the manner of Aristotle, as an important part of their characters.

Apelles specialized in easel-paintings, but none of these works have survived. It is possible, however, that his style is to a certain extent reproduced by some of the large pebble-mosaics of the period at places including Pella, Rhodes, and Chersonesus in the Crimea. One such mosaic at Pella, the capital of Macedonia, is signed by Gnosis, who was apparently Apelles' younger contemporary. Gnosis depicts a stag-hunt, one of a series of complex hunting and mythological compositions. Considering the comparative intractability of the medium, the realistic illusion of depth achieved by these foreshortened figures and shaded, wind-blown draperies is of remarkable quality, and suggests how good the wall-paintings that inspired such mosaics must have been. The same is true of the lost models of sophisticated three-dimensional-looking Delos mosaics of the later second century, likewise depicting animals, notably a panther on which Dionysus is seated.

Fortunately, a few of the original wall-paintings themselves have also now come to light. The finest of all such surviving Greek pictures of any period are from two tombs of *c*. 340–320, convincingly described as royal, and recently discovered at the former Macedonian capital Aegae (Vergina). The smaller, rectangular chamber tomb, though its contents had been completely pillaged, was found to contain a picture of Pluto (Hades), god of the underworld, carrying off the struggling Persephone, while Hermes runs in front of the chariot, and a maiden cowers below. The painting is drawn with inspired sureness of touch, and delicately coloured. Its free, swift brush-strokes have suggested attribution to a certain Nicomachus of Thebes; he is known to have painted such a scene, and was famous for the rapidity with which he worked.

The façade of the second of these tombs at Aegae, a larger, barrel-vaulted structure, revealed another very fine, richly coloured painting, evidently the work of a different artist. The scene is a lion-hunt, and the novel depiction of figures moving in space suggests that the artist was perhaps the same man who painted the lost original of a great mosaic of *c.* 150 at Pompeii, illustrating the defeat of the Persian King Darius III Codomannus by Alexander the Great at Issus or Gaugamela. The painter of the original battle-scene may have been Nicomachus' pupil Philoxenus of Eretria, whose inclusion of this theme in his repertoire is on record. Although the mosaicist seems to be introducing ideas of perspective that were not current in Philoxenus' time, he gives a fair idea of what the latter's picture must have been like. It is a complex and furious but admirably lucid composition, in which, by a series of recurrent oblique and criss-cross movements, an enormous mass of detail is superbly subordinated to a highly dramatic central effect: everything converges on the central figure of Alexander. The representation of a marvellous diversity of feelings is masterly and unerring: lust for the fight, the determination to conquer, compassion for the vanquished, faithfulness to death.

Less important wall-paintings of about 300, or a little afterwards, have survived at Pagasae (Thessaly), Lefkhadia Náousa (Macedonia), Kazanlik (Bulgaria), and Posidonia (Paestum in south-west Italy). The painted tombstone of Hediste at Pagasae shows the dead woman lying on her couch, with her family around her; the varying distances at which these persons are located from the viewer are cleverly indicated by intersecting lines and a slight diminution in the size of the figures that stand further back.

For the rest, third-century paintings have only come down to us in copies. One of the most remarkable was found at the Etruscan city of Vulci, where paintings from the François Tomb of Vel Saties (*c.* 250) depict not only the historical or legendary single combats of local heroes against their Italian enemies, but Greek myths from the Theban cycle, and Achilles' slaughter of the Trojan prisoners at the tomb of his slain friend Patroclus. This scene of Achilles evidently comes from a Hellenistic original, which had probably found its way to one of the Etruscan cities. Reproduced in Etruria on a number of occasions, this apparently embodied various elements from fourth-century Greek experiments in perspective, and must have been a masterpiece of disciplined violence and pathos.

Another imitator of earlier paintings identifies himself as Dioscurides of Samos. He is the signatory of panel mosaics at Pompeii, of which one represents street musicians and the other a group of actors, who are shown performing scenes from Menander's plays the *Theo-phoroumene* (*Woman Possessed*) and *Synaristosae* (*Women Breakfasting*) respectively. Both these mosaics are apparently copies or adaptations of third-century paintings from Pergamum. A more imposing original of the same epoch seems to be reflected in a remarkable series of imitations from a villa at Boscoreale, near Pompeii (*c*. 40 BC), perhaps depicting Alexander the Great's marriage to the Persian princess Statira (Barsine) in 324. Moreover, a wall-painting of early Roman imperial date at Herculaneum depicts Heracles and Telephus in a fine, idyllically calm, diagonal composition of self-absorbed beings that reflects what must have been a first-class Pergamene work of the second century BC.

A further impressive set of paintings of the same period were admirably, if loosely, reproduced on the walls of the Villa dei Misteri outside Pompeii in about 60 BC. They depict the rituals, terrors and glories of initiation into the Mysteries of Dionysus, and are notable for a special, peculiar brand of spirituality – and occasionally chill horror – in a magic, dream-like, shut-in world inhabited by people even more self-engrossed than Heracles and Telephus, people executed with brilliant life-like realism, though dwelling in a world unconcerned with our own. These paintings were perhaps inspired by pictures in the Shrine of Dionysus at Pergamum, though the central figures of the cycle (Dionysus and Ariadne, surviving in a fragmentary condition) may have been suggested by famous cult images at Smyrna. Yet the imitation cannot have been exact (indeed, some of the faces look like first-century portraits), since paintings of such ritual cycles were reserved for sacred places, which this rich man's villa was not. So perhaps the scenes are taken from a satirical mime centring upon the rites – in which case the original might be Alexandrian, rather than Pergamene.

Another tranquil, large-scale painting of second-century date was adapted in *c*. 170–150 BC by an Etruscan artist (or a Greek working in Etruria) who adorned the walls of the Tomb of Typhon (the grave of the Pumpu family) at Tarquinii, the modern Tarquinia. His picture depicts a finely composed procession of white-robed males. As for the more animated, violent type of Pergamene and Rhodian art – the type that produced the Pergamum Altar and the Laocoön – this, too, was favoured by certain groups of painters. Their work has disappeared; but it can to some extent be reconstructed from reliefs showing Greek mythological scenes on the innumerable cremation urns of the period (surmounted by reclining figures) from Volaterrae (Volterra), Clusium (Chiusi), Perusia (Perugia) and other centres in northern Etruria. Once allowance has been made for concessions and adaptations to local artistic and religious tastes, these vigorous reliefs must be regarded as imitations of Pergamene or Rhodian or south Italian mural paintings (or, sometimes, sculptures), known to the artists directly or through examples they had seen at Rome or elsewhere.

Vase-painting, which for earlier times had provided us with our only first-hand knowledge of the Greek painter's art, continued to proliferate, and once again illustrated the growth of realistic techniques. Delicate, fully polychrome scenes composed of several figures appear on vases from Centuripe in Sicily, with ornaments added in relief. Quite good vase-painters were also working in Apulia (south-east Italy); for example, in the last quarter of the fourth century we know of a group named after Gnathia (Fasano), where their work was first found. There were also continuing schools at Taras and partially Hellenized Canusium (Canosa); the engravings on some Praenestine caskets copy these vases. In Egypt, too, there was a production centre at Hadra, a suburb of Alexandria.

The strong movement of Hellenistic artists, in all media, towards realism inevitably involved a much sharpened and more sympathetic observation of nature. When earlier Greeks had shown an interest in natural beauty, they had done so not for its own sake, but to make a point. Thus in Euripides' *Bacchae*, natural details add to the eeriness of the horrible death of Pentheus. But at about the same date Socrates remarked that he found nature less interesting than people, implying that too much love of its attractions was a weakness showing an indolent character; and Menander still considered a non-participant in urban civilization a misanthrope. However, all that was now gradually changing. In an age which interpreted civic obligations less rigorously (and was concerned with people as individuals rather than as cogs in the social machine), an interest in one's natural surroundings could be cultivated and excused. Moreover, contemporary scientific studies of the physical world insisted that nature was something that ought to be understood; and the Stoics, taking their cue from certain aspects of Platonism, saw it as cosmic rhythm and the vehicle of world harmony. Anyte, Hermesianax, Callimachus and Apollonius Rhodius all wrote feelingly about natural scenes; while Theocritus' pastoral poetry elevated a contemporary longing for the countryside into a whole way of life (Chapter Four, section 3). Meanwhile the inhabitants of the great cities, when they felt weary of their bustle and turmoil, adorned them with parks interspersed with little shrines, pavilions and rockeries.

Such was the background of a new interest in nature which formed part of the current artistic drive towards life-like presentation. The Pella mosaic signed by Gnosis in 320–300 is decorated with fine borders depicting a variety of flowers – rose, crocus, lily, euphorbia and perhaps convolvulus; and a tent built in Alexandria for the drinking parties of Ptolemy II Philadelphus was fitted out as a great garden bower full of birds. The Telephus relief on the Altar of Pergamum (c. 200) introduces trees and rocks in an attempt to portray a few details of landscape upon rising ground, and similar landscape features gradually take their place in paintings (as copies at Pompeii and Herculaneum show), although at first such insertions are still only sketchy and secondary.

Landscape finally emerged as an autonomous artistic theme in the second century BC – perhaps in the first instance at the vastest urban conglomeration of all, Alexandria. The new idea is illustrated by a Pompeian copy of a Greek painting of that time, the *Lost Ram*, in which a man, pushing along the ram he has recaptured, is no longer the centre of the picture but only a small object in a large, varied, dramatic landscape and skyscape, illuminated by vivid lighting effects. The landscape is of a special, familiar kind, grouped round a shrine like the parks in the cities; but the tame contours of a park have been enlivened in order to depict a wilder aspect of nature. The original artist of this picture cannot be identified, but the movement as a whole is associated with the name of a second-century painter, Demetrius of Alexandria, known as the *topographos* or landscapist. He went to Rome and made the new art known there, while also giving shelter to his exiled monarch Ptolemy VI Philometor (164–163).

Demetrius may have been the artist of excellent paintings representing the Wanderings of Odysseus, which were copied a century later for a villa on the Esquiline Hill at Rome. The Odysseus theme was specifically associated (by the Roman architectural writer Vitruvius) with the landscape art; and rightly so, because in these paintings the series of human adventures, though seen against occasional architectural backgrounds, serve mainly as a pretext for romantic studies of the natural settings of land and sea. In the distance, the colours are faded away with a skill that betrays elaborate precedent and practice. True, some of the elements of nature, such as the rocks that figured frequently in paintings of this kind, have an artificial air about them, and, as usual, there is no unified aerial perspective; instead, light is introduced from various sides, and separate parallel receding lines and vanishing points are shown. Yet the trees and bushes waving in the breeze, the water reflecting the image of a goat as it drinks, the clouds drifting through the sky, and the strong light and shade, look true and real enough. And that was the blend between direct observation and artificiality achieved by Greek landscape painting at its best; it never combined them with the genius of Claude or Constable, but remained a secondary, quasi-realistic art of considerable charm.

The same quest after naturalism was pursued by mosaicists who designed works of their own account, including the well-known Sosus of Pergamum in the second century BC. Originals or copies of his extant works include an elegant study of doves drinking from a wine-cup, and an amusing representation of a floor strewn with the débris of a meal – a mosaic intended for the floor of a dining-room. The same medium was also employed for another type of joke, in which realism was blended with fantasy: the depiction of Egyptian, Nilotic scenery. One such exotic design, of about 130 BC, comes from the House of the Faun at Pompeii. The sparkling, rippling surface of the river teems with many specimens of local flora. But, above all, a fabulous variety of animals is to be seen, each executed with almost scientific precision, though jostling together in unnatural proximity. The artists – who may have had an illustrated treatise on zoology in front of them – perhaps came from Alexandria, like others who worked at Pompeii.

This type of artistic entertainment reached its height in another Nilotic mosaic created in about 80 BC for the sanctuary of Fortuna (Tyche) at Praeneste in Latium. Once again the Nile and its valley are swarming with life, and wild beasts are seen roaming in the half-desert lands around its fringes. But now the vast picture has become far more complicated, since its composer has crammed it with a great variety not only of animals but of people, structures, trees and rocky hills. All these things are closely and directly observed in themselves, but they are put together with total stylized artificiality, presenting an effect of extraordinary, lush lavishness. The idea of including a lot of buildings was soon afterwards taken over by Pompeian wall-painters, who probably borrowed their fantastic architectural scenes from stage sets. These mosaics provide an imaginative commentary and epitaph on the quest for realism which had preoccupied Hellenistic artists for a quarter of a millennium.

3 Biographers and Portraitists

An attempt has now been made to give some idea of what Hellenistic man was like. Despite all the troubles of the time, he was liberated from many earlier restraints, and more and more conscious of his own capacities and needs and rights. His life was changed, and had taken on a new autonomous meaning, because the hold and allure of the communal city-state had weakened, and the monarchical centres were often too far off to take its place. This meant that he fended much more for himself. He belonged to clubs. He lived (if he had the funds) in much better houses. He formed part of a large and better educated reading public, and the books he was given to read often appealed less to the high matters of principle that had been contemplated by the tragic dramatists of the past than to the reality of his own domestic and day-to-day interests.

Reality was one keynote of the time. The books and works of art that Hellenistic man demanded showed an increasing desire to give it expression: just as the scientists were making new efforts to explain what happens in the universe, so writers and artists wanted to show life as it is. And to show life as it is meant showing the individual as he or she is: this was the age, the first age, of the recognition, development and delineation of the individual person.

This tendency was given a great stimulus by the careers of unprecedentedly important individuals – and by an absorbed, officially encouraged, public interest in these potentates (however remote) and in their dramatic and picturesque personal qualities – which amounted to a veritable personality cult.

This was one of several converging trends that offered a special spur to the developing art of biography. The concept of the hero, distinguishable from other men by his greatness, had been laid down for ever, immutably, in the distant past by the never-to-be-forgotten verses of the *Iliad*. The Homeric hero, at all times, had to use his superior gifts to excel and win applause, for glory was the driving force and aim of his existence. Birth, wealth and valour confirm his title: his ideals are courage, endurance, strength, beauty, and then (in the *Odyssey*) cleverness as well. He is no god, but half-way between men and the gods. Every literate Greek was familiar with this ideal, and felt larger than life when he read about it, and followed after it as best he could. Nor did the tradition cease to retain its allurements. Plato was aware of it when he wrote of his Guardians who would look after the state; and Aristotle, reflecting upon them, declared his own view of the traditional hero – the man who is great-souled and superior: 'he will govern and we will gladly obey him'.[15]

These ideas could not fail to have a decisive effect on the attitude of the Greeks towards the writing of history. However devoted they were to the corporative institutions of the city-state, and however sophisticated an analysis Thucydides, in the fifth century, might apply to the historical process, they found it easy to follow the conviction of his older contemporary Herodotus that history is above all else a matter of significant people. And then, subsequently, amid the growing realistic interest in individual persons and their characters, this conviction led to the creation of the new art of biography. When Thomas Carlyle remarked in the nineteenth century that 'Universal History is at bottom the History of the Great Men who have worked here', the sum, that is to say, of innumerable biographies, he was voicing a doctrine that has become unfashionable today (under the influence of Marx and Engels, the fathers of Communism, and because modern 'great' men have been so unsavoury), but which would have been generally accepted by the great majority of people in the Hellenistic age.

Until then, in the old classical Greek world, the interest in biography had been limited, and it did not attain recognition as a separate branch of literature, for several reasons: a preoccupation with 'ideal' men hindered the study of what they were really like; there was a widespread tragic view that human beings were helpless before fate; and in any case it seemed to some (notably the physician Hippocrates of Cos) that it was hard for a man to rise above his environment and assert himself sufficiently to be of any real note. Yet it was a Greek characteristic to have a sharp eye for the different ways in which different people believe and behave, and the eventual emergence of biographical writings was inevitable. It started, perhaps, when Ion of Chios, who was born in c. 490, wrote his lost *Epidemiae* (*Journeys*, made by himself and others) incorporating anecdotal memoirs of a novel kind about the statesman Pericles, the dramatists Aeschylus and Sophocles, and others, ransacking literary sources and personal reminiscences to describe notable, idiosyncratic actions and sayings. Then, in the fourth century, Isocrates and Xenophon developed the art of the *encomium* – a standardized sort of biography of monarchs, concentrating (excessively) on the brighter features of their characters and careers (Evagoras I of Salamis in Cyprus (d. 374/3), for example, and Agesilaus II of Sparta (d. 360/59)).

Next, while Theophrastus (*c.* 370–288/5) was devising his fictional *Characters*, his remarkable and versatile contemporary Aristoxenus of Taras did much to create the biography of real people as a literary form. After various extensive travels, Aristoxenus established himself at Athens, where he transferred his philosophical allegiance from Pythagoras, the sixth-century mathematician and sage, to the person and teaching of Aristotle. In 322, however, Aristotle, contrary to Aristoxenus' expectation, passed him over for the succession to the school's directorship in Theophrastus' favour, and it is doubtful if he remained one of its members: though none of the others, it was said, had equalled him in learning.

Aristoxenus was a phenomenally prolific author (with an alleged 453 books to his credit), though very little of what he wrote has survived.

The outstanding musicologist of antiquity, he also wrote numerous works on historical themes. And, in particular, he wrote lives of Pythagoras, Archytas of Taras (a fourth-century member of his school), Socrates and Plato. He selected this biographical method in pursuance of the Aristotelians' interest in personal character, as well as out of a conviction that the close examination of these wise men's careers – or at least an attempt to interpret what earlier writers had said about their often picturesque personalities – was the best way of understanding and assessing their doctrines. By concentrating on philosophers in this way, Aristoxenus deliberately departed from the idea that heroes, men of action, were the only or even the most memorable 'great men'; and it was revealing that he should do so precisely at the time of the career of Alexander the Great, or very soon afterwards.

His studies inaugurated a long list of biographies of famous persons, constructed within a more or less fixed framework: background and birth, youthful years, actions revealing character (which was thought to be inborn ready-made, and not to change) and death. This episodic material was accompanied, in most of these Lives, by legendary tales (collected with scholarly zeal), discussions of ideas, moral reflections, and scandalous or otherwise provocative opinions and anecdotes thrown out in a detached or mildly humorous vein. Thus Aristoxenus, creator of this learned, worldly *genre*, saw Pythagoras of Samos as an Etruscan who had learnt his wisdom from the Persian sage Zoroaster, Plato as a writer who plagiarized his *Republic* from the fifth-century sophist Protagoras, and Socrates as a sensual, ignorant, selfish, hot-tempered money-lender and bigamist. Perhaps it was these 'debunking' views that caused him to be passed over from the directorship of the Aristotelian school of the Lyceum – unless he sharpened them after his rejection, to take revenge on more orthodox philosophers.

Another stage in the history of biography was reached with the work of the third-century writer Satyrus, who came from Callatis Pontica (Mangalia in Rumania), but worked mainly in Egypt. Four pages of his Life of the fifth-century tragic poet Euripides – framed, strangely enough, in dialogue form – have been found on a papyrus. These indicate that Satyrus employed Aristoxenus' broad headings, though he shows little awareness of his subject's development after the early years, and unscientifically deduces many biographical details from Euripides' plays, adding a lavish sauce of legendary material. However, he is a careful, attractive stylist, and shows a certain sense of literary history, for example by pointing out that Euripides foreshadowed Menander.

Satyrus also wrote about Pythagoras, Sophocles and the orator

Demosthenes. But, in addition, he widened his horizons from these intellectual figures in order to compose Lives of men of action as well – up-
to-date replicas of the heroes of antiquity. These selected personages
included two fourth-century monarchs, Dionysius II of Syracuse (367–
344) and Philip II of Macedonia. It was clear enough, from the deeds of
Philip and his son Alexander, that the contemporary Greek world had
fallen into the hands of 'great men': and Satyrus, while prudently
refraining from dealing with living people, showed that he saw that this
had happened. In other hands, the career of Alexander produced a
mass of almost wholly fictional biography, and the Lives of his Successors, written during their lifetimes, were for obvious reasons mainly
laudatory.

Antigonus of Carystus is perhaps identifiable with a sculptor who
helped to make the bronze statues celebrating the victory of Attalus I of
Pergamum over the Gauls. He wrote on the history of art, and he also
compiled *Lives of Philosophers*. Despite this restriction of range to one
single profession – which goes back to Aristoxenus' self-appointed limitation – Antigonus' biographies are important. For he not only wrote in
a fluent style that attracted admiration, but displayed a novel high
standard of accuracy, especially when he was describing contemporaries
from personal knowledge.

Biography was, by now, thoroughly launched as an integral feature
of the Hellenistic drive towards realism and individualism. Biographers
remained modest, however, conceding that their art was both different
from history and less grand and ambitious in scope. The distinction
remained firmly embedded in all future Greek and Roman literary
criticism (the embryonic art of autobiography, exemplified by the
Memoirs of Aratus of Sicyon (271–213), being classified as a second-rate
activity along with biography). The Hellenistic historians, for their part,
working on their admittedly wider canvas, no doubt heartily endorsed
this admission of their own superiority. Yet they too found themselves
greatly affected, all the same, by the current interest in biographical
material.

This was, of course, nothing new; Herodotus himself had long ago set
historians the fashion. But then the large-scale *Philippica* of Theopompus
of Chios (378–after 323), its subject being the reign of Philip II of
Macedonia, inevitably possessed a particularly strong biographical
character. Duris of Samos (c. 340–260) found the work dull, and his
own account of the period from 370 to about 280, while likewise placing
great emphasis on personalities, laid much greater stress on their more
sensational and emotional aspects. Hieronymus of Cardia, an important
officer and administrator for many decades following Alexander's

death, was far too sober and trustworthy to approve of such methods, but his interest in biographical methods was equally keen, and his depiction of the personality of Demetrius I Poliorcetes, in particular, presented a notable innovation: whereas most Greek writers were content to interpret character as fixed and static, Hieronymus innovated by preferring to trace the development of his subject's character. Polybius, too, laid much emphasis on individual personality, for example in his study of the Achaean leader Philopoemen.

Sculptural portraiture, the visual counterpart of the biographer's art, was likewise virtually an original creation of the Hellenistic world, though it retained a delicate balance between the old idealism and the new realism.

Just as the Greeks of the classical epoch (or earlier) had never evolved biography as an independent branch of literature, so also it scarcely occurred to them to produce visual likenesses of individual persons. In earlier times still, Egyptian and Babylonian 'portraits', though not usually seriously attempting to reproduce the features of individuals, had at least aimed at presenting an individual appearance and impression. But the Greek sculptors before the Hellenistic age retreated from this position. Their so-called portraits, often designed for funerary or votive memorials, tended to represent a generalized, synthetic ideal; they were not so much likenesses as assemblages of non-individual physiognomical elements, modified by only the barest minimum of real or imaginary individual traits. To make further, realistic concessions to purely personal distinctive facial features – so a sculptor of the fifth century might have said – would only mean emphasizing transient factors to the detriment of the essential, permanent aspects of human beings: that is to say, the aspects expressed in their *daimon*, the guiding life-spirit or vital principle inside or outside their bodies, which linked them with their destiny.

This classical tendency to avoid portraiture in favour of generalization was enhanced by several additional factors. For one thing, the customary subjects for portrayal were gods or semi-divine heroes, who obviously set an exalted, impersonal standard for the representation of human beings which followed later on – when, for example, statues of this same unindividual kind were made in 510–509 and 477–476 (copies of the later version have survived) to commemorate Harmodius and Aristogeiton, who had killed the Athenian 'tyrant' Hipparchus (514). Secondly, when the portrayal of less exceptional human beings got under way in the fifth century, it was limited to famous public persons, and this restriction again strengthened the impersonal trend: so did the fact that the portraits were always complete statues in which the face did not need too much emphasis and merely had to be made 'as handsome as possible'[16] in a general sort of way.

With a very few exceptions (notably a freakishly accurate head of Themistocles (462), apparently posthumous), portraiture retained these idealistic features until after 400. But then new possibilities opened up when Socrates popularized the idea of each person's soul as an existent, individual entity, shining through the body. Such provocative views offered a powerful invitation to sculptors to depict Socrates' own features, which were, moreover, peculiar enough to provide an additional incentive. The statues of him which they then proceeded to produce are to be seen in many copies; they dwell lovingly on his idiosyncrasies, but still with a touch of divine inspiration added, and a certain generalized home-spun quaintness as well.

Very different is a figure from the tomb of Mausolus (d. 353) (the Mausoleum) in Caria (south-western Asia Minor). Whether the sculptor is depicting Mausolus himself (in or after his lifetime) or, less probably, his father or an ancestor, it is the first major individualized portrait by a Greek artist to have come down to us. True, the individualization is still not complete; the portrait is intended to show the general grandeur of a monarch. Yet its features and poise show a considerable advance towards the plastic realization of personality. The features reflect the un-Hellenic appearance of this Asian ruling family, and it is no coincidence that this new accuracy of portrayal occurs on the outskirts of Greek civilization. In such partially Hellenized regions, under monarchs who were foreigners, it seemed easier for Greek artists to ignore the strong, invisible bonds tying them to the ancient, unpersonal, ideal traditions of Greek sculpture.

On another fringe of the Greek world, recent discoveries at the ancient Macedonian capital Aegae (Vergina) include a skilfully executed ivory head from a small relief figure that appears to be a portrait of Mausolus' contemporary Philip II of Macedonia: perhaps it is a copy of a gold and ivory portrait made by the Athenian (?) sculptor Leochares. Another ivory head from the same find represents his son, Alexander the Great. It was inevitable that the dramatic exploits and features of Alexander should have given a tremendous fillip to this whole activity of sculptural portraiture. His portrait type was created in Greece, to symbolize his leadership of the Greeks against the Persian empire. Alexander's favourite sculptor, for his own portraits, was Lysippus of Sicyon (Chapter Three, section 2), because Lysippus alone, the king believed, could truly capture the virile, leonine aspect of his appearance. Lysippus' delicate bronze portraits were regarded as consummately realistic. And so they no doubt were in comparison with most of his predecessors' works, although he himself remarked that 'while others made men as they were, he had made them as they appeared to be'.[17] Who the 'others' were we do not know, but in any case this was, and is, a significant answer to any sculptor who wishes to pursue realism to the point of totally exact reproduction: if he succeeds in doing so, the artist's transforming intervention will be lacking.

Thus a fine head from Sparta (now at Boston), which seems to date from Alexander's lifetime, strikes the subtle balance: while hinting at the monarch's extraordinary personal gifts, and endowing him with a well-observed, lifelike expression descriptive of a restless (and rather spoiled) character, the head still suggests a god (or the hero Heracles, whose lion's skin the king wears) rather than the man himself; and so do almost all the other innumerable heads of Alexander, executed for centuries to come, with their intense, deepset eyes gazing fierily upwards from beneath a heavy brow. In accordance with the same way of thinking other sculptors, too, while they once again injected a fair amount of realism, were really concerned with depicting not the individuals themselves whose portraits they were professing to undertake but the types or typical qualities that could be discerned in them, bearing in mind the ancient custom that sculpture should be concerned with the generic norm or ideal. Thus Silanion, a contemporary of Lysippus, made a bronze statue of a fellow-metalworker Apollodorus, which, according to Pliny the elder, 'represented in bronze not a human being but anger'[18] – personifying a quality rather than portraying the man.

Pliny reported that it was Lysippus' brother Lysistratus who introduced the practice of rendering actual likenesses (*similitudines*)[19], which is probably only a deduction from something else he had just remarked, namely that Lysistratus was the first person to have modelled a likeness in plaster of a human being from the living face itself (as well as from statues), after which he poured wax into this plaster mould and then made final corrections on the wax cast. In fact no immediate breakthrough to greater realism ensued. Thus the portrait busts of the earliest monarchs of the great Hellenistic kingdoms are not very highly individualized; Ptolemy I Soter, for example, is portrayed by sculptors in a much less individual style than we find on his coins.

Another example of this blend of idealism and realism is provided by a superb bronze bearded head of perhaps about 300 BC, possibly found at Rome, where it is preserved in the Capitoline Museum. The head is over-imaginatively labelled 'Brutus' (Lucius Brutus, founder of the Roman Republic), yet whether it even represents a Roman at all is uncertain. Rome, at this time as earlier, was culturally inextricable from Etruria, which was partially Hellenized, and the style of the head is Etruscan and Hellenistic at the same time. The forms into which its surface breaks up owe a lot to Etruscan tradition. But the agitated modelling, cleverly combined with a controlled expression of iron will behind a tranquil demeanour, is strictly in accordance with current Hellenistic taste, depicting a type rather more than an individual. (The contemporary heads on the mass-produced recumbent figures on Etruscan tombs, though individually touched up, remain types and nothing else, until the first century BC.)

At the time that the 'Brutus' was made, however, or not long afterwards, artists in Greek lands were shifting the balance in favour of a reduction of the impersonal element. A remarkable example is provided by full-length portrait statues of the orator Demosthenes, symbol of the great departed days when Athenians were independent and powerful, and spoke freely. Surviving examples are copies, but they go back to an original executed by Polyeuctus in about 280, some forty years after the death of their subject. Much thought has gone into the presentation of the orator, who stands motionless, head bent, in a moment of intense reflection. This is realism, but much more as well: figure and face mirror an intense, relentless inner life – compounded of passion and will-power, sadness and grim determination, physical weakness and intellectual strength movingly blended and contrasted. Yet the rhythm is as four-square, centripetal, simple and severe as that of the 'Brutus' head, for this is the statue of a man deemed worthy to rank among the classic heroes of Marathon and Salamis.

Recent philosophers lent themselves to the same sort of technique. A splendid head of Epicurus, probably copied from an original made at the time of his death, exploits the new capacity of artists to reproduce personal traits; but it also very markedly echoes the general theme of 'The Philosopher', wise and humane. The best of all, perhaps, among these statues of sages is a copy (or adaptation) of a statue (c. 200) of the Stoic Chrysippus by Eubulides (?), of which the head is in the Louvre and the torso in the British Museum. Here, once again, is the man, but also the archetypal thinker and teacher, imbued with a pathos appealing for our sympathy. Pose and costume are lifelike, and so are the features. Yet the powerful, restless structure of the brows, and the deeply scored wrinkles, are also reminiscent of the ideal figures of the gods portrayed on contemporary monuments at Pergamum. Later statues of philosophers are mostly less interesting: bristling with ideals and beards, but rather empty and non-committal of feature. Their artists were deliberately slow to throw off the old generalizing trends altogether and cautiously unwilling to be seduced by detailed peculiarities (if and when they knew of them), however alluring.

Portraits of Hellenistic monarchs, too, tend to depict not only their actual features, but also the providential foresight and care for his subjects that a king ought to show. There are some startling exceptions, however. One is a memorable head of Antiochus III the Great (223–187), arrestingly conveying a powerful inner tension. Another, of the same period, is a highly realistic, amusing portrait of the rugged-looking Bactrian monarch Euthydemus I Theos (*c.* 230–190), with a sun-hat on his head. This, as we shall see, is paralleled by a series of Bactrian and Indo-Greek coin-portraits that are likewise the finest in the whole Hellenistic series. Euthydemus' bust also prefigured portrait-sculptors of the second and first centuries BC, who achieved equally realistic effects on the commercially important island of Delos. Their work included marble heads of old and middle-aged men whose features are expressed with uncompromising, plastic exactness, made possible by increasing subtlety in the use of wax models. Delos was also famous for its workers in bronze.

The island, sacked in 88 and 69, became a Roman commercial dependency, and indeed even earlier the artistic fortunes of Delos and Rome had become inextricably mixed. Under various Hellenistic influences, introduced not only from Delos and other eastern Mediterranean centres, but from south Italy and Etruria as well, the Romans began to display a special and peculiar passion for accurate portraiture, as a record of the forebears who had made them what they were; and they expressed this taste by developing a novel and intensified realism, warts and all. This 'veristic' style, as it is called, had an enormous future ahead of it, very often in the hands of Greek sculptors, who were glad to grasp the opportunities that a powerful Roman patron and his knobbly physiognomy so readily offered to their talents.

Leading painters joined the sculptors in their drive towards realism, with such keenness that the Roman critic Quintilian accused Demetrius of Alopece (*c.* 400) – known as *anthropopoios*, 'maker of human beings' – of preferring realism to beauty,[20] which probably means that he sometimes verged on caricature. Aristotle, who saw all art as imitation – something for which every human being has a taste – found it natural in his *Poetics* (*The Art of Poetry*) to cite painting as a parallel example, subdividing its practitioners into those who depicted their subjects as better than they are, or worse than they are, or just as they are – 'the same kind of people as ourselves'.[21]

One famous painter of portraits was Aristotle's contemporary Apelles, whose likeness of Antigonus I Monophthalmos (d. 301) depicted him in three-quarter view, so as not to show his empty eye-socket. It was about Apelles that the grammarian Apion told the story that physiognomists employed his painted portraits not only to determine how old his subjects were at the time of their portrayal, but even to forecast the year in which they were going to die.[22] This was typical of a thousand exaggerated tales or legends illustrating the realism that the public found so particularly admirable in these artists.

There were interesting sketches of Darius III and Alexander in the battle painting – perhaps painted by Philoxenus of Eretria in the later fourth century – which is reproduced on a Pompeii mosaic. But to judge the originals of these incidental portraits of Hellenistic date for ourselves, the best we can do is to go to Etruria, where Greek styles were taken over and ingeniously adapted to Etruscan tastes and circumstances. And there we find that the somewhat sketchy and allusive likenesses of Vel Saties and his dwarf Arnza, in mid-third-century paintings from the François tomb at Vulci, and the representations of the people buried in the Tombs of the Shields and of Typhon at Tarquinii, once again display a judicious blend of individuality and classicism.

And that, indeed, is the keynote of the portraits that Hellenistic painters included in their works. Like the sculptors, they still chose to modify their realistic effects by an overall, traditional preoccupation with showing what a face *ought* to represent: a type of character, or exemplar of social behaviour. Even at the end of the Hellenistic period, we have no painted portraits to compare with the new 'verism' of Delian and Roman sculpture.

Much greater advances towards lifelike portraiture are to be found on the coinage of the Hellenistic period.

In the classical period, true portraits had not appeared on the coins of the Greek city-states any more than on their statues. An individual portrait would have been out of place on so corporate and communal a product: its appearance would have been *hubris* – a sign that the individual in question, living in a community that enjoyed a republican government, was getting above himself. By tradition, the appropriate head to be placed on a coin was that of a god or goddess; and despite all a hero's striving to climb close to the gods (and his not-infrequent admission to the coinage as a substitute deity), a gulf still remained between gods and human beings.

But easterners had no reason to cherish these convictions so sharply, and the first coin-portraits of living people to be executed by Greeks are those of a Persian satrap (regional governor) and a local prince, Khäräi, on coins of Lycia (southern Asia Minor) in the later fifth century BC[23] (the time when gems, too, begin to show their first portraits). More realistic heads of further Persian satraps in the same peninsula followed shortly afterwards (c. 412–360). These coins were intended for the payment of the Greek mercenaries employed by the Persians. Thus individual portrait coinage began in an area in which the artists, although Greek, were unhampered by Greek prejudices against such a development: a point they emphasized by their willingness to make their subjects look un-Greek, just as the Carian prince Mausolus was given a non-Greek appearance in his marble statue from the Mausoleum at Halicarnassus.

As in other media, the career of Alexander the Great gave a massive encouragement to coin-portraiture. In his exceptional case, the traditional ban reserving personal representations on coins for the gods and heroes was deliberately blurred, since the heads of Heracles wearing the scalp of the Nemean lion on his abundant coinage frequently display an exalted approximation to his own features, accompanied by his name. After Alexander's death, his portrait appeared on the coins of his Successors, to legitimize their claims. The most famous of these issues was a silver series of Lysimachus on which Alexander is shown sprouting the ram's horns of Zeus Ammon: and at his foundation Alexandria, too, he was posthumously depicted in an elephant's skin, with tusks and trunk, as the conqueror of India. The features on all these pieces are more or less idealized.

Ptolemy I was probably the first of the Successors to replace Alexander's head by his own, in about 300, and this portrait of a living ruler is a landmark. A new theme has been pronounced: the depiction of the reigning warlord, with beetling brow and formidable jaw. Ptolemy's features are simplified, and he wears the aegis (goatskin) of Zeus. But the basically truthful, uncompromising toughness and ugliness of the representation considerably exceeds any known contemporary sculptural portrait in fidelity. It was the Seleucids, however, who first made a regular practice of showing the ruling monarch's head. A coin-portrait of Antiochus I Soter (d. 261) attained a degree of realism that had never been aimed at before. This is the depiction of power, but of very human power: the king's expression manifests anxious care and attention. More forceful is the appearance of the heavy-jowled Philetaerus (d. 263), founder of the breakaway kingdom of Pergamum, whose successors continued to portray him on their coins.

The designers of such coin-portraits were operating on a small scale that did not have to conform to the conventions binding the artists of major works, and were less strongly bound than the sculptors to the ties that linked Hellenistic art with the classical past. Moreover, the monarchs who caused these coinages to be made possessed a far greater appreciation of the powers of propaganda than had ever existed before. True, the Greeks had always been alert to the potential of coins for this purpose, as they had shown by the admirable, highly paid artists whom they had chosen to make them; they realized that the public, unlike its modern mass-media-nourished counterpart, looked at these pieces carefully, and admired them if they were good. But a Hellenistic monarch had something much more ambitious in mind. For what he intended to do was to stamp his own personality on the eyes and hearts of his peoples – not quite (as yet) warts and all, but still with considerable recognition of whatever individual, distinctive characteristics he possessed – and clearly the best possible means of conducting this operation was provided by the coins, which circulated in every town and village of his kingdom.

It was only around the year 200 BC that Hellenistic coin-portraiture, stimulated by these requirements, reached its memorable climax. The result was a series of heads that equalled not only a photograph, but a really first-class, imaginative but unmendacious photograph of genius in their ruthless fidelity to the intriguing, formidable, and sometimes unprepossessing or even brutal appearance of the monarchs they were depicting; while at the same time they infused their creations with more than a touch of unusual artistic originality and talent. Unusually expressive, for example, is a head of the Seleucid monarch Antiochus III the Great (223–187), displaying in paradoxical juxtaposition (more clearly than his marble bust) a strong intellectual forehead, imperious brow, but almost gentle mouth – a penetrating, restrained study of a personage in whom force and weakness met. And once again the heads of the remarkably ugly monarchs of the rising kingdom of Pontus, Mithridates III (c. 220–185) and Pharnaces I (185–169), display a surprising realism enhanced by acute insight into character; and they are made to look very foreign. Partially Hellenized Parthian coin-portraits, too, include a remarkable frontal head, perhaps representing Mithridates III of that state (c. 57–54), which foreshadows a long tradition of such frontality.

The outstanding achievements of coin-portraiture during this epoch, however, are the masterpieces presented on the coinages of the Bactrian and Indo-Greek kingdoms that lay even further out upon the periphery of the Hellenistic world (Chapter One, section 5). As we saw, the earliest of all realistically inclined coin-portraits had been produced by Greeks under un-Hellenistic influences in Asia; and then in the course of the third century, and later, the high-water mark of this trend was once again reached in Asian regions. For these Bactrian and Indo-Greek rulers, living so very far from the centre of the Hellenistic world, felt relatively uninfluenced by ancient Greek traditions of idealistic impersonality, and were correspondingly willing to sponsor something new; though it was a happy coincidence that truly admirable portrait artists, with styles exhibiting extraordinary firmness and assurance, happened to be available at the right time.

One fine example of this art depicts the Bactrian king Euthydemus I Theos (c. 220) as elderly and rather toothless, with pursed-up lips. A masterly portrait bust of the same monarch was noted earlier. It had shown him wearing a wide sun-hat, and this hat reappears on a coin of Antimachus I Theos Nicephorus (from c. 171), ruler in east Gandhara and the Punjab. His features convey a very clever suggestion of strength of personality combined with humorous sophistication. Another expert character-study is provided by the largest ancient gold piece in existence (it should probably rather be described as a commemorative medallion), issued by Eucratides I (c. 170-155), monarch of Bactria and west Gandhara, the first Greek king to describe himself as 'the Great' on a coin. In more heroic vein is a head-and-shoulders bust on a silver piece showing a back view of the same ruler helmeted and bare-shouldered, looking round with a scowl and brandishing a spear. There are also a few equally distinguished gem and intaglio portraits of Bactrian and Indo-Greek rulers.

After the great imperial career of Menander Soter Dikaios, the Indo-Greek and Bactrian kingdoms gradually split apart in the later second and first centuries BC, amid intense dynastic strife and external pressure. Yet it is at this unpromising period that the largest known monetary or quasi-monetary silver piece of the entire ancient world was struck, by the otherwise undocumented Indo-Greek monarch Amyntas Nicator (c. 100-75). His eccentric features are unflinchingly reproduced; as on other pieces in this exceptional series, facial oddities are adroitly employed to accentuate aspects of character. Then, as the entire region was falling into the hands of various nomad peoples, the aggressive posture of a heavily armed bust of the equally unrecorded Archebius (c. 100) captures the defiance of this final, belated and isolated outpost of Hellenism.

The great Roman series of coin-portraits that followed was often no less realistic than those of the Bactrian and Indo-Greek monarchs, and no less skilful. But if the Romans rivalled their brilliance, they could not exceed it, either in realism (even the best Roman veristic techniques do not outdo them in that) or in skill, because that was almost impossible.

4 The Hellenistic Woman

Inevitably the literary and artistic media that have been discussed in the earlier parts of this book tended to concentrate largely on men rather than women, who still played a less influential part in society. But it would be strange if the various changes described in the foregoing pages had not affected the position of women as well. Indeed, they affected it very considerably, and this is one of the outstanding novelties of the Hellenistic world.

Among the earlier Greeks there had been certain signs of the emergence of women, but they were signs that remained sporadic and patchy. Women were liberated, within their own circle, among the society of Sappho (born *c.* 612) on the island of Lesbos, which gave its name to the homosexual practices in which they probably indulged. The tragic dramatists – notably Sophocles, who showed women as capable of shaping their own destinies, and Euripides, who was an expert on the sex – chose to give their female characters an astonishing prominence (in a thoroughly heterosexual context) that did not correspond to the much humbler status of women in real life. Considerable freedom, it is true, came to be enjoyed by high-class prostitutes (*hetairai*). Yet in classical Greece women as a whole led extremely limited lives. They received no schooling outside the home (except at a few cities such as Sparta and perhaps in distant Etruria), spent most of their lives in their own quarters, were often prevented from rearing their own children, and possessed no more legal rights than slaves. 'She knew', said the conservative Xenophon (*c.* 428/7–354) with depressing satisfaction about his own teenage wife, 'that it was her job to be neither seen nor heard. What more could I want?'[24]

All this was to alter greatly in the Hellenistic epoch. For one thing, it was an age in which, for the first time in Greek history, there were very powerful women indeed: the widespread realization that some women, at least, had reached these dizzy heights in the community boosted the hopes and expectations of womanhood as a whole. The Hellenistic world was to a large extent a world of kingdoms, and the kingdoms produced queens of enormous ability, freedom of action, and power. The kingdoms stemmed from Macedonian precedents, and in Macedonia – which in so many ways developed independently of Greek traditions – queens of terrifying force had already made their appearance in earlier times.

In the Macedonian ruling family, the relation between mother and son was much stronger than the relation between husband and wife, so that a Macedonian queen stopped at nothing to secure the succession of her own son, which would bring her a dominant position in the state. A prime example of this phenomenon was Alexander the Great's mother Olympias, of the Epirote (Molossian) royal family. This mystical, ungovernable, passionate woman murdered her step-son Philip III Arrhidaeus so as to secure sole rule for her infant grandson Alexander IV. But she was killed in 316, with the connivance of one of the Successor commanders, Cassander. As for Cassander's influential sister Phila, she married two principal leaders in turn, first Craterus and then Demetrius I Poliorcetes, whom, in spite of all his infidelities, she presented with a son (Antigonus II Gonatas), founder of a great dynasty; she also maintained a court of her own in southern Asia Minor, perhaps in Lycia (there had long been female rulers, notably Artemisia and Ada, in neighbouring Caria).

Thereafter, too, the tradition of powerful (and learned) queens was amply maintained, in almost every Hellenistic kingdom, and most notably of all in the Ptolemaic house. The most remarkable woman of the age was a member of that family, Arsinoe II Philadelphus, daughter of Ptolemy I Soter and Berenice I. First of all, at the age of about seventeen, Arsinoe married one of Alexander's Successors, Lysimachus (c. 299–298), who had the greatest respect for her talents and gave her a group of important cities (including Cassandrea) as her personal dominion. After Lysimachus had been defeated and killed, Arsinoe II – after a one-day marriage to a step-brother Ptolemy Ceraunus (Thunderbolt), who slew her two younger children but failed to make away with their mother – took refuge in Egypt, where she married her own brother Ptolemy II Philadelphus in c. 276–275(?) and remained his queen, and the dominant personality of the country, until her death five or six years later.

A forerunner of the Roman empresses of the future, Arsinoe II was practical, shrewd, hard-working, relentlessly ambitious, and a far stronger character than her husband-brother, whose caution she overcame by her vigour and diplomacy, qualities she had inherited from both of her parents. She taught Ptolemy II how to use his fleet, and transformed his reign from comparative ill-success into the glories of the Ptolemaic Golden Age of maximum expansion. During her lifetime she received wholly unprecedented honours for a woman. For one thing, she was the subject of superb sculptural portraits, so that it is from her time (with only minor earlier exceptions) that female portraiture takes its place as part of the rapidly rising portrait tradition (Chapter Three, section 3). Furthermore, even while she was still alive, she was singled out to receive the official worship which Phila, too, had been accorded at Thria in Attica, and which was to become a feature of the Ptolemaic and other Hellenistic régimes. It was not enough that people identified Arsinoe II with Aphrodite and Isis. For, in addition, her husband Ptolemy II declared himself and herself, together, to be a pair of Theoi Adelphoi, Brother and Sister Gods. As such, their heads were later to appear on the coins of their son Ptolemy III Euergetes (together with those of earlier 'gods', Ptolemy I Soter and his wife Berenice I). Ptolemy III also depicted Arsinoe II alone on a coin (the type was imitated by Hiero II of Syracuse, in honour of his wife Philistis); a youthful bronze bust and a superb amethyst ringstone also appear to portray the same queen.

From this time on, the Ptolemies very often, indeed quite regularly, continued to marry their sisters. The practice ensured that their wives were sufficiently noble and royal to meet their exacting social requirements, and also made it less likely that they would be unfaithful and treacherous – since the great queens, though powerful and quick to use poison or the knife, were habitually chaste (more chaste than the Roman empresses of the future): not least because they, like their brothers, would have found it hard to acquire lovers worthy of their grandeur. The Pharaohs of earlier Egypt, like some of the rulers of other near-eastern royal houses, had likewise practised brother-and-sister marriage. When Ptolemy II married Arsinoe II, the satirical and scurrilous poet Sotades, who invented or gave literary form to a new genre of obscene ('cinaedological') poetry, wrote a coarse verse in condemnation of the unnatural act.[25] He was punished, and perhaps executed. The court poets, on the other hand, including Theocritus, rallied round the monarchs (from whom they desired patronage), explaining that the theology of Greece – like that of Egypt – offered highly appropriate models, notably Zeus and Hera themselves. The inbreeding which subsequently characterized the Ptolemaic house for generation after generation caused its queens to repeat and magnify a pattern of physical beauty, marked ability, purposeful passion for power, and murderous cruelty – the last-named quality being frequently needed, because kings often lacked the nerve to declare decisively who was their most important wife and who, in consequence, was their heir.

Several successive Cleopatras continued to set the tone. Cleopatra I, of Seleucid birth, survived her husband Ptolemy V Epiphanes and ruled the kingdom for four years (180–176) as regent for their infant son Ptolemy VI Philometor ('lover of his mother'). Then Ptolemy VI's daughter Cleopatra Thea (d. 121 BC), residing in Syria for twenty-nine years, married and promoted to the kingship at her pleasure three successive Seleucid monarchs (Alexander I Theopator Euergetes Epiphanes Nicephorus (Balas), Demetrius II Theos Philadelphus Nicator, and Antiochus VII Euergetes Sidetes the Great). Moreover, Cleopatra Thea was the only Seleucid queen who minted coins with her own portrait and in her own name, as the 'goddess of fertility' (*Thea Eueterias*), a title to which her nine children gave her obvious entitlement.

The Seleucid kingdom was in a state of political decay when Cleopatra Thea lived out her career, and for all her gifts she could not avail to halt its decline. The same was true of the Indo-Greek kingdom under her contemporary Agathocleia Theotropos ('god-like in character') whose dominant role, at times, in the régime of her consort Strato I Epiphanes Soter Dikaios (after *c.* 130) could do little to avert the collapse of the huge state established by Menander Soter Dikaios a few decades earlier.

Decay, to the point of near collapse, was also undermining Ptolemaic Egypt, bullied by ruthless Romans eager to grab its still very extensive wealth. Cleopatra III (sister of Cleopatra Thea), ruling at intervals for fifteen years (116–101), exercised her quarrelsome, lethal passion for dominance by promoting a series of violent rebellions in which she succeeded in supplanting her first son Ptolemy IX Soter II (Lathyrus, 'chick-pea') by her second son Ptolemy X Alexander (107). As things went from bad to worse in the country, the frequently humiliated Ptolemy XII Theos Philopator Philadelphus, known as the New Dionysus and the Oboe-Player (Auletes), was succeeded in 51 by his far more decisive daughter, the famous Cleopatra VII. Fired by the exploits of earlier queens, and educated to admire the glory of Greek civilization in which the bygone Ptolemaic empire had played such a magnificent part, Cleopatra VII was determined to devote her great talents and charms to the revival of that empire under her own dominance.

This seemed an extraordinary ambition at a time when the kingdom was so desperately weak. However, taking stock of the situation, she decided that she could attain her purpose, not by clashing with the ever-encroaching Romans, but by allying herself with the men who dominated their Republic – first Julius Caesar (whose new libraries and canals and calendar her officials helped to create), and then Marcus Antonius (Antony). Her aims were nearly achieved in 37–34, when considerable portions of the Roman dominions were detached, on Antony's orders, to form a reconstituted Ptolemaic empire in the names of herself and her infant children by Antony and Caesar (?) (Caesarion, or Ptolemy XV Caesar). When her lover's clash with Octavian (the future Augustus) came to a head (31), Cleopatra, though disliked by his commanders, made herself indispensable to his strategy as a source of ships and supplies. But the battle of Actium, off the north-west coast of

Greece, went the other way, and in the following year Cleopatra, like
Antony, killed herself.

She had possessed a number of titles. Among them was Thea Neotera,
the New Goddess, an echo of that great earlier Cleopatra Thea; and
Philadelphus, lover of her brothers, which she scarcely deserved since
one of her youthful half-brothers, Ptolemy XIII Philopator Philadelphus,
met his death at her hands, and the other, Ptolemy XIV Philopator, was
killed in battle against Caesar, her ally. Moreover, like these youths she
herself had taken the title Philopator, lover of her father, whose humi-
liations she was determined to avenge – a determination which provides
a guide to her whole career. Finally, as we learn from a recently
discovered papyrus, she assumed the designation of Philopatris[26] (lover
of her country), which she adopted in order to counteract the impression
among her subjects (not greatly benefited by her ambitious policies)
that she was too pro-Roman. And yet because of her defeat and death
the Ptolemaic kingdom, instead of regaining its empire, was annexed by
Rome and vanished for ever. The last of the major states that had shared
out Alexander's inheritance had gone, and with its disappearance (even
though an Indo-Greek principality continued to survive for some three
decades) the Hellenistic epoch is generally said to have come to an end.

The reverence accorded to these powerful Ptolemaic queens was
closely related to the worship of the great goddess Isis, and often formed
its direct reflection. There were other great mother-divinities presiding
over nature, but none enjoyed the widespread veneration accorded to
Isis. And, above all else, she was the patron of women, the divinity into
whose worship women entered heart and soul. Although there had
always been revered and mighty goddesses, it was only in a few cults
that women had fulfilled a prominent role – notably the worship of
Dionysus, in which his mythical union with Ariadne, and following of
maenads, played such a leading part. But Isis was emphatically theirs,
in a very special sense. With the infant Horus or Harpocrates in her
arms (like the Virgin and Child of later times), she was the universal
mother, the 'Glory of Women',[27] mothers and young girls alike – conferring upon them power and strength that equalled the power and
strength of men. In sexual terms, the worship of Isis was ambiguous. It
beckoned towards unrestrained sensuality – her rites provided meetings
for lovers – and yet, at the same time, her sacred figure was imbued
with a strange and wonderful purity.

The doings of the great Hellenistic queens, their prestige, and their
relationship to the major contemporary cults of Isis and other deities,
could not fail to make important contributions to the emancipation of

women in general, although there were also potent factors still operating in the opposite direction. Things were not yet all that good for most Hellenistic women. They often still led very confined lives. For example, when Greek men went overseas as colonists and settlers, they frequently did not take their wives and families with them. Sometimes, however, they did. Thus we happen to know that 79 families migrating to Miletus in the third century took along 118 sons and 28 daughters. The disparity between these two figures is sinister, since it shows that the exposure of female infants was common – probably even commoner than it had been earlier, now that it seemed safer, amid the disturbances of the Hellenistic epoch, to restrict one's family to a single child, if any.

Nevertheless, there were improvements. For example, whereas most marriages had hitherto been matters for agreement between father-in-law and son-in-law, the new era witnessed a gradual diminution in the role of the bride's father. Divorce, too, was now foreseen in numerous marriage contracts, which brought wives a good deal closer to equality. But the contracts were subject to interpretation by social equals, and in an agreement of 311 BC between two Greeks in Egypt, Heraclides and Demetria,[28] it emerges that whereas extramarital sex by the wife is out of the question (her infidelities, incidentally, could be detected by putting a magnet in the bed, in which case if she was guilty she would fall out), the husband is allowed casual adultery, especially with slaves and prostitutes. He is debarred, on the other hand, from setting up a home with any other woman whom his wife would find offensive. Moreover, guidance on such subjects – with particular reference to how a woman should behave if her husband was adulterous – were found in a series of pamphlets of *Advice for Young Ladies* of various Hellenistic and Roman epochs, written under the pseudonyms of Theano, Periction and Melissa, female relations or supporters of Pythagoras – the names of members of this school being selected for the purpose because it had made a point of encouraging female participation.

There were considerable variations in the treatment of women from place to place. Athens, the city of Plato and Aristotle, remained relatively conservative. Under Demetrius of Phaleron, who ruled the Athenians in an authoritarian fashion from 318 to 307, the appointment of Supervisors of Women (*gynaeconomoi*) – to oversee their public life, costume, behaviour at religious ceremonies and so on – must have caused a good deal of resentment. In some other cities, on the other hand, women's property-owning rights almost equalled those of men. Indeed, the process had already been under way before the Hellenistic age began, although legal rights tended to lag behind a more general trend towards economic emancipation.

The women of Sparta were the first Greeks of their sex to win victories with their horses at Olympia: more important, by the later third century they owned much of the wealth of their state – including two-fifths of the land – and in consequence opposed the attempts of King Agis IV to redistribute and equalize allotments (Chapter One, section 1). The king's mother Agesistrata (along with her mother Archidamia) was the richest Spartan woman of all, possessing a stranglehold over numerous debtors, so that he made it his top priority to try to win her over. At Delphi, the numerous statues of Aetolian women dedicated at the shrine show that their social position, too, was relatively free of restrictions.

In Ptolemaic Egypt – possibly under the indirect influence of the royal house, in which the queens were so prominent – liberation had at least gone far enough for two ladies whom Theocritus brings to the festival of Adonis to grumble about their husbands in a highly undeferential manner. Herodas deals frankly and coarsely with the sexual aspects of women's lives in some of his *Mimiambi*. The Alexandrian females depicted by such writers are intended as joke figures in the tradition of Sophron of Syracuse, who in the fifth century had written 'women's' as well as 'men's' mimes. The women of Theocritus and Herodas seem sharp enough in wit but not very cultured. However, from at least the fourth century onwards, an increasing number of respectable girls in some of the cities began to obtain a formal education at all levels. We have evidence, for example, from Chios, and also from Teos, where the courses were co-educational: the gymnasium of the place appointed 'three teachers of letters to give instruction both to boys and to girls'.[29] And this spread of education meant that women became increasingly avid readers: there are strong signs that the novelists of the period (Chapter Three, section 2) were catering for their tastes.

The development of private houses also made women's lives more agreeable. Outside the home, too, not only were women sometimes admitted to clubs, but much wider possibilities of employment had begun to open up for their benefit. In the fifth century, women of good repute (with the single exception of priestesses) had worked away from their homes only if they were forced to, because they needed the money – and even then they only got jobs that were unskilled. But in the Hellenistic age, quite a number of Greek ladies are found taking a full part in outside activities. For example, they now participated to a certain extent in civic life. For the first time in history, they appeared as public functionaries (magistrates) in their communities; we have decrees rewarding them with civic honours. They are also found seriously pursuing other professions before or during marriage, or even as its alternative. One such profession was medicine. Women had already practised as midwives at an earlier date, but Hagnodice, in fourth-century Athens, was described as the first female physician; her work probably lay in the same obstetrical field. Several women also composed treatises on gynaecological subjects.

Moreover, they embarked on the practice of the arts and letters in much larger numbers, and with considerable success. From as early as the fourth century half a dozen women artists are recorded, mostly the daughters of men of the same calling. And then Laia of Cyzicus, who painted portraits of members of her own sex (including herself) at Rome shortly after 100 BC, enjoyed a particularly impressive reputation; and Phile of Priene, in the same period, was the first woman to work as an architect; among the structures she designed was a reservoir. Meanwhile a few women had also become well-known musicians, notably the Theban harpist Polygnota who scored a success at Delphi not long after 200 BC, though she had to take a male relation with her as her escort and chaperon.

Women poets also made their appearance. One was Erinna of Telos. She was not, as the ancients sometimes believed, a contemporary of Sappho (born c. 612) – who was inevitably always thought of in such connexions – but apparently lived nearly three hundred years afterwards, at the end of the fourth century BC. Erinna died while still in her teens. Her three-hundred-line piece known in later times (though not apparently by herself) as the *Distaff* was composed, mainly in the Doric dialect, in memory of her friend Baucis, who had got married and then died. Although the poem only survives in a fragmentary condition, it is still possible to discern the skill and tenderness with which Erinna evokes the childish occupations and pleasures the two girls shared, and her jealousy when Baucis went off to a husband. These must have been fairly familiar themes of female poetry, but Erinna, for all her fresh, spontaneous manner, is carrying out a subtle, conscious adaptation of the traditions she had inherited. For in fact, although so young when she died, she was a very sophisticated poet, blending poetic modes and conventions with artful concealment and mastery. Her *Distaff* won her a quite distinct reputation second only to Sappho's; and Antipater of Sidon, a leading second-century epigrammatist, dedicated a moving epigram to her memory. Another writer whose ancient attribution to an earlier period (this time the fifth century) must once again, many think, be moved some hundreds of years later – perhaps to about the year 200 – is Corinna of Tanagra in Boeotia, who wrote narrative lyrical poems on Boeotian themes (and for the most part in Boeotian dialect) for a circle of her own women friends.

Anyte of Tegea in Arcadia (*c.* 300), on the other hand, had represented a Doric or Peloponnesian school of epigrammatists (a genre of which more will be said shortly), concerning themselves with local and country life, and reflecting a new interest in nature; her surviving verses breathe a quiet beauty and simple grace. Anyte was famous enough to have her portrait sculpted by Cephisodotus and Euthycrates, the sons of Praxiteles and Lysippus respectively. A second woman of the same poetic school, perhaps writing a few years later, was Nossis, whose epigrams offer fleeting, moving glimpses of the world of domestic duties and rites which made up the life of her home town, Locri Epizephyrii in south Italy. Then, in the same century, Aristodama of Smyrna and Alcinoe of Thronium both built up successful careers writing poetry, which earned them honours in various cities.

Women do not seem to have made their mark in the rhetorical profession, but were acceptable and prominent, though not very numerous, in a number of philosophical schools. They figured extensively in the quasi-religious revivals of the Pythagorean sect or movement in Greek south Italy and Alexandria, in pursuance of the tradition that Pythagoras himself, in the sixth century, had numbered 17 women among his 235 disciples (hence the choice of neo-Pythagorean women to provide the *noms de plume* of authors offering guidance to women readers). There were also two female Platonists (though one of them, Axiothea, dressed like a man), but the first teacher to allow members of the sex to become regular members of his group was Epicurus, who admitted them on equal terms from the beginning – mainly *hetairai*, well-educated prostitutes, but some others as well. Hipparchia, a woman of respectable and prosperous origins, entered with gusto into membership of the Cynic school, which she shared with her husband Crates. The Peripatetics kept women out because Aristotle did not believe that they were one hundred per cent rational beings, and the Stoics, too, refused to accept them, because even in his most Utopian phase Zeno felt unable to regard them as equals.

Although Sophron of Syracuse, in the fifth century, had given women an equal place with men as subjects of his mimes, and although the tone of the great Athenian tragic drama of the same epoch had been so thoroughly heterosexual, the dialogues of Plato, in which Socrates plays a leading part, reflected a society in which not only was all political life and most worthwhile social life reserved for men, but in which there was general acceptance of an attitude envisaging love affairs between older men and youths or boys. True, as the ribald jokes of Aristophanes' Old Comedy about such affairs indicate, less rarefied persons were 'normal' enough; breeding went on. Nevertheless, the encouragement of emotional friendships in battle, the popularity of all-male athletics, and a communal male life in general, had stimulated the existence of a strong homosexual element in cultivated Greek society. Yet changes were on their way, even in Plato's lifetime: and indeed, apparently, even in his own mind. For by the time he wrote his *Laws* he had come to hold the view (ascribing it to an unnamed Athenian speaker, with whom he evidently agrees) that his ideal city cannot tolerate the homosexual activities that were so prevalent in Dorian communities – Sparta and the cities of Crete.[30] He came to this conclusion partly on political grounds, because communally organized meals and gymnastics encouraged the formation of seditious groups and secret societies, but on moral grounds, too, because he now regarded these practices as contrary to nature.

Zeno, the founder of Stoicism, did not agree. Indeed, he declared that love both with the opposite sex and with one's own was permissible under appropriate circumstances, and he positively encouraged the latter, provided that 'the wise man will love boys whose physical beauty shows the goodness innate in their character'.[31]

Yet attitudes were still shifting, for various reasons. Politico-moral considerations, so prominent in Plato's later thinking, probably did not play a very big part: but fewer men than before were interested in homosexual love, because fewer led the old social life which had existed entirely for the benefit of males. Despite the strong physical element that still persisted in Hellenistic education, the transformation of adult athletics from an amateur into a professional activity meant that young men spent less time admiring each other's naked bodies; while the conversion of war into a business for mercenaries offered less occasion for romantic camaraderie among compatriots at the battle front. Thus Menander and his fellow-playwrights of the New Comedy, as Plutarch noted, do not refer to homosexual attachments at all.[32] Nor had the tragedians in the past, but the transfer of this total avoidance to the domestic life which these New Comedy dramatists depicted evidently reflects the character of that life as it was lived at the time. To turn to the epigrammatists, it is true that Callimachus' openly professed homosexuality was authentic enough; and even poets whose work suggests a strong interest in women can still contrive a homosexual epigram, either because their personal tastes were ambivalent or because they were conforming to an established tradition. Yet Asclepiades of Samos now declares that he finds associations between males productive of unhappiness, Glaucus of Nicopolis complains how expensive boys have become, and Meleager of Gadara, while admitting his own bisexuality, decides to make an end to relations with males. What Meleager is principally rejecting is sex with grown men. Greeks of the classical period had favoured athletic adolescents. Already in the fourth century BC, however, their successors were shifting their own tastes away from these juvenile athletes towards effeminate boys and youths, because they looked more like women; and the tendency continued, finding its strange ultimate stage in the sculptors' popular invention of the Hermaphrodite, who had masculine genitals and female breasts.

Homosexuality, of course, did not cease. Indeed, it continued on a large scale, pederasty in particular – Polybius remarked that young Romans mostly liked male or female prostitutes, and that 'alluring boys commanded a higher price than pieces of land'.[33] But then Plutarch, in the second century AD, composing his dialogue *On Love*, expressed a dislike for the idea of relations with his own sex, which only piety towards Plato's Socratic dialogues, he declared, enabled him to countenance at all.[34]

The cultural background for this shifting of attitudes was a tremendous new discovery, strongly reflected both in literature and art, that women were actually interesting, not merely as remote figures in tragedies, but as real and attractive persons: and preoccupation with their looks, and with feminine standards of beauty, increased out of all recognition.

Plato had believed that women were *usually* inferior to men, but with the proviso that this was not necessarily the case. In consequence of this proviso, he argued that both sexes should be allotted the same duties and the same education – after all, he said, we make no distinction between the sexes of animals. Aristotle took a more conservative line. To him, the husband was naturally the dominant partner, and the relations between man and wife, as he saw them, were those of benefactor to beneficiary. Yet Plato and Aristotle, though evidently so interested in the social nexus between men and women, did not have a great deal to say about sex or sexual attraction, which they and their fellow-Greeks tended to regard as a more biological phenomenon not requiring discussion, like hunger or thirst.

However, Antisthenes, the forerunner or first founder of the Cynic school, although regarding female gratitude as worth having, also stated that he would rather be mad than feel physical pleasure. His successor Diogenes went back to the Platonic idea of the communal ownership of wives. Yet he also held that among sensible people sexual intercourse, like everything else, should be a matter of agreement between the two parties, since both possess equal freedom of choice. In other words, he broke new ground by making the revolutionary assumption that the will of the woman plays an essential part in the matter. And he added that she was perfectly entitled to have sex with anyone she could induce to cooperate.[35] Moreover, since the Cynics believed in behaving naturally, their adherent Hipparchia, despite her reputable background, was quite ready to make love with her husband Crates in public; though when they were preparing to cohabit in a convenient portico, the young Zeno of Citium, at this time an adherent of the Cynic school, thought it best to cover up their bodies with a cloak. And yet Crates delivered scathing attacks on sexual immorality. If Eros, he said, is not checked even by hunger – or the passage of time – we had better let the hangman's noose do the trick.

When Zeno of Citium left the Cynics to become the founder of Stoicism, he reverted to the Platonic idea of a community of wives (later abandoned by his followers), on the grounds that the truly wise man would find a matrimonial household quite unnecessary. Friendship, he felt, was really what counted, though he did not try to brush sex aside, recognizing that physical excitement is the commonest 'violent fluttering of the soul' (pathos), and that its satisfaction is undoubtedly enjoyable. Epicurus, on the other hand, who was even keener on friendship but particularly averse to emotional entanglements, emphasized the distress caused by intense desire. Indeed, he did not propose to forbid sexual intercourse, and conceded that it does not do actual harm, provided that it is suitably promiscuous and entirely unaccompanied by disturbing passion (which seemed to him ridiculous). Yet he also believed that sex never does anyone any positive good, since it makes no genuine contribution to the absence of pain – which should always remain our ideal goal (Chapter Four, section 2).

But meanwhile a more humane, and by modern standards ordinary, approach to matters of the heart was being presented on the Athenian stage by Menander's New Comedy. In all his plays, said Plutarch quite rightly, there is one common element, and that is Eros. For having read about the erotic passion in Euripides, whose dramas enjoyed especial popularity, Menander was perfectly clear that it is love which makes the world go round; and the conviction was echoed and encouraged by his audience and readership, which included many more women than ever before. Love, therefore, is a theme on which he plays with numerous variations, ranging from the crises and estrangements of married life to a young man's adoration for a prostitute (hetaira). In particular, very often indeed, the happy endings in which the plots terminate turn on the discovery that the hero's beloved, who has been forced to live as a hetaira (or was thought to be a slave), is really of no such base origins, so that she is therefore matrimonially attainable after all.

This prominence of hetairai (who were often quite well off) was a reflection of Athenian society as Menander knew it. Although he presents women as far more lifelike personages than, say, the joke-figures of Aristophanes' fifth-century Old Comedy, it is significant that he only has two possible roles for them: as wife or *hetaira*. It was still a society in which women of good reputation met very few men, and custom almost entirely prevented respectable youths from getting to know marriageable girls. The world of the *hetairai*, who were not in this eligible category, was quite a different one, so that Menander finds it possible to endow them with feelings regarded as justifiable for themselves but not permissible for respectable young females.

Yet, granted these limitations, the world of love that he depicts also contains a substantial amount of consideration for women. Marriage is seen as a link between two individuals, and no longer between two families; love triumphs over parental opposition; and weddings arranged by the two fathers never come off. In several plays, too, a good, nice woman is hastily misjudged and wronged by her husband or lover; but there is room for remorse, and things get put right.

In this picture there is also room for chivalry. In Menander's *Misoumenos* (*Hated*), Thrasonides loves the captive girl whom he has in his power. But he does not force his sexual attentions upon her when she has taken a dislike to him, and he frees her without a ransom as soon as her father appears. Moreover, the playwright's handling of the emotions of his young couples is not unsubtle. They are not afraid to utter romantic sentiments and talk of what they feel, but when they do so they do not err on the side of heavy-handed directness or mawkish over-emphasis, but build up the picture by a series of oblique touches and allusions.

The generation that followed witnessed the rapid development of elegy as a poetic medium for displaying this new literary interest in the analysis of love. The elegiac couplet (hexameter and pentameter), which had first made its appearance as early as 700 BC, was a subtle and tempting metre full of rhythmical tensions and counterpoints, capable of witty and suggestive effects, but tender and poignant as well. One of the various uses to which it found itself rapidly adapted was to celebrate the emotion of love. But poems on the subject apparently remained rare until the third century, when this became elegy's most characteristic theme – though its Hellenistic exponents have left few surviving works. First and foremost among them, according to a somewhat dubious tradition, was Philetas of Cos (born *c.* 320 or later). His pupil Hermesianax of Colophon (*c.* 300), though apparently a poor writer, was famous for poems about passion's all-conquering power; in the three books of his *Leontion* he told his mistress (after whom the poem is named), with a wealth of learned allusions, that all great men of the past had felt the force of love.

It was Callimachus of Cyrene, however, in the same generation, who firmly established the Hellenistic elegy as a major form of poetic expression. Mournful reflections on love and death are the elegiac themes to which he devotes his incomparable technique and romantic expressiveness; though he always remains the outside observer. A very popular elegist of the first century BC, Parthenius of Nicaea, who wrote *Metamorphoses* (mythological pieces and dirges), passed on the Callimachean elegy to the Roman literary world, though it remains doubtful how far the personal Latin elegy – concerned not only with stories of love but with the poet's own love – corresponds with any lost Hellenistic prototypes.

The most successful and original Hellenistic medium for the analysis of heterosexual love was an offshoot of elegy, and once again made use of elegiac couplets. This was the epigram. Its origins, it is true, had lain in subjects other than love: the inscriptional dedications and epitaphs of writers such as Simonides of Ceos (*c.* 556–468) were concerned with themes of a different kind. In the fourth century, however, poets produced a new literary form which became independent of inscriptions and was thus able to cover a much wider range of material, including, especially, emotional and erotic relations. Thus expanded in scope, the epigram continued to find clever exponents for many hundreds of years to come. Their works were collected in a series of anthologies, of which the *Garland* of Meleager of Gadara (*c.* 80 BC), though not the first ever to be compiled, is the earliest major example of which we have any knowledge, and is represented in later collections that have survived.

The epigram's contribution to the search for the Good Life, for the widely desired attitude which could keep one going regardless of all external vicissitudes (Chapter Four, section 2), was intimacy. It condensed feelings and reflections and pathos and wit into a very few lines. Typically enacting or suggesting some little stock scene, it was an incomparably neat medium both for looking inwards into one's own self or for commenting on the world outside with concise detachment. As to looking inwards, the exploration of love, which was such a favourite feature of the Hellenistic age, seemed ideally suited to the methods and possibilities of this kind of poetry, which achieved its greatest successes in touching upon these matters of the heart (and is therefore being discussed in the present section). Indeed, the epigrammatists treated of a vast range of amorous situations – some of them, as we saw earlier, homosexual, but many others relating to men's love for women – in terms all the way from sterile cliché to sparkling wit, and the occasional poignant expression of heartfelt emotion.

This love epigram, one of the principal discoveries of the Hellenistic world, outlived many other kinds of poetry because it did not try to compete with them or obey their rules: it could be written from a personal viewpoint without restraint. True, it echoes past writings, slyly adapts, elegantly experiments, and displays antiquarian learning, like other literature of the age (Chapter Four, section 3). Yet it also very often strikes a note of unhampered, appealing directness which the rest of Hellenistic literature cannot rival. Poems with this particular blend of qualities present a stiff challenge to translators, since they depend on an infinitely subtle range of variations and counterpoints of tone and rhythm and phrase, concentrated into the briefest possible dimensions.

Two schools of Hellenistic epigram developed; a Doric school based on the Peloponnese, south Italy and Thebes, and an Ionian school centred on Samos and Alexandria. Of the Doric woman poet Anyte something has been said; but it was in the hands of an adoptive Alexandrian, Callimachus of Cyrene, that the epigram firmly emerges as a new literary type, free from the old traditional link with inscriptions. His sixty-four surviving pieces deal with various subjects, oscillating interestingly between a simple, moving, classical sympathy and feline mockery displayed, for example, in parodies of religious belief. Other epigrams by Callimachus express personal emotions or depict lovers' troubles, including his own – though, like his elegies, they present such disturbances with an air of malicious detachment.

At the same period (c. 290), Asclepiades of Samos seems to have been the leader of another Alexandrian group of writers of light verse. He and one of his associates, Posidippus of Pella, were attacked by Callimachus for admiring long epics. Nevertheless, Asclepiades became best known as a writer of brief epigrams, of which he, Posidippus, and a fellow-Samian, Hedylus, published a collection they called *The Heap of Grain (Soros)*. Asclepiades' best epigrams are erotic, written in a direct, compact style in which the genuine lyrical, personal feelings seem to offer a deliberate contrast to the more controlled and perhaps cold-blooded Callimachus. Asclepiades knows the violent obsessions of love very well, and explores them with original, dramatic talent. But love, to him, means sex much more often than romance. The women he writes about are mostly attractive *hetairai*, and he comments on them in satirical and scandalous language, frequently obscene in its content, though never in form. He was weary of living, he said, at the age of scarcely twenty-two.

The Hellenistic epigram reached the climax of its development in the hands of Meleager of Gadara (Jordan) (*c.* 140–70 BC). The anthology he collected, the *Garland*, which is no longer extant, was said to have contained works by more than forty poets. His own preface is still extant, and a hundred of his epigrams have survived in subsequent collections. Nearly all of them are about love. Their structure is taut and adroit, their manner subtle and sure, and Meleager displays an inventive ingenuity and lavish taste for experiment which diversify and transform the whole epigrammatic tradition. What is peculiar to him is his profuse, exotic, Syrian imagination, displayed in a wide range of sugary, ornate, amorous imagery, amid a steamy mist of fantastic perfumed metaphors. Meleager, like the writer of the Hebrew *Song of Songs* (*Song of Solomon*), written in the same epoch and country, is one of the great poets of heterosexual love. He knows that some women are promiscuous, and that others drink too much. Yet his love for the female sex still assumes a hundred shapes, and he exalts it into something like a religion.

Equally intense and exciting was the treatment of love by a contemporary of the first Hellenistic epigrammatists, Theocritus of Syracuse. He, too, wrote excellent epigrams, but it is his longer poems, known subsequently as his idylls, that say most about women and love; and the theme stands close to the centre of his complex lyrical vision of people and their place in the world.

However, Theocritus does not seek to interpret love as an ennobling or purifying passion, for there is nothing he does not know about the misery of erotic frustration, the agony of the heart. In his first poem (*Thyrsis*), he tells how the goddess Aphrodite sneered at his passion. He himself, in more contemplative moods, would agree, for he sees capitulation to love as an illness, a lapse of the intelligence, a lunatic sinking-down into the fragmentation and disorder to which humankind are in any case all too prone: and, except when fatalistic resignation is sometimes his mood, he dedicates himself to the task of coming to terms with the menace.

He attempts this, at times, with a measure of his usual detached humour and irony, making the frustrated lover's agonized indignities into parodies of grandiose heroic struggles. But in one poem he reaches more sharply to the heart of the matter. This is the second piece in the collection, *The Sorceress* (*Pharmaceutria*). Revealing some of the vivid techniques of the mime (of which he was a master – Chapter Three, section 2), Theocritus tells of the disappointed love of Simaetha, and describes the incantations she employs to recover the affections of her lover. Up to a point, the poet is a discerning, sensitive feminist. Yet one of the contrasts and contradictions which obsessed his mind – and such contradictions were the essence of the Hellenistic scene – was the basic, ultimate irreconcilability of male and female, and that is what he is trying to express here. In this passionate and splendid poem, Simaetha, crying out feverishly and unrestrainedly to the moon, fails to come to terms with her rejection by her man, like other abandoned heroines of literary tradition. And those mythological heroines are enumerated here, with a typical Hellenistic erudition that might have turned the poem to dust. In Theocritus' hands, however, the opposite happens, and she emerges more vividly than any of them, exposing her inmost thoughts and feelings with an overwhelming, pathological force.

Unlike other Theocritean lovers, Simaetha does not turn to song for consolation. She turns instead to magic. But magic, says Theocritus (and it would have been better if countless people of the Hellenistic world had listened to him), is a bad and profitless antidote, and cannot help her lamentable derangement in any way at all. What she says at the end of the poem is movingly sympathetic. She does not, it is true, renounce magic; she is too deeply upset for that. Yet: 'My desire I'll bear as best I can – as I have until now.' [36] Perhaps sheer endurance, a falling back on her ultimate resources of strength, will bring her through the unbearable crisis that magic can do nothing to resolve. Theocritus has his own alternative recipe for this (Chapter Four, section 3).

In the next generation, Apollonius Rhodius, by depicting Medea's passion for Jason in his poem the *Argonautica*, became the first poet to use love as the central theme for an epic poem – romantic love, too, characterized by early, shattering visual impact, violent obsessive agitation, idealization of the beloved, and readiness to battle against all obstacles for the sake of the long-term future. With the single exception of Sappho four hundred years earlier, no other Greek poet ever depicted the beginnings of a girl's heartfelt passion with such sensitive sympathy, or followed its future dramas with so much care – with an insight and sympathy no writer of the preceding classical epoch would have cared or felt able to show, not even Euripides, whose tragic heroines had been so memorable. Euripides had developed the idea that to portray an individual emotion is the most important thing, more important than the presentation of a rounded, complete picture of a whole personality. Apollonius gave this perception a new and hitherto unimagined profundity and vividness:

> So without voice, without murmur, they stood there face to face,
> As oaks or towering pine-trees stand rooted in their place

Side by side, unmoving, high up among the hills,
When winds are hushed – but, sudden, a gust through their branches thrills,
And they whisper with infinite voices. So now before Love's gale
Those two were doomed, in a moment, to tell their whole hearts' tale.[37]

By portraying, with almost painful psychological intensity, this young Medea who is desperately in love, Apollonius has created romantic passion as a major literary theme, or rather he has used the manner and matter of heroic epic to present a fantastic tale in which high romance is adventurously blended with the equally novel Hellenistic taste for descriptive realism. The blend is somewhat surprising and discordant, just as the poem itself is too disjointed to achieve a traditional epic unity (Chapter Four, section 3); and these inconsistencies offended the highly developed sense of form cherished by some of his critics. Yet no less an epic poet than Virgil paid the *Argonautica* the compliment of deliberate imitation, and it was largely due to Apollonius that love became, as it has ever since remained, the principal subject of imaginative literature.

Love, of a more middle-brow and saccharine nature, was once again the main feature of the novels that were now being launched upon the world, melodramatically separating earnest heroes from their coy heroines only to reunite them in a happy ending – the *Ninus Romance*, *Joseph and Aseneth*, *The Dream of Nectanebus*, predecessors of Heliodorus' *Aethiopica* and Longus' *Daphnis and Chloe* of Roman imperial times, and forerunners of a thousand best-sellers of today. Furthermore, in the early first century BC, Parthenius of Nicaea (who became a prisoner of war of the Romans, and considerably impressed them by his talents) took time off from his elegiac poetry to compile a book of *Sorrowful Love-Stories* gathered from various Greek writings, so that the Latin elegist Cornelius Gallus could use them as material for his poems.

Much more spicy, however, and catering for a more prurient type of public, were the sex-orientated short stories that came into fashion at the same time. They were inaugurated, or popularized as a literary form, by Aristides of Miletus (*c.* 100), and consequently became known as *Milesian Tales* (*Milesiaca*). Such stories, stimulated perhaps by anecdotes told by speakers at dinner parties, tended to be immoral and ironical. In the early first century BC, Aristides' *Tales* were translated or adapted into Latin by Sisenna, whose version greatly shocked the Parthians when they found it in the baggage of Roman officers captured at the battle of Carrhae (53 BC). But the writings of Sisenna as well as Aristides are lost, and the best way to reconstruct their intentions is to read the *Milesian Tales* inserted by Petronius and Apuleius in their Latin novels of the first and second centuries AD respectively, the *Satyricon* and the *Golden Ass*. Magic and sorcery help to add a bizarre seasoning, but the basic theme was love – in the somewhat specialized, cynical sense that no woman's chastity is proof against sufficiently ingenious assaults upon its defences; and the joke becomes better because the stories misleadingly start amid the starry-eyed, sugary atmosphere of a romantic novel, only to develop later in this entirely different and far less edifying direction.

In visual art, the new Hellenistic interest in women took enormously vigorous shape. It expressed itself, above all, in terms of Aphrodite, goddess of love and of the entire cosmic force that animates nature. When sculptors and painters portrayed her in altogether novel, imaginative fashions as part of their search for greater physical realism (Chapter Two, section 2), they had another purpose in mind as well; the depiction not only of a female body, but of womanhood itself – seen often in nudity, which may not have contributed to a greater respect for women, but certainly made for a better understanding of what sort of people they really were.

Moreover, from about 370 BC, and with increasing momentum as the Hellenistic age got under way, the ideal picture of what a woman ought to look like was changing: a new feminine physical type came into fashion, deliberately rejecting the old classical lines. This new Greek woman has narrower, sloping shoulders and tiny breasts but she boasts broad and swelling hips. These were all evidently considered attractive features at the time, for the softer, sculptural moulding now in fashion is deliberately intended to stress sensual appeal. The aim, in these days of the discovery of womanhood, is to design a woman's form that is not so much beautiful as (according to the ideas of the age) seductive. It was the lifelike sexiness of these artistic endeavours that appealed to the Greeks. The fifth-century painter Zeuxis of Heraclea in Lucania, planning a painting of Helen of Troy for the city of Croton, was said to have held a parade of the local girls and chosen the best features of five of them for incorporation in a single one of his figures, in order to achieve the utmost possible degree of realism; and in the following century Apelles' Aphrodite Anadyomene (Aphrodite Rising from the Sea) was hailed as a masterpiece of fidelity. It was the same with the sculptors. Praxiteles reputedly employed his mistress Phryne as a model for his Aphrodite of Cnidus, ready for her bath, which was regarded as the finest statue ever to have been made because it was seen as totally realistic. Indeed, it was considered so sexually exciting – though the dull surviving copies make it an effort to appreciate this – that lewd legends grew up to describe the excitement experienced by men who gazed at its charms.

Aphrodite was traditionally abetted by her son Eros, who stands for sexual desire, regarded by philosophers as a disease. There had long been tributes to his mighty power, and Theocritus and Menander associated themselves passionately with the conviction of its horrifying nature. Later, however, writers and artists more comfortingly transformed him from a lethally dangerous youth into a mischievous, whimsical imp – or pluralization of imps, the Erotes, illustrating the multiplicity of the ravages he performed on Aphrodite's behalf.

Chapter Four

The Search for Peace of Mind

1 Despair and Faith

The Hellenistic age, as we have now seen, devoted a new, sympathetic attention to the individual man and woman. In consequence, an enormous proportion of the best thought of the time was concerned with analysing the extensive problems and predicaments that disturbed him and her, in order to solve them and dispel the anxieties that they caused. This, by definition, should have been a practical, realistic pursuit; and indeed, as the previous chapter emphasized, the age witnessed an unprecedented grasping after realism, a determined search for the realities of life in all their various forms, free from idealizations and illusions. And yet, by virtue of the greatest contradiction of an epoch that was full of them, the quest for these individual solutions at times veered right away from rationality. As at other times in the world's history, it seemed as if people, having looked at reality, could take just so much of it and no more, so that for the further satisfaction of their yearnings they had to plunge into the irrational, or at least reveal intense disbelief in all that reason could achieve – a feeling which, despite the philosophers, had never been far below the surface of Greek life.

For one thing, tens of thousands of people were gripped by an unreasonable, dismal, desperate conviction that everything in the world was under the total control of Tyche: Fortune, Chance or Luck. There was a deep-seated feeling that men and women were adrift in an uncaring universe, and that everything was hazardous, beyond human control or understanding or prediction. And so the cult of Chance swept conqueringly over the Mediterranean. It was not a new concept, and it covered various ideas: one and the same lyric passage of Pindar (518–438) had interpreted Tyche both as what a man attains on his own, and what happens to him by luck.[1] Nor could the poets and philosophers agree whether the gods were Tyche's masters, or whether her existence and power excluded belief in their existence altogether; in a play of Euripides, the herald Talthybius wondered whether it was Zeus or Chance that governs the world[2] – and it was the latter idea that increasingly gained strength as the old religion tended to lose its hold. Centuries later, the Roman poet Lucan summed up this conclusion:

> There are no gods: to say Jove reigns is wrong.
> 'Tis a blind Chance that moves the years along.[3]

For to many people it seemed, in the Hellenistic and Roman worlds and long before, that Chance or Fortune was some order of affairs beyond the comprehension of human beings. There was nothing theoretical about her, however; it was all too easy to see her in action, raising men and women up and striking them down: today to me, tomorrow to thee.

In the fourth century BC, and afterwards, the idea that we prosper or suffer unforeseen and unmerited disasters in an entirely arbitrary fashion gained currency. It was significant that a successful local prince, Alexander of Pherae in Thessaly (d. 358), was worshipped by his people as Tychon (Lucky – and the name of a fertility god). By the time of Alexander the Great, the potency of Fortune or Luck – Aristotle sought to find a difference between them[4] – was well established; and one of the best-worn debating points was whether that mighty king himself owed his achievements to merit or merely to Chance. As to his immediate successors, they were seen by many contemporaries and historians to be engaged in a grim and meaningless game of hazard, in the course of which every possible seesaw of fortune afflicted them in turn. Demetrius I Poliorcetes, who was accustomed to quote the tragic poets on Tyche's hazards, himself looked like the supreme example of her vicissitudes. But in a gambler's world of war and stress and disorientation everyone else, too, felt that they were wholly at the mercy of blind luck.

An altar in the Agora at Athens had four panels, each depicting a piteous situation induced by a reversal of Fortune. In the same city, too, at the outset of the Hellenistic age, the poets of the New Comedy were repeatedly emphasizing Tyche's ruthless power in the pessimistic, melancholy vein that had always been prominent in Greek literature. Menander, especially, dwelt over and over again on her incalculable strokes, and the unfavourable odds that confront us in dealing with her – the helpless victims of force that, despite all the efforts we have to make, we cannot resist. As one of his characters despairingly cries: 'Each single thought, each word, each act of ours is just Chance. All you and I can do is sign on the dotted line'.[5] Even so, Menander, or one of his fellow dramatists, declares it wrong to blame Chance for ills that we ourselves have brought about: 'It's clear Fortune can have no bodily existence – but those who can't bear the natural course of events apply the name of Fortune to their own character!'[6]

The philosophers tried to come to terms with Tyche, and the Aristotelians (Peripatetics) in particular made great efforts to convert this great antagonist of philosophy into its servant. Not that they denied her existence. Theophrastus, for example – implying criticism of his master Aristotle's belief in a purposeful universe – stressed that there is much that happens at random and without an aim; and another Peripatetic, the Athenian leader Demetrius of Phaleron, was the first man, as far as we know, to dedicate a whole treatise to the operations of Fortune. Epicurus angrily dismissed the belief that she was a divine being as a popular fallacy.[7] But he was very much in a minority, for many people saw her as a goddess, and were extremely ready to identify Tyche with Cybele and Isis, or make her Aphrodite's attendant – the embodiment of feminine whim.

Every individual person, too, was believed to have a *private* Fortune peculiar to himself or herself. The idea developed from the ancient concept that everybody had a private spirit or *daimon* watching over him, seen as a power for good or evil; and so the term Tyche, used rather in the same sense, came to personify someone's own distinctive individuality, being variously interpreted as a providential gift – the Tyche of a king could be worshipped – or an entirely capricious force.

By an extension of this idea, not only every individual, but every city, too, was ascribed its own Tyche; and the cults allotted to these Fortunes were aimed at appeasing the unpredictable and uncontrollable elements that might buffet these communities in the future. It was hoped that Good Luck (Agathe Tyche, Agathodaimon) would protect and bless the cities and their soil. The earliest of these cults of which we have any knowledge was at Thebes, in Boeotia, where her figure was shown holding the child Plutus (Wealth). Later on, similar worships spread to many smaller places as well.

Many endeavours were made to give visual shape to the idea. Praxiteles created a statue of Agathe Tyche for Athens. But the most famous and influential figure of Tyche in the entire ancient world belonged to a sculptural group made by Eutychides of Sicyon for the recently founded Seleucid capital of Antioch in Syria (296–293). The original has disappeared, but we can see from Roman copies and coins that Tyche was shown seated on her mountain with the river-god Orontes at her feet, while the Seleucid kings Seleucus I Nicator and Antiochus I offer her wreaths. Gazing thoughtfully into the future, she stands for the success of the new city, wearing a turreted crown that symbolizes its walls, and holding the palm-leaves of victory.

The historian Polybius of Megalopolis (*c.* 200–after 118) deliberately

placed Tyche in the very centre of the world he was depicting, because
he felt that the transformation of the Mediterranean into a unified
Roman lake was an epoch-making event that could only be explained
in this way: 'For fruitful as Fortune is in change, and constantly as she
is producing dramas in the life of human beings, yet never assuredly
before this did she work such a marvel, or act such a drama, as we have
witnessed'[8] (Chapter Three, section 2).

However, his interpretations of what 'Fortune' actually means are
varied and shifting, like most people's views on the subject. Sometimes
he sees Tyche as everything that lies beyond human control, or displays
no rational causes. Sometimes her name is his label to describe purely
haphazard coincidences – or to reflect the fact that anything can happen
to anyone at any time. Occasionally there is a hint of a purposive
Providence, or of the old Greek idea, so familiar from the tragic drama,
that it is Fortune's task to see that mortal wickedness, or even excessive
prosperity, is penalized. Yet Polybius also views Tyche as basically
amoral, and just as likely to injure the virtuous. But it is in large-scale
operations that his Tyche really comes into play: when huge and capricious events upset the balance of history, and the fortunes of nations are
abruptly and sensationally reversed. However, when another, rational,
cause is perceptible, he prefers to invoke that instead, calling upon
Tyche only when no such rational cause can be detected. He feels that
human beings genuinely overcome by Fortune (as opposed to mere
self-destructive fools) deserve our pity. All they can do is to yield, with
such dignity as they are able to muster.

In this presentation of Tyche or Fortune, Polybius also offers two
lessons to people pursuing his own professions of politician and historian.
The politician must learn from history, not only to foresee what can be
foreseen, but also (as far as is humanly possible) to predict the unpredictable. The historian must not only know his facts – and the causes
and effects that are associated with them – but he must also note how
men and women have met vicissitudes quite outside the usual run of
causality, and what means, therefore, they should employ to confront
such hazards if they occur again. Moreover, Tyche is fundamental to
his entire historical approach. It was she who, by giving the Romans so
much power, created a unified world; and in consequence Polybius
(rejecting limited monographs) had produced the unified work of history that was the outcome and counterpart of this new world, and was
given its decisive pattern by this central event. Indeed, it had only been
through pondering on the part played by Tyche in the rise of Rome
that he decided to undertake the writing of his great history at all.

By invoking and discussing its connexion with Rome, Polybius had endowed the concept of Chance (despite its ambiguous features) with intellectual respectability. Here once again, however, there is that touch of ambivalence hinging on its relationship to Providence. For Polybius saw Rome's conquest of the Hellenistic world as *destined* to happen, so that Tyche is to this extent a power working towards a conscious goal, a providential planner like the producer of a play – in which human beings can control the sectional scenes and sub-plots, but are unable to influence the Grand Design (a comfort, incidentally, to his humiliated fellow-Greeks, who could thus shift the blame for their defeats at the hands of Rome on to impersonal forces). With this Design in mind, Polybius noted how Rome had built up its empire with smooth, irresistible and apparently inevitable ease. Yet merit, as well as Chance and Providence, enters into the matter, for the historian is also (not altogether consistently) very sure that Rome's success could be *rationally* explained, and was the fitting outcome of superior gifts. Although Polybius was well aware that so many of his fellow-Greeks resented the Romans intensely, he still maintained that the conquered are in the wrong: it is nature's well-known ordinance that inferiors should be governed by their betters.

The inconsistency could be ironed out by explaining that the gods help those who help themselves – and the historian traces the stages by which the Romans did just that. And yet, pro-Roman though Polybius is, he sees no reason why Rome should be spared, at some unknown date in the future, from the eventual decline that comes to every person and community alike.[9] And indeed the Romans themselves were not unaware of the need to placate Fortune: noble friends of Scipio Africanus built shrines in her honour after the Second Punic War (218–201), and the Temple of Fortune at her old oracular centre in Praeneste (Palestrina) was the most splendid sanctuary ever to be erected in Italy. In the imperial epoch, too, as countless writers bear witness, she still had not lost any of her sinister allurement.

However, during the centuries immediately before and after the beginning of the Christian era, people were starting to speak less about Fortune and more about the Fate or Destiny which had already been the subject of Polybius' meditations. Fate was often viewed as a general scheme ruling the world and creating a chain of remorseless mechanical causation. Certainly, there was not always much difference, in people's minds, between 'chance would have it so' and 'it was fated to be so'. But some writers, realizing that it is illogical to believe in them both at one and the same time, tried to distinguish between them. Thus Zeno (d. 263 BC), the founder of Stoicism, saw belief in Fate as the more respectable doctrine of the two, offering a cause and series of causes 'like a fine thread running through the whole of existence';[10] and his follower Cleanthes coupled Destiny, to which he wrote a famous hymn, with Zeus himself. For the Stoics identified Fate with the Divine Reason, which determines everything and demands our total joyous acceptance and assent, though we can choose *how* we shall obey it, at least in detail. Their opponent Epicurus, however, believed it was worse to be enslaved to this philosophical and moral Fate than to serve even the useless gods revered by the vulgar: the wise man, he says, laughs Fate to scorn. And many others, too, felt daunted and oppressed by its inescapable, intolerable, boring despotism, which so ruthlessly restricted the ultimate value of human behaviour. Nevertheless, millions of people accepted its tyranny without question.

Millions, too, including some of the best educated people of the day, accepted an even more lamentable doctrine: belief in the power of the sun, moon and stars. For the movements of such celestial forces, it seemed overwhelmingly certain, must affect the lives and deaths, fates and fortunes of humankind. The foundation for this belief was a widespread, profound conviction that some kind of harmony exists between the earth and these heavenly bodies – some cosmic 'sympathy' which meant that the earth and all the orbs seen shining in the sky must possess the same laws and behaviour in common. People felt sure – and philosophers encouraged them in this conviction – that the cosmos is a unity, whose parts are interdependent: that is to say, behind the huge and spectacular processions of the sun, moon and stars, like the marchings of the Homeric armies before the walls of Troy, some underlying solidarity and order has to exist – an order which must correspondingly prevail on earth as well. For it was believed that the heavenly bodies were nourished by emanations or effluvia from their counterpart the earth, and it therefore seemed only sensible to conclude that emanations also proceeded in the opposite direction, too, and influenced the earth and the human beings who dwelt on its surface.

A clear proof that what happens above affects what happens below seemed to be provided by the visible influence that the heavenly bodies exert on the world: the sun makes the vegetation grow and die, and causes animals to sleep and go on heat; storms and floods come and go according to the rise and fall of constellations; and the moon appears to control the tides like a magnet – the laws of tide-generating gravitation being unknown, this relationship (in so far as it interested the dwellers round an almost tideless sea) was explained by cosmic sympathy between a supposedly watery planet and the element of water in earth. So the whole doctrine seemed to hang together neatly, completely, and rationally, in coherence with the sciences. Yet it is based on a complete fallacy. The generalization that links all human activities, as well as the physical properties of the earth, to the heavenly bodies is quite without foundation.

The pedigree of this set of beliefs had been antique and complex. The Greek tragic poets described sun, moon and stars as deities, and Plato accepted this belief, weaving an elaborate astral theology into the fabric of his ideal state. Aristotle, too, far from hostile to a relationship between earth and the stars, regarded the latter as intelligent, divine beings – an interpretation that almost all Hellenistic writers shared. People were learning with fascinated interest about the star-worship and astrological practices of the ancient Babylonians, for example from Eudoxus of Cnidus (*c.* 390–340); and once Alexander the Great had absorbed Babylonia into the world of the Greeks, professional astrologers began to transmit and adapt its traditions to the west.

The first of these practitioners was said to be the Babylonian priest Berossus, translator of *The Eye of Bel*, who moved to Cos and founded an astrological school on the island (*c.* 280). But it was not until after 200 that the movement reached the proportions of a flood. This was the time when Bolus of Mendes in Egypt (a country that had learnt its astrology from Mesopotamia) compiled a treatise *On Sympathies and Antipathies* which explained and justified the fictitious correspondence between heavenly bodies and human beings. His book became one of the most influential best-sellers of all time. Another successful work was an astrological textbook, probably written *c.* 150–120, which went under the probably fictitious Egyptian names of Nechepso and Petosiris.

These beliefs fitted all too easily into the doctrines of the contemporary Stoic school of philosophy, especially at this time when science was beginning to fade. Thus its leader Diogenes 'the Babylonian' from Seleucia on the Tigris (d. 152), maintaining, as Stoics did, that the souls of men and women contain a spark of the power that rules the heavens, and building on his forerunner Cleanthes' veneration of the sun and the celestial bodies, became the traitor within the gates who welcomed astrology for its apparently convincing proof of this 'Sympathy of all Creation'. It is true that another important Stoic, Panaetius of Rhodes (*c.* 185–109), although willing to accept the validity of divination, rejected the idea that the sun, moon and stars causally affect the affairs of the world. But soon afterwards this pseudo-science was given even more impressive sanction by the favour lavished upon it by the outstandingly influential Stoic Posidonius of Apamea in Syria (*c.* 135–50 BC), whose belief in a unifying cosmic sympathy caused him to agree with Diogenes the Babylonian in welcoming the basic astrological principles as keys to the harmony of the universe.

Those who believed in such fallacies (even if they allowed a limited scope for free will) were voluntarily reducing their own power of action to very little, preferring to consider themselves ruled by the unfeeling, unchanging, inescapable heavenly spheres, predestining all that will happen. Yet many revolted against this pitiless mechanical inevitability, and sought urgently to discover whether the oppressiveness of these astral powers could not somehow be circumvented or reduced. The first step towards such an evasion or mitigation was to find out, by enquiry, what the powers had in store; and then to discover how to determine, arrange, and time one's own future activities so as to avoid subjecting oneself to their most hostile intentions.

These arduous tasks, however, could only be undertaken with the assistance of experts – namely the professional astrologers, who thus became a highly influential class. Their primary task was to devote careful study to the seven planets – currently identified as Saturn, Jupiter, Mars, the Sun, Venus, Mercury and the Moon – since it was these that were believed to jointly influence all that lay beneath them, particularly the earth – still for most people the supposed middle-point of the system (Chapter Three, section 1) – and all the human beings that it contained. Alongside the planets, the second major elements in this fantasy were provided by the twelve signs of the Zodiac or 'Houses of the Sun', which were likewise believed to exert potent influences over events.

It was therefore towards these planets and signs, seen as the principal controllers of the human race, that astrologers had to turn their attention. Aristotle's successor Theophrastus remarked on the extraordinary gifts of these Chaldaeans, as they were called (after the southern region of Mesopotamia), who could predict future events including the careers and deaths of individuals; and then the historian Diodorus Siculus, in the first century, declared how wonderful it was that they could 'foretell all changes, good and bad, affecting not only the nations and regions of the world, but also monarchs, and ordinary men and women'.[11] In so doing, these astrologers provided numberless believers with the main interest, consolation and excitement in their lives. And, after all, if a prophecy turned out wrong, these believers could always argue that it was merely an individual practitioner who had been at fault, and not the principles of the system themselves.

One of the astrologers' main activities was the casting of horoscopes. This was done by the working-out of patterns which, by noting the arrangement of the heavenly bodies at the time of a person's birth (or conception), indicated what his future destiny was to be. The earliest horoscopes of which we have any knowledge date from the fifth century BC and employ techniques of Babylonian origin; thereafter the practice became rapidly more widespread, especially in Hellenistic Alexandria.

This overwhelming vogue was due not only to the Chaldaeans' alleged ability to prophesy future destinies, but also, and to a far greater extent, to their additional and exciting assertion that they were able to counsel *how to outwit* what had been destined – how to coerce and manipulate the powers into actually changing their intentions. And so the oppressions of the sun and moon and stars did not seem to be so substantially inescapable after all, since the astrologers, by discovering the days, hours and minutes of the influences these celestial bodies were going to exert, could effectively advise a client how to evade their dictation by planning, or refraining from planning, his or her activities at the times and seasons the experts declared to be appropriate. There were of course people who doubted the authenticity of such claims, but compared to the credulous they were a drop in the ocean.

With such beliefs in astrology went an equally persistent belief in portents and prodigies of every form and kind, and above all an acceptance of magic, which sought to influence the course of nature by constraining its activities through the performance of occult, esoteric practices. After the great dramatic monologue of Theocritus' second poem, invoking magical powers (Chapter Three, section 4), and Menander's *Thessalian Woman* who draws down the moon, Bolus of Mendes linked his astrology with this sort of occultism and alchemy and magic, all of which were hailed as purely scientific subjects – as manifestations, indeed, of practical science in action.

The subsequent taste for magical procedures was enormous and long-lasting. In particular, they gave a shady living to a whole series of professional miracle-workers and charlatans, such as the 'sage' Apollonius of Tyana (d. after AD 96?), a product of the Neo-Pythagorean movement which glorified Pythagoras as author of a religious revelation. Neo-Pythagoreanism had not appeared in Rome and Alexandria until the first century BC; but long before that gurus of various persuasions had found it easy to obtain funds from the credulous, notably Eunus, Syrian leader of the first slave-revolt in Sicily (135–132), who claimed magical gifts in support of his rebel régime.

Once again, there were people who disbelieved in magic. The tone and outcome of Theocritus' second poem seems to show that he was among their number; and the popular philosopher Lucian of Samosata (born *c.* AD 120) became the most famous of all the scoffers. But once again, too, there had been a feeling ever since Hellenistic times and earlier still – and it was a feeling which was far more widespread – that, even if one individual practitioner or another might be fraudulent, the fundamental principles on which magical practices were based could not be all that unsound.

The growth of all these half-worlds clinging to the fringes of science, history and religion was part and parcel of a general waning of hope, a generally declining belief in the potentialities of real scientific research, that became apparent in the second and first centuries BC. At the beginning of that period, an intelligent observer, noting recent advances in the sciences, would have seemed justified in thinking that an epoch of increasing knowledge, something approaching an Age of Reason, was on its way, and lay not too far in the future. If so, he would have been totally wrong.

Euripides, in his overwhelmingly powerful *Bacchae* (*Bacchants*) (*c.* 405), had warned that reason and reasonableness are not enough, and Aristotle, too, deliberately left room for the irrational. But now there was a danger that irrationality would take over altogether: the desire for reality felt by scientists, writers and artists alike was arrested by this formidable counter-current that had no scientific basis whatsoever.

Astrology and magic, then, were two of the false sciences which promised escape, not only from unpalatable reality, but from the horrors of fate and destiny. Meanwhile countless other people pinned their hopes of escape and equanimity instead upon a passionate belief in gods and goddesses – or in some of them.

The Greeks were traditionally a religious people. Yet there had always been a tendency, at the same time, to treat the gods with a certain familiar flippancy – this is already very apparent in the *Iliad* and the *Homeric Hymns*. The rationalist movements of the later fifth century had subjected the reputation of the divine personages to a further battering. The inquisitive spirit of Euripides, when not (as in the *Bacchae*) interpreting the gods as profound psychological forces, was capable of presenting them as shady seducers or discredited figures of fun. And at the same time Socrates was questioning the whole traditional fabric so indefatigably that his prosecutors, who secured his death sentence, were hardly wrong to accuse him of 'not believing in the gods in whom the city believes'.

Then the early Hellenistic age that followed produced numerous slighting references to the Olympian powers. Many people had come to regard them as merely symbolic, and even the Stoics, for all their belief in divine Providence, reinterpreted and accommodated many

individual deities as merely allegorical explanations of natural phenomena. Like Hellenistic sculptors, who began to represent some of these
gods, and above all goddesses, in much less idealistic forms than those
their predecessors had favoured, the poets Callimachus and Theocritus
showed that they were living in an age when the old gods were no longer
a matter of belief or serious concern.

Other writers were even more specific. Thus the idea of Euhemerus
that the gods Uranus, Cronus and Zeus had once been great human
kings upon the earth may have been a flattering gesture in favour of
worshipping living monarchs as their equals (Chapter One, section 6),
but it was also, in another sense – like the suggestion that Aphrodite
had been the first prostitute – little more than a rationalization of
atheism; and his younger contemporary Strato of Lampsacus (d. 269)
declared that he did not need the help of the gods at all in order to
construct an understandable world. Meanwhile, an Athenian's hymn
to Demetrius I Poliorcetes had asserted that the gods of the city, if not
non-existent, were at least indifferent: and both Menander (in passing)
and Epicurus (in an elaborate series of philosophical arguments) found
this latter conclusion an obviously correct one, since the traditional gods
seemed able to do nothing to ease men's daily encounters with the
vicissitudes of Hellenistic life. St Paul, after such ideas had been going
round for three or four centuries, understandably saw pagan Hellenism
as a 'world without hope – and without God'.[12]

All the same, his impression was misleading. Pagan religion was not
already dying or dead when Christianity overtook it; it had remained
very lively indeed. But it had deviated, and continued to deviate
throughout the Hellenistic age, from the traditional mainstream of the
classical Olympian cults. They continued, it is true, to receive impressive
ceremonial worship, but a person of this epoch no longer pinned his or
her faith on those gods, but on a number of Divine Saviours. These
Saviours were relied on, passionately, for two quite distinct miraculous
gifts, of which their various cults held out hopes in varying proportions:
the conferment of strength and holiness to endure our present life upon
this earth, and the gift of immortality and happiness after death. And so
religion was not moribund at all, but turned out to be one of the most
vital elements in the Hellenistic world.

The guarantees for the hereafter offered by the Mystery cults enormously impressed the Hellenistic public mind. An epoch had begun –
it lasted for more than two millennia – when the chief anxieties of society
centred round the afterlife. Fear of what was going to happen when one
died had already been on the increase among the Greeks during the
fifth century BC, and was strong in the fourth, as Plato bears witness.

The earlier belief had been that the life after death was only a pallid reflection of life on earth, inhabited by the feebly, dimly flitting souls of dead men and women. But now such ideas had been transformed in favour of an almost universal conviction that the afterlife was the scene of wonderful rewards and terrifying punishments.

This greatly annoyed certain philosophers, notably the Epicureans, who refused to believe a word of it. However, the unphilosophically-minded now felt very differently indeed, and cast round for an assurance that when the time came they would be on the right side. The elixir that was called upon to dispel their anxieties was religion – a special sort of religion, characteristic of the age. It dispelled them, not by arguing that the punishments never take place, but by removing believers from within the menaced area. That is to say, the appropriate cults' processes of *ecstasis* (the soul becoming clear of the body) and *enthusiasmos* (the god entering his worshippers), and an accompanying series of ordeals and penances, would initiate them into divine mysteries and privileges which meant that, after they were dead, these horrific punishments could touch them no longer. Magic might change your destiny, but initiation – *musterion*, so that these were called Mystery religions – raised you outside its clutches altogether; and the soul of the initiate was elevated beyond the reach of the hateful stars, too, or brought together with them in harmony so that they could no longer do it damage.

This miracle was effected by personal union with a Saviour God, who was often himself believed to have died and risen again in the past. He had been saved, and initiation into his Mysteries would bring your salvation too. The supposed transformation was carried out with the aid of detailed and binding precepts, baptisms and sacramental banquets. By such means the initiations were designed to provide an overwhelming conviction of holiness, accentuated sometimes by a new sense of conscience and sin, and above all by an intensity of emotional experience and dependence from which flowed ineffable comfort and tranquillity of mind – a tranquillity which came from an absolute assurance that the terror and power of death would be, and indeed already had been, overcome.

The germ of these proceedings had been present from very early times in the elaborate annual rituals of the earth goddess Demeter at Eleusis near Athens. The secret rites apparently included a cult-drama, enacting the sacred marriage of the Grain-Maiden Persephone with Hades (Pluto), the god of the underworld. Originally linked with the annually recurrent cycle of nature, these mystic rites came in due course to possess a new significance: participation by initiates ensured the favour of the deities who rule beneath the earth – that is how a happy afterlife would be ensured, and all anxieties about what it had in store effectively dispelled.

During the procession in honour of Demeter at Eleusis the participants called upon a god Iacchus, identified with Dionysus, who became one of the principal symbols of the Hellenistic epoch. Long ago, itinerant devotees had brought his savage, frenzied worship from Thrace. Dionysus was the Liberator (*Lysios*) of men and women. At one time, in the sixth century BC, the orgies performed in his name may have become so violent and agitated that they almost seemed to threaten the subversion of the whole social structure. Later, in the classical epoch, the Greek city-states tried to make these manifestations respectable by incorporating them in official cults: but the profoundly disturbing behaviour of the Dionysiac devotees lives on in the *Bacchae* of Euripides.

Soon the cult of Dionysus, like that of Demeter, became the setting for elaborate Mysteries. In the kingdoms of Alexander and his Successors they gained widespread popularity: Dionysus is the distinctive deity of Macedonian and Greek expansion into the east. For he, too, so legend recounted, had made a triumphal progress through Asia – like Alexander, who was assured by the inhabitants of Nysa in the Koh-i-Mor valley of Swat in northern Pakistan that they were descended from the god Dionysus' soldiers. But Dionysus, once his conquests had brought peace, was believed to have turned to the pursuit of pleasure and enjoyment, which were also in store for his faithful devotees, perhaps already in their lifetimes, and certainly in the world to come.

So the Mysteries of Dionysus became one of the leading religious cults of the age, assimilating many foreign faiths. He stood for all life that rises in the spring, for the sap in the trees, for the seed in animals and men, so that by worshipping him men hoped that they themselves would rise again after the winter of death, and revel intoxicated for all time to come. The return of Dionysus to Europe after his eastern victories signified the annual return of fertility, and his mystic marriage with Ariadne (whose prominence helped to give women their place in the cult) told how the initiate, redeemed from Hades, would celebrate throughout the afterlife in the company of his divine deliverer and guide (Kathegemon), an everlasting triumphal symposium of the blessed, himself 'becoming Dionysus'.

Demetrius I Poliorcetes was happy to worship this god of joy and release. But it was the house of the Ptolemies in Egypt which went to special pains, for their own dynastic purposes, to canalize the worship of Dionysus, from whom they claimed descent so as to legitimize their own royal claims; and so his ecstatic cult was encouraged and jealously domesticated under the auspices of the court, to prevent it from becoming a potential counter-culture instead. A small bronze bust of Dionysus seems to show the features of Ptolemy I Soter. His son Ptolemy II Philadelphus staged particularly lavish and ostentatious processions in honour of the god, whom he saw as the patron of his own luxurious image – and the promoter of carefree liberation from daily cares by wine, which was calculated to keep his subjects happy and content. It was Ptolemy IV Philopator, however, who was Dionysus' most zealous and extravagant servant and initiate of all, and who, despite the distaste of his fastidious wife Arsinoe III Philopator, did much to stimulate still further the popularity of the cult. There was also financial method behind Ptolemy IV's enthusiasm, since his regulation of the procedure of the Mysteries by edict included the insistence that their priests should register – and render accounts.

Famous since early times as the supreme inspirer of the Greek drama, Dionysus now presided over the Alexandrian symposia where Hellenistic poetry was recited, and female entertainers gave performances. Pre-eminent among religious guilds were associations in Dionysus' honour, which devoted themselves to the promotion of music and theatre, the lead being taken by Athens in the early third century BC; and itinerant musical performers were banded together 'in the service of Dionysus'. The visual arts mirrored these Dionysiac fashions. The traditional representation of the god's female devotees, the maenads, goes back to the sculptor Scopas, and satyrs or fauns, too, became commonplaces of Hellenist art. A bronze mixing-bowl of c. 320 from Dherveni in Macedonia gives a splendid representation of maenads and satyrs alike in the train of Dionysus and Ariadne. In due course Dionysiac cults spread very strongly, by way of Campania, to Etruria and then Rome, where governmental checks were at first lacking: the emergence of these associations from semi-secrecy into fanatical activity caused considerable official alarm, and produced measures of senatorial repression (186).

While Ptolemaic Egypt became one of the principal homes of the imported religion of Dionysus, it was also the centre of an even more popular faith of native origin, centring round the worship of Isis.

The country was still the home of innumerable rituals of its own, which enjoyed the prestige of remote antiquity and impressed the immigrant Greeks with their imposing, venerable traditions. The rites and sacred dramas and myths relating to Isis enjoyed much of this prestige and reverence and constituted one of the few Egyptian cults that became substantially Hellenized. This process was already well advanced in the early fourth century BC, when Plato saw a kind of kinship between the Athenians and the people of the Egyptian town of Sais, where the statue of the local deity Neith was identified not only with Athena but with Isis as well.[13] Then the Greeks became better acquainted with Isis in the 330s BC, when her cult was established at Piraeus by Egyptian residents. But it was Ptolemy I Soter who saw the potentialities of Isis, 'the queen of the entire land'.[14] It was he too – now that Alexandria was founded – who transformed her holy drama into Mysteries of the Greek type, which rapidly became enormously popular among his immigrant subjects.

Isis' partner in her liturgical drama was the god of the lower world, Osiris (identified with Hades or Pluto), who introduced into the cult a tradition of his former earthly rule when civilized order had first become a part of human life. He also stood for the birth and death of the year; and the 'Finding of Osiris', in mid-November, was the climax of this whole, deeply emotional ceremony, and the occasion for ecstatic jubilation. Indeed, all the rituals of Isis, with whom Osiris was thus associated, came to exercise a unique theatrical appeal. In addition to the major festivals, elaborate ceremonies were staged daily, almost hourly, throughout the entire year: the impact of Isis' exciting worship forcefully struck eye and ear alike, as her penitents paraded through the streets chanting hymns and performing melodramatic acts of piety and self-mortification.

Yet this was also a faith of contemplation, as the worshippers at the roadsides stood in awed silence while the image of Isis, in linen robe and fringed mantle, passed amidst a solemn procession. Her graciously feminine, compassionate countenance seemed to incarnate the veritable female principle in nature, and her worship appealed to women with unparalleled force and directness (Chapter Three, section 4).

Moreover, all the magic that was so much the spirit of the age was hers: for she was an enchantress of overwhelming power, not *a* divinity but all divinities in one, the 'Goddess of Ten Thousand Names'. This was an age of popular syncretism – the equation or fusion of deities, at a time when the differences between one god and another, a single god or many, were gradually fading away into a sort of comprehensive monotheism. Thus it was Isis above all who absorbed every other divinity into herself, not only in Egypt but in every Mediterranean land: 'in your own person', declares a hymn of the first century BC, 'you are all the other goddesses named by the peoples'.[15] And so there are great lists of the divine figures of Asia Minor and Syria and elsewhere with whom she came to be assimilated. Among them was Tyche (Fortune), whom people of this epoch so consummately feared; seen as Isis she became beneficent, the bestower of fertility. Fate, that other terror of the age, seemed to be defeated by Isis for ever. 'I overcome Fate,' she was said to declare, 'and Fate obeys my will.' [16]

Isis came to people in dreams. Ptolemy IV Philopator and his wife Arsinoe III Philopator knew she came to haunt her temple at night and show herself to those who slept in its precincts. Such 'incubation' was held to be highly therapeutic; she told the sick, in their dreams, about the many health-giving drugs she had discovered. She also revealed the wider secrets of the universe: she was Wisdom itself, the Wisdom that conferred a knowledge of the highest – a universal civilizing force. But above all, she came to people who suffered distress and gave them *compassion and pity*, described with incomparable vividness by the Latin novelist from north Africa, Apuleius. She showed pity because of the trials and tribulations which she herself had once endured, and which were re-enacted in her Mysteries.

From Isis, then, people could learn how to triumph over their sorrows here and now. Above all, however, she brought them comfort and salvation not only in this world but in the next. From the outset her cult had stressed that she will 'save the universe' and everyone in it; her gift was personal immortality and the poignant, overwhelmingly appealing message of this redemptive union between humankind and divinity, conveyed through ritual dramas enacting the simulation of death, seemed to more and more people of the Hellenistic and Roman worlds to be the fulfilment of their deepest emotional needs.

When Ptolemy I Soter developed the worship of Isis, he did another remarkable thing as well: he created a new kind of worship of a male Egyptian god, Sarapis, to be the partner and male counterpart of Isis at her rituals. Sarapis was perhaps the only god of historical times successfully devised by deliberate official thought and direction – a move typical enough of the contemporary mood of religious inventiveness and empiricism, and typical also of the Ptolemies' desire to control every aspect of their subjects' lives. It is true that Sarapis was not new to Egyptian religion. The sacred bull Apis worshipped at Memphis, the best-known of the numerous sacred animals traditionally venerated in the country, had already been identified by the Egyptians after its death with Osiris, under the name of Osor-Hapi. Greeks arriving in Egypt in pre-Ptolemaic times began to revere him, first as Oserapis and then as Sarapis, grafting Greek elements on to his figure and cult in the process.

The new name of Sarapis may have dated from the time of Alexander the Great, who discovered the god at the Egyptian village of Rhacotis, the site of the later Alexandria, and was then said to have enjoyed his divine companionship on his subsequent journey throughout Asia.

Next, Ptolemy i Soter thought out a whole new cult for the god, as patron and symbol of the Hellenistic dynasty he was seeking to consolidate in Egypt. His aim in developing the worship of Sarapis was not, as was once thought, to reconcile the Greek and Egyptian elements in his kingdom, since the new forms of worship made no impression among the Egyptians, who did not find them appealing. His purpose was rather to give the Greek population of Egypt, and especially of Alexandria, a patron deity of their own – a deity who conveniently already had his roots in the country where the new Ptolemaic state was seeking to found itself, and served as a counterpart and counterblast to the cults of Memphis and other ancient Egyptian holy cities.

For this purpose a new artistic type of Sarapis was evolved by the Greeks. Even before 300, it would appear, the leading Athenian sculptor Bryaxis made him a huge cult-statue, loaded with precious stones, which – as far as we can judge from copies – gave him the appearance of Zeus or Poseidon, but added a bushel on the top of his head to represent his rulership of the fertile earth. The statue stood in his shrine at Alexandria, the great complex of the Sarapeum erected on an eminence towering over the city, begun by Ptolemy i Soter and completed by Ptolemy iii Euergetes.

In this temple of Sarapis, strange wonders could be seen. They included the sight of an iron statue of Ares propelled into the embrace of a lodestone Aphrodite by the combined action of magnets and invisible wires. This was one of the ingenious gadgets invented by Ctesibius, Philo of Byzantium and Hero to impress worshippers. It was likewise in Alexandrian shrines that the principle of the siphon was applied to making water into wine; and when the congregation arrived in the temple, hidden hydraulic bellows ingeniously caused fanfares of trumpets to blare out, or the altar-fire to burst into a seemingly miraculous blaze. Moreover, the expansive force of hot air created by burnt offerings was utilized to throw open the temple doors and propel the image of its god forward, so that he came to meet and greet his devotees; and a variety of novel lighting effects included the internal illumination of statues so that light shone out of their eyes. The historian Polybius no doubt approved: he thought it a good thing to impress and frighten the populace by religious means in order to keep it loyal.

The shrine of Sarapis at Alexandria, like the temple of Isis, was a notable centre of cures for those who slept and dreamt on its premises, and perhaps provided the service of oracles as well: for Sarapis was above all a healer, assimilated to Apollo and Asclepius – the Greek patrons of all such activities – and presiding over the great Alexandrian medical school. The Athenian leader Demetrius of Phaleron testified how the god had restored his sight, and wrote, we are told, a five-volume work on his miraculous curative powers. Sarapis, like Isis, became immensely popular not only in Egypt but in the rest of the Hellenistic world as well. They were regarded by tens of thousands of people as a supreme universal pair.

Cybele the Earth-Mother, assimilated to immeasurably ancient Anatolian deities (Ma, Enyo), was revered by annual religious dramas that were equally spectacular, but offered a more savage and uninhibited allurement. They centred upon the shrines of the temple states in Asia Minor, such as Pessinus in Galatia, and the two Comanas in Cappadocia and Pontus. The ritual performances undertaken in such shrines celebrated the death and rebirth of Cybele's youthful consort Attis, who (like Osiris in Egypt) was god of all that grows and perishes.

The rites of Cybele and Attis presented the most elaborate and complex pageantry ever witnessed in the ancient world, carrying indulgence in orgiastic emotionalism to sensational lengths and raising hopes of immortality to a fever-heat of excitement. Seven fast-days were followed by a magnificent procession, of which the centre-piece was a newly cut pine, representing Attis who had perished. Then, after a day of lamentations for his death, came the Day of Blood when the priests lashed and lacerated their own bodies, while fanatical novices castrated themselves before the public gaze. At the end of the whole proceedings came the proclamation: 'Be of good cheer, initiates, since the god is saved: for we too, after our labours, shall find salvation!'[17] And that was the signal for frenzied rejoicing.

The tragic, sanguinary cycle, and its ineffably happy culmination, were celebrated by the third-century poet Hermesianax of Colophon. His verses have not come down to us. However, we do have an astonishing, almost hysterically unrestrained adaptation of some Hellenistic poem on the same subject – not necessarily the piece of Hermesianax – by the Latin lyricist Catullus (d. 54), whose whole movement, that of the 'singers of Euphorion' – poet-librarian at Antioch under Antiochus III the Great – was largely inspired by the Hellenistic tradition: Catullus' incantation to Cybele gives us unique insight into the power her rites exercised over the minds and emotions of the whole age.

2 The Philosophers' Solutions

Astrology, magical practices and mystic initiations were all evoked by millions to avoid the tyrannies of the stars and Chance and

Fate, and the terrors and despairs they imposed. But the knowledge or commonsense of others told them that such panaceas were useless and hopeless, and urged that some other means of avoiding or overcoming these despotic anxieties were needed.

Among people like the Greeks, who were much given to discussing and arguing, philosophy was the natural medium to provide such an alternative: and, employed for just this purpose in Hellenistic times, it penetrated the educated public more thoroughly than ever before. Of course, philosophy had long been searching for plausible, generalized explanations of human beings and their environment. The view that it might find them, by the exercise of reason, had gained new importance when the fifth-century sophist Protagoras of Abdera declared that Man, the individual human person, is the measure of all things. From that time onwards, philosophers turned people's attention more and more imperatively to the need to care for and improve their own souls. According to Plato, that is what Socrates (d. 399) tried to induce the Athenians to do; and that was what prompted his prosecutors to assert that he was, by implication, denying the validity of religious beliefs by advocating his own, different design for living instead. Nor were they pleased by his suggestion that no city-states and their organizations were necessary, since goodness, he maintained, is independent of any such social manifestations.

Convinced that one's soul and not one's body was what mattered, Socrates became noted for the ascetic life he chose to lead, caring nothing for luxury or personal safety or the needs of the body, and comparing himself jokingly to the hero Heracles, about whom similar tales were told. This Socratic asceticism helped to lead the way to the philosophies of retirement which became so prominent later. In this tendency a decisive part was played by Socrates' slightly younger contemporary Democritus of Abdera (famous for his theory that the universe is composed of material atoms). He spoke in favour of *euthumia*, which is often translated 'cheerfulness' but is, more accurately, imperturbability and invulnerability in face of all the misfortunes that Fortune (Tyche) may choose to inflict (later the Romans called it *tranquillitas*); and Democritus also employed for this concept the term *ataraxia*, freedom from disturbance, which was to be the keynote of all the Hellenistic philosophies to come.

Antisthenes (c. 445–360), the son of an Athenian and a Thracian slave-woman and founder or forerunner of the Cynic school, dwelt upon just the same aim, which he defined as *to apathes*, absence of suffering or feeling. In his consequent distaste for all physical pleasure, he was harking back to the ascetic remoteness of Socrates, and Cynic tradition remained full of stories of how Antisthenes scored debating points at the expense of the fastidious élitist Plato. And yet Plato's belief in another eternal, immutable world outside this one – a world consisting of Forms or Ideas, the contemplation of which was the highest human good – likewise and equally encouraged withdrawal and abstraction. Although for Aristotle the correct starting point was the description of the world as it is, he too once again hailed Contemplation and *to apathes*, seeing them as expressions of his Doctrine of Mean, the avoidance of extremes, which is what one needs to make oneself impregnable to circumstances and Chance.

This goal was in line with the Indian *karma*, which emphasized individual responsibility and was favourable to self-culture and meditation. The ascetic brotherhood of Pythagoras of Samos, in the sixth century BC, seemed to display a good deal in common with the beliefs of contemporary Jains (a recently founded offshoot of Hinduism) and with the doctrines of the Buddhists as well, and it was later maintained that he and Democritus and then Plato too had all travelled to India. But probably the first learned Greeks to visit the country were those in the company of Alexander the Great, who was himself reputedly impressed by the Indian sages he met at Taxila in the Gandhara. Their physical self-control appeared admirable, and their self-sufficient view that each man possesses just as much of the earth as he stands on appealed equally to philosophical Greeks: so that Megasthenes, the Seleucid envoy to Chandragupta Maurya (*c.* 321–296), was able to develop a comparison between the Indian and Greek ways of thinking.

For there was, indeed, an obvious point of convergence in their mutual pursuit of the goal of imperturbable, invulnerable *ataraxia*. All the same, actual Indian influence on Hellenistic thought remained slight. The Greek philosophers had their own similar driving imperatives, in the world that they were able to see around them. Men and women were crying out for their guidance in a disoriented society where the mirror of unchangeable order seemed to have been shattered. And that guidance was just what the new philosophers believed they could supply. Moreover, they had separated themselves off from the sciences, which they left to the experts, so that philosophy had an imperative need to justify itself on its own account, as an entirely autonomous, streamlined discipline. It was now, for the first time, a specialized subject; and the speciality of its practitioners (in contrast to their cosmically minded forerunners of earlier periods) was to be guides and friends and spiritual directors. Surrounded by crowds of passionate admirers, Hellenistic philosophers became famous men. Two thousand students attended Theophrastus' morning public lectures, and when Stilpo (*c.* 380-300), leader of a popular dialectical school at Megara, paid a visit to Athens, people would run from their work to catch a glimpse of him.

These philosophers, like their predecessors, claimed to present truth and reality. Yet their systems were by no means logically attack-proof, and what they really offered was not far from the opposite – *withdrawal* from reality in order to attain peace of mind: this could be argued to represent a higher reality, contrasted with the more obvious, palpable and protrusive sort. Xenocrates (d. 314), head of the Academy founded by Plato, was speaking for his whole profession when he declared that 'the reason for discovering philosophy is to allay what causes disturbance in life';[18] and followers of Aristotle – the Peripatetics, at their centre, the Lyceum – said much the same thing. To escape helpless subservience to Chance, self-sufficiency is essential. So Stilpo was greatly admired because of an answer he gave Demetrius I Poliorcetes. Demetrius' troops had wrecked Stilpo's home town, Megara, and the king asked him if he needed any help. 'No', replied Stilpo. 'I carry everything within myself.' [19]

People wanted this invulnerability and self-sufficiency urgently and *instantly*, so that schools claiming absolute and total certain knowledge had to be run up as an emergency measure to provide them.

The most influential of these schools, in the long run, was Stoicism, named after a public hall, the Stoa Poikile (Painted Portico), at Athens, in which its founder Zeno (335-263) taught; the Stoa's remains have recently been excavated. Since Zeno came from Citium in Cyprus, in which many of the population were Semitic (Phoenician) by language and race, he may well have been, wholly or partly, of similar origin. Certainly he numbered many non-Greeks among his adherents; and his written Greek is far from attractive. Nevertheless, this gaunt, middle-aged man, who enjoyed sitting in the sun and eating green figs, was an excellent teacher, of imposing personality and presence.

A master of vivid illustrative effects, he relied heavily on the forceful impact of brief, unqualified, vehement assertions. And he boldly found his inspiration in that concentrated love (*eros*) of the ideal, a love which all true Athenians, it had often been claimed, must feel for their city of Athens, but which Zeno – coming from far away, and living at a time when the city-state ideal was fading – passionately felt for his own doctrines and convictions instead. In many ways Stoicism was more like a religion than a philosophy, especially under Zeno's fervent, poetic successor, Cleanthes. The next leader of the school, Chrysippus, wrote just as badly as Zeno (and their views are not always easy to distinguish);

but he became the great scholar and dialectician of Stoicism, which he turned into a highly technical philosophy.

Zeno's fundamental innovation had been to stress the prime importance of sense-perception. Vividness of perceived experience, he asserted, is the sufficient and only criterion of truth, for he believed (in total revolt against the idealism of Plato) that everything in existence is material. There are two sorts of material things, he conceded: on the one hand the ordinary passive sort, and on the other the active, dynamic, intelligent, all-controlling matter which is God, Providence, Fate, and Necessity, the wonderful, all-powerful divinity of nature. But he argued that even this dynamic force is material – a ruling principle, yet at the same time a material entity to which everything else, all the passive kind of matter (being essentially of the same origin), is directly and totally linked by an ineluctable chain of connexions. The link extends to ourselves as a portion of this passive matter, so that we too, literally and physically, have a share of the divine, providential nature and cherish sparks of it in our souls. That is to say, cosmic events and human actions both belong to one single, indissoluble process. In consequence, it is incumbent on us to live 'according to Nature', in agreement with the great purposeful sacred law to which we inextricably belong. This marvellous whole, maintained the Stoics, makes perfect sense, and so will we if we gladly accept our part in it – but not otherwise.

Zeno also felt, on the basis of sense-perception and empirical observation, that his ruling principle is evidently and wholly animated by, and identified with, Reason. This must be so, firstly because the beauty and order we see in the universe are surely the work of an all-powerful rationality; and secondly because its products include things possessing rational qualities – namely ourselves, whose reasoning faculty, therefore (if correctly used), will enable us to choose and pursue the courses of action that are right.

'Right', once again, means in accordance with Nature, since only by so living can we behave in a way that is morally good: for seeing that Nature, being God and Providence, must inevitably be governed by a principle of goodness and justice, then to live in accordance with Nature must, with equal inevitability, mean to behave well. And behaving well, added Zeno with epoch-making force, is all that matters: it is the only real good and real happiness, beside which everything worldly is meaningless. Here is the moral law of Socrates and Plato, discoverable by reason but now endowed with a novel, imperative, urgency. In Stoicism, ethics come far ahead of anything else.

However, its moral imperative, modern philosophers maintain, is impossible to demonstrate logically. And as to how this moral self-improvement was to be put into practice, there were certain ambiguities. Later Stoics developed the noble doctrine of the brother-hood of man – the idea that since we all have a share of the divine spark we must treat each other decently. Zeno, however, apparently limited this brotherhood to the wise, the people who think 'rightly'. There was also a second complication. If the world is already directed by a providential guidance, ordering everything for the best, what room is left for us to choose whether to behave well or badly, and why should we try? The Stoic answer (a difficult one for many to swallow) was that we have to learn to want, and accept, what we are inevitably going to get anyway: if we accept fate, it cannot hurt us. A man is like a dog tied to a cart; if he does not walk, he will be pulled, and that is not so good as walking of his own free will.[20] Unfailing submission to all that happens, on the other hand, will present him with that armour against suffering, that inner tranquillity and peace of mind, which was what the Stoics, like all the other schools of the time, were really after.

The way to achieve this desirable submission was by neglecting everything bodily and therefore 'indifferent', and concentrating entirely on the all-important affairs of the soul, so as to stamp out every trace that it retained of disturbing hopes and fears and passions. The admirable absence of feeling (*pathos*) that would thus be created was the famous Stoic 'apathy' (*apatheia*, a term that harked back to Antisthenes). It does not mean *total* impassivity or insensibility, since that is obviously beyond our reach: but it signifies the elimination of every one of the soul's irrational, excessive, impulsive 'flutterings' (among which Zeno included sexual excitement). By avoiding these disturbances, even a beggar can be triumphantly independent of Fortune.

The Stoics were charged with shrouding themselves in the grave-cloth of their highly starched virtue: they seemed to have made a desolate solitude and called it peace. Yet they offered a compelling world picture, and one must either ignore it or swallow it whole. Despite its logical flaws, Cicero pointed to 'the remarkable [inner] coherence of the system and the extraordinary orderliness of its components'.[21] It evoked heartfelt admiration; the dramatic ideal of the imperturbably Stoic sage caught the imagination of a considerable number of people, especially those who had some innate strength of character – and found that Stoicism confirmed their confidence and self-respect. It remained a significant intellectual and social influence for five centuries. It also gave the word 'philosophical' important parts of its dictionary definition: wise, calm, temperate, resigned.

Moreover, in the last two centuries BC, when the doctrine of the brotherhood of man was gaining strength, Stoicism became gentler, more human and less uncompromising. Thus Panaetius of Rhodes (*c.* 185-109) grappled with the aim of attaining a properly harmonious relationship between the various powers and instincts of human beings, not as perfectly wise sages (who are, obviously, not to be found on this earth), but as men and women actually are, in all their variety. And so it was probably he who abandoned the term *apatheia* as misleading (because unattainable), reviving instead Democritus' term *euthumia*, by which he wanted to define a peace of mind derived from a proper harmony between natural impulses.

Panaetius also brought Stoicism into focus as a guide to political careers. Despite the remoteness of the imperturbable sage, the Stoic school had never, unlike others, been wholly averse to public life. As Chrysippus remarked, reason requires that human beings should co-operate to serve the purposes of the world; although he added that Stoic participation would very likely be unenthusiastic and lukewarm – and that the wise man would not commit himself to any particular state or government or condition of society.

And indeed, despite this concession that public activities could not be evaded altogether, the Stoic attitude to the glaring social problems of the time had never been entirely helpful (Chapter Two, section 2). It was true that Zeno himself had seen no objection to accepting poor and dirty people among his followers. On the other hand, the disregard of outward circumstances professed by himself and his followers easily turned into passive acceptance of inequitable conditions. Furthermore, their ideal of the perfectly wise, virtuous and capable man tended to favour right-wing institutions: notably monarchy, about which so many textbooks were being written instructing rulers to display just those qualities. When a Stoic, Persaeus of Citium, attended the court of King Antigonus II Gonatas of Macedonia, and another, Sphaerus of Borys-thenes (Olbia), stayed as the guest of Ptolemy II Philadelphus, Stoicism truly seemed to have become the philosophy of social conservatism. (Sphaerus only advised the archaizing reformist Cleomenes III of Sparta (Chapter One, section 1) because Stoics always admired the traditional Spartan constitution.)

Panaetius gave these political implications of Stoicism much more concrete expression. As befitted the first Stoic to possess ample material resources of his own, he laid special stress on the virtues, or aspects of virtue, which were particularly appropriate to the ruling class of each monarchy and city, such as justice and bravery and liberality. He also performed a historic task by introducing and commending these elements in the Stoic ideal to the Romans. For after living for a time at Athens, he moved to Rome (*c.* 144), and before long joined the cultured circle which gathered round its national leader, Scipio Aemilianus. Like the historian Polybius, Panaetius was eager to encourage such powerful, sympathetic Romans to use their authority well, and his conversion of Stoic rigidity into a code for a gentleman – stressing not so much Zeno's ideal sage as the imperfect leader searching for a workable way of life – greatly appealed to this Roman ruling class, and exercised a major influence over the future of its moral and political thinking. Roman lawyers and leaders made great use of the Stoic Law of Nature as well, seeing it as a universally valid set of precepts; for they identified the concept with their own *ius gentium*, which had originated as a much more limited and concrete idea, comprising that part of the law that was open to citizens and non-citizens alike, but which was elevated under Stoic influences to become a philosophical justification of Roman imperial rule.

Posidonius, the immensely influential, widely enquiring polymath of the early first century BC, was another who gave the Roman cosmopolis a Stoic background; and in his hands the rigours of Stoicism were watered down once again. For Posidonius humanized its morality by reverting to Plato's view that the psyche contains both rational and irrational elements, and he insisted that moral failings are implanted by nature, so that evil and the emotions and passions that operate in its company cannot be eliminated but only brought under control. But to subsequent generations of Roman writers, with their strong practical bias, it seemed more important to perform the arduous enough task of suppressing passions without trying too hard to analyse the causes that lie behind them; though Stoics such as Seneca (d. AD 65) and Epictetus and the emperor Marcus Aurelius in the second century AD were a good deal more eloquent than any of their forerunners – the first in Latin, and the other two in Greek. Moreover, none of them (despite the worldly responsibilities of Aurelius and Seneca) lost sight of that original kernel of the Stoic philosophy, the quest for imperturbable, impregnable peace of mind.

The principal rival and opponent of Stoicism, Epicurus, was born on Samos; but after his father had been expelled from that city, the son became a citizen of Athens, where the place in which he taught, a piece of land adjoining his house, was known as The Garden. Epicurus was the complete pragmatist, impatient of all knowledge which lacked relevance – that is to say, which seemed irrelevant to the single purpose of securing well-being, which he saw once again as *ataraxia*, peace of mind, invulnerability to circumstances and fortune. For all other purposes he held education, including the whole mathematical and dialectical training so dear to Plato, to be a complete waste of time. Eloquence and logical subtlety seemed wholly beside the point: it all looked like part of the intellectual pretence and presumption which he hated, including all attempts (except his own) to force any orderly system on other people, and line them up to be counted within its ranks.

Like his Stoic competitors, Epicurus approached the ideal of peace of mind from the material viewpoint of sense-perception: 'if a man allows himself to enter into a struggle against the self-evident testimony of the senses, he will never be able to avoid uncertainty and confusion, and thus attain true peace of mind'.[22] Yet the path which led him to that desirable end of ataraxy was strangely different from that of the Stoics. Like the fifth-century scientist-philosophers Leucippus of Miletus and Democritus of Abdera, Epicurus asserted that sensation contacts objects by 'effluences' thrown off by those objects through the movements of atoms – moving mechanically in a straight line and a downward direction – of which he held everything in the universe (except the void) to consist. Although this doctrine differed so strongly from the beliefs of the Stoics, it was none the less as basically materialistic as theirs, allowing no room for anything non-material.

The understanding that there is nothing which is not material seemed to Epicurus to remove automatically the two greatest hindrances to human peace of mind. These hindrances, he believed, are fear of death and fear of the gods. It was the widespread fear of death that the Mystery religions had been designed to dispel (Chapter Four, section 1). Epicurus' method was different. For since he believed that the soul, like everything else, is part of the wholly material (atomic) structure of the world and the universe, souls must obviously come to an end at the same time as the bodies containing them, so that there could not possibly be any reason to fear what was going to happen to them afterwards. Religious people would not find this consoling, but to Epicurus it seemed the greatest and most logical of all possible consolations.

The other great obstacle to peace of mind he identified as fear of the gods; his view of the gods was a peculiar and arbitrary one. The Stoics had not permitted their materialism to get in the way of a belief in cosmic providence. Epicurus did not allow his equally materialistic view to prevent him from believing that gods existed 'between the worlds', made of atoms like everything else but nevertheless gods, since he maintained that their existence is demanded on the grounds of 'universal consent' (accepted also by Aristotle), because people generally believe that they exist, and so they must.[23] Yet nothing disquieted Epicurus more profoundly than the idea that these supernatural beings control earthly phenomena or affect human affairs, an idea which he believed to be the second of the major, destructive, universal terrors, and an utterly false idea at that, because the gods must by definition lead lives of undisturbed *ataraxia* – which could not be the case if they intervened in the affairs of the world.

With these two great fears out of the way, *ataraxia* as splendid as that of the gods will be within our grasp as well, since according to Epicurus we shall now have thrown off the main hindrances to our becoming captains of our own souls. Yet – as in the competing philosophy of Stoicism – there was a logical snag all the same. For if we, as Epicurus believed, like everything else in the universe, are composed of material atoms moving mechanically in a straight line and downwards, then surely we can have no freedom of movement or will whatsoever, and cannot ultimately be captains of our souls. He got out of the dilemma by allowing that the atoms sometimes make a swerve (*parenklisis*), permitting us free will after all. For Epicurus will not allow us to be slaves either to Fate or to Chance. *It is up to us to strive for what we want.*

What we want turns out, once again, to be unshakable ataraxy, which was everyone else's goal too. Adopting this ideal, like others in his repertoire, from Democritus' pupil Nausiphanes of Teos, who had called it 'undisturbedness' (*akataplexia*), Epicurus himself interpreted the concept to mean undisturbedness 'to oneself' (as well as not being a nuisance to anyone else); that is to say lodgment in a tranquil, passive equilibrium from which all baseless sufferings, terrors, desires and opinions are removed. 'The end of all our actions is to be free from pain and fear, and once we have attained all this, the tempest of the soul is laid.' [24] This might seem to be an ideal of low tension, of a life that is only half alive, and it is true that none of the other philosophical schools stressed withdrawal so completely: 'live in hiding', 'out of the news' (*lathe biosas*) is what Epicurus uncompromisingly counsels. He exalts the *galene*, the smooth calm amid the disturbing gales of the storm. Yet he does so in full awareness that the storm's peripheral swirls – pleasures and sorrows – cannot be eliminated completely.

Indeed, he has even gone down in history as an apostle of pleasure. This is due to the attacks of his sect's enemies, who liked to pretend that its self-regard took the form of luxury, described, for this reason, as 'Epicurean' or 'epicure'. This was entirely untrue of the master himself, who saw pleasure (*hedone*) – sometimes 'joy' seems a better translation – not by any means as debauchery or self-indulgence, but merely as the absence of trouble from body and soul alike; in fact, once again, as *ataraxia*. Looking at the matter in this way Epicurus was prepared to concede, from the evidence of the senses, that the 'pleasures' of taste, sex, sound and scent are normal conditions of well-being, and indeed actually make it easier to secure and maintain self-sufficient peace of mind. Nevertheless, he urged that they should always remain controlled by careful insight and right calculation, and must never become shackling, binding emotions or infatuations – which, if one's soul is unfortunate enough to be invaded by them, have to be expelled from it just as medicine expels diseases from the body.

So the poet Abraham Cowley felt able to observe:

> Whoever a true Epicure would be,
> May find there cheap and virtuous luxurie.

Virtuous? It seems to those who have been brought up in the Judaeo-Christian tradition that ethics come rather a bad second here. For Epicurus regarded virtue not as an end in itself, but only as the means to an end – which is ataraxy. 'Injustice', he even observed, 'is a bad thing not in itself, but in respect of the fear and suspicion of not escaping the notice of those set in authority concerning such things.' [25] In other words, you had better behave decently or you may get caught out, and then bang goes your ataraxy: which for *that* reason is unattainable if virtue and justice are lacking!

This seems an amoral way of looking at the matter. Yet Epicurus was a moralist, in quite another and more idiosyncratic fashion: he believed with enormous force in friendship and affection. For the ancients, friendship, not necessarily including sexual feelings, played a far larger part than it usually does today, and among the Greeks in particular it reached a famous degree of intensity. Plato's *Symposium* and *Phaedrus* are extremely enlightening on the subject, to which he also devoted an entire dialogue, the *Lysis*; and then Aristotle had accorded the same theme systematic treatment, demonstrating that friendship is a necessary ingredient in our lives as social beings. It is necessary, that is to say, to our happiness, our peace of mind. The happy, undisturbable man cannot be a solitary recluse or associate only with strangers. He must have friends as well: paradoxically, if he has no friends he will not be self-sufficient, since his life will be the life of the jungle, where no safety is to be had anywhere.

Menander, too, constantly praised friendship, and so did the epigrammatists – Callimachus' epigram to a friend, 'They told me, Heraclitus, they told me you were dead',[26] is particularly moving – and the Stoics were gradually enlarging the concept into that of a universal brotherhood. Epicurus, however, taking exactly the opposite direction from his Stoic rivals, preferred to narrow friendship down into a small-scale way of living, shared by only a few people. True, he declared that 'Friendship, affection, dances round the earth, announcing to us all that we should bestir ourselves for the enjoyment of happiness!' [27] And yet, though friendship was so powerful all over the earth, he was convinced that it had to be put into practice within a very restricted human circle. He was surrounded, in his Garden, by a group of devoted supporters and intimate friends, not unlike the clusters of followers who live with a guru today. The group was deliberately kept small, because Epicurus felt that a large one would have been too complicated and demanding – besides, he believed that philosophers should not court crowds.

It was this cultivation of friendship between congenial characters that gave the Garden its special and peculiar tone (and subsequently attracted the approval of Karl Marx, who admired not only its materialistic philosophy, but its fraternal, charitable spirit). Epicurus, despite his dislike of exaggerated emotional involvements, wrote with effusive enthusiasm about the close relations of mutual kindness that living in his sort of group demanded; *apatheia*, absence of feeling, in the sense of reluctance to form *this* kind of tie, seemed to him much less likely to produce the peace of mind he was after.

The key to his success was his own personality; for although he had suffered from a painful and incurable internal illness since his early years, he remained a tranquil man, dispensing and inspiring abundant affection. Certainly, the standards of this cosy, mutually admiring little society ('Act always as if Epicurus is watching') must have been somewhat oppressive. It was also strange that the constant advocacy of gratitude and kindness to one another, urged by the master himself and by his followers, was accompanied by unprecedentedly virulent abuse of rival philosophers, including some to whom Epicurus was deeply indebted. For example, he calls Nausiphanes – from whom he had learnt a great deal – an illiterate deceiver and a prostitute and a lungfish (a dumb animal insensitive to the truth). To admit an obligation to any sort of forerunner or model was evidently out of the question. Moreover, while Epicurus did regard his much-praised friendships as *intrinsically* desirable, in order to keep egotism at bay, this was only, so to speak, a secondary consideration. For he also admitted quite frankly that their real basis was self-interest: 'there is none who feels affection for another, except for his own benefit' – that is to say, for his own peace of mind.

So that is what *lathe biosas*, live out of the news, is intended to mean: achieve ataraxy by living in a small, close, likeminded group. Epicurus' idea came at a time when the Greek family was losing some of its strength and appeal. It also owed something to current disillusionment with the hitherto all-embracing, universally effective city-state. True,

Epicurus saw some useful features in the city. It helps us to make the friends we need, and it serves as a useful policeman and barrier to keep disturbing external interferences away. There is good cause, therefore, to obey civic laws and customs, since that is the best way to make sure that one's life will not be buffeted or overturned by disorders. Indeed, for the same reason, even participation in public life is not to be condemned in all its forms, but only in so far as the worldly success it might involve would be an obstacle to attaining peace of mind.

For to win this we do need to be protected from our fellow citizens and human beings – outside the circle of our friends – as Epicurus was careful to point out.[28] By this assertion he was implicitly condemning the historic Greek subordination of the individual to the good of the community, and thus accelerating a destructive process which the questions raised by the fifth-century sophists or popular philosophers, and then by Socrates, had first set in motion. But they, and subsequently Plato and Aristotle, had still been speaking within the context of the city-state which they assumed must continue to provide the basic structure and framework for the well-being of every individual who formed part of it. To Epicurus, on the other hand (whose Garden was significantly well away from the market-place) the city-state was only an entirely secondary aid to a main purpose which rejected its overriding demands, political, ethical and religious alike. Nor was he any more interested in the monarchies than in the cities: his contribution to the literature on the subject was merely to warn philosophy students to have nothing to do with such leaders. Thus no political system at all seemed particularly attractive to the Epicureans. Indeed, the most important of the master's followers, Metrodorus of Lampsacus (c. 331–278), summed the matter up by actually advising his pupils 'not to trouble to save Greece'.[29]

The Epicureans felt able to stand on their own, regardless of anything that went on outside their ranks. Like their Stoic rivals, they formed a sort of secular church with infallible, undeveloping dogmas. Yet, inward-looking though Epicureanism seemed to be, many people found its sweeping simplification of life's problems an exciting and liberating experience, splendidly free from superstitious cant, and its doctrines soon spread widely and deeply. It appealed to the oppressed and fearful and to those who wanted a quiet life: but not only to them, either, for Julius Caesar's murderer Cassius, for example – who felt that Epicurus would have wanted a state based on consent, and not ruled by a dictator – was very far from a quietist.

However, the logical flaws that could be detected in Epicurus' doctrines aroused great indignation among other philosophers, and his lack

243

of communal spirit offended official circles both in the Hellenistic world and then in Rome as well. Cicero, it is true, was not disposed to under-estimate him, but was shocked all the same by his casual treatment of moral and patriotic values alike.

The Hellenistic quest for *ataraxia* had also been brought into equally great prominence by Diogenes of Sinope (*c.* 400–325 BC), who de-veloped the Cynic way of thinking. He was generally regarded as its founder, though others attributed its foundation to his older contem-porary Antisthenes, to whom much of Diogenes' attitude went back, as he himself admitted, declaring that 'he had never been a slave again since Antisthenes set him free'. When Alexander the Great supposedly went to see Diogenes at Corinth (Diogenes was said to have asked him not to block the sunlight from coming into the wooden barrel in which he was residing), the latter had already been challenging the basic conventions of classical Greek life for a good many years.

Like other philosophers of the day, he saw no point in the state. He criticized its current forms of education, censuring their stress on ath-leticism. He deplored the pursuit of wealth and marriage, citing tradi-tional Sparta as a model for the avoidance of such institutions. He would have agreed with Rousseau: decide what society is doing, and do the exact opposite. 'Deface the currency', he urged; that is to say, call in the artificial coinage, the customs that pass as valuable in the tradi-tional city-state communities. Rules are a bondage, he said, live as nature commands. Incest, for example, seemed to him a matter of indifference, and so did the eating of human flesh. Socrates, who held the central place in the list of those revered by the Cynics, had already assumed a withdrawn and ascetic attitude: but Diogenes, as Plato remarked, behaved like 'Socrates gone mad'. He detached himself from all but the barest necessities with much greater deliberation and gusto, living as straightforwardly and shamelessly as a dog (*kuon*, hence Cynic) – he even slept and made love in the public gaze – and inuring himself to hardship by lying in the winter snow embracing a marble statue, or in summer-time by rolling about in the scorching sand.

He scarcely professed any philosophical doctrines at all, and refrained from the fashionable pursuit of trying to explain what goodness was. Indeed, what he claimed to offer instead (and expounded in lost tragic dramas) was what the other schools, in their different ways, offered as well: a way of life that could bring peace of mind. But he offered it without the encumbrance of all their untenable theories – just throw away conventions, he said, and everything will be all right. He was a snapping dog, brave and faithful, who needed nothing but his own natural endowments to fight the wild beasts he confronted; and the same, he maintained, could and should be possible for everyone else as well.

'Your fame will live for ever, Diogenes,' pronounced his epitaph at Sinope, 'because you taught humankind the lesson of self-sufficiency.' For the most important things in existence, he believed, are complete, uninhibited freedom of speech and freedom of action, and the truly wise and self-fulfilling people are those who use these freedoms, with total self-discipline, to make their own decisions about their own lives. The mythical hero whom he cited as a model was Heracles – the favourite of Socrates as well – who had lived hard and simply from one day to the next, without house or country, practising the endless training and exercise (*askesis*) that seemed to be needed for the acquisition of virtue and liberty.

Now Heracles had also subjected the Augean stables to the thorough cleaning operation they needed; and the social analogy to this process brings us to the one positive feature in Diogenes' teaching. What had to be cleaned away most urgently, he believed, was poverty, since the love of money seemed to him the mother of most evils. To this extent Cynicism improved on all contemporary schools in its preoccupation, not merely with purely theoretical questions, but with the actual predicament of the human condition. In other words, although Diogenes did not evolve a doctrine, and presented no solutions for the elimination of the poverty he deplored, he at least pointed the way to a new attitude, and this gave his followers the conviction that they were entitled to give guidance to others.

They duly imitated the marvellous bad manners of their successfully eccentric master and produced all kinds of new and even more provocatively shocking deviations that soon gave the term 'cynical' its present significance. Moreover, they invented a method of serio-comic popular preaching; their lecturers – often in trouble with the authorities of the various cities – did not trouble to give regular courses, but accosted and harangued casual or curious bystanders, hurling all manner of abusive challenges and exchanging crude and spicy repartee.

Anti-bourgeois Cynic lecturers of this type became very well-known figures in the early Hellenistic age. The most popular of them was Crates of Thebes (*c.* 365–285), a hunchback who came to Athens and was converted to Cynicism by Diogenes. In the company of his aristocratic wife Hipparchia he wandered about offering instruction; and Hipparchia's brother went with them, too, because Diogenes' courses cost so little, unlike those of the more orthodox sects. Crates created the image of the Cynic who went visiting from house to house – as the members of the other leading schools would never have done – 'joking and laughing, as if life was a game',[30] and preaching that the best way to achieve freedom from care was to cast off one's possessions, in imitation of himself, who had thrown his money into the sea and claimed to confront Fortune with nothing but his courage. He also developed a new, softer, more compassionate element in Cynicism, displayed by the consolation of people in distress and the reconciliation of enemies, activities which gained him a widespread and affectionate reputation for humaneness.

Crates evolved a remarkable, influential style of vivid anti-establishment writing. His writings included tragic dramas, from which a few lines have survived, expressing cosmopolitan sentiments based on a distaste for traditional city-state conventions. Another of his specialities, a curious one, was to revise many poems by well-known earlier poets, twisting and burlesquing them by the insertion of his own radical views. An original poem of his own, of which part has come down to us, is his *Beggar's Wallet* (*Pera*): it names an imaginary country as the symbol of Cynic self-sufficiency and sole refuge for honest men and women, rising like an island from the sea of universal humbug. But whether, like Diogenes, he also denounced poverty as an evil, we do not know.

Crates was one of the major influences on Bion of Borysthenes (Olbia in south Russia) (*c.* 325–235 BC), the son of an ex-slave and a former prostitute. After his father had been convicted of fraud, the family was sold back into slavery, but Bion received a good education from his master and inherited his money, moving subsequently to Athens. It was there that he absorbed, among a variety of other views, the social criticism and caustic humour of the Cynics, though he did not specifically adopt their creed. The importance of Bion lay in the fact that he was the first really effective popularizer of philosophy, which, according to the polymath Eratosthenes, he tried to 'tart up', clothing it in the gaudily embroidered dresses of loose women.[31] Bion was also called *theatrikos*, a man who played to the gallery.

His chosen medium was the 'diatribe', philosophical conversation or fictional dialogue, which he converted into a literary form. In so far as we can tell from surviving fragments, these were witty, vulgar, stinging and vituperative pieces of street-corner rhetoric, denouncing the passions or prejudices of others with an air of coarse and sturdy commonsense. Bion, like others who had imbued Cynic opinions, was interested in conduct rather than philosophy. The arresting manner in which he spoke ensured him a hearing, so that even crowds of Rhodian sailors paused from their work to hear what he had to say. But they heard no new message, and no suggestions about social improvement. Be content, he told them, with what you have, however little it may be. Grasp your fortune without flinching or complaint.

A generation or two after Bion came a more positive, radical Cynic, Cercidas. Although probably identifiable with a high official from Megalopolis who helped defeat the reformist Spartan king Cleomenes III at Sellasia (222), Cercidas cared genuinely for the poor, and wrote passionately denouncing the oppressions from which they suffered, though we do not know what solution for the problem he offered (Chapter Two, section 2). Combining Bion's 'diatribe' style with echoes of Homer, Aristophanes' Old Comedy and archaic satirical poets (whose iambic metre he imitated), Cercidas scoffed at the folly of pretentious high-flown speculations, and made fun of over-refined ways of satisfying one's desires.

Also active at about the same time was Menippus of Gadara (Jordan), who had been a slave at Sinope, and studied under a Cynic professor. He was credited with originating a new form of diatribe, described as serio-comic (*spoudogeloion*) – a kind of earnest philosophical jesting in prose interspersed with verse, a blend also found in the Semitic languages of his native land. He also succeeded in gaining a readership of unprecedented dimensions, which recognized his achievement as a specific literary form ('Menippean satire'). Only fragments of Menippus' homilies now survive. They apparently contained criticisms and mockeries and caricatures of all manner of persons and religions and philosophical follies. The scornful sharpness of his style caused the Roman emperor Marcus Aurelius (d. AD 180) to call him 'a mocker of man's ephemeral existence', while in the same period Lucian, although sympathetic to Cynic attitudes, described Menippus himself as 'a frightening dog with a treacherous bite'.[32]

Another practitioner of the diatribe was the Cynic Teles (c. 235), who probably came from Megara. Have no dependants, Teles advised, have no wife or children or friends whose loss would cause you grief; do not bother to try to acquire luxuries unless circumstances place them easily within your reach. If there is a wind to blow your ship onwards, then take advantage of its help, but if there is none, be content to stay where you are. Fortune, he suggested, is like a playwright who designs a number of parts: just play your part as well as you can, and *ataraxia* will be yours.

The Cynic way of thinking possessed healthy enough aspects, because it swept away outworn conventions and hierarchical distinctions. There was real force and power in this counter-culture that proposed to break all the attachments that seemed to make men and women weak and afraid: fear nothing, desire nothing, possess nothing, and then life cannot disappoint you. Cynicism was stimulating because it urged people to stand on their own feet. But it did not offer them positive enough solutions to enable them to take this stand with any firmness or certainty.

Indeed, many Greeks considered that the same applied to all the philosophical schools, with their various logical and social deficiencies. So people who felt like this took refuge in the comforts of Scepticism (from *skepsis*, speculation).

This was by no means an entirely new road for the enquiring, critical Greek mind to take. Doubts concerning the ability of human beings to attain knowledge, amid the welter of conflicting beliefs, were traditionally traced as far back as the sixth-century poet-philosopher Xenophanes of Colophon. Protagoras of Abdera (*c.* 485-415), too, when he declared that 'man is the measure of all things', seemed to assert the *relativity* of all knowledge and opinion; in other words, he was refusing to regard any belief, or supposed piece of knowledge, as universally valid. Thus Protagoras found himself unable to say, for example, whether God exists or not. And Socrates' whole trend, too, according to the early dialogues of Plato, was to say 'I know that I don't know'. Later, the discussions of knowledge by Aristotle's pupil Theophrastus raised a number of similar questions which foreshadowed the detailed Sceptical viewpoints of the future.

These doctrines were first formulated, it was said, by Theophrastus' younger contemporary Pyrrho of Elis (*c.* 365/60-275/70). Pyrrho apparently taught that in practice nothing can be known, so that speculation is merely a waste of time and an unnecessary cause of anxiety; and it is therefore better to suspend one's judgement about everything without exception. For although Pyrrho's methods and conclusions, in other respects, were so different from those of the Stoics, Epicureans and Cynics, his ultimate aim was just the same as theirs: how to achieve *ataraxia*, peace of mind, invulnerability to circumstances. 'We assert', declared Sextus Empiricus, in his *Outlines of Pyrrhonism*, 'that the Sceptic's purpose is quietude in respect of matters of opinion. ... The man who determines nothing as to what is naturally good or bad neither shuns nor pursues anything eagerly: *and in consequence he is unperturbed.*' [33] Since he found dogma abhorrent, Pyrrho had no desire to adopt completely extremist or intransigent positions. He was prepared to admit that even a Sceptic will not attain *complete* imperturbability – he will still be troubled by unavoidable things like cold and thirst. But because he refuses to hold any strong view about their badness, they will only 'moderately affect him', and will not significantly diminish the basic unconcern and indifference which alone will lead him to *ataraxia*.

The 'quietude in respect of all matters of opinion' which he must adopt in order to reach this goal will necessarily imply that he has to doubt everyone and everything, preserving utter unconcern and indifference. Since Pyrrho put nothing in writing (probably to avoid any impression of dogmatizing), and since he founded no formal school, it is not entirely clear how much of what later constituted Scepticism actually went back to his own initiative; but it is likely that he formulated its main lines. Anecdotes gathered around his name. Like other philosophers, he was reputed to have met Indian sages, and to have been inspired by what they told him: and it was said that he had to be stopped from being run over by carts and falling over precipices, since he could not accept knowledge of their existence.

The Sceptical approach contains two different but related elements: the conviction that nothing can be known, and the recommendation that one should suspend decisions on all matters (*epoche*). That is to say, Pyrrho sought to undermine both belief and knowledge at the same time. With these two aims in mind, he withheld judgement, made no positive statements, and remained uncommitted to any definite or permanent attitude. His quietism, based on indifference to outward things (*adiaphoria*), did not necessarily amount to total lethargy, but was merely non-identification with the issues involved. *That*, he declared, was the way to achieve the happiness, the well-being – in other words, the peace of mind – which everyone was after. It comes, as if casually or fortuitously, once you have stopped actively trying to grasp it – in other words, once you have stopped trying to make up your mind about anything whatever.

It was easy to condemn Scepticism as wholly negative and nihilistic. In the second century AD Lucian effectively made fun of its views in *The Sale of Philosophers*, and other ancient critics, too, declared that the Sceptical way of life could not, in practice, be lived, and should not therefore command assent. Nevertheless, its practitioners displayed powerful intellectual gifts and a new philosophical integrity in rejecting the dogmas which seemed to them so fatuous, and not infrequently were.

In the fourth century BC Metrodorus of Chios (a follower of the atomic scientist-philosopher Democritus) declared that 'none of us knows anything – not even whether we know anything or not'.[34] But the man who principally saved the Sceptical approach for posterity was Timon of Phlius (*c.* 320–230). As a young man he had been a professional dancer, but then he studied philosophy at Megara and Elis –

under Stilpo and Pyrrho respectively – after which he moved on to Athens. Only fragments of his abundant and varied works have survived. The most influential of them were his *Silloi* or 'squint-eyed' pieces – that is to say, mockeries or lampoons, full of ridicule and invective. Following the example of the satirical *Silloi* written three hundred years earlier by Xenophanes, whom he respectfully engages in a fictitious dialogue, Timon launched a clever attack on the credulity of all dogmatic philosophers, living and dead. The three books of hexameter poetry containing these onslaughts cannot have been intended for an entirely popular audience, since they presuppose a wide knowledge of the history of philosophy; nevertheless, public interest in the subject was apparently strong enough to enable him to attract a good many readers.

Timon composed a poem in elegiac verse dealing with the beliefs of his master Pyrrho, whose legendary role as an innovator he did much to popularize. The title *Indalmoi*, 'Fantasies', which he gave to this composition refers to the illusory doctrines of all the rival philosophical schools. In addition, Timon was the author of a prose treatise named *Python*, describing his career as one of Pyrrho's followers. He defends the Sceptic standpoint with colourful vividness, concluding with the acceptance of a pragmatic and, practically speaking, not too immoderate position. Since, he declares, everything is unknowable, a person should, for the purposes of day-to-day life, accept the laws and traditions he finds around him – without any fervour (or indeed much respect) but with a good enough grace to escape disturbing conflicts, so that he will be free to concentrate on the pre-eminently important task of grasping the *ataraxia* which his Scepticism will bring into reach.

Timon also wrote an essay entitled *The Funeral Banquet of Arcesilaus*, dealing appreciatively with a philosopher of that name from Pitane (316/15–c. 241), who was head of the Platonic Academy between 268 and 265. Timon had mocked him on earlier occasions, but now he changed his line and treated him with respect. For Arcesilaus, having learnt of Pyrrho's teaching (perhaps from Timon himself), and wishing to attack the vulnerable views insisted on by the Stoics, gave the Academy a bold new turn by deserting Plato's dogmatic, transcendental idealism in favour of a Sceptical insistence that no perception can ever be reliable, so that all judgements, on every matter whatever, must be avoided and withheld. Arcesilaus was able to justify this sharp departure from the Academy's Platonic traditions by citing Socrates' sceptical 'I know I don't know' – though he went further, and remarked that even Socrates had been mistaken when he claimed to *know* that he did not know.

Arcesilaus was a complex man, with many friends, who spiced his teaching with a famous wit – directed somewhat harshly against his fellow-philosophers – and who was not above courting popularity in unintellectual circles. Although he wrote nothing down, the novel Pyrrhonic twist he gave Platonism had come to stay, so that henceforward the Academy laid much more emphasis on doubts of this kind than on the search for absolute, cosmic truth that had been its original aim.

Carneades of Cyrene (214/13–129/8 BC), who became head of the Academy nearly a century later, shared the same determination to attack Stoic dogmas, singling out their gods and providence and fate as especially ridiculous concepts; and he fully agreed with Arcesilaus that no proposition can be certainly established as true or false. Yet he also hedged by concluding that in most matters it is at least possible to decide what is persuasive and convincing, what *appears* to be true, and to act on the basis of that. In other words, he worked out a theory of probability, and this rescued Scepticism from the dead end to which its negativeness would otherwise have ultimately condemned it.

Following the example of Arcesilaus, Carneades did not write down his opinions, with the result that his pupils were sometimes extremely uncertain what they actually were. But it is clear that he, like his predecessor, laid bare Stoic inconsistencies and implausibilities with devastating skill. At Rome in 155 he gave an eloquent speech in favour of justice, and on the next day an equally eloquent one directed against it. This acrobatic achievement made a very profound impression, but it also shocked many Romans, to whom it seemed typically Greek – too clever by half.

Thereafter Sceptical views – usually in a more scholarly and theoretical form – continued to be taught in the Academy until the first century BC, when they were dropped. However, they continued to be taught outside Academical circles, and were taught in the original, more uncompromising, Pyrrhonian form. This was the approach, for example, of Aenesidemus of Cnossus, who upbraided the Academy for its defection from Sceptic ideas. Aenesidemus wrote with such force that his hard-line approach, reinforced by a variety of new arguments, caused him to be regarded as one of the last original thinkers of antiquity – the last being Plotinus, in the third century AD, who sought his *ataraxia* in quite another direction, by an astonishingly original enhancement of the mystic elements of Platonism.

3 The Literary Escape Routes

While many writers and artists were seeking to take a firmer grip on reality, the philosophers, while claiming to do the same, were in fact teaching how to *resist* its incursions by cultivating a remote, impregnable, invulnerable peace of mind. Another way, however, in which the same escape from real life could be achieved inwardly was by inventing a better world instead, in which all the obstacles in the way of good living had been finally broken down, and this was a popular exercise in the Hellenistic age.

The emphasis was on an imaginary country in which the desired peace of mind had been reached by universal goodwill and collaboration among its inhabitants. For this was an age, in spite of or because of all its wars, in which the concept that all men and women share a common humanity had gained considerable strength. Already in the fifth century the Athenian orator Antiphon and the philosopher-scientist Democritus of Abdera had enunciated this doctrine with force. Since then, the growing lip-service to pan-Hellenic ideas led by Isocrates (436–338) (Chapter Two, section 1) had operated both on behalf of and against such cosmopolitan conceptions: on behalf of them, by helping to demolish the barriers between the various Greek states, and against them, by stressing that the purpose of pan-Hellenism was to make war – to fight the traditionally condemned 'barbarians' (Persians). Pan-Hellenism of this chauvinistic, anti-cosmopolitan kind was also implied by Aristotle, who described the Asiatic races, for all their gifts, as naturally 'enslaved and subject'.

His pupil Alexander the Great, however, evidently did not agree. For it was he above all others whose conquests – given glory by a remarkably enlightened ideal of partnership with the Persians – established the conditions in which a kind of international régime might have come into being. He himself, though, was evidently more interested in transcending race by the creation of a mixed élite and ruling class: while God is the father of all human beings, he is reputed to have said, it is the noblest and best whom he makes especially his own.[35]

Alexander's portentous expansion, following sharply upon the suppression of the Greeks by his father Philip II, had breached the walls and ideals of the city-state, and exposed its traditions to criticisms inspired by a wider point of view. The new Greek Dispersion inspired thinking about 'the world' (*oikoumene*), a kind of universal spiritual empire which was not only pan-Hellenic – though Hellenic life had been extended over vast territories where a common dialect of Greek (*koine*) was now spoken – but cosmopolitan in a wider sense. The latter idea, as well as the former, exercised a marked effect on literary and philosophical attitudes. 'No honest man', declares Menander, 'I call a foreigner: one nature have we all.' And: 'if a man has a noble character which prompts him to a good life, then he's of noble birth, even if he's a black African'.[36] Aristotle's chief pupil Theophrastus likewise stressed the kinship of all living creatures in a world that is the common home of gods and men.[37]

In this new, huge Greek or partly Hellenized world, many philosophers travelled and migrated a lot from place to place, which made them feel rootless and awakened their susceptibility to international points of view. Thus Diogenes the Cynic, a typical exile, declared 'I am a citizen of the universe'[38] – and so not by any means of one particular state or another. He did not, it is true, manage to look as far as the unity of mankind. Yet he decisively rejected the city as just another unnecessary limitation to the uninhibited life. In the same spirit his pupil Crates of Thebes could declare that he had no one city (his knapsack was city enough for him); for the entire world was his citadel and his house.[39]

Epicurus, too, had spent fifteen years in banishment without a fixed home before he settled in Athens, so that his rejection of current political and social values likewise bears the marks of a refugee philosopher. The clue to detached attitudes in the rival Stoic school, as well, lay in the similar expatriate history of its founder Zeno and his followers. They were migrants who had abandoned the rights and duties of their own cities, accepting life as aliens and second-class residents in the states where they finally settled. That is one of the reasons why Zeno's early work *The Republic* (*Politeia*), of which fragments survive, was evidently of a sharply radical, revolutionary character, recommending – in forceful, Cynic terms that his Stoic followers later tried to water down – the abolition of everything typical of the traditional city-state, such as marriages, temples and coinage.

However, the cosmopolitan ideal state he advocated instead was by no means an egalitarian one. On the contrary, the wise and good were to play a predominant part in its management; they may even have been intended to be the only citizens it had. At all events the cosmopolis was to be in their hands and theirs alone, since, as both Zeno and his successor Chrysippus declared, only the wise man is able to rule, judge and speak. They were looking forward to an ideal state which might be established in the future. But they were also conveying a message to the contemporary world: it must place the control of affairs in the hands of the wise and good, who, for their part, far from retreating into the contemplative, sage withdrawal idealized by subsequent Stoicism, must gird themselves for this active task.

That was also the clue to the famous Stoic doctrine that all human beings are brothers and sisters, since all have a share of the divine spark. Such a doctrine was only fully developed under later Stoic philosophers (Chapter Four, section 2): to Zeno himself, once again, only the wise and good 'are godlike and have something divine in them, whereas the bad man is without divinity'.[40] So Zeno, in his early days, had a vision of these élite people living together in Concord (Homonoia, a fashionable concept), as the directors of a new kind of ideal state. Later in his life he was prepared to admit that the city might provide a convenient framework after all. Even so, what seemed to him much more important was one's own self-cultivation within the favourable climate that the wise men's imaginary régime would provide, with a considerable degree of indifference to everything else.

In about 250 Ariston of Chios, who founded an independent branch of the Stoic school, moved back towards less qualified Cynic simplicities when he roundly asserted that, by nature, we none of us have any fatherland at all: the true division is not between nations but between people who are good and people who are bad. Ariston exercised an influence on Eratosthenes of Cyrene (c. 275–194), who became head of the Alexandrian Library and was the most versatile scholar of his age. Writing at a time when relations between Greeks and Egyptians in Egypt were tense, Eratosthenes asserted once again that humankind should be divided not according to races but according to qualities. Eratosthenes spoke with particular conviction since he was an expert in geographical studies, which testified, like the remarkable travels of Pytheas and others, to the unity of the world created by Alexander's conquests.

Polybius (c. 200–after 118) transferred the idea of this cosmopolitan unification to history, in which he saw it as *already* provided by the Romans. And then the *Histories* of the Stoic Posidonius of Apamea (c. 135–50), a polymath on a scale even outdoing Eratosthenes, gave vigorous philosophical life to this same Rome-oriented interpretation of the cosmopolitan union. Unwaveringly determined to see the world as an integrated, indivisible, harmoniously organic whole, unified and united by universal sympathy, Posidonius felt it his duty to make an equally unified, orderly narrative of this orderly system that Providence had established on earth. Like Polybius, he placed this grand plan in the service of Roman imperialism, since he too believed that the potentially world-wide Roman state was the only possible earthly embodiment of this providential cosmopolis: so that less civilized nations should be persuaded (or forced) to accept Rome's control, for the sake of their own evolution and improvement. Evidently a readable, entertaining and highly influential writer, Posidonius did much to recommend this pro-Roman variety of the Hellenistic cosmopolitan idea to a host of universal historians who came after him.

Long before Posidonius' time cosmopolitanism had also got off on quite a different tack. This took the form, not of envisaging a future or present cosmopolitan state on earth, but of inventing and describing quite imaginary Utopias instead, to use the term – from *ou* (not) and *topos* (place) – invented by Sir Thomas More (1516). These are generally ideal and perfect places, for the contrary depiction of ideally horrible societies (in the near future), *dystopias* or *kakotopias*, is a modern literary device.

Such perfect mythical Utopias had been devised by the Greeks for many centuries previously, including the Blessed Islands, the Garden of the Hesperides, the home of the Hyperboreans, the equally fictitious Homeric island of Scheria inhabited by the Phaeacians, and the country of Aea or Aeaea towards the Rising Sun which was the goal of the Argonauts. In the bad times of the Peloponnesian War between Athens and Sparta (431–404), such happy never-never lands had been dwelt on with loving nostalgia by dramatists of the Old Comedy such as Aristophanes, whose masterpiece *The Birds* reflects the perennial desire to escape reality in this kind of way.

It was a source of never-ceasing satisfaction among the Greeks to envisage the attributes of an imaginary ideal community. Some of their thinkers, conservatives and radicals alike, professed to find them mirrored in the archaic institutions of Sparta. In the fifth century Hippodamus of Miletus, the famous town-planner, enumerated the characteristics that this perfect society ought to possess, and Phaleas of Chalcedon (*c.* 400) listed its aims, which included equality of education, communal ownership of goods, and the nationalization of industry. Plato's imaginary island of Atlantis (in his unfinished dialogue the *Critias*) is our oldest surviving philosophical wonderland in Greek; and there was also, apparently, a strong Utopian element in a strange book, now lost, written by Onesicritus of Astypalaea, who was with Alexander in India and wrote a historical romance suggested by the king's achievements.

Henceforward, Utopias inspired by the Alexander legends proliferated. On the whole they exercised no influence on practical politics, though a curious attempt to bring such ideas into effect was made by Cassander's brother Alexarchus, when he established a 'City of Heaven' (Uranopolis) in Macedonia, though little is known about how things developed among the Uranidae who were the citizens of this ambitiously

named foundation. Meanwhile another member of Cassander's entour-
age, Euhemerus of Messene, was writing a fictitious travel-book which
returned Utopianism to the realms of make-believe. As the surviving
fragments of his *Sacred Scripture* indicate, the work described a visitor's
account of the way of life on the imaginary island of Panchaea in the
Indian Ocean. Euhemerus, like so many others, was fired by the exciting
situations and unexpected, instructive foreign societies opened up by
the discoveries of Alexander – and he encouraged the recognition of
Alexander's Successors as divinities by his famous theory that all the
gods had once lived upon the earth (Chapter One, section 6). In
Panchaea, like the isles of ancient myth, everything abounds in ideal
profusion, though the island is not a completely isolated laboratory
specimen, since it retains some small trading relations with the outside
world. Euhemerus' Utopia attained widespread popularity when rendered into Latin prose by Ennius (better known as a poet) early in the
second century BC; and it became the ancestor of many other works,
including Swift's ironical *Gulliver's Travels*.

It may have been at about the time of Ennius' translation that a
certain Iambulus, who appears to have been an Arab (Nabataean),
wrote another fantastic Greek account of a journey to a fictional island
– this time the Island of the Sun, reached by way of Ethiopia, where the
traveller writes how he was kidnapped by the inhabitants; it was they
who then took him to the island, where he lived for seven years. Echoing,
as usual, the old fairyland myths and more recent Alexander legends,
Iambulus also introduces a significant social note in keeping with contemporary ideas. For although upon his island the Sun God (Helios,
who was fashionable in the monotheistically inclined Hellenistic world)
is master, liberator, and guardian of justice, he presides over a community founded on brotherhood and the dignity of free labour: under
the influence of Cynic principles, communistic lines of conduct are
introduced, including the common ownership of women, and the
general abolition of class distinctions. Utopias enjoyed some popularity
among the lower orders of society, because they lent respectability to
ideas of social change. Thus when Aristonicus sought to win over
popular support for his resistance to Rome's annexation of Pergamum
(133-130 BC), he chose to call his proposed new state the City of the
Sun (Heliopolis), deliberately taking a leaf from Iambulus' book, out of
social as well as religious motives.

Meanwhile the exotic settings of Greek novels were bearing witness
to similar Utopian hankerings, but without any such desire to give them
practical effect.

To write about ideal Utopias was one way of resisting, or ignoring, the encroachments of the existing world, and of seeking what everyone wanted, that imperturbable peace of mind (*ataraxia*) that disregarded them altogether (Chapter Four, section 2). The intellectuals of the Hellenistic age had another escape route as well: if they were able to claim the necessary qualifications, they could pick up their baggage and physically decamp to the sheltered, cloistered 'ivory tower' provided for them by the Ptolemies in the Museum in Alexandria.

The word *mouseion* originally signified a place associated with the Muses, or with the arts over which they presided. Sometimes a *mouseion* included, or was synonymous with, the temple of these deities. More often, however, the implications of the term were literary or cultural, relating to a school or research centre designed to be a centre of inspiration and creative imagination. Such were the 'Museums' in Plato's Academy and Aristotle's Lyceum. But by far the most famous of all of them was the Museum at Alexandria, established on some site (not yet identified) in the neighbourhood of the royal palace. The founder seems to have been Ptolemy I Soter, acting on the advice of Aristotle's pupil Demetrius of Phaleron, after the latter had been expelled from the rulership of Athens; and, although he had ruled it in an authoritarian manner, the influence of his Aristotelian school prompted the spirit of relatively free investigation which permeated the new institution at Alexandria. Under the early Ptolemies, the Museum developed into an ever more impressive focal point of learning, the greatest single centre of Greek culture that had ever existed or would ever exist again. It placed both scientific research (Chapter Three, section 1) and the pursuit of letters on a firmer footing than they had ever enjoyed before in Greek lands, and made Alexandria the cultural rival of Athens.

The Museum was designed to house a group of scholars, perhaps thirty in number, to whom the monarchs paid generous enough salaries to attract first-class men. They were presided over by a director, who was a royal appointment. The establishment, which included a communal dining hall, a crescent-shaped portico for meetings, and a colonnaded garden lined with trees, was intended primarily for writing and research rather than for teaching. The members also held discussions in which the Ptolemies, who were nearly all cultured men, would take part; and literary prizes were awarded and presented. In addition, there were numerous dinners and drinking parties, at which problems were debated in an atmosphere of epigrammatic wit. The Sceptic Timon of Phlius (*c.* 320–230) had scathing words for the 'fatted fowls that quarrel without end in the hen-coop of the Muses'.[41] Yet it was a place where the happy few could escape the anxieties and boredoms of the age, and get on with some important work.

The same was true of the Alexandrian Library, which adjoined the Museum but was more or less distinct from it, and later became the more renowned of the two institutions. Aristotle had established an organized library in his Lyceum at Athens, and this provided a model for the epoch-making sequel at Alexandria. Like the Museum, it was initiated by Ptolemy I Soter – once again assisted by the advice of Demetrius of Phaleron – though Ptolemy II Philadelphus may have played an even larger part than his father in launching the project. The contents of the Library are variously assessed between 100,000 and 700,000 volumes; an estimate of something like half a million may not be too far from the truth.

The books were made from the papyrus plant which grew plentifully in the Nile delta. It was cut vertically into very thin slices, each of which was overlaid crosswise by a second slice which adhered to it by means of the natural gum of the plant. Next, a number of these two-layered slices were stuck together into a long strip, averaging twenty or thirty feet in length and eight or nine inches in width. A reed pen and carbon ink (vegetable gum mixed with soot and water) were employed to inscribe the writing on the surface of the strip in vertical columns, and it was then rolled up on a stick. To read it, one held the roll in the left hand and unrolled it with the right, rolling up each part of the papyrus again as one finished perusing its contents. The Library was equipped with a series of pigeon holes in which the rolls were lodged, each identified by a label attached to its cover.

The Chief Librarians were a succession of eminent scholars, appointed by the kings, like the Directors of the Museum, and mostly required, at the same time, to act as tutors to the royal children in the palace. The first known occupants of the post were Zenodotus of Ephesus (c. 284), a pupil of the poet-scholar Philetas of Cos, who had himself been tutor of Ptolemy II Philadelphus; and then the epic poet Apollonius Rhodius (c. 260). Apollonius' assistant, the poet Callimachus – his former teacher, and hostile literary rival – produced a scientifically planned catalogue of the Library in 120 volumes. Who, if anyone, was allowed to take the books out is unknown; but their consultation was probably limited to scholars, scientists and poets, and particularly to the people residing in the Museum, though a smaller branch establishment adjoining the Temple of Sarapis may perhaps have been available for members of the public, or at least for teachers in the city's schools.

The early Ptolemies spent large sums, and employed numerous agents, to purchase manuscripts of the profoundly admired Greek classics wherever these could be found in any part of the Hellenistic world. Thus Ptolemy III Euergetes, advised by Eratosthenes who succeeded Apollonius as Chief Librarian, was able to buy works by Aeschylus, Sophocles and Euripides; while Ptolemy IV Philopator founded a whole branch of the library exclusively dedicated to Homer. Such acquisitions enabled scholars to collect, collate, edit and amend the texts of the famous earlier authors, which had never been done before.

Zenodotus led the way by working on the epic and lyric poets of the past and initiating the first scientific attempt to get back to the original text of the Homeric poems. Then Aristophanes of Byzantium (d. 180), following Eratosthenes as Chief Librarian, produced much-improved critical editions of Homer, and edited many other poets as well. It was with his pupil, Aristarchus of Samothrace (d. 145), however – a monumentally versatile producer of commentaries and treatises – that truly accurate literary scholarship may be said to have begun; later writers pronounced him the greatest critic of all time.

Although signs of a growing sense of literary history had already been apparent before Hellenistic times, it was these Alexandrian men of learning who virtually created scholarly, philological criticism – at a time when so much crass superstition was flourishing all around. Their familiarity with the whole of extant Greek literature was dazzling and unrepeatable. In an age when learning was keenly admired, their achievements won an existence for scholarship not merely as an adjunct but in its own autonomous right. Their methods became canonical in determining the forms of book-production and literary analysis in all Hellenistic centres, and the earlier writings they had so carefully preserved and studied were handed down to the Romans, and thus to ourselves.

Yet disaster fell on the Library, and on the Museum as well, in 145 BC, when Ptolemy VIII Euergetes II (Physcon, 'Fat-paunch') turned against the intellectuals who worked in these institutions because they had sympathized with his brother Ptolemy VI Philometor, whom he hated. The two centres of learning suffered a purge (from which they never really recovered), and the scholars fled elsewhere. They took with them the techniques in which they were so expert, and introduced them into the other cities to which they migrated.

Some of these cities already had important libraries of their own: for example, the royal foundation at Antioch, under the auspices of the Seleucid monarchs (where the over-elaborate but influential poet Euphorion of Chalcis was made librarian by Antiochus III the Great), and the library in Antigonid Macedonia (in which King Perseus took a keen interest). Alexandria's most serious rival, however, was the library founded at Pergamum by Attalus I (241–197) and developed by his son Eumenes II Soter (197–160/59), with the help of links with the Platonic Academy and the Aristotelian Lyceum at Athens. This Pergamene Library (the earliest in the Greek world to have been traced by archaeologists) stood next to the temple of Athena, who was its presiding deity, just as she presided over Pergamum itself. Eventually the building lodged 200,000 volumes. The Ptolemies and Attalids were keen rivals in support of their respective libraries. In the hope of crippling his competitor's book acquisitions, Ptolemy V Epiphanes clamped down an embargo on the export of papyrus from Egypt, but Eumenes II Soter retaliated by producing a new writing material made of sheepskin parchment (named after his city of Pergamum), which was expensive but had the advantage that it could be used on both sides. The very high prices that both royal houses were prepared to pay for important books encouraged the production of numerous forgeries.

The Alexandrian Library was of importance not only because of the scholars who collected its classical texts, but because of the poets who, residing in the Museum, used these texts as the bases and stepping-off points for their own distinctive work.

In the immediately pre-Hellenistic years the only successful Greek poetry had been the Athenian Middle and New Comedy, which had little 'poetical' about it except its employment of verse. Otherwise, poetry had fallen far below prose as a literary medium. Now, in this new world of cultural stimuli, there were radical changes. For the thousand Hellenistic writers whose names have survived (though little enough of their works) included very many poets indeed. Basking gratefully in the exceptional patronage accorded by the Ptolemies, poetry reassumed its earlier primacy, creating what has sometimes been described as a new, poetical, Alexandrian Golden Age between 290/80 and 240 BC.

Yet the old tragic poetry, to which people had flocked in earlier times, did not regain its leading role. It is true that the names of 130 Hellenistic tragic dramatists have come down to us; but as far as one can judge from their 400 surviving lines, they did not embark on any important new courses of development, and it was not they who became famous and imposed their stamp on the age. Indeed, the dramatic stage as a whole – apart from the brief climax of Menander's New Comedy – no longer came first in people's minds as a serious cultural institution. In these days, they were reading much more than they were sitting and listening. And there were now two different sorts of public. What the vast middle-brow public were interested in we have seen elsewhere (Chapter Two, section 2). But a few extremely well-educated poets, and the élite that supported them, looked inwards rather than outwards in order to revive their art, which became a much more refined and recondite and withdrawn affair – divorced, as never before, from the political, social and religious roles it had traditionally played. Poets were willing and glad to admit that they no longer dealt with life as a whole. Instead, a new, intellectual art for art's sake emerged, setting and trying to solve its own esoteric problems, and nobody else's.

For one thing, almost every poet of the day showed a keen and often obsessive concern with form; with the encouragement of analyses such as Aristotle's *Poetics*, this was a technical literary age preoccupied with fixed rules. In metre, simplicity was favoured; yet it was a simplicity that was far from spontaneous, but highly polished and sophisticated, only attainable by masterly skill. As models for their language and style the Hellenistic poets had the entire range of ancient Greek literature to call upon, from heroic times onwards; and they had the great new libraries in which they could read its masterpieces. However, far from allowing this wealth of material to daunt them, they drew upon it for what it had to offer, adding ingenious variations of their own with elaborate erudition and refined self-consciousness. The trick was to revive the words, phrases and rare poetical usages of authors of the past – in addition to making clever, allusive adaptations from the works of contemporaries – and to give them a cunning twist, bringing them together in piquant new combinations and endowing them with novel nuances of meaning.

These scholar-poets took not only their language but their subject matter from the past, once again with clever diversifications. They ransacked the most recherché myths and legends, antiquarian histories and obscure points of local topography for whatever titillating details and psychological angles they might be able to provide. For the widening of spatial horizons, combined with the diligence of the scholarship industry, signified a new freedom for the poet to journey both far and wide in a geographical sense and far backwards into time, selecting what he best felt able to assimilate and exploit from all those generations of past literary experience. He had consciously begun to use, instead of being used by, the tradition – of which he no longer regarded himself as a living part, but rather as a self-conscious descendant and successor.

The imitativeness and allusiveness that were inevitable results of such methods set a hard problem to those who are trying to assess this literature today: for in order to do so we have to master a huge and recondite vocabulary, and understand what these words had meant to poets of earlier times and how intricately and subtly, therefore, the Hellenistic poets were investing them with novel shifts of meaning. But this difficulty was already freely admitted, indeed deliberately embraced and vaunted, in their own times and by themselves. Only those who had received the most elaborate education in earlier Greek literature could grasp and appreciate all these backward allusions. Unable, and unwilling, to seek after the large audiences who had listened to the poetical dramatists of the past, the Hellenistic poets were the few writing for the few; aiming to please small groups of connoisseurs, fellow-initiates and fellow-professionals who soared upon the same exceedingly rarefied cultural levels as themselves. For this purpose they were granted their residences and subsidies by rich and generous monarchs, who were only too glad to see their writers abdicating from the public roles that might have led them to criticize the régime.

However, these industrious Hellenistic poets, thus munificently provided for, had much more than mere refinement or over-refinement or technical brilliance to offer. They also provided abundant thematic variety, highly original treatment within their chosen conventions, close and almost clinically exact observation, a novel range of the gentler emotions, and a desire to bring poetry into relation with smaller, more intimate interests: into relation with what people thought and felt, in a world which was now too large for the recovery of a full synthesis. They also, quite frequently, spiced the dish with sly touches of humour – notably in the softening of erudition by pseudo-naïve jokes and surprises, and the deliberately shocking humanization of gods and myths. Within their self-imposed limits, and in their own way (though it may not be ours), they were formidably competent performers who treated poetry as a very serious discipline and exploited its possibilities to chronicle their own personal tastes, moods and characters in ways that had never been seen or heard or read before.

The complete, outstanding dweller upon these Hellenistic literary heights was Callimachus of Cyrene (c. 310/305–240). While still young, this phenomenally gifted man moved to Alexandria, where he became a school-teacher in one of its suburbs. Later he was introduced to King Ptolemy II Philadelphus, who gave him a secondary post in the Alexandrian Library. In response, Callimachus composed court pieces for his patron; but he also wrote a great many other poems as well.

His most important work was the *Aitia* (Causes), of which parts have survived. In the prologue of its second edition he reports advice given him by the god Apollo: 'Walk on the path where the carriages do not journey, do not drive in the tracks of others, do not travel the broad way, but on a road of your own, even though it be a narrow one.' *I detest all common things*, Callimachus declares in an epigram.[42] There could be no better way of describing the Hellenistic poetical ideal of esoteric exclusiveness, and of the desirability of following one's own tastes and inclinations. A poem must be different, and no matter – indeed, all the better – if it is artful and acrobatic, and far above the heads of the public. Let the road, by all means, be narrow. In this connexion Apollo went on to advise that the poet should 'keep the Muse slender. . . . For we sing among those who love the thin piping of the cicada and not the noise of donkeys.' Callimachus was very ready to agree. Only small-scale compositions, he felt, could embody the specific Hellenistic qualities of delicacy and high finish: poems are sweeter for being short: a big book is a big evil.[43]

His opponents, with Apollonius Rhodius (his Director in the Library) in the forefront, vigorously criticized this literary policy, declaring that the reason why Callimachus did not like long poems was because he lacked the ability to write them. Yet he hit back with a mocking malevolence and contempt that characterized this new generation of men of letters. He did so with conviction (although otherwise not a violent person), because he believed it imperative to turn away from the antique tradition that had produced the long, heroic and in his view hackneyed and bombastic poems of the Epic Cycle. 'I hate the cyclical poem.' 'The great stream of the Assyrian river Euphrates carries much filth and refuse.' 'Don't come to me for thunder: go to Zeus – that's *his* job.'[44]

The *Aitia* described a dream-journey to Mount Helicon, where the Muses, we are told, instructed the poet in many kinds of mythical learning. For ancient myths were habitually employed by these poets (as by Ovid and other Roman poets later on) as a vehicle for the fashionable, scholarly pursuit of causes – *aitia*, hence aetiology, the art of tracking them down, by the collection of facts, fancies and traditions that would throw light on the origins of Greek names or historical events or relics or rites or curious customs. In the course of these investigations (which recurred in Callimachus' *Hymns*), he treated the gods and their adventures with a new familiarity, learnt, to some extent, from Homer and the tragic dramatist Euripides and deliberately opposed to the normal Greek practice of reverent idealization.

Although thickly packed with literary and mythical references (which helped to provide the required brevity), the *Aitia* maintains a style that is sharp and neat, aimed at setting traps and administering little, unexpected, teasing stabs. 'Truly,' the poet remarks, 'much knowledge is a grievous ill for him who does not control his tongue.'[45] This is an endearing, and not untypical, self-criticism, since his own erudition does sometimes unmistakably run riot. Nor did the *Aitia* quite constitute the short poem that he himself advised us to admire, since it amounted to 7,000 lines; though it was not so much a continuous, 'cyclical' poem as a series of short vignettes strung together.

Callimachus also developed a miniature epic of a more unitary character, a type of work later known as the epyllion. His most famous achievement in this field was the lost *Hecale*, which dealt with the hero Theseus and his conquest of the mythical bull of Marathon. The poem adopts a novel, up-to-date narrative method and attitude, emphasizing not so much the traditional bloody struggle between hero and beast as the more intimate theme of the poor old woman Hecale who hospitably offered Theseus a rustic meal on his way to fight the monster.

Despite the small proportion of his output that has survived, it is evident that Callimachus possessed a peculiarly original talent, displayed in an abundance of bold and versatile experimentation, interspersed with many lively and piquant personal touches. True, his superlatively polished virtuosity and his exploration of the most curious byways of learning inevitably leave us cold. Yet in ancient times he earned a more persistent and admiring reputation than any other Hellenistic poet, receiving the compliment of imitation by Catullus. Indeed, Callimachus had made a serious attempt – the first for centuries – to give Greece a 'new poetics', insisting on poetry that derived its validity not from any transcendental truths it might contain but from its own inherent, immanent form.

Callimachus' rival Apollonius Rhodius (*c*. 295–215) was born either at Alexandria or at another, older Greek city in Egypt, Naucratis, and succeeded Zenodotus to become the second Director of the Alexandrian Library under Ptolemy II Philadelphus (260–246). His principal work was his epic the *Argonautica*, which has survived. It tells how the Argonauts, under the leadership of Jason of Iolcus in Thessaly, sailed the *Argo* to the remotest corner of the Black Sea in order to seize the Golden Fleece from King Aeetes of Colchis on the sea's far shores. Apollonius was the first poet to make romantic love the central theme for an epic poem. For an epic poem, of a kind, the *Argonautica* was – yet not of the old heroic sort which belonged irrevocably to the past, since Apollonius' epic was infused with every possible novel Hellenistic trend and device. For one thing, the poet seizes upon every chance to parade the fashionable learning for which his subject gives him ample scope; extensively indulging, for example, in the modish pursuit of investigating causes and antiquities, to which he contributed a genuine passion for the sparkling variety of the ancient myths. Apollonius also shows extraordinary sleight-of-hand in adapting Homer's language and style to his own new and quite un-Homeric literary world. In addition he displays an un-Homeric superciliousness, making his hero Jason, for example, a rather contemptible lightweight. And finally he does not attempt to achieve even the loose kind of unity of the Homeric masterpieces, but allows his poem to fall apart into a series of disjointed, though often beautiful, details.

Nevertheless, the *Argonautica* must have been anathema to Callimachus, because it *was* a long epic all the same, which was what he hated above all; and by endowing it with that form, Apollonius was deliberately launching a revolt against Callimachus' newly framed and fashionable 'Alexandrian' ideals extolling the short poem. According to tradition, this revolt involved him in a serious dispute over matters of principle with Callimachus – an older man, and formerly his teacher, but now his subordinate in the hierarchy of the Library. Apollonius, we are told, called Callimachus a wooden-head; while Callimachus accused Apollonius of plagiarism. That was an easy charge at this time, when it was fashionable to reproduce and cunningly reframe the writings of other poets, past and contemporary alike: moreover, it was a charge capable of plunging Apollonius into some embarrassment, since he did retell and rewrite long passages of Callimachus himself. Indeed, it is not impossible that the whole episode of their feud was thought up by some critic who had noticed these adaptations, and just inventively deduced the story from their existence. However, it is more likely that there is some truth in the tradition of their dispute, and that Callimachus gained the upper hand, which was why Apollonius left Alexandria (as he did) and retired to Rhodes, thus becoming known as the Rhodian.

Nevertheless, even if Callimachus won a temporary victory, the honours were not so one-sided in the times that lay ahead. For long epics continued to be written and to find favour in the next generation of Greeks; and in Latin this type of poem was to experience a mighty revival, first in the somewhat archaic heroic poems of Ennius, and then, above all, in the *Aeneid* of Virgil, which owed many conspicuous debts to the romantic tale of Apollonius.

The *Argonautica* includes some clever touches of a realistic, naturalistic character. Yet the poem presented an escape from reality as well, in two ways; firstly, because it was a supreme product of the school of Alexandrian poets who wrote entirely for a fellow élite with their own refined tastes, and secondly because the Colchis of King Aeetes, which formed the goal of Jason's quest, was a Utopian wonderland like the islands of Euhemerus and Iambulus (though recent excavations of the magnificent, partly Hellenized city of Vani in Colchis (now Soviet Georgia) have shown that there were some facts to build upon).

Such escapes were contributions to the widespread hankering for *ataraxia*, that peace of mind that would make a man superior to the vicissitudes of the age (Chapter Four, section 2). However, a contemporary poet, Theocritus, had the same purpose in mind but produced an entirely different recipe altogether, and it is a recipe which had more than a touch of original and profound genius. Expressed in the simplest (but entirely inadequate) terms, Theocritus' prescription was withdrawal into communion with nature and the countryside. The idea was not entirely unknown, but Theocritus gave it a wholly new life, and thereby handed down to modern times an entire set of ideals - which, as created by himself, were replete with potent dramatic and emotional content, and only in much later epochs degenerated into pastoral triviality.

Theocritus seems to have been born at Syracuse (Siracusa) in Sicily. But he apparently spent most of his life away from his native island (where King Hiero II does not seem to have helped him), first perhaps in southern Italy and later at Cos and Alexandria; and there he composed a panegyric for King Ptolemy II Philadelphus, though it is not evident how much patronage he gained in return. Thirty-one poems (in addition to brief epigrams) are attributed to him with some certainty. Some two centuries later they came to be described as idylls, *eidullia*, the diminutive of *eidos* (piece), a name given earlier to the *Odes* of the fifth-century lyric poet Pindar. The diminutive form has a certain convenience as a description of Theocritus' small, highly finished works of art, each of which is detachable and complete in itself, for he was a wholehearted supporter of Callimachus in his rejection of long poems - the work of crows (one of his characters declares) who are trying to behave like nightingales.

Theocritus is keen to dissociate himself from the grandiose epic, heroic, Homeric tradition: but to his readers, all of whom knew their Homer, his way of doing so raised an intriguing and paradoxical point familiar from the acrobatics of Apollonius and others. For Theocritus' poems, in the same typical Hellenistic manner, are crammed with Homeric references, but they turn them all upside down. Thus on the one hand, although he writes in a blend of non-Homeric, artificially Doric dialects, his metre is still the hexameter of the *Iliad* and *Odyssey*; and incidents and themes, too, are adapted from those poems. Moreover, Homeric proper names and words and phrases continually make their appearance. Yet these borrowings are also continually and deliberately jumbled together and sharply contrasted with un-Homeric usages, so as to create a hotch-potch of inversions that would instantly strike his cultured readers as highly incongruous, shocking, and amusing. Thus Theocritus allows his humble or vulgar herdsmen to indulge in ludicrously unsuitable epic reminiscences; and he ironically transposes the old Homeric situations into modern and highly unheroic, comic forms. In the characteristic Hellenistic manner (which his like-minded friends could appreciate), he is reviving mythological epic – but reviving it in very modern and dizzyingly subversive terms.

Theocritus' surviving poems may be divided today (though he probably did not do so himself) into those that are literary versions of mimes, and those that are pastoral or 'bucolic' (from *boukolos*, cowherd). The mimes, and their contribution to the realistic trends of the day, have already been commented on (Chapter Three, section 2). The pastoral pieces deliberately got away from realism altogether, and made their own highly individual and profound contribution to the current quest for *ataraxia*. On the surface, it is true, they deal with such apparently unprofound topics as singing contests and quarrels and banterings between shepherds, lamentations for rustic lovers, and the narration of old folk-tales about legendary cowherds and shepherds and their joys and sorrows. There had already been traces of this sort of poetry in Homer; but its true creator was said to have been an early, legendary Daphnis in Sicily or Euboea, though in historical times the men who first developed the theme were the fifth-century Sicilian poets Epicharmus and Sophron. In the Hellenistic age, nature was becoming an increasingly fashionable theme for both literature and art (Chapter Three, section 2); and some of its earliest writers – notably Anyte of Tegea – may, in a limited sense, have been forerunners of Theocritus' pastoral manner. It is also conceivable that he was influenced by the everyday songs of contemporary Sicilian herdsmen, derived directly (so Greek tradition believed) from the herdsmen-singers of the past. However that may be, Theocritus' pastoral poems – even at this relatively late stage of Greek literary history – virtually amounted to a new literary form, as he himself proudly suggests,[46] and it was a form that despite all changes became the inspiration of Virgil's *Eclogues*, Milton's *Lycidas*, and Shelley's *Adonais*.

The localities of Theocritus' rustic goings-on are hard to pin down. It is uncertain just how Syracuse, Cos and Alexandria were distributed in Theocritus' life, and the scenery of these various places is ambiguously distributed in his extant poems. Thus whereas his themes and characters are sometimes Sicilian or south Italian, certain of the poems are instead staged in Cos (VII and probably II); it is from this Aegean region that he appears to have drawn most of his visual detail, either by direct observation or, perhaps, through the medium of other men's poetry.

However, the pleasant country scenes of Theocritus are not designed to lend themselves to detailed localization. They are generalized yet selective arrangements of what may be described as stage properties, like the rural sacred precincts that are the habitat of the gods in Greek lyric poetry and Hellenistic epigram and art: stop in the grove and take your ease. For Theocritus' poetry is the pastoral verse of an urban civilization, written for the townsman. His countrymen are intensely conscious of the rustic beauties around them, which they describe in eloquent terms – like townspeople on a fine day out for a country excursion. Theocritus, who knew both urban and rural life, is registering a protest against the grim and desolating aspects of existence in great towns such as Syracuse and, above all, Alexandria. Many of Alexandria's multitudinous residents had only recently moved in from the country, and were expatriates like Theocritus himself. The city needed a myth to make good its deficiencies, and here it is. It is presented without the explicit moralization of later pastoral writers, but the moral is there for those who care to look for it:

> Not so much hurry. You're not on fire. You'll sing much better
> If you relax here among the trees, beneath this olive.[47]

In the subtle, enigmatic, densely structured seventh poem, *The Harvest Feast*, the goat-herd Lycidas, an impressive figure, is able to lead his friend Simichidas to this alluring destination. Lycidas may or may not be intended to represent some actual poet of the time. Simichidas is to a very real extent Theocritus himself. When Lycidas says to his friend (characteristically echoing Hesiod, who had written about the countryside nearly half a millennium earlier), 'I will give you my stick, for you are a sapling whom Zeus has fashioned all for truth',[48] Theocritus is identifying this pastoral personage as the source of the inspiration and poetic skill that will lead Simichidas (himself) to this goal. The poem ends with a triumphant, lavish assertion of the fecund life force of which Simichidas-Theocritus will then take possession, proclaiming Demeter, harvest goddess, as the embodiment of the sweetness of nectar and joy of creation, and as the epitome of the translucent evocations of the Mediterranean sea and sky which it was Theocritus' exquisite gift to evoke: she is the symbolic welcomer at the end of the poetic and human quest.

Elsewhere he subjects the rural scene to the humorous, startling technique at which he was so adept, contrasting elaborately refined and

THE SEARCH FOR PEACE OF MIND

coarsely rustic turns of phrase and forms of speech, so that country life at one moment seems idealized and at the next is presented with gross, lusty realism; the peasants who have been speaking in refined literary commonplaces suddenly dive into strident, unfragrant farmyard bathos, which was the sort of shock that appealed to Hellenistic poets and their readers. But that is merely one of Theocritus' jokes – one of the various conjuring tricks by which real and artificial, actual and imaginary are wittily blended and juxtaposed in a language of selective, concentrated, delicate precision, in which every superbly ordered word, Homeric and colloquial alike, is placed just where it ought to be with the lightest and most telling of poetic touches.

This relation that Theocritus creates between the two lives, the real life of the city and the poetic imaginary life of the countryside, is subtle and hard to pin down. Up to a point his pastoral scene is a limited world of the rustic bower, closed to everything that lies beyond its bounds, in which the ordinary, prosaic laws of nature are timelessly suspended; one has to escape from ordinary human society in order to find where this magic territory lies. Yet the oasis is not entirely cut off from the world outside. Theocritus, when we look beyond his piquant ironies, is not just longing for wild nature, but for a human community which will realize its true potential in these invigorating, healing surroundings – or in their symbolic equivalent, in which men and women will be able to live a life of freedom, concord and love in a perfect landscape, a landscape in which spiritual harmony can be set up as an ideal, can be put to the test as a yardstick for other kinds of society, *and can be triumphantly achieved*.

The poet, then, is trying to present issues and solutions that lie right at the centre of intellectual and aesthetic experience. He is reaching out to an all-embracing, cleansing, redeeming vision of humankind in which the hitherto repressed, unrealized individual can awaken his or her liberated, reborn self. In other words, Theocritus is trying to reconcile people to the stresses and realities of their situation by propounding a solution which is not, in his opinion, merely Utopian and unattainable, but is there for those who can grasp it – grasp it not necessarily or only in his chosen rural countryside, but in heart and soul.

One key word is *hasuchia* (the Doric form of *hesuchia*), peace and quiet, precisely the ataraxy everyone was seeking. In the fifth century Pindar had praised it as a political aim, but Theocritus sees it as a far more generally applicable goal: 'on *hasuchia* be our minds set', sings one shepherd to another,[49] and what he refers to is the whole lovely ideal that the poet is propounding. A further word which occurs over and over again in Theocritus is *hadus* (*hedus*), literally 'sweet' – its noun is *hadona*, pleasure or joy – but intended to describe the whole peace-bringing purpose that Theocritus has conjured up out of nature – which, he declares, is *hadus* itself.[50]

Hadus, again, is the very first word spoken by the shepherd Thyrsis in the programmatic showpiece which is the first of Theocritus' poems, a dramatic dialogue in form and framework interspersed with a long narrative description, and further varied by Thyrsis' lament for the death of Daphnis. The myth of Daphnis, as told by Theocritus, is designed to demonstrate the powerful efficacy of the poetic art as a harmonizing catalyst of the potent forces of nature. Thyrsis' song strongly affirms the joy and sweetness of life. Yet it is still a lamentation, and the whole idyll breathes a sense of death and doom: for this paradise, Theocritus wants to tell us, is a very fragile and precarious place or idea. The song sung by Thyrsis presents both peace and conflict at the same time, very close to one another. Indeed, Theocritus' whole pastoral vision is perpetually conscious of conflicting and opposing forces. While presenting the picture of tranquillity and harmony in a green pasture, he constantly, ironically, qualifies or questions the veracity of his own vision. Peace is threatened not only by the external world, but by an inner disharmony in human beings themselves. Like the whole Hellenistic world in which they were written, Theocritus' poems are full of contrasts, replete with a whole variety of dynamic counterbalancing tensions. There are contrasts between town and country, male and female, nature and society, nature and art, aspiration and fact, and above all between stern reality and the world of dreams – and it is that contrast, as much as anything else, which truly epitomizes the whole age he so brilliantly represented.

At times his pastoral landscapes are so deliberately unreal that they seem only to be luring us on to the impossible and unrealizable. But the clash between hard facts and dreams, says Theocritus, *may* lead to a reconciliation, the antithesis to a synthesis. The peace of mind that everyone wanted is elusive indeed; yet it can be found somewhere, all the same, if only we can muster the strength and imagination to lay our hands on this wonderful blessing. It is the alluring, moving beauty of this message that makes Theocritus the only Hellenistic poet who can still communicate powerfully with modern readers, if they are prepared to look carefully beneath the apparently trivial rustic surface to the depths that lie within. The dual role of Theocritus, bridging the contemporary urge towards reality and the no less urgent desire to escape from it altogether, need not surprise us since it was he, too, who led the quest towards realism in his mimes. But above all it was he whose pastoral world created the most moving and profound of all the escapes from ordinary living into ataraxy – an escape, however, which he insists is not an evasion, since the peace of mind he offers is the only true life: and it is, or can be, within our reach.

Epilogue

So Theocritus, in his own unique person, combined the greatest contradiction of the age: its urge to see things as they truly are, and its counter-urge to withdraw from this reality into the peace of mind that is invulnerable to its blows.

The same contradiction is apparent over the whole field of Hellenistic life. Scientists sought to see things as they were, and many writers and artists, too, tried increasingly to depict men and women in a far more realistic manner than had ever been seen before. Yet in sharp opposition to this trend, the mystery religions set up fantasy worlds to rescue people from having to suffer from existence as it is; and the philosophers almost unanimously saw it as their duty to satisfy a pressing, universal longing for *ataraxia*, freedom from disturbance, impregnable emancipation from the troubles of this world. In the earlier years of the present century it became the practice to emphasize this withdrawal and its symptoms as peculiarly characteristic of the Hellenistic world. More recently, writers have preferred to stress its more positive, active, constructive features. Both views are right; each is only half of the story.

Of course, there is nothing unique about such a simultaneous co-existence of these or any other two contradictory tendencies in a human society. Communities are well used to harbouring, at one and the same time, persons whose hearts and minds pull, destructively or usefully, in opposing directions. Furthermore, it is even thoroughly customary for one single individual to combine two opposite, contrasting and perhaps unreconciled characteristics in his own personal, emotional and intellectual experience – as Theocritus seems to have done. The 'Double-think' practised in the anti-utopian society forecast in George Orwell's *1984* meant the power of holding two contradictory beliefs in one's mind simultaneously, and accepting both of them. In *1984* this was a terrible unconscious process; but powerfully creative personalities are able to harbour the contradictions with deliberate consciousness. One of them was Theocritus, and another was the poet Catullus, one of the greatest

Roman heirs of the Hellenistic age, who said of his beloved: *Odi et amo*, 'I hate her and I love her at the same time', and spent his poetic life explaining how this could be.

The especially Hellenistic opposition between seeking reality on the one hand, and seeking to rise above it and escape it on the other, is an important aspect of the same phenomenon. It is a contrast, and clash, that can be found – though not usually to the same extent – in any society possessing an imaginative literature which impels individuals to withdraw into another world than their own, so as to fend off for a time the rigours of ordinary practical existence. As T.S. Eliot observed, humankind cannot bear very much reality. But when another poet, William Wordsworth, earlier said the same thing – that the world is too much with us – his words deserve consideration; for it was perhaps his late eighteenth-century and nineteenth-century England, above all, which is most directly comparable with the world of the Hellenistic Greeks for its contrast between an ebullient forward drive (the industrial revolution) and a simultaneous, by no means unconnected, retreat into imaginary escape-routes (exemplified by the novels of Sir Walter Scott). There are, of course, countless differences between the two epochs, but they are alike in their sharp contradictions between two simultaneous, co-existent phenomena: on the one hand, buoyant, realistic activity, and on the other the healing retreat into inaction which seemed the only means of keeping the excessive pressures of this exacting realism at bay.

On looking more closely at the Hellenistic world it becomes clear that this is only one of a number of unprecedentedly sharp paradoxes that the period presents. There was also, for example, a glaring and novel contrast between the hugeness of the dominating, remote states and the helpless smallness of the individuals who lived in them. Stimulated by the earlier advice of Socrates and men of his temper, each individual fended for himself and developed and fostered his own personality and potential, becoming conscious of what he could be and achieve. Cities, which in the past had provided such a cosy community protection, were now lacking a lot of their previous glamour, so that the individual – man and woman alike – correspondingly counted for more.

Here is another, incidental, contradiction as well. This was an age of great monarchies, beside which the cities (unless occasionally grouped together in federations) for the most part played a subordinate role. Yet the cities persistently survived; and even a monarchy, with rare exceptions, was likely to build its society around them. However, this is only one particular aspect of another, the most general and most elusive confrontation of all, the clash and blend between novelty and tradition.

273

This, of course, is a frequent phenomenon in many epochs and territories: but it constitutes the basis of the Hellenistic achievement in a very special sense. People never ceased to be conscious of the portentous classical past; and yet, while inevitably clinging to that past, they were also thoroughly eager to get away from it, and introduced striking and varied innovations in order to further that aim.

With the classical past behind it and Rome's empire lying ahead, the Hellenistic age has sometimes been rated dismissively as a merely transitional period. Yet this is a curiously mistaken conclusion. We cannot, it is true, tell whether and when, if there had been no Rome at all, the internal stresses and weaknesses of the Hellenistic world would have caused it to fall apart in any case: though it would surely not have been so soon, even if, as the historian Polybius realized, no society goes on for ever.[1] Nevertheless, while the Hellenistic states and societies lasted they constituted a civilization in their own right, one of the most significant in the history of the world – the western world, one should add, for despite the huge polyglot populations of the great states its noteworthy creations mostly remained Greek, with only moderate infusions of the other cultures they temporarily overran.

When this age was replaced (according to our modern terminology) by the epoch of Roman imperial domination, we come to a larger and stranger contradiction, perhaps, than any of those that have hitherto been enumerated. For defeat and political subordination to Rome came to mean not the suppression but the maintenance and perpetuation of the Hellenistic society. Rome had, of course, been partially Hellenized for centuries: in the words of the poet Horace, 'Greece, the captive, made her savage victor captive'.[2] He was referring to the distant past in which the Romans had adapted Greek culture for their own purposes. But by Horace's time another trend, too, had become clear: the Greek world, though politically subjected to Rome, had not been Romanized at all – and was not going to be, either. Extended rather than diminished in size, it was going to remain Greek.

Virgil – in this respect reproducing the views of Augustus, and of countless other Romans as well – coupled a reverent admiration for the cultural tradition of the Greeks with an equally firm belief that the Romans must remain their political masters.[3] Yet the Greeks, eventually, got their revenge. It began to be evident when Constantine the Great (AD 306–337) replaced Roman paganism by the Christian faith that Paul had introduced into Greek lands. Constantine gave the Greeks another successful revenge as well: when he created Constantinople, on the site of the Greek city of Byzantium far outside the Latin-speaking sphere – and the new foundation replaced Rome as the imperial capital.

In the following century, when the empire was divided into two parts, the western, Latin part succumbed to German invaders, and the 'Roman empire' – for so it continued to call itself – that survived was the eastern, Greek half of that world. Romanness, *Romanità*, persisted partially for a time at the court of Constantinople: in the sixth century, Justinian I was still codifying his laws in the Latin tongue. After the passage of another three hundred years, however, even the inscriptions on the coins had become Greek. Moreover, from the territories of Byzantium the power, language, art and thought that had formerly been the proud possessions of the Hellenistic world spread far and wide, with ineradicable persistence; that world had not only survived, but won.

Table of Dates

Eastern Europe	Western Asia	Egypt
336 BC. Alexander III the Great succeeds Philip II as king of Macedonia and suzerain of Greece	334-332 BC. Alexander III the Great conquers Asia Minor (part), Syria and Palestine from the Persians	332 BC. Alexander III the Gre conquers Egypt from the Persians; foundation of Alexandria (331)
	328. Zipoetes founds state of Bithynia (king 297)	
323. Antipater in Macedonia and Greece; defeats Athens in Lamian War (322)		323-283. Ptolemy I Soter; defeats Demetrius I Poliorce at Gaza 312 (king 305-30
319. Cassander succeeds Antipater	321. Antigonus I Monophthalmos in Asia (king 306, killed at Ipsus 301)	
315-281. Lysimachus in Thrace etc.	312-281. Seleucus I Nicator (king 305-304) defeats Lysimachus at Corupedium (281)	
304/3. Spartocus III king of Cimmerian Bosphorus		
	301. Mithridates I Ktistes founds kingdom of Pontus	
297-272. Pyrrhus I king of Epirus		c. 295. Foundation of Museur and Library at Alexandri
294-288. Demetrius I Poliorcetes in Macedonia and Greece (siege of Rhodes 305-4)	282-263. Philetaerus ruler of Pergamum	283-246. Ptolemy II Philadelphus
284-239. Antigonus II Gonatas king of Macedonia; defeats Gauls at Lysimachia (278/7), Athens and Sparta in Chremonidean War (267-262), Egypt off Cos and Andros (258, 245)	281-261. Antiochus I Soter; defeats Gauls (Galatians) (c. 273) 263-241. Eumenes I at Pergamum; throws off Seleucid suzerainty 261-246. Antiochus II Theos	c. 279. Construction of Pharo of Alexandria c. 276-270. Arsinoe II in powe 262-c. 242. Apollonius financ minister
245-213. Aratus dominant in Achaean League; seizes Corinth (243)	c. 255. Ariaramnes recognized as king of Cappadocia	246-221. Ptolemy III Euerget
244-192. Reformist kings at Sparta (Agis IV d. 241), Cleomenes III (defeated at Sellasia 222), Nabis (d. 192)	241-197. Attalus I at Pergamum; defeats Gauls (c. 230), named king	

Eastern Europe	Western Asia	Egypt
229–221. Antigonus III Doson		
229, 219. Roman interventions in Illyria		
221–179. Philip V; wars with Rome (215–205, 200–197: Cynoscephalae); 'freedom' of Greece, rewards to Rhodes	223–187. Antiochus III the Great; defeats Egyptians at Panion (200, reversing Raphia defeat 217); defeated by Romans (191, 190: Treaty of Apamea 188)	221–205. Ptolemy IV Philopator; defeats Antiochus III at Raphia (217)
192–182. Philopoemen dominant in Achaean League	197–160/59. Eumenes II Soter king of Pergamum	205–180. Ptolemy V Epiphanes; defeated by Antiochus III at Panion (200)
189. Aetolian League becomes subject ally of Rome		
	175–163. Antiochus IV Epiphanes; forced to evacuate Egypt (168)	180–145. Ptolemy VI Philometor
179–168. Perseus; war with Rome (Pydna); end of kingdom	167–142. Maccabean (Hasmonaean) revolt in Judaea	
167. Romans deport Epirotes and declare Delos a free port	160/59–138. Attalus II Philadelphus at Pergamum	
	150, 146, 138. Cleopatra Thea marries successive Seleucid kings	164–163, 145–132, 127–116. Ptolemy VIII Euergetes II
146. Romans sack Corinth, dissolve Achaean League, and annex Macedonia and Greece	133. Attalus III Philometor Euergetes; leaves Pergamum to Rome	
	120–63. Mithridates VI Eupator Dionysus the Great in Pontus; three Roman wars end in annexation	
	103–76. Alexander Jannaeus king of Judaea	
	94–74. Nicomedes IV Philopator; leaves Bithynia to Rome	107–89/8. Ptolemy X Alexander I placed on throne (for third time) by Cleopatra III
88, 69. Delos sacked (by Pontic fleet and then by pirates)	83–66. Tigranes I the Great; loses Syria to Romans (annexed 63)	
c. 60–44. Burebistas of Dacia: Balkan empire		
48. Caesar defeats Pompey at Pharsalus		51–30. Cleopatra VII Philopator Philadelphus Philopatris; with Caesar in Egypt (48–47); with Antony (41–40, 37–30); Egypt annexed by Rome (30)
	42–30. Antony rules Rome's eastern provinces	
31. Octavian (Augustus) defeats Antony off Actium	37–4. Herod I the Great king of Judaea	

The East	Western Europe	America
331–326 BC. Alexander III the Great conquers Babylonia, Persia and Bactria and extends frontiers to Indus	Late 4th cent. BC. Pytheas of Massalia circumnavigates Britain 345–337. Timoleon at Syracuse	(dates are conjectural)
323. Revolt of colonists in Bactria		
312–281. Seleucus I Nicator (king 305–304); cedes eastern territories to Chandragupta Maurya (c. 303)	317–289. Agathocles at Syracuse 310. Romans penetrate Ciminian forest into Etruria	c. 300 BC. Pottery in south-we New Mexico (etc), and Cochise (Desert) culture evolves into Mogollon (agricultural)
	294, 281. Roman victories over Volsinii (Etruria) 290. Romans conclude Samnite Wars and control central Italy	after 300 BC. Kaminaljuyú centre (Guatemala City) reaches first climax in Miraflores phase
281–261. Antiochus I Soter	288–278. Hicetas at Syracuse 280–275. Pyrrhus I of Epirus in Italy and Sicily	300 BC–AD 150. 2nd phase of literate Monte Albán cen in Zapotec territory, with elements from late pre-Classic Maya culture (Oaxaca, Mexico)
c. 274–232. Reign of Asoka in Mauryan empire	c. 269–215. Hiero II king of Syracuse 264–241. First Punic War; ends with Roman annexation of most of Sicily and of Sardinia	300 BC–AD 300. Izapa (Chiapas, Mexico) centre new style c. 300 BC–AD 400. Hopewell (Woodland) Indian cultu in Illinois and Ohio
c. 235–200. Euthydemus I Theos; greatly expands Bactrian state	237–206. Carthaginian empire revived in Spain; Carthago Nova founded (228) 225. Romans defeat Gauls (invaders from northern Italy) at Telamon	

The East	Western Europe	America
	218, 211, 195. Emporion (colony of Massalia) landing port of Roman expeditions to Spain	
223-187. Antiochus III the Great; eastern expedition (212-206)	218-201. Second Punic War: Hannibal's invasion of Italy defeated	
221-207. Ch'in dynasty in China (founded by Shih Huang Ti)	215-214. Hieronymus at Syracuse; goes over to Carthage	
202 BC-AD 221. Han dynasty in China	213-212. Siege and sack of Syracuse by Romans	c. 200 BC. First Maya pyramids in central Guatemalan lowlands (Tikal, Uaxactún)
c. 185. Mauryan empire falls to Sunga dynasty (Pusyamitra); Greeks rule east of Khyber Pass	206. Scipio Africanus by victory at Ilipa drives Carthaginians from Spain	
c. 171-138. Mithridates I; expands Parthian empire.	149-146. Third Punic War: destruction and annexation of Carthage	
c. 170/65-155. Eucratides I the Great; breaks away from Euthydemid dynasty		
Second quarter of 2nd cent.-140/30. Maximum expansion of Indo-Greek state under Menander Soter Dikaios	c. 135-132. First Slave Revolt in Sicily	
	133, 123-122. Attempted reforms by Gracchi at Rome	
	125-121. Appeal by Massalia prompts Roman annexation of southern Gaul	
141-87. Wu Ti greatly expands Chinese empire; travels of explorer Chang Ch'ien (138-125)	c. 125-100. First large fortified settlements from Gaul to Bohemia	
138-129. Antiochus VII Euergetes Sidetes; invasion of Parthian empire (130-129)	c. 113-101. Southern migrations of Teutones and Cimbri	
	104-100. Second Slave Revolt in Sicily	c. 100 BC-AD 300. Late Formative or Proto-Classic period of Maya art; urbanization of Teotihuacán
c. 130. Bactria falls to Scythians (Sacae) and Yüeh-Chih	102-101. Marius destroys invading Teutones and Cimbri	
	82-80. Sulla dictator at Rome	
	73-71. Slave Revolt of Spartacus in Italy	
53. Parthians defeat Roman triumvir Crassus at Carrhae	58-51. Caesar's Gallic War	
	49-45. Civil War between Pompey (d. 48) etc. and Caesar (dictator 49, d. 44)	
c. 40-1. Hermaeus Soter the last Indo-Greek King	36. Octavian (Augustus) takes Sicily from Lepidus	

Notes

Preface

1 John Gustav Droysen, in the 1830s and 1840s, played a major part in defining the term 'Hellenistic': C. Préaux, *Le monde hellénistique*, I, pp. 7ff. For its earlier background, ibid. pp. 5ff. Confusion is caused by the term 'Hellenism', which only means (or should mean) 'Greekness' in English, but is sometimes used to translate the German 'Hellenismus', which can refer specifically to the Hellenistic world.

Chapter One: The Hellenistic Kingdoms

1 Polybius, XVI, 13, 1; Livy, XXXIV, 31, 11ff. and 32, 9
2 Theocritus, XVII, 13ff., 85ff.
3 B.P. Grenfell, A.S. Hunt, etc. (eds), *Tebtunis Papyri*, III, 703, 230
4 Diodorus Siculus, III, 12–14
5 W.L. Westermann and E.S. Hasenoehrl (eds), *Zenon Papyri*, I, 66, lines 19–21; J.F. Oates, A.E. Samuel and C.B. Welles (eds), *Yale Papyri in the Beinecke Rare Book and Manuscript Library*, 46, column 1, line 13
6 U. Wilcken, *Urkunden der Ptolemäerzeit*, 7, 8, 15; *Papiri greci e latini*, IV, 421
7 B. Grenfell and A.S. Hunt (eds), *Hibeh Papyri*, II, 198
8 Plutarch, *On the Fortune or Virtue of Alexander the Great*, 5 = *Moral Essays*, 328E
9 Pliny the elder, *Natural History*, VI, 30, 122
10 Malalas, XVIII, 418
11 Arrian, *Anabasis*, VII, 9–10
12 *Corpus Papyrorum Judaicorum*, 4
13 I Maccabees, 1, 11
14 II Maccabees, 4, 9
15 Josephus, *Jewish Antiquities*, XIII, 318
16 Y. Meshorer, *Jewish Coins of the Second Temple Period*, pp. 118ff., nos 1ff.
17 *Oracula Sibyllina*, III, 271
18 N. Davis and C.M. Kraay, *The Hellenistic Kingdoms: Portrait Coins and History*, nos 174, 175, 178
19 Lucan, *Civil War*, X, 141ff.
20 Plutarch, *Should an Old Man Engage in Politics?*, 11 = *Moral Essays*, 790A

21 Pseudo-Plato, *Alcibiades*, 107E
22 Plato, *Politicus*, 294A (cf. 296ff.)
23 Pseudo-Isocrates, *To Demonicus*, 36
24 Aelian, *Varia Historia*, II, 20
25 Pindar, *Nemean Odes*, VI, 5f.
26 Aelian, *Varia Historia*, II, 19
27 Plutarch, *Alexander*, 27
28 Athenaeus, VI, 253
29 *Orientis Graeci Inscriptiones Selectae*, 212
30 Plutarch, *On Isis and Osiris*, 24; *Sayings of Kings and Emperors* (Antigonus), 7 = *Moral Essays*, 182C

Chapter Two: City-States and Leagues

1 Polybius, III, 59
2 Polybius, XV, 24
3 W. Dittenberger, *Sylloge Inscriptionum Graecarum*, 527
4 Plato, *Laws*, I, 626A, *Republic*, V, 471A–B
5 Apollonius Rhodius, *Argonautica*, II, 541
6 Aristotle, *Politics*, VII, 1327B
7 Plutarch, *Camillus*, 22, 3
8 Menander, *Fragments*, 537 Kock = 614 Sandbach
9 Polybius, XXXVI, 17
10 F. Jacoby, *Fragmente der griechischen Historiker*, A 112ff., 72
11 Isocrates, *Archidamus*, 50
12 Aeneas Tacticus, *Poliorcetica*, 14
13 Pseudo-Demosthenes, XVII, 5
14 W. Dittenberger, op. cit., 526, lines 22ff.
15 Polybius, XX, 6
16 Pseudo-Aristotle, *Oeconomica*, 1344A–B
17 Philemon, *Fragments*, 39 Meineke = 95 Kock
18 Menander, *Fragments*, 563A Körte
19 F. Jacoby, op. cit., A87, 108C and F
20 Homer, *Iliad*, IX, 443
21 Plutarch, *Lucullus*, 22
22 Plutarch, *On the Education of Children*, 8 = *Moral Essays*, 5E
23 Julian, *Against the Galileans*, 229E
24 Aristotle, *Rhetoric*, 1413 B 12
25 F. Jacoby, op. cit., C 697
26 *Inscriptiones Graecae*, II, 2nd ed., 1368
27 Athenaeus, VII, 276B–C
28 Cicero, *On Divination*, II, 86–87

Chapter Three: Reality and the Individual

1 Theophrastus, *Metaphysics*, 11B 24–12A 2
2 Plato, *Republic*, VII, 528C
3 Simplicius, *Commentaries on Aristotle's Physics*, 1110, 5
4 Vitruvius, IX, 11
5 Pliny the elder, *Natural History*, XXVI, 24, 95
6 Aristophanes, *Plutus*, 653–744
7 Alexis, *Fragments*, 30 Kock
8 Polybius, X, 47, 12
9 Plutarch, *Marcellus*, 17, 3
10 Syrianus, *Commentaries on Hermogenes of Tarsus*, 2, 23
11 F. Jacoby, op. cit., A76, 1; cf. Diodorus Siculus, XX, 43, 7
12 Polybius, V, 33
13 Pliny the elder, op. cit., XXXIV, 19, 52
14 Xenophon, *Memorabilia*, III, 10, 1–3
15 Aristotle, *Nicomachean Ethics*, IV, 3, 1–34
16 Pliny the elder, op. cit., XXXV, 44, 153
17 Ibid., XXXIV, 19, 65
18 Ibid., XXXIV, 19, 82
19 Ibid., XXXV, 44, 153
20 Quintilian, XII, 10, 9
21 Aristotle, *Poetics*, 2
22 Pliny the elder, op. cit., XXXV, 36, 88
23 I. Carradice, *Ancient Greek Portrait Coins*, p. 2, fig. 2
24 Xenophon, *Oeconomica*, 7, 30, cf. 14
25 J.U. Powell, *Collectanea Alexandrina*, 238, 45
26 *Ägyptische Urkunden aus den Staatlichen Museen, Berlin (Griechische Urkunden)*, XIV, no. 2376 (Heracleopolis)
27 B.P. Grenfell, A.S. Hunt, etc., *The Oxyrhynchus Papyri*, 1380, line 130
28 O. Rubensohn, *Elephantine-Papyri*, 1
29 W. Dittenberger, *Sylloge Inscriptionum Graecarum*, 578
30 Plato, *Laws*, I, 636
31 Diogenes Laertius, VII, 129
32 Plutarch, *Table Talks*, VII, 8 = *Moral Essays*, 712C
33 Polybius, XXXI, 25, 3
34 Plutarch, *Treatise on Love*, 23 = *Moral Essays*, 768–769
35 Diogenes Laertius, VI, 3
36 Theocritus, II, 164
37 Apollonius Rhodius, *Argonautica*, III, 967–972 (translated by F.L. Lucas)

Chapter Four: The Search for Peace of Mind

1 Pindar, *Olympian Odes*, XII, 2–12
2 Euripides, *Hecuba*, 488–491

3 Lucan, *Civil War*, VII, 445-7
4 Aristotle, *Physics*, II, 4-6
5 Menander, *Fragments*, 482 Kock = 417 Sandbach
6 Ibid., 594 Kock
7 Epicurus, *Letters*, III (*to Menoeceus*), 134
8 Polybius, 1, 4
9 Polybius, VI, 57
10 Zeno, *Fragments*, 87 Arnim
11 Diodorus Siculus, I, 49, 5
12 Paul, *Epistle to the Ephesians*, 2, 12
13 Plato, *Timaeus*, 21E
14 Diodorus Siculus, I, 27, 4
15 *Supplementum Epigraphicum Graecum* VIII, 548
16 Apuleius, *Metamorphoses*, XI, 6, 15
17 Firmicus Maternus, *About the Error of Profane Religions*, 22ff.
18 Xenocrates, *Fragments*, 4 Heinze
19 Diogenes Laertius, II, 115
20 J. von Arnim, *Stoicorum Veterum Fragmenta*, II, 975
21 Cicero, *De Finibus*, III, 22, 74
22 Epicurus, *Principal Doctrines*, 22, 23
23 Epicurus, *Letters*, III (*to Menoeceus*), 123
24 Ibid., 128, 4-5
25 Epicurus, *Principal Doctrines*, 34
26 Callimachus, *Epigrams*, 2
27 Epicurus, *Vatican Sayings*, 22
28 Epicurus, *Principal Doctrines*, 14
29 A. Körte, *Neue Jahrbücher, Supplementband* XVII, 536
30 Plutarch, *On Tranquillity*, 4 = *Moral Essays*, 466E
31 Diogenes Laertius, IV, 52
32 Marcus Aurelius, *Meditations*, VI, 47; Lucian, *Twice Accused*, 33
33 Sextus Empiricus, *Outlines of Pyrrhonism*, 12
34 H. Diels and W. Kranz, *Fragmente der Vorsokratiker*, 70A-B (2, 231-4)
35 Aristotle, *Politics*, VII, 7, 1327B; Plutarch, *On the Fortune or Virtue of Alexander the Great*, 6 = *Moral Essays*, 329D
36 Menander, *Fragments* 602 Kock, 533 Kock = 612 Sandbach
37 Cf. Porphyrius, *De Abstinentia*, III, 25
38 Diogenes Laertius, VI, 63
39 Ibid., VI, 85-93
40 J. von Arnim, *Stoicorum Veterum Fragmenta*, III, 13
41 Athenaeus, I, 22D
42 Callimachus, *Aitia*, I, 1, 25-28 Trypanis; *Palatine Anthology*, XII, 43, 4
43 Callimachus, *Aitia*, I, 1, 24, 29-34 Trypanis; *Athenaeus*, II, 72
44 *Palatine Anthology*, XII, 43, 1; Callimachus, *Hymns*, II, 108-109; *Aitia*, I, 1, 20 Trypanis
45 Callimachus, *Aitia*, III, 75, 8-9 Trypanis
46 Theocritus, XVI, 106-110

47 Ibid., V, 31-32
48 Ibid., VII, 43-44
49 Ibid., VII, 126
50 Ibid., VII, 143

Epilogue

1 Polybius, VI, 5, 8; 57, 1-9
2 Horace, *Epistles*, II, 1, 156
3 Virgil, *Aeneid*, VI, 847-853

Bibliography

— ■ —

Ancient Sources

1 *Greek Writers*

The information about the Hellenistic world provided by Greek writers adds up to an abundant quantity and variety (M.M. Austin, *The Hellenistic World from Alexander to the Roman Conquest: A Selection of Ancient Sources in Translation*, Cambridge 1981). Nevertheless, this mass of information remains extraordinarily patchy, arbitrary and fragmentary. Only one first-class historian has left us a substantial part of his work – namely Polybius – and he only covers a period of three-quarters of a century. An immense proportion of Hellenistic literature has failed to come down to us altogether, although in some cases more or less isolated excerpts of varying dimensions have been preserved. In the following list of contemporary and later authors who throw some light on the period, those of whose works considerable portions are still extant are shown in **bold type**.

Aelian (Claudius Aelianus) of Praeneste. *c.* AD 170–235. Rhetorician and moralizing philosopher. His surviving works include the *Varia Historia*, a collection of excerpts and anecdotes about human life, and a similar collection *On the Nature of Animals*.

Aeneas Tacticus, probably an Arcadian general from Stymphalus. First half of 4th cent. BC. Military writer. His *Poliorcetica*, about fortified positions, has survived.

Aenesidemus of Cnossus. 1st cent. BC. Sceptic philosopher.

Agatharchides of Cnidus. 2nd cent. BC. Historian and geographer. Writer on Asia under the Successors, on European history from 323 (?) to 146, and on the Red Sea. Extracts survive.

Alexis of Thurii (lived at Athens). *c.* 375–275 BC. Dramatist of the Middle and New Comedy. Writer of 245 plays, of which 140 titles and 340 fragments survive.

Antipater of Sidon. Later 2nd cent. BC. Epigrammatist. About seventy-five of his epigrams survive.

Anyte of Tegea. *c.* 300 BC. Poet. Her lyrics are lost but about eighteen of her epigrams (in Doric dialect) survive.

Apollonius of Perga. Later 3rd cent. BC. Mathematician and theoretical

288

astronomer. The first four books of his eight-book *Conics* survive in Greek and the next three in Arabic translation. The names of his lost works are preserved.

Apollonius Rhodius. Born in Egypt. *c.* 295-215 BC. Director of the Alexandrian Library. Writer of epic poem in four books, the *Argonautica.*

Appian of Alexandria. 2nd cent. AD. Writer of twenty-four-book *Romaica* describing Rome's conquests. Books 6-7 and 11-17 are complete, and 1-5 and 8-9 fragmentary.

Aratus of Soli. *c.* 315-240/39 BC. His best-known work is an astronomical poem, the *Phaenomena.* The names of lost poems are known.

Archimedes of Syracuse. *c.* 287-212 BC. Mathematician and astronomer. Nine works, mainly on mathematics, survive in Greek originals and two in Arabic adaptations. His astronomical books are mainly lost.

Aristarchus of Samos. 1st half of 3rd cent. BC. Astronomer. Author of the heliocentric hypothesis, though his only extant treatise, *On the Sizes and Distances of the Sun and Moon,* is based on the geocentric view.

Aristarchus of Samothrace. *c.* 217-145 BC. Director of the Alexandrian Library. Literary and linguistic critic. The most famous of his eight hundred works was an edition of the Homeric poems, with commentaries.

Aristides of Miletus. *c.* 100 BC. Author of erotic short stories, the *Milesian Tales.*

Ariston of Ceos. Later 2nd cent. BC. Peripatetic (Aristotelian) popular philosopher and biographer. (The Stoic Ariston of Chios left no writings except letters.)

Aristophanes of Byzantium. *c.* 257-180 BC. Director of the Alexandrian Library. Literary and textual critic and grammarian.

Aristoxenus of Taras. *c.* 375/60-after 300 (?) BC. Musicologist, biographer and antiquarian. Parts of his *Principles and Elements of Harmonics* and *Elements of Rhythm* are preserved.

Arrian of Bithynia. 2nd cent. AD. Author of *Anabasis* (History of Alexander), *History of Successors* (large fragments survive), and *History of Parthia* and *Indice* (lost).

Asclepiades of Samos. Early 3rd cent. BC. Epigrammatist. Published a collection of epigrams, the *Soros,* with Hedylus and Posidippus.

Athenaeus of Naucratis in Egypt. *c.* AD 200. Author of the encyclopaedic *Learned Banquet* (*Deipnosophistae*), now in fifteen books.

Berossus of Babylon. Early 3rd cent. BC. Author of three-book history of Babylon, the *Babyloniaca.*

Bion of Borysthenes (Olbia). *c.* 325-after 239 BC. Popular philosopher and author of *diatribai* (short, familiar ethical addresses combining seriousness and humour). Fragments survive.

Bion of Phlossa (near Smyrna). *c.* 100 BC. Seventeen fragments of his *Bucolica* are extant. A ninety-eight-line *Lament for Adonis* is often attributed to him.

Bolus of Mendes. 3rd cent. BC. Paradoxographer; also a pharmacologist.

Callimachus of Cyrene; lived at Alexandria. *c.* 310/305–240 BC. Poet. *Hymns* and *Epigrams* survive complete, *Aitia* (*Causes*), lyrics and elegies in fragments; his miniature epic the *Hecale* is lost.

Callisthenes of Olynthus, Aristotle's nephew. Historian, d. 327 BC, executed by Alexander.

Cercidas. Poet; probably identifiable with statesman and general of Megalopolis, *c.* 290–220 BC. Cynic philosopher and poet. Nine fragments of his verse have survived.

Chrysippus of Soli. *c.* 280–207 BC. Head of the Stoic school, whose philosophy he defended in numerous works.

Cleanthes of Assos, 331–232 BC. Head of the Stoic school. His *Hymn to Zeus* and fragments of other works, in verse and prose, have survived.

Clitarchus of Alexandria. Late 4th and early 3rd cent. BC. His *History of Alexander* is preserved in abbreviated form in Diodorus Siculus' *World History*.

Corinna of Tanagra. Probably *c.* 200 BC. Lyric poet. Previously-known fragments of her poetry have been augmented by a papyrus discovery.

Crates of Mallus. At Rome in 168 BC. Literary and linguistic scholar.

Crates of Thebes (Boeotia). *c.* 365–285 BC. Cynic philosopher and poet; fragments survive.

Dicaearchus of Messana in Sicily. Late 4th and early 3rd cent. BC. Peripatetic (Aristotelian) philosopher and writer of *Life of Greece* (*Bios Hellados*), *Tripoliticus* (a constitutional study) and *Circuit of the Earth*. Fragments survive.

Diodorus Siculus of Agyrium in Sicily. 1st cent. BC. His *Library* (*Bibliothece*) is a forty-book history of the world down to Caesar's Gallic War (54 BC). Books 1–5 and 11–20 survive intact and the rest in fragments.

Diogenes of Seleucia on the Tigris ('of Babylon'). *c.* 240–152 BC. Head of the Stoic school and expounder of its grammatical doctrines.

Diogenes Laertius. 3rd cent. AD (?) Author of ten-book *Lives and Opinions* (or *History*) *of the Philosophers*.

Duris of Samos. *c.* 340–260 BC. Author of *Histories* in at least twenty-three books, probably covering the period 370–280 BC. Fragments survive.

Epicurus of Samos. 341–270 BC. Founder of the Epicurean school of philosophy ('The Garden'). Out of his three hundred volumes two letters, forty *Principal Doctrines* (*Kuriai Doxai*), and eighty-one similar short statements (*Vatican Sayings*) have survived.

Erasistratus of Ceos; worked in Alexandria. First half of 3rd cent. BC. Writer of books on medicine, especially comparative anatomy.

Eratosthenes of Cyrene. *c.* 275–194 BC. Director of the Alexandrian Library, and author of works on mathematics, geography (*Geographica*), mathematical geography (*On the Measurement of the Earth*); also *Chronographies*, and poems.

Erinna of Telos. Late 4th or early 3rd cent. BC; died at age of nineteen. Writer of poem *The Distaff* and epigrams.

Euclid of Alexandria. Late 4th and early 3rd cent. BC. Author of thirteen-book mathematical textbook the *Elements* (*Stoicheia*) and other works on geometry.

Euhemerus of Messene. Late 4th and early 3rd cent. BC. Writer of traveller's tale, the *Sacred Record* (*Hiera Anagraphe*). Fragments and epitome survive.

Euphorion of Chalcis. Born *c*. 276/5 BC. Writer of miniature epics (epyllia) and other poems on mythology, etc., of which fragments survive.

Eupolemus of Judaea. Mid-2nd cent. BC. Hellenized Jew; wrote popular *History of the Kings in Judaea*.

Firmicus Maternus of Syracuse. First half of 4th cent. AD. Astrologer and Christian convert. His work *On the Error of Profane Religions* has survived.

Hecataeus of Abdera. *c*. 300 BC. Author of History of Egypt (*Aegyptiaca*).

Hegesias of Magnesia by Sipylus. Early 3rd cent. BC. Historian (*History of Alexander*, fragments) and orator; chief exponent of 'Asianic' style.

Heraclides Ponticus of Heraclea Pontica. *c*. 388–315 BC. Platonic philosopher, physicist, astronomer and eschatologist. Fragments are extant.

Hermagoras of Temnos. Mid-2nd cent. BC. Leading rhetorical theoretician.

Herodas (Herondas) of Cos (?). Later 3rd cent. BC. Writer of mimes, of which seven – and fragments of others – have survived.

Hieronymus of Cardia. 4th and 3rd cent. BC. Writer of *History of the Successors* from the death of Alexander (323) to 272 or 263.

Iambulus, probably from Nabataea (Arabia). 3rd cent. BC (?). Writer of fantastic tale of travel to an Island of the Sun.

Josephus (Flavius). AD 38–after 93/4. Jewish historian (in Greek). Among his surviving works are the twenty-book *Jewish Antiquities* and seven-book Jewish War.

Leonidas of Taras. Late 4th cent.–*c*. 260 BC. Writer of epigrams, of which about a hundred are still extant.

Lucian of Samosata. *c*. AD 120/5–180. Satirical popular philosopher. His voluminous writings provide extensive information about the philosophical schools, notably the Cynics.

Manetho, chief priest at Heliopolis (On). Early 3rd cent. BC. Wrote History of Egypt (*Aegyptiaca*) down to 323, into which two (?) subsequent writers (including one who was strongly anti-Semitic) inserted interpolations.

Megasthenes of Ionia. *c*. 350–290 BC. Writer of four-book *History of India* (*Indice*).

Meleager of Gadara. *c*. 100 BC. Writer of epigrams, of which about a hundred survive, and of Cynic 'Menippean' satires in mixed prose and verse, now lost. Compiler of the first major collection of Greek epigrams, the *Garland*.

Menander of Athens. *c.* 342–292 BC. Writer of more than a hundred plays of the New Comedy. Substantial passages or fragments of ten plays survive.

Menippus of Gadara. First half of 3rd cent. BC. His thirteen books of mixed prose and verse originated the serio-comic style of the 'Menippean satires'.

Metrodorus of Chios. 4th cent. BC. Follower of scientist and philosopher Democritus of Abdera. Writer of meteorological and astronomical studies and of historical works on Troy and Ionia (*Troica, Ionica*).

Metrodorus of Lampsacus. *c.* 331/30–278/7 BC. The most important of Epicurus' followers. Considerable fragments of his numerous writings survive.

Mnaseas of Lycia. 3rd cent. BC. Writer of geographical and antiquarian works and compiler of collection of Delphic oracles.

Moschus of Syracuse. Mid-2nd cent. BC. Poet and grammarian. Excerpts from his *Bucolica* and *Runaway Love*, and an epigram, have survived. None of his grammatical works has come down to us.

Nausiphanes of Teos. Born *c.* 360 BC. Follower of Democritus of Abdera, student of Pyrrho, first teacher of Epicurus. Fragments survive.

Nicander of Colophon. After *c.* 150 BC. His epics and *Georgica* have not survived, but two didactic poems are extant: *Theriaca* (*Treatise on Beasts*) and *Alexipharmaca* (*Curative Herbs*).

Nicolaus of Damascus. *c.* 64–after 4 BC. Historian and philosopher. The most important of his numerous works was his 144-book *Universal History* from which substantial passages survive in quotations and adaptations.

Nossis of Locri Epizephyrii. *c.* 300 BC. Poet. Twelve of her epigrams are extant but her lyrics have vanished.

Onesicritus of Astypalaea. Later 4th cent. He was with Alexander in India and wrote a historical romance with the king as Cynic hero.

Panaetius of Rhodes; lived in Athens and Rome. *c.* 185/80–109 BC. Stoic philosopher. His writings, of which only fragments survive, include studies *On Providence* and *On Appropriate Action*, which can largely be reconstructed from Cicero's *De Officiis*.

Parthenius of Nicaea. 1st cent. BC. Numerous poems, extant only in fragments, included *Metamorphoses, Iphitus, Heracles* and dirges. His prose collection of *Sorrowful Love Stories* survives.

Pausanias of Lydia. 2nd cent. AD. Writer of ten-book *Description* (*Periegesis*) *of Greece*.

Persaeus of Citium. *c.* 306–243 BC. Stoic philosopher and writer of *On Kingship, On the Spartan Constitution*, and of *Dialogues*. Fragments survive.

Philemon of Syracuse; lived in Athens. *c.* 365/60–264/3 BC. Writer of nearly a hundred plays of the New Comedy, of which sixty titles and more than two hundred fragments survive.

Philetas of Cos; lived in Alexandria. Poet and scholar. Born not later than 320 BC. Five titles and fifty fragments of his poems have survived, and thirty fragments of his prose *Lexicon of Unclassifiable (?) Glosses.*

Philinus of Acragas. Historian of the First Punic War (264–241 BC), in which he supported the Carthaginian cause.

Philinus of Cos. *c.* 250 BC. Credited with the foundation of the Empirical School of Medicine.

Philo of Byzantium. Late 3rd cent. BC. Writer of nine(?)-book compendium of technology, of which books 4 and 5 and parts of 7 and 8 survive.

Philo Judaeus. Jew. *c.* 30 BC–AD 45. Writer of numerous works on Hebrew religion and philosophy, which he sought to reconcile with Greek culture.

Philodemus of Gadara; lived in Italy. *c.* 110–40 BC. Epicurean philosopher and poet. Two-thirds of a collection of four hundred (out of eighteen hundred) carbonized papyri discovered at Herculaneum have been identified as his philosophical monographs. Twenty-five of his erotic epigrams are extant.

Phylarchus of Athens. His works include twenty-eight-book *Histories* covering the period 272–220 BC. Fragments survive.

Plutarch of Chaeronea. Before A D 50–after 120. Philosopher and biographer.

Polybius of Megalopolis. *c.* 200–after 118 BC. His forty-book *Histories* covered the period 220–146 BC. Books 1–5 are complete, and excerpts, often substantial, survive from the others.

Posidonius of Apamea, *c.* 135–*c.* 51/50 BC. Philosopher and historian.

Pytheas of Massalia. Late 4th cent. BC. Geographer and explorer. His treatise *On the Ocean* has only survived in later quotations and adaptations.

Rhinthon of Taras. *c.* 300 BC. Comic playwright of Doric farces (*Phlyax* plays), of which thirty-eight were ascribed to his authorship. Nine titles but very few fragments survive.

Satyrus of Callatis Pontica; lived in Egypt. 3rd or 2nd cent. BC. Writer of biographies of which only fragments have survived, including portions of a Life of Euripides.

Serapion of Alexandria. Founder or second founder of the Empirical school of medicine (*c.* 200–150 BC) and writer of medical works.

Sextus Empiricus. *c.* AD 200 (?). Member of the Empirical school of medicine and the Sceptic philosophical school, of which he wrote a history, as well as criticisms of other schools and professions.

Simplicius of Cilicia; 6th cent. AD. Commentator on Aristotle.

Sopater of Paphos. Late 4th and early 3rd cent. BC. Writer of parodies and farces (*Phlyakes*).

Sosylus of Sparta. Writer of seven-book history of the career of the Carthaginian Hannibal (247–183/2 BC).

Sotades of Maronea. 3rd cent. BC. Writer of scurrilous and obscene poems, of which a few survive.

Sphaerus of Borysthenes (Olbia). *c.* 285 or 265–at least 221 BC. Stoic writer on all branches of philosophy.

Stilpo of Megara. *c.* 380–300 BC. Third head of the Megarian philosophical school. Writer of at least twenty dialogues, of which some names have been preserved.

Strabo of Amasia. *c.* 63 BC–at least AD 21. Author of seventeen-book *Geography* (extant) and forty-seven-book *Historical Sketches* (of which minor fragments survive) covering the period 146–44 BC (or later).

Syrianus of Alexandria. 5th cent. AD. Neo-Platonist philosopher. Two commentaries on works by the 2nd cent. rhetorician Hermogenes of Tarsus survive.

Teles of Megara (?). 3rd cent. BC. Author of Cynic *diatribai* (see Bion of Borysthenes). Fragments survive.

Theocritus of Syracuse; lived at Cos and Alexandria. *c.* 300–260 (?) BC. The thirty-one poems (other than epigrams) attributed to him include six bucolic (pastoral) 'idylls', and pieces resembling mimes, and mythological items.

Theophrastus of Eresus. *c.* 370–288/5 BC. Successor to Aristotle as head of the Peripatetic school. His 240 writings covered rhetoric, ethics, politics, logic, religion, metaphysics, and physics, but only two survive complete: *Inquiry Concerning Plants* and *Causes of Plants* in nine and six books respectively.

Xenocrates of Chalcedon. Head of the Platonic Academy 339–314 BC. Writer of philosophical works formalizing Plato's thought.

Zeno of Citium (in Cyprus). 335–263 BC. Founder of the Stoic philosophy which he expounded in numerous writings. He also wrote a *Politeia* or *Republic* (an early work), *Homeric Problems* in five books, and a study of Hesiod's *Theogony*.

Zenodotus of Ephesus. Born *c.* 325 BC. First director of the Alexandrian Library; critical editor of the *Iliad* and *Odyssey* and of works by Hesiod (*Theogony*), Pindar and Anacreon; and compiler of a Homeric *Glossary* and *Foreign Terms*.

The writers of the following works are unknown: *Alexander Romance, Dream of Nectanebus, Joseph and Aseneth, 'Letter of Aristeas', Nechepso and Petosiris* on astrology, *Ninus Romance, Oracula Sibyllina*.

2 *Latin Writers*

The following Latin writers have been mentioned in the book:

Apuleius of Madaurus (Numidia). Born *c.* AD 123–125. His most important work was the eleven-book *Metamorphoses* (or *Golden Ass*), of which the last book is a major source of information about Isis worship.

Cato the elder of Tusculum. 234–149 BC. Out of his many works, only the *De Agricultura* or *De Re Rustica* (*On Agriculture*) is extant. His *Origines*, a Roman history down to his own times, only survives in fragments. His speeches are not preserved.

Catullus of Verona. *c.* 84–54 BC. His varied poetry echoes Hellenistic Greek models and includes a *Hymn to Attis*.

Cicero of Arpinum. 106–43 BC. Orator, philosopher, rhetorician, poet. Major source of information for Hellenistic philosophy and rhetoric.

Ennius of Rudiae. Six hundred lines of his eighteen-book epic the *Annals* survive, twenty titles and numerous fragments of his tragedies, and seventy lines of his *Satires*. He adapted and popularized Euhemerus' prose work the *Sacred Scripture*.

Gallus, Cornelius, of Forum Julii (southern Gaul). 69–26 BC. Writer of four books of elegies, the *Loves*, partly based on Parthenius' *Sorrowful Love Stories*, and a miniature epic on Apollo's shrine at Gryneium (Aeolis) modelled on Euphorion.

Horace of Venusia. 65–8 BC. His *Odes*, *Epodes*, *Satires* and *Epistles* owe many debts to Hellenistic literature.

Lucan of Corduba. AD 39–65. His *Civil War* (*Bellum Civile*) (also known as the 'Pharsalia') breaks off in the tenth book, at the time when Caesar and Cleopatra VII are together in Alexandria.

Plautus of Satsina. *c.* 254/50–184 BC. His twenty-one attributable plays borrow and adapt the main lines of their plots from Menander and other writers of the Athenian New Comedy.

Pliny the elder of Novum Comum. AD 23/4–79. Five of the thirty-seven books of his *Natural History* deal extensively with Hellenistic and other Greek art. The thirty-one books of his contemporary *Roman History* have disappeared.

Pompeius Trogus of Vasio (southern Gaul). Later 1st cent. BC. Writer of a forty-four-book universal history, of which the last thirty books dealt with the Hellenistic period down to Augustus.

Quintilian of Calagurris (Spain). *c.* AD 35–100. Educationalist. The tenth of the twelve books of his *Institutio Oratoria* (*Education of an Orator*) offers a Greek and Latin reading list.

Sisenna. Early 1st cent. BC. Writer of twelve- (or twenty-three-) book *History* of his own times and translator or adapter of the salacious *Milesian Tales* of Aristides of Miletus. Fragments survive.

Terence of Carthage. *c.* 195/85–159 BC. His six plays borrow their themes (more closely than those of Plautus) from Menander and other writers of the Athenian New Comedy.

Virgil of Andes (near Mantua). 70–19 BC. Although Virgil's talent was entirely original, his *Eclogues* (*Bucolics*) display the inspiration of Theocritus' bucolic (pastoral) 'idylls'; his *Georgics* owe much of their contents to Nicander and Aratus; and the love-story of Dido and Aeneas in the *Aeneid* is strongly influenced by the romance of Medea and Jason in Apollonius Rhodius' *Argonautica.*

Hebrew, Indian and Chinese literary sources are also of assistance.

3 *Inscriptions*

Moretti, L. (ed.), *Iscrizioni storiche ellenistiche* (Florence 1967). See also bibliography in C. Préaux, *Le monde hellénistique*, vol. I (Paris 1978), pp. 20–24.

4 *Papyri*

Primary source for Ptolemaic Egypt. C. Préaux, op. cit., pp. 24–27.

5 *Coins*

Ibid., pp. 27–31; G. K. Jenkins, *Ancient Greek Coins* (London 1972); C. M. Kraay and M. Hirmer, *Greek Coins* (London 1966); C. T. Seltman, *Greek Coins*, 3rd ed. (London 1960); M. R. Alföldi, *Antike Numismatik*, I–II (Mainz 1978). Primary, and often the only, source for the Bactrian and Indo-Greek kingdoms: M. Mitchiner, *Indo-Greek and Indo-Scythian Coinage*, vols 1–9 (London 1975-6).

Some Modern Books

Aalders, G. J. D., *Political Thought in Hellenistic Times* (Amsterdam 1976)
Adcock, F. E., *The Greek and Macedonian Art of War* (Berkeley 1967 [1957])
Alexander the Great (Greece and Rome, 2nd ser., XII, 2, Oxford 1968)
Allen, R. E., *The Attalid Kingdom: A Constitutional History* (Oxford 1982)
Anderson, G., *Ancient Fiction: The Novel in the Graeco-Roman World* (London 1984)
Armstrong, A. H. (ed.), *Classical Mediterranean Spirituality* (London 1986)
Arnott, W. G., *Menander, Plautus and Terence* (Oxford 1975)
Astin, A. E., Walbank, F. W., Frederiksen, M. W., and Ogilvie, R. M. (eds), *Cambridge Ancient History, VIII: Rome and the Mediterranean to 133 BC*, 2nd ed. (Cambridge 1989)
Austin, M. M. (ed.), *The Hellenistic World from Alexander to the Roman Conquest: A Selection of Ancient Sources in Translation* (Cambridge 1981)
Badian, E., *Roman Imperialism in the Late Republic*, 2nd ed. (Oxford 1968)
Baldry, M. C., *The Unity of Mankind in Greek Thought* (Cambridge 1965)
Bar-Kochva, B., *The Seleucid Army* (Cambridge 1976)
Barnes, J., Brunschwig, J., Burnyeat, M. and Schefold, M., *Science and Speculation: Studies in Hellenistic Theory and Practice* (Cambridge 1982)
Bartlett, J. R., *Jews in the Hellenistic World* (Cambridge 1985)
Bengtsson, P., *Fouilles d'Ai Khanoum*, I–V (Paris 1973–86)

Berve, H., *Die Herrschaft des Agathokles* (Munich 1972)

Bevan, E. R., *A History of Egypt Under the Ptolemaic Dynasty* (Amsterdam 1967 [1927])

Bevan, E. R., *The House of Seleucus* (London 1902)

Bichler, R., *Hellenismus* (Darmstadt 1983)

Bickerman, E. J., *Religion and Politics in the Hellenistic and Roman Periods* (E. Gabba and M. Smith eds) (Como 1985)

Bieber, M., *Alexander the Great in Greek and Roman Art* (Chicago 1964)

Bieber, M., *The Sculpture of the Hellenistic Age*, rev. ed. (New York 1969)

Boardman, J., *Greek Art* (London 1985 [1974])

Boardman, J., Griffin, J., and Murray, O. (eds), *The Cambridge History of Classical Literature* (Cambridge 1985)

Bonnard, A., *Greek Civilisation, III: Form Euripides to Alexandria* (London 1961)

Bosworth, A. B., *Conquest and Empire: The Reign of Alexander the Great* (Cambridge 1988)

Bouché-Leclerq, A., *Histoire des Lagides* (Brussels 1963 [1903–7])

Bouché-Leclerq, A., *Histoire des Seleucides* (Brussels 1963 [1913])

Burstein, S. M. (ed.), *The Hellenistic Age from the Battle of Ipsos to the Death of Kleopatra VII* (Cambridge 1985)

Buschor, E., *Das hellenistiche Bildnis*, 2nd ed. (Munich 1971)

Cary, M., *History of the Greek World from 353 to 146 BC*, rev. ed. (London 1977 [1951])

Cerfaux, L., and Tondriau, J., *Le culte des souverains dans la civilisation gréco-romaine* (Paris 1957)

Charbonneaux, J., Martin, R., and Villard, F., *Hellenistic Art* (London 1973 [1970])

Chesterman, J., *Classical Terracotta Figures* (New York 1974)

Cloche, P., *La dislocation d'un empire: less premiers successeurs d'Alexandre le Grand* (Paris 1959)

Cohen, G. M., *The Seleucid Colonies* (Wiesbaden 1978)

Cook, J. M., *The Greeks in Ionia and the East* (London 1962)

Cook, R. M., *Greek Art*, 2nd ed. (Harmondsworth 1979)

Davis, N., and Kraay, C. M., *The Hellenistic Kingdoms: Portrait Coins and History* (London 1973)

De Sainte Croix, G. E. M., *The Class Struggle in the Ancient Greek World* (London 1983 [1981])

Deininger, J., *Der politische Widerstand gegen Rom in Griechenland 217–86 v. Chr.* (Berlin 1971)

Delorme, J., *Le monde hellenistique 323–133 BC* (Paris 1975)

Downey, G., *A History of Antioch in Syria from Seleucus to the Arab Conquest* (Princeton 1961)

Drachman, A. G., *The Mechanical Technology of Greek and Roman Antiquity* (Copenhagen 1963)

Dunand, F., *Le culte d'Isis dans le bassin oriental de la Méditerranée* (Leiden 1973)

Easterling, P. E., and Knox, B. M. W. (eds), *The Cambridge History of Classical Literature* (Cambridge 1985)

Easterling, P. E., and Muir, J. V. (eds), *Greek Religion and Society* (Cambridge 1985)

Eddy, S. K., *The King is Dead: Studies in the Near-East Resistance to Hellenism* (Lincoln, Nebraska, 1961)

Ehrenberg, V., *The Greek State*, 2nd ed. (London 1969)

Ehrenberg, V., *Man, State and Deity* (London 1974)

Ferguson, J., *Callimachus* (Boston 1980)

Ferguson, J., *The Heritage of Hellenism* (London 1973)

Ferguson, J., *Utopias of the Classical World* (London 1975)

Fine, J. V. A., *The Ancient Greeks: A Critical History* (Cambridge, Mass., 1983)

Finley, M. I., *Ancient Sicily*, rev. ed. (London 1979)

Finley, M. I. (ed.), *The Legacy of Greece: A New Appraisal* (Oxford 1985 [1981])

Finley, M. I. (ed.), *Slavery in Classical Antiquity: Views and Controversies* (London 1960)

Forbes, R. J., and Dijksterhuis, E. J., *History of Science and Technology*, vol. I (Harmondsworth 1963)

Forrest, W. G., *A History of Sparta 950–192 BC* (London 1968)

Fox, R. Lane, *Alexander the Great* (London 1973)

Fox, R. Lane, *The Search for Alexander* (London 1981 [1980])

Fraser, P. M., *Ptolemaic Alexandria*, 3 vols (Oxford, 1986 [1972])

Fuks, A., *Social Conflict in Ancient Greece* (Jerusalem 1984)

Fyfe, D. T., *Hellenistic Architecture* (Chicago 1974 [1936])

Gajdukevič, V. E., *Das Bosporanische Reich* (Berlin 1971)

Garlan, Y., *War in the Ancient World: A Social History* (London 1975)

Garnsey, P. D. A., and Whittaker, C. R., *Imperialism in the Ancient World* (Cambridge 1978)

Giangrande, G., *L'humour des Alexandrins* (Amsterdam 1975)

Giannantoni, G., and Vegetti, M. (eds), *La scienza ellenistica* (Naples 1984)

Giuliano, A., *Urbanistica delle città greche*, 3rd ed. (Milan 1978)

Godwin, J., *Mystery Religions in the Ancient World* (London 1981)

Goldberg, S. M., *The Making of Menander's Comedy* (London 1980)

Grant, M., *Cities of Vesuvius*, rev. ed. (Harmondsworth 1976 [1971])

Grant, M., *Cleopatra*, rev. ed. (London 1974 [1972])

Grant, M., *The Visible Past: Greek and Roman History from Archaeology 1960–1990* (London 1990)

Grant, M., and Kitzinger, R., *Civilisation of the Ancient Mediterranean: Greece and Rome*, 3 vols (New York 1988)

Griffith, G. T., *Alexander the Great: The Main Problems* (Cambridge 1966)

Griffith, G. T., *Mercenaries of the Hellenistic World* (Cambridge 1935)

Grimal, P. (etc.), *Hellenism and the Rise of Rome* (London 1968)

Habicht, C., *Gottmenschentum and die griechischen Städte*, 2nd ed. (Munich 1970)

Hadas, M., *Hellenistic Culture: Fusion and Diffusion* (New York 1959)

Hägg, T., *The Novel in Antiquity* (Oxford 1983)

Halperin, D., *Before Pastoral: Theocritus and the Ancient Tradition of Bucolic Poetry* (New Haven 1982)

Hammond, N. G. L., *Alexander the Great* (London 1981)

Hammond, N. G. L., *Epirus* (Oxford 1967)

Havelock, C. M., *Hellenistic Art* (Oxford 1971)

Hengel, M., *Judaism and Hellenism* (London 1974 [1969])

Herm, G., *Die Diadochen* (Munich 1978)

Heuss, A., *Stadt und Herrscher des Hellenismus* (Leipzig 1963 [1937])

Holt, F. L., *Alexander the Great and Bactria* (Leiden 1988)

Hornbostel, W., *Sarapis* (Leiden 1973)

Howatson, M. W. (ed.), *The Oxford Companion to Classical Literature*, 2nd ed. (Oxford 1989)

Hutchinson, G. O., *Hellenistic Poetry* (Oxford 1988)

Inwood, B., and Gerson, L. P. (eds), *Hellenistic Philosophy: Introductory Readings* (Indianapolis 1988)

Jones, A. H. M., *The Greek City from Alexander to Justinian* (Oxford 1981 [1940])

Jouguet, P., *L'impérialisme macédoine et l'hellénization de l'Orient*, rev. ed. (Paris 1972)

Kuhr, A., and Sherwin-White, S. (eds.), *The Interaction of Greek and non-Greek Civilisations from Syria to Central Asia after Alexander* (London 1987)

Larsen, J. A. O., *Greek Federal States* (Oxford 1968)

Launey, M., *Recherches sur les armées hellénistiques* (Paris 1949–50)

Lawrence, A. W., *Later Greek Sculpture and its Influence in East and West* (London 1927)

Lesky, A., *History of Greek Literature* (London 1966 [1957–8])

Levi, M. A., *L'ellenismo e l'ascesa di Roma* (Turin 1969)

Levi, P., *The Pelican History of Greek Literature* (Harmondsworth 1985)

Lewis, N., *Greeks in Ptolemaic Egypt* (Oxford 1986)

Ling, R. (ed.), *Plates to Cambridge Ancient History, VII, Part 1: The Hellenistic World*, 2nd ed. (Cambridge 1984)

Long, A. A., *Hellenistic Philosophy: Stoics, Epicureans, Sceptics* (London 1974)

Long, A. A., *Problems in Stoicism* (London 1971)

Long, A. A., and Sedley, D. N., *The Hellenistic Philosophers* (Cambridge 1987)

Longega, G., *Arsinoe II* (Padua 1968)

McShane, R. B., *The Foreign Policy of the Attalids* (Urbana 1964)

Macurdy, G. H., *Hellenistic Queens* (Baltimore 1932)

Maehler, H., and Strocka, V. M., *Das ptolemäische Ägypten* (Berlin 1976)

Mahaffy, J. P., *Greek Life and Thought from the Age of Alexander to the Roman Conquest*, 2nd ed. (London 1896)

Marlowe, J., *The Golden Age of Alexandria* (London 1971)

Marrou, H. I., *A History of Education in Antiquity* (London 1977)

Martin, L. H., *Hellenistic Religions: An Introduction* (Oxford 1987)

Martin, R., Bandinelli, R. B., and Moreno, P., *La cultura ellenistica* (Milan 1977)

Mastromarco, G., *Il pubblico di Eronda* (Padua 1979)

Ménandre (Entretiens Hardt, vol. XVI, Vandoeuvres-Geneva 1970)

Meyer, E., *Blüte und Niedergang des Hellenismus in Asien* (Berlin 1925)

Momigliano, A. D., *Alien Wisdom: The Limits of Hellenization* (Cambridge 1975)

Momigliano, A. D., *The Development of Greek Biography* (Cambridge, Massachusetts, 1971)

Momigliano, A. D., *Hochkulturen im Hellenismus* (Munich 1979)

Moreau, J., *Stoicisme, epicurisme: tradition hellénique* (Paris 1979)

Mossé, C., *Athens in Decline, 404–86 BC* (London 1973)

Murray, G., *Five Stages of Greek Religion* (London 1935)

Narain, A. K., *The Indo-Greeks* (Oxford 1957)

Newell, E. T., *Royal Greek Portrait Coins* (Racine, Wisconsin 1961 [1937])

Nicolet, C., *Rome et la conquête du monde méditerranéen* (Paris 1977)

Nilsson, M. P., *The Dionysiac Mysteries of the Hellenistic and Roman Age* (New York 1975 [1957])

Nock, A. D., *Conversion: The Old and the New in Religion from Alexander the Great to Augustine of Hippo* (Oxford 1961 [1933])

Oliva, P., *Sparta and the Social Problems* (Amsterdam 1971)

Oliva, P., and Burian, J. K. (etc.), *Soziale Probleme im Hellenismus und im römischen Reich* (Prague 1973)

Onians, J., *Art and Thought in the Hellenistic Age* (London 1982 [1979])

Palanque, J. R., *Les impérialismes antiques* (Paris 1960)

Pelling, C. B. R. (ed.), *Characterisation and Individuality in Greek Literature* (Oxford 1990)

Peters, F. E., *The Harvest of Hellenism* (New York 1970)

Petit, P., *La civilisation hellénistique*, 2nd ed (Paris 1965)

Pohlenz, M., *Der hellenistische Mensch* (Göttingen 1946)

Pollitt, J. J., *Art in the Hellenistic Age* (Cambridge 1986)

Polybe (Entretiens Hardt, XX, Vandoeuvres-Geneva 1974)

Pomeroy, S. B., *Goddesses, Whores, Wives and Slaves* (New York 1975)

Pomeroy, S. B., *Women in Hellenistic Egypt: From Alexander to Cleopatra* (New York 1984)

Préaux, C., *La civilisation hellénistque*, 2nd ed. (Paris 1965)

Préaux, C., *L'économie royale des Lagides* (Brussels 1939)

Préaux, C., *Le monde hellénistique* (Paris 1978)

Richter, G. M. A., *Greek Portraits* (Brussels 1955–62)

Richter, G. M. A., *Handbook of Greek Art*, 7th ed. (New York 1974 [1959])

Richter, G. M. A., *The Portraits of the Greeks* (London 1972 [1965])

Rider, B. C., *Ancient Greek Houses*, rev. ed. (Chicago 1964)

Rist, J. M., *Epicurus* (Cambridge 1972)

Rist, J. M., *The Stoics* (London 1978)

Robertson, C. M., *History of Greek Art* (Cambridge 1975–6; *Shorter History* 1981)

Robertson, D. S., *Greek and Roman Architecture*, rev. ed. (Cambridge 1969 [1945])

Romilly, J., *A Short History of Greek Literature* (Chicago 1985)

Rosenmayer, T. G., *The Green Cabinet: Theocritus and the European Pastoral Lyric* (Berkeley 1969)

Rostovtzeff, M., *Iranians and Greeks in South Russia* (Oxford 1922)

Rostovtzeff, M., *The Social and Economic History of the Hellenistic World*, rev. ed. (ed. P. M. Fraser, Oxford 1957 [1941])

Russell, D. S., *The Jews from Alexander to Herod* (Oxford 1967)

Sandbach, F. H., *The Comic Theatre of Greece and Rome* (London and New York 1977)

Sarton, G., *History of Science*, vol. II: *Hellenistic Science and Culture in the Last Three Centuries* BC (Cambridge, Massachusetts 1979 [1959])

Schlumberger, D., *L'orient hellénisé* (Paris 1970)

Schneider, C., *Kulturgeschichte des Hellenismus*, 2 vols (Munich 1967, 1969)

Schofield, M., Burnyeat, M., and Barnes, J., *Doubt and Dogmatism: Studies in Hellenistic Epistemology* (Oxford 1980)

Schürer, E., *The History of the Jewish People in the Age of Jesus Christ: 175 BC–AD 135*, I, rev. ed. (G. Vernes and F. Millar, Edinburgh 1973 [1890–4])

Sedlar, J. W., *India and the Greek World* (Totowa, New Jersey 1980)

Sevenster, I. N., *The Roots of Pagan Anti-Semitism in the Ancient World* (Leiden 1975)

Shimron, B., *Late Sparta and the Spartan Revolution 243–146 BC* (Buffalo 1972)

Skeat, T. C., *The Reigns of the Ptolemies*, 2nd ed. (Munich 1969 [1954])

Smith, R. R. R., *Hellenistic Royal Portraits* (Oxford 1988)

Solmsen, F., *Isis among the Greeks and Romans* (Cambridge, Massachusetts 1980)

Stambaugh, J. E., *Sarapis under the Early Ptolemies* (Leiden 1972)

Tarn, W. W., *Antigonus Gonatas* (Oxford 1969 [1913])

Tarn, W. W., *The Greeks in Bactria and India*, 3rd ed. (ed. F. L. Holt, Chicago 1984 [1938])

Tarn, W. W., *Hellenistic Military and Naval Developments* (Cambridge 1930)

Tarn, W. W., and Griffith, G. T., *Hellenistic Civilisation*, 3rd ed. (London 1974 [1927])

Tcherikover, V., *Hellenistic Civilisation and the Jews* (Philadelphia 1959 [1931])

Trendall, A. D., *South Italian Vase Painting*, 2nd ed. (London 1976 [1966])

Treu, K., *Die Menschen Menanders: Kontinuität und Neuerung im hellenistischen Menschenbild* (Berlin 1976)

Turner, E. G., *Greek Papyri: An Introduction*, 2nd ed. (Oxford 1980 [1968])

Vermaseren, M. J. (ed.), *Studies in Hellenistic Religions* (Leiden 1980)

Vidman, L., *Isis und Serapis bei den Griechen und Römern* (Berlin 1970)

Vigilio, B. (ed.), *Studi ellenistici*, I (Pisa 1984)

Vogt, J., *Ancient Slavery and the Ideal of Man* (Oxford 1974 [1965])

Walbank, F. W., *Aratus of Sicyon* (Cambridge 1934)

Walbank, F. W., *The Hellenistic World* (London 1981)

Walbank, F. W., *Philip v of Macedon* (Cambridge 1940)

Walbank, F. W., *Polybius* (Berkeley 1972)

Walbank, F. W., Astin, A. E., Frederiksen, M. W. and Ogilvie, R. M. (eds) *Cambridge Ancient History, VIII, Part 1: The Hellenistic World*, 2nd ed. (Cambridge 1984)

Walker, S. F., *Theocritus* (Boston 1980)

Ward-Perkins, J. B., *Cities of Ancient Greece and Italy: Planning in Classical Antiquity* (New York 1974)

Wardman, A., *Rome's Debt to Greece* (London 1976)

Webster, T. B. L., *An Introduction to Menander*, 2nd ed. (Manchester 1974)

Webster, T. B. L., *Hellenistic Art* (London 1967)

Webster, T. B. L., *Hellenistic Poetry and Art* (London 1964)
Welles, C. B., *Alexander and the Hellenistic World* (Toronto 1970)
White, H., *Essays in Hellenistic Poetry* (London 1980)
White, H., *New Essays in Hellenistic Poetry* (Amsterdam 1985)
Wiedemann, T., *Greek and Roman Slavery* (London 1981)
Will, E., *Histoire politique du monde hellénistique*, 2 vols (Nancy 1981 [1979])
Will, E., Mossé, C., and Goukowsky, P., *Le monde grec et l'orient*, vol. II: *le quatrième siècle et l'époque hellénistique* (Paris 1975)
Winkler, J. J., and Williams, G., *Later Greek Literature* (Cambridge 1982)
Witt, R. E., *Isis in the Graeco-Roman World* (Ithaca 1971)
Woodcock, G., *The Greeks in India* (London 1966)
Zanker, P. (ed.), *Hellenismus in Mittelitalien* (Göttingen 1976)
Zanker, P., *Realism in Alexandrian Poetry: A Literature and its Audience* (London 1987)

Index